ANY OTHER WAY

HOW TORONTO GOT QUEER

Coach House Books, Toronto

first edition

 Canada Council Conseil des Arts
for the Arts du Canada

 ONTARIO ARTS COUNCIL
CONSEIL DES ARTS DE L'ONTARIO
an Ontario government agency
un organisme du gouvernement de l'Ontario

Canadä

Published with the generous assistance of the Canada Council for the Arts and the Ontario
Arts Council. Coach House Books also acknowledges the support of the Government of
Canada through the Canada Book Fund and the Government of Ontario through the
Ontario Book Publishing Tax Credit.

The views expressed by the contributors do not necessarily reflect those of the editors or
Coach House Books.

LIBRARY AND ARCHIVES CANADA CATALOGUING IN PUBLICATION

Any other way : how Toronto got queer / edited by Stephanie Chambers, Jane Farrow,
Maureen FitzGerald, Ed Jackson, John Lorinc, Tim McCaskell, Rebecka Sheffield, Tatum
Taylor, and Rahim Thawer.

Issued in print and electronic formats.
ISBN 978-1-55245-348-3 (softcover).

1. Gay liberation movement--Ontario--Toronto. 2. Gays--Ontario--Toronto.
3. Essays. I. Chambers, Stephanie, editor

HQ76.8.C3A59 2017   306.76'609713541   C2017-902856-1
                                        C2017-902855-3

ARRIVING

SPACES

ORIGINS

DEMIMONDE

EMERGENCE

RESISTING, SHARING, ORGANIZING

RIGHTS AND RITES

PRIDE

CONCLUSION

My arrival in Toronto as a young tomboy from Hong Kong in the late autumn of 1975 was an experience marked with banality. Grey skies, grey sidewalks, grey buildings, including the one where I now work: Toronto City Hall.

Coming from the tropical hustle of an Asian metropolis, I felt a sense of haplessness amidst Toronto's brooding, hurrying crowds. Like a fish out of water, I couldn't find my place in the city's mainly white, Anglo-Saxon Protestant east end.

Forty-two years later, an amalgamated city with a growing population of over 2.8 million people is recognized as the most diverse place in the world. And Toronto has more than grown on me. In many ways, we grew up together. Or it feels like we tumbled out of the closet together.

Kristyn Wong-Tam

Foreword

People from around the globe have found their way here. By logical extension, LGBTTIQQ2SA people or queers exist in every Toronto community, speaking over 140 languages. Yet the city's mainstream queer narrative remains predominantly white, male, cis, middle-class, and able-bodied. Only by pulling back the lavender headlines will we truly reveal the hyperdiversity and immense intersectionality of Toronto's full queer community and history.

Organizations large and small have either merged or morphed into something bigger and unrecognizable. Others have disappeared and, with them, the seldom told or understood histories about a community once broadly persecuted for its sexual-minority status. Gone are grassroots groups with descriptive names such Lesbian and Gay Youth of Toronto, Asian Lesbians of Toronto, Lesbian Youth Peer Support, Queer Nation, Glamorous Outcasts, Asian Canadians for Equal Marriage. Each contributed to the dynamic queering of this maturing city.

It was the unique cross-pollination of these community groups that forged solidarity with notable political partners, such as Black Action Defence Committee, Chinese Canadian National Council Toronto Chapter, Coalition for Lesbian and Gay Rights in Ontario (now Queer Ontario), Egale Canada, and others that helped coalesce these social movements to build strength in numbers to resist police violence, institutional racism, and government oppression.

Queers in Toronto have loved, fought, and rioted together. On Halloween, we pranced around in our colourful costumes, only to have our street parties interrupted because that specific night also attracted the most hateful gay-bashers to the Village and Yonge Street. There was a time when our anger flooded the streets to protest the Toronto Police after they raided the bathhouses, first in 1981 and then again in 2000, when six male officers crashed the women's bathhouse, Pussy Palace. Lesbians in Toronto were instrumental in creating women's shelters and rape-crisis support services. They struggled in the decade-long battles for women's reproductive rights. Queer women have been leaders in the women's movement since the very beginning.

Without ever getting much credit, queers helped push Toronto toward a more inclusive and just future. Respect, human rights, and basic dignity were hard won. The mythology of urbanism remains simplistically focused on the architecture, urban design, land use, and transportation planning of a city. The cultural, political, and social contributions from sexual-minority people have never emerged in any significant way in the conventional histories of Toronto. Which is why this particular anthology is so important.

From early European explorers and missionary records about Two Spirit peoples to the Alexander Wood sculpture commemorating the gay Scottish magistrate's vast landholdings, queer culture is interwoven in Toronto place-making. Gay cruising in parks from Allan Gardens to Queen's Park and Marie Curtis Park are examples of the queering of Toronto's public spaces.

During World Pride in 2014, Toronto's Casa Loma hosted the world's largest interfaith gay wedding, for 120 couples. The event garnered international media attention from Australia to Wales. Determined and joyful newlyweds, Cindy Su and Lana Yu, took their Toronto marriage licence home to Taipei, where they have been advocating for marriage equality for over three years. As of 2017, Taiwan is on the verge of becoming the first Asian country to legalize same-sex marriage. When Black Lives Matter Toronto halted the Pride parade on Yonge Street in 2016, Justin Trudeau, the first Canadian prime minister to participate in a sexual-liberation march, took notice, as did the rest of Canada.

Toronto's queer reach has gone beyond the local. It's a messy social miracle and also a work-in-progress that is no longer dull and grey. Now I can't imagine living anywhere else.

'It's just about that time for the star of our revue, ladies and gentlemen, Little Jackie Shane!' It was the fall of 1967, and Jackie, backed by Frank Motley and the Hitchhikers, was recording an album live from the Saphire Tavern in downtown Toronto. Jackie packed the house, appearing in a shimmering sequin pantsuit, full makeup, false eyelashes, and a fabulous do. 'I sing sexy, too,' Jackie tells us. 'That helps.'

For the last number of the evening, Jackie performed 'Any Other Way.' Originally released in 1962, the record climbed to #2 on the local CHUM chart and was a 'regional breakout' in places like Baltimore, St. Louis, and Washington, reaching #124 on Billboard's 'Bubbling Under the Hot 100.' Jackie started in, slow and seductive, with just the right quaver. And then that enigmatic hook: 'Tell her that I'm happy, tell her that I'm gay, tell her I wouldn't have it any other way.' This night, Jackie punctuated the song with several spoken lines: 'Tell her that I'm happy *... be sure and tell her this ... tell her that I'm gay.*' A moment later, Jackie interrupted again: 'I hear them whisper, they say, there Jackie goes with a broken heart ... *but they're wrong, darlin', I'm having a good time, me and my chicken.*'

Jackie's Black-fem fabulosity, the winking double entendre, rhapsodizing about chicken, all in nominally straight clubs in Toronto of the 1960s – the brazenness and bravery astound and impress even today. How many in the audience caught Jackie's references? Russ Strathdee, a straight white saxophone player active on the city's thriving R&B scene during the sixties, saw Jackie perform several times, even snapping some pics of Shane at the west-end dance club Ascot Hall. 'When Jackie made reference to the word *gay*,' he recounts, 'none of the people I knew back then were using that word in connection with the "homosexual" scene, including one of my friends of that persuasion.' Surely, though, others among the 'gay set' who flocked to Jackie's shows got the reference. There's a reason gay gossip columnists in the local tabloids kept tabs on Jackie, their interest peaking in the year 'Any Other Way' debuted.

It's tempting to read the song as autobiography. The liner notes on the *Jackie Shane Live* LP invite this: 'You'll be inspired as Jackie tells you his life story in "Any Other Way."' And what was that story? As Jackie tells it, 'You know what my woman told me one night? She said, "Jackie, if you don't stop switchin' around here and playing the field and bringing that chicken home, you gonna have to get to steppin."' I said, "Uh huh," and I grabbed my chicken by one hand, baby, and we been steppin' ever since that night.'

Steven Maynard

'A New Way of Lovin'':
Queer Toronto Gets Schooled by Jackie Shane

Jackie Shane at Ascot Hall.

The popularity of 'Any Other Way' and how it spotlights 'gay,' then and now, has overshadowed other aspects of Jackie's identity. Today, Jackie lives as a woman. In many of the historical sources, as well as people's reminiscences quoted in what follows, Jackie is referred to as 'he.' I leave these as is, because they capture important features of transgender historical experience. When I refer to Jackie, I'll take my cue from *her*. While I believe Jackie properly belongs to a Black-trans past, we need to keep in mind that throughout her courageously unconventional life and career, Jackie moved across a range of gender and sexual identifications, always in complicated relation to race and class, in ways that fascinated many and mystified others.

'Her face is his fortune'

In the fall of 1963, in an entertainment roundup for the *Varsity* student newspaper, a sophomoric writer informed University of Toronto students, 'Peppered along Yonge are a series of night clubs offering brass and boobs. The Brass Rail features beautiful babes who aren't quite. Blonde and buxom Brandy brays on the main floor, if you dig him/her/it. Upstairs Frank Motley and his crew perform, with little Jackie Shane doing the vocal. Is he or isn't she? Only its mother knows for sure.' Brandy, a popular female impersonator and star at the Warwick, a seedy hotel and strip joint at the corner of Dundas and Jarvis, met Jackie at the Brass Rail and remembered her as 'terribly feminine' – she was 'one great big sequin!' Brandy recalled you could spot Jackie about town, eating a ham sandwich at the twenty-four-hour lunch counter of Ford Drugs on Yonge. At the same time, Brandy found Jackie 'kept to himself' and seemed 'secretive,' a shield, perhaps, against those who'd refer to others as 'it.'

There's no doubt Jackie's gender perplexed people. In December 1967, a woman wrote to the *Star* with a burning question: 'My friend and I saw a group called Jackie Shane and the Hitchhikers, and he says Jackie Shane is a girl. I thought he was a boy. We've been arguing about it and he wants to bet me. Could you find out?' The *Star* was only too happy to oblige: 'When you're stuck, go straight to the source. So we went to the Palais Royale and popped the question. "I'm a boy of 23," Jackie declared, with just a touch of irritation.' The reporter wondered 'if the question was not, perhaps, a little embarrassing.' Jackie replied, '"No, I'm used to it. It's part of my act. When you're in show business, you have to depend on glamor, you know – and I know I have a feminine kind of face, so why not capitalize on it?"'

This did not settle matters. Several weeks later, another writer to the paper, referring to the 'article on whether Jackie is a he or a she,' doubted both Jackie's reported age and Jackie's claim to be a man: 'If he didn't give his age correctly, perhaps none of his answer – that Jackie's a he – is correct.' The paper checked again: 'Jackie repeats that he's a he of 23 and has been singing since the age of 13.' Despite being ambushed and slightly irritated by the *Star*, Jackie didn't pass up the chance to pose for the paper's photographer. In the photo, Jackie is all lipstick and eyeshadow; the caption read, 'her face is his fortune' – one of the only references I found to allow Jackie to inhabit the feminine pronoun, if only in part.

Jackie seemed in no rush to straighten out people's puzzlement. As Jackie explained to audiences, 'I'm going to enjoy the chicken, the women, and everything else I want to enjoy … that's how I live.' Jackie continued, 'My credo, I live the life I love, and I love the life I live … as long as you don't force your will and your way on others … I hope you'll do the same.' You get the distinct sense Jackie never bothered much with labels, even if others did.

'I've got a lot to work with here'

Some people placed Jackie in the camp of female impersonators, cross-dressers, and transvestites. As Strathdee, echoing Jackie on gender as an act, tells us, 'My perception of Jackie is that he had the persona of a transvestite … I thought it was all part of his shtick as an entertainer.' Certainly a lot of work went into performing Jackie. As she put it, 'I'm standing up here perspiring, getting all hot, workin' hard.' In a review of a show with Jackie on the bill at Massey Hall in September 1968, a writer zeroed in on the '[s]howmanship [that] is almost as important in soul music as its roots in the blues. After all, soul should show that a real man is at work … Any gimmicks he uses are supposed to seem like a natural part of his style.' The reviewer went on to note that 'Toronto's Jackie Shane and the Hitchhikers, who play hard soul with singing that ranges from a smooth baritone to a falsetto, all from Shane,' looked good, 'although I thought his eye makeup could have been more dramatic.' The simultaneous demand for a 'real man' and for more eye makeup, for baritone and falsetto, captures the double bind of gender Jackie must often have been forced to negotiate – and pulled off with such panache.

At the same time that Jackie's performance threw into question for audiences exactly what was 'real' when it came to gender, Jackie could also work it in ways that made femininity seem – to borrow from the Massey Hall show critic – 'like a natural part of his style.' Jackie's incredible 1965 appearance on *Night Train*, an all-Black televised music show out of Nashville, Jackie's hometown, suggests that Jackie did not so much impersonate a female as embody one. In the only footage known to exist, Jackie is looking good, made up but with neither the exaggerated femininity of drag nor the flashiness of some of her own shows. She's totally comfortable in her skin, looking – dare I say it? – like a 'natural woman,' not born this way but, as Aretha would tell us in two years, a way you're made to *feel*, by a lover, or maybe even by a short, collarless jacket that looks just right as you're 'walking the dog.' More than a decade later, in a different musical era, another Black, gender-bending, gay performer by the name of Sylvester (and I'm not the first to draw the parallel) called it feeling 'mighty real.'

Jackie's realness was rooted in her relationship with the audience, particularly with the women. Jackie spoke directly to women, dispensing advice, in true blues fashion, on how to deal with men and heartache. 'I'm talkin' to you, girls,' she says at the end of the live show. 'Hold on to your man, baby ... Makes no difference what your best friend, your mother, your father, your sister, your brother says about him, if he loves you, and you know you love him, baby, get a good grip on him because you're gonna need him in the midnight hour.' And if your man goes with your best friend? Well, 'just kick him out into the streets, baby.' Talking to the 'girls,' Jackie emphasized, 'You see, I'm a witness to this,' and then told the tale about being given the boot for stepping out with chicken.

'Gorgeous chicken'

Realness also registered in the fact that Jackie was Jackie whether onstage or off. Jackie understood perfectly well that Toronto could be a 'cruel, cruel world.' During the live performance of 'Money,' Jackie explains to the audience, 'You know, when I'm walkin' down Yonge Street, you won't believe this, but you know some of them funny people have the nerve to point the finger at me and grin and smile and whisper. But you know, that don't worry Jackie, because I know I look good. And every Monday morning I laugh and grin on my way to the bank.' Money could be sweet revenge. 'I see some people sitting out in the audience sometime, they

Toronto Star ad, 22 February 1967.

be rolling their eyes and looking all funny, but, baby, I like that because they come here each and every night to watch me, paying my way through.'

You took your chances heckling at a Jackie show. As Laima, who saw Jackie perform, recalls, she 'would challenge people in the audience if they got mouthy.' Humour and charm were Jackie's weapons of choice against 'Sticks and Stones' (flipside of 'Any Other Way'). She could defuse an insult by inviting and mocking it: 'Listen, baby, when you see Jackie walking down the street or I walk into a restaurant you're in, I want you to laugh and talk and grin and point the finger at me, because if they didn't point and whisper [I'd think] I done lost my touch!'

Money was important to Jackie for other reasons. 'The way I live, me and my chicken,' Jackie explained, 'I need the money, honey.' Chicken, of course, was gay slang for young men, often available as trade. The November 1964 cover of *GAY*, Canada's first gay tabloid, which hit the streets of Toronto earlier the same year, promised a piece on 'How to Be a Chicken Queen,' but it doesn't sound like Jackie needed any lessons. During the spoken break on 'Money,' Jackie tells us she wanted to take a six-month vacation. 'I don't want to have to do nothin' but have breakfast brought to me in bed by gorgeous chicken … That's going to take a whole lot of money.' In the Toronto music scene, in which Black performers were routinely paid less than white acts, Jackie usually got her price, and it was one of the highest. 'I'm takin' care of business,' Jackie assured fans.

According to the album liner notes, 'Jackie likes "chicken." Even where food is concerned Jackie likes chicken. The only problem is when Jackie suggests "let's go out and get some chicken after the show," you can't be too sure what he has in mind.' Whether or not we fully believe this banter, the question is, where did one look for chicken in Toronto?

Remembering the early sixties, the pioneering gay activist Jim Egan (see pages 136–139) recalls 'street kids … sixteen- or seventeen-year-olds, and there were lots of them around in Toronto in those days if you knew where to look.' You could find them at 'the Corners' of Queen and Bay, hanging out around the Municipal and Union House, grungy beverage rooms popular with working-class gays, hustlers, and drag queens. Egan fondly recalls one hustler: 'Frances was a Black guy who weighed two hundred pounds at the absolute minimum and was always plastered with makeup, including green eyeshadow and lipstick. He dressed in a unisex way so that it was difficult to tell whether you were looking at a man or a woman.'

'Ain't nobody sanctified and holy'

Jackie's base at the Saphire Tavern, on Richmond just east of Yonge, was only a stone's throw away from the Corners. George Hislop remembered the Saphire as a destination for him and his gay friends as early as the 1950s, and *Hush Free Press*

The Saphire Tavern, Richmond and Victoria.

reported in March 1952 on the story of a man who picked up a seventeen-year-old male prostitute at the Saphire.

It's doubtful Jackie, a Black singer from the U.S., working in Canada and frequently crossing the border, would risk spending much time around beverage rooms known for their gay clientele and closely monitored by liquor board inspectors, or in the first exclusively gay clubs, such as the Music Room and the Melody Room, 'featuring Toronto's finest female impersonators,' and which were routinely raided and harassed by the police. And then there was the racism of the clubs, particularly the more refined hotel bars popular with white gay men, such as the King Edward and, right across the street, the Nile Room of the Letros Tavern, known to deny entry to men of colour and men who didn't dress in conventional masculine fashion. Despite the stage banter about aspiring to the high life – French perfumes and diamond rings – it seems pretty clear Jackie's real sympathies lie with the lower orders; as she put it, 'ain't nobody sanctified and holy.'

Jackie played all manner of venues, from the Holiday Tavern at Queen and Bathurst to a curling rink in Scarborough, but her world revolved most around Black music and clubs. Eric Mercury, singer for the Soul Searchers, remembers that Jackie was 'appreciated by Black people, in Black clubs, in the Black community.' That appreciation might have started with Jackie's undeniable musical talent, but the Black community took Jackie at face value or, better, with her face on. The Reverend Larry Ellis, former bass player for Frank Motley and His Motley Crew (as the band was known before the mid-sixties), explains that Jackie 'didn't hide that he was gay … People were falling in love with him knowing he was gay.' While embraced by the Black community, Jackie's world, like many of the R&B bands and clubs, was racially mixed and far from genteel. Edjo, a big white biker and head of the Vagabonds motorcycle club, remembered Jackie as a 'fun guy to be around … gay and all that, but he never came on to me, we were just good friends.'

Laima recalls hopping in a taxi with Jackie after the show at the Saphire and speeding up the Yonge Street strip to the Club Bluenote in time to catch its popular floor show. The Bluenote featured some of the city's best Black women singers: Dianne Brooks, Kay Taylor, Shawne Jackson, and Shirley Matthews. In the early seventies, Jackson would release 'Just as Bad as You,' a Black-feminist anthem, proclaiming there was a time she'd have been 'just another young girl for you to treat like a fool, but the times are a-changin' and you're no longer in control … Just as bad as you, there ain't nothin' I can't do, I'm as bad as bad can be, ain't no man gonna mess with me.' In 1963, Matthews, a Bell office worker by day and soul singer at the Bluenote by night, shot to fame with her debut single 'Big-Town Boy.' This was Jackie's world, and she sometimes joined the floor show. She must have gotten a real charge out of the shows in March 1963. As an entertainment writer for the *Star* noted: 'Female impersonator Jackie Shane now has a female impersonating him. Shane has a record that's proving to be very hot on the charts called 'Any Other Way.' Shirley Matthews sings it à la Shane.'

'With Jackie, *gay* meant a whole different thing'

It's said that at some point in the late sixties, Jackie left Toronto and wasn't seen again. True, Jackie did relocate to Los Angeles, where she was also a well-known performer, before ultimately moving home to Nashville, where she still lives today. But Jackie never entirely said goodbye to Toronto. She was back at the Saphire Tavern for several months in the spring of 1970 and at the Club Concord for another long run in the fall of 1971.

Since then Jackie has made other kinds of returns. In 1981, a writer for the *Star* declared 'rhythm 'n' blues born again in Toronto.' Recalling 'black music's long and deep roots in the city,' the writer conjured up 'little Jackie Shane, the city's own Little Richard.' In 1988, in a review of the Lakeview Restaurant for the *Globe and Mail*, John Allemang sampled the music on offer in the diner's jukeboxes, which included 'the epicene Jackie Shane crooning "Any Other Way."' In 1992, another journalistic profile of Toronto as the 'Soul City in the '60s' singled out Dianne Brooks, Eric Mercury, and 'the smooth soul stylings of Jackie Shane.' And so it goes. In recent years, Jackie's been the subject of radio and television documentaries, videos, and dozens of blogs. In 2016, Jackie's portrait was included in a twenty-two-storey-high mural on Yonge Street, a tribute to the strip's musical past.

I believe there are other reasons, beyond the significant musical contribution, that Jackie has returned once again. During the 1960s, Jackie Shane dramatized some of the distressing and enduring dilemmas of transgender existence, perhaps especially the public's prying and persistent demand to know – 'is he or isn't she?' At the same time, Jackie was a glittering sequin of hope. Laima remembers: 'He was pretty openly "out" and in fact was probably my introduction to gay people.' Today, the blogosphere is sprinkled with testimonials from those who recall their sexual- and gender-questioning youth in the stultifying suburban Toronto of the 1960s. They remember the revelation and validation of seeing Jackie at one of the many teen-dance clubs she played in Don Mills, Newmarket, and elsewhere. And then there's Jackie's pioneering place in the long line of Black divas, from Elle Mae to Michelle Ross, some of whom began performing in Toronto in the late sixties and went on to play foundational roles in the city's Black queer communities and beyond. All this is legacy enough. But there's more.

One standard (read: dominant) account of how Toronto got queer typically begins in the 1950s and 1960s with the emergence of the first (class-stratified and often racially segregated) gay clubs, the gay tabloids and physique mags (with their endless pages of white beefcake), and the (mostly white, male) homophile activists. This early community formation set the stage for the subsequent development (or decline, depending on your point of view) from gay liberation to gay marriage, a decades-long process in which *gay* was whittled down to signify primarily as white, middle-class, masculine, straight-acting/straight-looking, no fats/no fems. And, for just as long, this has been at the root of the ongoing political struggles around gender and race within Toronto's queer communities.

The Reverend Ellis recalls that 'with Jackie, *gay* meant a whole different thing,' and indeed the story of Jackie Shane suggests a different way to tell this history. It's a story that begins in Toronto's Black and racially mixed R&B clubs and dance halls, centres on a fierce femininity, even proto-feminism, and embraces chicken, working-class trade, fat Black street queens, bad-ass women, and burly white bikers. Jackie's is a truly trans history – in the original meaning of the term – *across* genders, sexualities, classes, and races, a scrambling of boundaries that, in our own time, often seem impossible to cross.

In 1969, on the last single Jackie recorded, she belts out in gut-wrenching, driving soul, 'I gotta new way of lovin' baby … lemme teach you tonight.' Almost a full half-century later, the question is, are we finally ready to really listen and learn?

***

How This Book Got Queer

The essays that follow pick up on the provocation Jackie Shane poses to the story of how Toronto got queer. They proceed in any way other than straightforward. Starting the collection with Jackie – Black and trans in the 1960s – and covering Jackie's chart-topping hit on our cover signals our desire to switch up perhaps more familiar ways of approaching Toronto's queer history.

There are other starting points: 1810, 1838, 1882, 1969, 1981. The events and historical personages represented by those key dates are not ignored here, but we've chosen not to line them up in linear fashion. Doing so seems almost always to privilege a history that begins with and dwells on homosexuals of distinction – notable white men. Jackie would have called them 'squares.' But Toronto's queer history is anything but square. And so, like the sequins on one of Jackie's outfits, the essays presented here dazzle as they distract from conventional chronologies of Toronto's queer past, and they cover varied facets of queer existence: bar life; print culture and performance; the making of queer space and the queering of mainstream space; the gulf separating the 'rough' from the respectable; the interplay of social stigma and queer defiance. Readers will find all this and much more featured in the following pages.

The recent rediscovery of, and interest in, Jackie are surely related to how Jackie's multivocal performance of gender speaks to our present. Jackie leaps out of the 1960s to speak directly to, for instance, the remarkable upsurge in transgender organizing in the Toronto of our own day. But no single person can speak for everyone or cover everything, not even Jackie Shane. What follows is an eclectic mix; we make no claim to be definitive or comprehensive.

There's a risk, too, that commencing with one exceptional *individual* – after the success of 'Any Other Way,' Jackie was regularly referred to as the 'recording star' – will obscure the more *collective* forms of queer life, from the domestic to the political. The contributions here balance profiles of the 'stars' of Toronto's queer past with an appreciation of the social and political desire of many queer people for community.

Whether they come to us as individuals or members of communities, we must ask, why do we want these historical figures? What do we want from the queer past? The answers offered here are as varied as our contributors. Some register a real ambivalence about plucking predecessors out of the past. For others, there's a deeply felt need to build an archive, especially for those who've been marginalized or ignored in existing queer historical narratives. Still others offer a thanks-but-no-thanks to the archival impulse and its status-conferring discriminations.

If Jackie seems to speak to an astonishing array of experiences in Toronto's queer past, she is also a vital link between that past and our present. To take just one example, consider the protest led by Black Lives Matter during the 2016 Pride

Toronto parade. Intended to draw attention to how queers of colour experience the presence of police in the parade and to their struggle to maintain Black space within Pride, the reaction of many white queers revealed long-standing cleavages along lines of race within Toronto's queer communities. It's a history for queer people of colour filled with determined and principled resistance, but also with exasperation and exhaustion. In 1967, Jackie told an audience, 'Sometimes it's fatiguing being a Jackie Shane.' The past echoes in the present. We might equally be talking about the fraught history of relations between lesbians and gay men, sometimes working together, other times the lesbians doing it for themselves.

For some white queers, the police surveillance and harassment of queer communities, a leitmotif in Toronto's queer history and hence also in these pages, is not viewed as a shared historical experience with which to make common cause with those who still feel the brunt of it. Rather, it's discarded in the proverbial dustbin of history. For these people, a few of the following pieces may read like so much unnecessary dredging up of a lamentable but best-forgotten past. So be it.

No matter how you conceive it, an always illuminating, sometimes vexed, and often inspiring relationship between past and present beats at the heart of queer Toronto, and it animates much of what follows.

ARRIVING

St. Charles TORONTO

FOR FINE FOODS

"MEET ME UNDER THE CLOCK"

In 1960, when I was three, my mom moved us from Nova Scotia to Toronto. We soon ended up in a small apartment near the corner of Queen and Sackville, south of Regent Park. It was near public housing and a lot of Scotians lived there. But my mom was determined to own her own place. She started making money the well-known Cape Breton way – bootlegging and running card games until she raised enough to buy a cheap tarpaper house on Trefann Court. The whole downtown was pretty much working-class in those days: old Cabbagetown, the east end, Yonge Street, Yorkville. Rich people didn't want to live there.

Faith Nolan

A Whole Other Story

When I was about eleven, she got a place on Wellesley Street. A few blocks away, in a basement at Yonge and Wellesley, there was a dance club called Soul City. All the young Black kids went there. The music was James Brown and soul. We girls would get all dressed up, very femme. If you didn't get femmed up, the soul sisters and men would call you a lesbian.

Then, Soul City changed into a gay establishment called the 511 Club, and there was a big hullabaloo. Why was this gay club coming and taking over one of the few spaces we had in the city? The city itself, like the country, was racist, homophobic and, of course, classist. There weren't many places where Black or poor people felt welcome. People didn't like these white queers coming and taking over. They were angry. But I had had my first sex with a woman when I was twelve, so when I heard that's where queers hung out I said, 'I've got to go back here.'

It wasn't a huge transition. The 511 played Donna Summers and musicians like her. Black music was very popular. We called it soul music; the white gay guys called it disco. I guess the white gay DJs who played there didn't want to be called soul brothers. That's where I heard there were lesbian bars.

I was underage, but at that time you didn't have to show ID to get into a bar. Because I was Black, I don't think they noticed I was so young. Black people didn't have age. I was just a black dot floating through, so if I said I was eighteen, that was fine.

The first place I went to was Lola's, in the east end – the lesbian clubs tended to be far from Yonge because rents were cheaper. Lola was this big stone butch woman who rented a space at Carlaw and Eastern, down in the basement of a factory, on Friday and Saturday nights. She was probably 250 pounds, in her fifties, men's pants, shirt, and haircut, really strong, lots of tats on her arms.

Lola's had tinfoil on the ceiling and different-coloured light bulbs and cheap folding tables and chairs. Most of the clientele were working-class and poor. You didn't hardly see middle-class women in bars at that time, certainly not at Lola's. They must have had private parties or whatever.

Most of the butches passed as men and dressed as men – pants, suit jackets, white shirts, men's shoes; that was the cool look. At first, I wasn't sure they weren't really men, until I got closer and I could see they had a little more chest than men, flattened down but thicker. The butches would work in factories. The femmes were typists or cashiers. They wore short skirts and tops.

The Blue Jay was a bit more upscale – no tinfoil on the ceiling, and nicer chairs, those black leather ones with steel frames like they have in restaurants. There were little round tables that could sit four. When you went through the door you would pull back a curtain and pay your money to the owner-operators, two English dykes, Patty and Ed. The cops would come in and hassle them, so they made sure they always had protection: they had two big Dobermans. I think there was payola, though. Otherwise we probably would have been raided and closed down.

On the first level inside the door, there were maybe twenty tables, and the bar to the side. Then you'd walk down a couple of stairs, and there was a walkway to the circular dance floor, with a disco ball and soft lighting and chairs on the sides, and at the back of the room was the DJ spinning records. The space could hold 150 women or so. There were no men allowed. Sometimes women's bands played there. One was called Lady, with Sherry Shute on lead guitar and Lynda Lesny on bass.

I met some girls at school who came out about the same time. My friend Heather was native. Mary was Italian, and Italians weren't really considered white

Faith Nolan, left, with friend outside Eve Zaremba's bookstore on Harbord Street

either. So we started to going to clubs together and hanging out. In those days, anybody who wasn't white would hang out together. Queer Black and Indigenous people met with a lot of racism. Everything was white. A good-looking woman was white with blond hair and blue eyes. White girls thought they were just all that. A lot of people didn't want to go out with someone who wasn't white. Everything else was exotic, unless you had a fetish.

I knew three Black lesbians in the city at the time: Teerea, Greta, and me. Teerea was a Scotian and more of a hoodie, like me. That was cool 'cause we could hang a little bit, but she was pretty much my cousin from Nova Scotia so nothing more than that was going to happen. Greta was a Canadian Black from some little hick town somewhere. She was more popular because she was femmy and more like a white girl, so the white girls liked her. She was very nice but wasn't interested in young Black women. So for me, the pickings were slim.

At first when I went out, I got all dressed up, very femme, because that's the way we'd dress to go to Soul City. I'd just ask women to dance who I thought were pretty, the feminine ones, but they wouldn't dance with me because I was looking femme myself, and that was a no-go. That's when I recognized I was kind of butch, too. My friends had always told me I had to wear clothes that were more femmy to go out with them. But when I realized I could dress butch, that was it. It wasn't like stone butch. Styles were changing. The younger 1970s dykes were more androgynous, with the long hair and the low-cut jeans and construction boots and sneakers and T-shirts.

Nevertheless, I was still kind of the last chance. People would say, 'If you can't get anyone, ask Faith.' So I would go with older women who weren't too discerning. I had a lot of one-night stands. I would tell them that I was eighteen because I knew that nobody would go with me if I told them my real age. But after we went to bed together, I'd tell them, and that's when they'd say, 'Get lost.'

My first relationship was with Robin, a white girl I met at the Blue Jay at a twenty-four-hour dance marathon. (I should have won that marathon but I don't think they wanted to give the fifty-dollar prize to a Black girl, so they split it between me and the second-last dancer, who was white.) Robin was seventeen. She would come to my house after school and we necked in my bedroom. I kept the door locked, and my mother started to ask why. I said we were doing homework. But she started making jokes and saying, 'What are you? Some kind of queer?' After about six months of that, I finally had enough and said, 'Yeah, I am.' I was trying not to say it because I knew if I did, she was going to throw me out. And she did. She said, 'Get the fuck out. You're sick. You're disgusting.' I was fourteen.

At that time, in the queer community, we would help each other out, like Black people. There really weren't community organizations, so people took care of each other. If there was a young homeless queer, somebody would put them up.

In 1971, I moved in with Dee Dee. She was trans. I had met her at Momma Cooper's, one of the bars, and she said I could come and stay with her. She fed me. We were pretty poor, so we ate a lot of chili. Most of the trans and butches and drag queens that I knew, even if they had come from money, were poor by the time they got downtown. Just about all the gay guys I met were working-class, too, especially those hanging on Yonge Street. The good thing with Dee Dee was that her apartment was at Church and Wellesley, so I was able to continue going to school at Jarvis Collegiate.

One of my gay school friends used to occasionally give me five dollars for food. I also made some money singing and playing the guitar. I had started playing when I was twelve or so. I had found an Odetta record – a Pete Seeger/Woody Guthrie songbook – so by the time I was fourteen, I knew a few songs. I also started writing some of my own. One was called 'I Want to Love Someone Who's Just Like Me.' I guess that was calling out for another butch woman. I played at the Nervous Breakdown Cafe on Carlton at Parliament, and would pass the hat to get some change. Or I'd play on the street corner in Yorkville. People would jam a lot, and we shared folk songs back and forth. Everyone was hanging out on the street, smoking joints, not like now. If you show up with a guitar now, the police arrive and ask for your permit.

By the time I was seventeen, I had finished high school. Around Regent, we were mostly Black Scotians. Since it was segregated when I came out, a lot of people in my community were homophobic, like everywhere else. But I still wanted to be around Scotians, so I thought I would return and go to university down there.

But that's a whole other story.

I grew up in Dinorwic, a town of about two hundred people east of Dryden above Lake Superior. My grandfather was Italian and my grandmother was Ojibway. Because of the laws at the time, she lost her status when they married. My dad never had status, and when he married my mom, she lost her status too. Indians like me without status were thought of as Métis. Nevertheless, I grew up very traditionally, woken at sunrise for ceremonies. As youngsters we were told to pay attention and observe and be part of it.

During my teenage years, we would pick wild rice. My job was to be in the front of the canoe, paddling. My mom or a relative would be in the back, thrashing the rice into the boat. On the first day people went out, they would give what they picked to a community pot.

Art Zoccole

Agokwe

One year, we were getting ready to do the ceremony, sitting on a blanket with the meal in the middle, the women on one side and the men on the other. The elder who was to conduct the ceremony had been drinking. Suddenly he said to me, 'How would you like to fuck me up the ass?'

When I was really young, I had begun to realize I was different. I exhibited both feminine and masculine qualities, but I kept that to myself. The women came to my defence and put the elder in his place. But I had been outed in my community.

I didn't really sense any hostility. People looked after me. One family invited me for meals and treated me very well. When I was about eighteen, they explained, I was exactly like their brother, who passed away as a teenager. I understood then there had been somebody else before me who was gay.

Shortly before she died, my mom called me 'Agokwe.' She only used that word once. I never had the opportunity to sit with her and get a full explanation of what it meant. I only found out when I was researching homosexuality among Indigenous peoples in Toronto in the seventies. The lights went on, and I realized she knew.

When I finished the trauma of high school, there were two options – to be a truck driver or a woodcutter. I knew I needed to leave town and get an education, but my father refused to pay the registration fee, and because I wasn't a status Indian, there was no government support.

I moved to Ottawa and worked a series of mindless jobs there, and then in Toronto. But I finally saved enough to enrol in an accounting course at Confederation College in Thunder Bay. Thunder Bay had a very small gay community. That's where I was introduced to other gay people for the first time, and heard about the wonderful gay world in Toronto, and especially the St. Charles Tavern. When I had been in Toronto, I'd walked by it but had no idea it housed a gay scene.

After finishing my course, I moved back to Toronto, arriving late in October 1979. I heard that Halloween was a big festival where people dressed up in costumes like women and went to the St. Charles. I was excited about going and celebrating, and stood across the street from the tavern to see the show.

But what I observed was absolutely horrifying. People started yelling obscenities and throwing eggs at those going in or out. I was devastated, and sat on a bench near Alexander Street for several hours, thinking, 'What have I done? Is this my life? Is this what's going to happen to me?'

But I stayed. At the end of the 1970s, the scene was still largely limited to the St. Charles and the Parkside Tavern. You'd go from one to the other, usually along a back alley parallel to Yonge Street, because it wasn't safe to walk down Yonge. Even in the alley, there could be bashers. One of the three times I was bashed was in that back alley, standing behind the Parkside with a friend. Somebody came along and started punching us.

I went to work for the Chiefs of Ontario, and I wasn't out there. I remember hearing one of my bosses, a regional chief, saying, 'We don't have a gay Indian problem.'

Some Aboriginal people came to the bars, but at first I didn't know who they were. Everybody tried to keep a low profile in those days. There was a lot of racism – you'd be taunted by other patrons yelling rude remarks. But there were also Caucasian guys who were totally enthralled by us: it was the 'noble Indian' versus the 'drunken Indian.' You had to try to figure out, is this person going to be rude or nice? It got worse as the evening went on and people got drunker. Sometimes the Indigenous people became confrontational. Many of us carry a lot of baggage – residential schools, the Sixties Scoop, the loss of language and culture, plus being gay and ostracized by our communities.

But as we got to know each other, we stuck together. We had a core group who met on Friday or Saturday evenings, starting at the Parkside and then going up to the St. Charles to cruise, and finally maybe to Boots, at Sherbourne and Bloor.

Around this time, we noticed people were starting to get sick and we organized care teams to go into people's homes. When they passed away, some communities wouldn't even accept the body back home because of the stigma around AIDS. We had to do our own ceremonies – celebrations of life with traditional ceremonies, often at the Native Canadian Centre on Spadina.

Around 1987, the writers Tomson Highway and Billy Merasty and I started talking about organizing an Aboriginal group. We booked a room at the 519 Church Street Community Centre (now simply the 519), made a poster, and put them up in all the gay bars.

The first meeting was set for a Sunday in January 1989. I can still see that tiny room at the 519 suddenly filling up, mostly with men. We had no idea what we were going to do. Out of the corner of my eye, I saw LaVerne Monette, who worked for the Union of Ontario Indians. 'Oh my God,' I said to myself. 'The Union of Ontario Indians has sent their lawyer to see what we're doing.' I feared infiltrators. But as the meeting went on, people started expressing themselves, and when I looked at LaVerne again, I realized she was a lesbian. At that time I knew all about gay men but nothing about lesbians.

At the meeting, we tried to come up with a name for our group. But we all had different languages and different words to describe Two Spirit people, so we settled on an English term that everybody understood: Gays and Lesbians of the First Nations in Toronto.

In those early stages, we wanted it to be a social group where we could come together and play pool, join a baseball team, or go on camping trips. We used to have tea and bannock potlucks, sometimes at the Native Canadian Centre.

At first, we didn't focus on HIV/AIDS, but then Frank McGee from the AIDS Bureau asked if we would like $50,000 to do HIV/AIDS work. That's where our focus shifted. After a long fight with the bureaucracy, we incorporated as 2-Spirited People of the 1st Nations and got charitable status. I don't think a lot of people realize how the system prevented us from getting stuff done. Today, we're integrated into both AIDS service and Aboriginal networks. In 2014, we were the Honoured Group at World Pride.

As a kid growing up in Saskatoon, I saved my allowance for months so I could buy a VCR: a beautiful four-head Hi-Fi Panasonic that cost nearly $300.

That machine was worth every penny because it provided a conduit to *Another World*, NBC's long-running soap opera, whose characters and storylines preoccupied my pubescent brain. In particular, I was enamoured with Vicky and Marley, identical twins separated at birth – one raised poor and one very wealthy. Every morning I set my VCR to record the daytime drama so I could revel in their schemes after school. But on April 30, 1997, I used that same VCR to record the sitcom *Ellen*, to preserve forever the moment when Ellen Degeneres's character told her friends and the world what all of us already knew: Ellen was gay. And by 1997, I was gay, too.

Rebecka Sheffield

Take Me Away to Another World

The following year, I moved to Toronto, leaving on a 2:45 a.m. train with my girlfriend, a Siamese cat, and my VCR in tow. I wanted to get as far away from the prairies as I could, and arrived just as Mayor Mel Lastman was summoning the army to dig whining Toronto out of a snowstorm.

When I got to Toronto, I did all of the things that young gay people do when they move to the big city: wandered up and down Church Street, sat on the cruising steps, played pool at Pope Joan's. We lived in an Annex basement, with a dirt-floor bathroom. Some evenings, I'd rent obscure queer films from Suspect Video and watch them on my old VCR.

Despite the digs, Toronto was a generous town. I ate well, danced many nights at Boots, and fell more deeply in love with the person I eventually married. By 2000, a profession materialized, and things seemed to be going well.

For my birthday, I bought tickets to see Ellen Degeneres at Massey Hall. But, to be perfectly honest, I wasn't as excited about seeing Ellen as I was about the fact that she was touring with her then-girlfriend, Anne Heche.

Heche plays an important cameo in my tale that I've neglected to mention. From 1997 until their fiery breakup in 2000, Ellen and Anne were Hollywood's Most Famous Lesbian Duo. Yet Heche had also played Vicky and Marley on *Another World* during my formative years. Her relationship with Ellen validated every queer feeling I had ever had. I almost swooned when I caught a glimpse of her at the show.

I had much more than a glimpse of Heche a year later, in September 2001, when she released an autobiography entitled *Call Me Crazy*, in which she reflected on her experiences on *Another World* and her mental health struggles.

Every lesbian I knew was talking about the book.

Heche was scheduled to give a reading at the Indigo bookstore near my office, the headquarters of a feminist publisher. Several of my colleagues and I decided to go to the reading on our lunch break. But that very morning, two planes struck the World Trade Center in New York. Despite a stepped-up police presence downtown and an evacuation order in my building, we decided to make our way to the reading.

There we were, four queer girls standing in a packed bookstore an hour after the North Tower collapsed. Heche arrived late, flustered and apologetic. She had flown in from Boston that morning, but Pearson security had held her plane on the tarmac for an extensive check before releasing the passengers.

She had found out about the Twin Towers in the taxi on the way here, Heche explained somberly. And as she read, a well-dressed businesswoman in the front row wept. I scanned the room and noted a high presence of lesbians. We acknowledged one another with nods.

When the reading ended, I grabbed a copy of *Call Me Crazy* and brought it to Heche for an autograph. I don't remember what I said to her. Afterwards, I stood back and watched the crowd, spotting Heche's fiancé, the cameraman she'd left Ellen for amidst much scandal. (All the lesbians were talking about it!) Star-struck and overwhelmed, we stumbled out onto Bay Street. I forgot to pay for the book, and no one noticed. I did not go back in.

The morning's events left me feeling nervous about the subway. I decided to walk back to my apartment, past the Annex's sushi restaurants and knick-knack shops, and then the Korean eateries west of Bathurst. When I reached Christie Pits, I lay down on the park's grassy slopes, clutching my signed book.

It was nearly supper by the time I got home. I sat on my balcony, looking out at the evening's calmness while those buildings fell over again and again on the TV inside. Amidst the oddly entwined tragedy and excitement of that day, I felt something I have experienced many times since – when something you've long anticipated finally comes to pass in a way that you never imagined, and does so in a city where everything is just a little bit queer.

I was Miss General Idea.

If this doesn't surprise you, it should: my name doesn't appear anywhere in the annals of General Idea.

Miss General Idea was a character, a conceptual caprice. Jorge Zontal, Felix Partz, and AA Bronson – the three Toronto artists who comprised the General Idea collective – created her in the late 1960s, and she flits through the following fifteen years of their work.

General Idea were Warhol's Canadian cousins, making art, magazines, and installations that mocked and mimicked the machinery of stardom. Miss General Idea was the brightest star in their sky from the moment she was conceived until the mid-1980s. She was the beauty queen to end all beauty queens, a parody of Miss America and other pageant glamour-pusses.

Miss General Idea was a figure as real as any beauty queen – that is, not real at all. Through her, the artists in General Idea were able to plunge themselves into an aspect of stardom that they loved and loathed: glamour. They designed dresses for her, and a boudoir. They drew up plans for a pavilion that would be built in her honour. They staged pageants in which men and women would win her title, at least for a time.

Derek McCormack

I Was Miss General Idea

In 1971, General Idea created an 'artist's conception' of her: a silkscreen on rubber of a woman – at least, I think it's a woman – in a skirt, killer heels, and what looks to be a black rubber bodysuit. She had lots of looks. There was the 1940s-style dress worn by Miss General Idea Pageant participants in 1971. There was the VB dress of 1975, which consisted of three Robert Smithson-esque pyramids – a hat, a blouse, and a skirt – constructed from venetian blinds.

General Idea produced glamour in order to parody it; the artists inhabited the world of fashion in order to fuck with fashion. Of course, being fashionable complicated their critique of fashion: was the critique for real, or were they simply co-opting criticism for fashion, furthering fashion's reach? Miss General Idea embodied this ambiguity; she made fashion seem as complex and intellectual as I always wanted it to be.

Which is why I stepped into her stilettos. In 1985, I proclaimed myself Miss General Idea. I had to: she wasn't real, and I needed her to be.

In 1985, I went to the Art Gallery of Ontario to see a survey show of General Idea's work. I was sixteen. I had heard of the artists, but not of Miss General Idea.

I was smitten. She was a creature of glamour, and for me glamour was a synonym for fashion, and fashion was a synonym for gay. Her duties: perverting and playing with beauty, fame, and sexuality.

These were duties I knew I could discharge. She was the ambassadress of artificiality and abasement; I was a spotty teen who longed for glamour and wanted badly to be abased. She wasn't real, nor was I.

I crowned myself. Then I bused back to Peterborough, my hometown. I did my best to embody the title. I was faggy. I was condescending. With a friend, I published a zine, *The Aquamarine Poodle*. The title was inspired by a triad of poodles – one pink, one gold, one aquamarine – that appeared in several of General Idea's pieces. More often than not, the poodles were engaged in a ménage à trois.

My friend and I sold our zine in the school cafeteria. It included my reviews of the recent prêt-à-porter shows in Paris. I hadn't been in Paris for the shows, but that didn't stop me. I also penned an essay about Paris. I tried to simulate the style of General Idea's writings, which parroted and parodied the academese of *Artforum* and blended it with the bon mots of Diana Vreeland's *Vogue*: 'Have you ever been to Paris?' I wrote. 'Paris is an object, a twentieth-century icon imbued with the trappings of glamour, its characteristics, and gestures.' It goes on and on. I discuss image and violence and surveillance. I couldn't dress up in Miss General Idea's garments, so I tried a different kind of drag: words.

I lost myself in Miss General Idea. What I didn't grasp was that she was already lost.

'Miss General Idea has fled.' So wrote General Idea in 1984. The artists said she had abandoned them; in truth, they had abandoned her. She had amused them, but she was no longer their muse. They had turned their attention to other matters; for a while, it was the media and TV; then it was AIDS. In 1994, both Partz and Zontal died of AIDS-related illnesses; General Idea was lost, too.

In 2011, I went back to the AGO to see another General Idea survey. It was all there: the architectural plans for the 1984 Miss General Idea Pavilion; the relics from the ruins of the pavilion, which burned down in 1977 (it didn't really burn down, since it was never really built: the pavilion was a ruse, as were the relics). Oodles of fucking poodles. It was fun, all fancifully perverse, though the later AIDS art casts a long shadow on the rest. There were three titanic AZT pills. The mirrored surface of Felix Partz's big Mylar handbag (1968) is reflected by the mirrored surfaces of the pill-shaped Mylar balloons of *Magi© Bullet* (1992).

From purse to prescription, General Idea reflected the fashion world, the art world, the gay world, and their mirrors mirrored me, mirroring their mirrors.

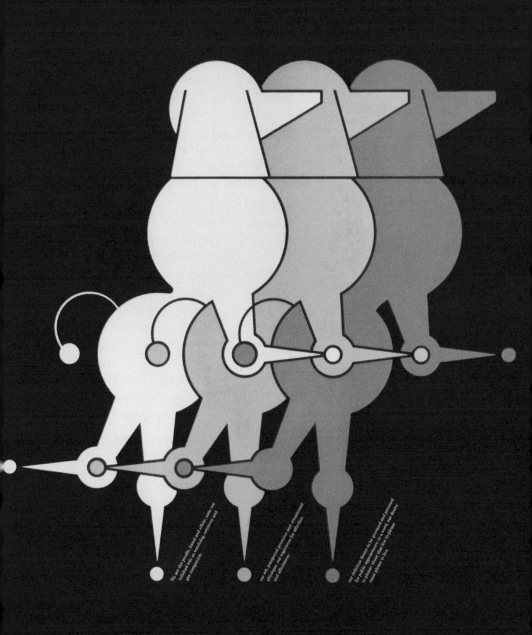

THE 1984 MISS GENERAL IDEA
PAVILLION ✷ APRIL 26 - JUNE 23
1985 ART GALLERY OF ONTARIO

Sunday, August 23, 1998

HUNGOVER. I had … nine drinks? Eight? Maybe ten. Stopped counting after a while. Just tried to match Millie, drink for drink. Surely I couldn't let her drink me under the table. For shame.

Plus, Ah Jun was there. Came late as usual, walked in smoking. We were all already stuffed into every available space on the tiny couches of the karaoke room. She dared insert herself next to Millie (I was, of course, on Millie's other side), and her songs in front of everyone else's. I was fully aware we were both flanking Millie like disgusting wolves. But I couldn't help myself.

Karen B. K. Chan

Uptown/Downtown:

Diary of a Hong Kong

Dyke in Nineties Toronto

Ah Jun's dominance is so selective. A tiny, whimpering shrimp in English spaces (school, the mall, even at fucking McDonald's – which I'm still boycotting), and then a bucking bronco on Cantonese turf. She was sneaking feels of Millie's side boob all night. UGH! That fuckin' infuriated me! Fear not, misogynists: the patriarchy is alive and well, thanks to Ah Jun.

Which is why I taught her a lesson. In the middle of all her gung-ho drinking and rubbing up everything in a skirt, I suggested we play 15/20, a Chinese drinking game. One catch: losers do push-ups in addition to drinking. I knew she wouldn't refuse. Any chance to fluff her feathers. I also knew she did push-ups religiously (yes, me too, ahem) as a chest/breast control strategy. I've seen her triceps.

Once we had a few rounds, I went in for the kill. I suggested the loser had to do push-ups while hovering over the winner, who would lie on the floor. The obvious reference is that we'd look like we were fucking. Everyone laughed and squealed. They were so into it!

Ah Jun shook her head, *hard.* Complained of the filthiness of the floor, joked how the ugliness of my face would make her vomit. Blah blah blah. Her final, ineffectual appeal was simply about how 'gay' it all would be. But by then everyone was chanting, 'Do it! Do it! Do it!'

I feigned backtracking: 'No, no, let's not. Your knees will get weak from finally getting to mount me in the missionary position,' which made her tell me to *PK and die* and immediately start the next round.

She lost three sets in a row. That's thirty push-ups, huffing and puffing over me. For the last ten, I opened my legs and moaned. Everyone went wild. I was tearing from laughing so hard. Ah Jun scoffed and lost much of her bravado.

If in no other way can I compete with that rich, slightly attractive and moderately charming uptown dyke, I can always beat her at gender fluidity. She can rule Highway 7 and Bayview but she can't rule me. Ha!

Plus, Millie came home with me. Which just goes to show that to get the girl, it's best to make her feel safe enough to laugh at you.

I turn twenty-three in eight days! Maybe I should write a memoir.

Monday, August 24, 1998

So. Yesterday Millie and I woke up in the same bed. It was a bit awkward. What's worse is, it became obvious once I went to the bathroom that she or I – or both of us – had thrown up before we, um, got busy. Which means we did some major and unexpected fluid-swapping of the vomitous kind. I can't even think about it.

But thank god it all came back to normal tonight at the organizing meeting. Asian Youth HIV Outreach. It was like nothing had happened. All the usual suspects were there – Bao, Jenny, Fiona, Cheuk, Ava – all of us except for Rita. She's in Hong Kong visiting her grandma, who got sick suddenly last week. We read out an email from her. She was having a hard time explaining to her family why her head was shaved. In a panic, she told the truth (no!), saying it was because she is a radical feminist unshackling from feminine beauty expectations. And then Rita overheard her mom explain to the nurses privately that she was becoming Buddhist. Rita was both relieved and, as usual, deeply offended.

We spent most of the meeting figuring out how to get the uptown dykes to come downtown for the next event. They think of us as angry, dirty, unfashionable *bananas*. And we talk about them like they're plastic dolls who stick only to themselves. When that *Toronto Star* article about anti-Black animosity from Chinese people in Toronto came out last summer, there was so much outrage. I get it – framing it so antagonistically doesn't help, we need to dialogue! But I was like, honestly, there's some truth to it.

Sometimes I forget that, technically, I too live uptown. Squarely in the 905 with my mom in a new Markham subdivision. And I know how to play the part – wear brand names, use Canto slang, don't get too uptight about politics. But, for some reason, I don't always pass. Somehow they see through my address to where I'm angry and dirty.

The committee decided our Bubble Tea House event will be different from other queer events, which all seem so loud and proud. That's what keeps the uptowners away. It's so obnoxious – all these pronouncements of one's identity. People need the slack to be anonymous or in the grey, you know? On the flyer and the volunteer training, we'll emphasize that it's for 'LGBT Asian youth *and friends*.' And you never have to say whether you're a gay, a grey, or a friend. Brilliant, right?

Wednesday, August 26, 1998

Shit fuck. Worst day ever.

Turns out I seriously offended someone on Saturday night: Pack and her girl-friend, whom I had just met. When we said goodbye, I hugged them both. Even through my drunky haze, I remember Pack stepping in between Oriana and me. Right there in the parking lot, she put one hand around Oriana's body and continued smoking with the other hand. It was straight out of an HK triad movie. Groan!

The Bubble Tea House event planning continues. Getting a sinking feeling now that many uptowners won't come. It's too far downtown. Too Church 'n' Wellesley. Too English. And TOO. MUCH. HUGGING.

I'm so done with event planning!

Friday, August 28, 1998

Helping Melissa move out of her parents' house tomorrow. It'll be nice to get her settled in after the hell she's been through.

At the same time – what a dream! – to live at Church and Maitland. It doesn't get gayer, does it? I'd like to do that at some point, live in the gaybourhood. Just stumble home after clubbing. Buddies and Slacks and Fly – and the Golden Griddle, most importantly – all within five minutes.

But I wouldn't take it for that high a price – she's basically been disowned. Her poor parents and their suburban bomb shelter don't know what hit them. I'm sure they're thinking, *How did we raise such an anti-society ungrateful brat?*

And all of this fell out of Melissa refusing to lock the front door and her parents freaking out about all the robbers in Mississauga lining up to pillage them. I'm like, your parents survived war, and the mean and poor streets of 1950s HK! How can you not understand why they're scared of everything? What's the big deal with locking a door? She makes it like a political statement, but they're not even the enemy.

But seriously, how will I ever move out without getting married or without my parents thinking it's treason? My freedom seems like a personal insult to them.

Monday, August 31, 1998

I'm twenty-three tomorrow!

To celebrate, I'm going to a BDSM workshop at the 519, dropping posters off at the Women's Bookstore, bringing Melissa some egg tarts, and *then* having dinner with my parents.

Haven't started, already tired. Fuck, I'm so old.

grew up in 1950s Toronto when the Junction was still dry and TV was brand new. As a teen, I loved songs like 'It's My Party' (Leslie Gore), 'Never Be Anyone Else But You' (Ricky Nelson), and 'My Boyfriend's Back' (the Angels).

I only broadened my musical taste when I met my now ex-husband. For our first fateful date in December 1967, Tom, a passionate R&B fan, invited me to an Otis Redding concert. Sadly, that date never happened, as Redding, just twenty-six, died in a plane crash only days before his Toronto appearance. But Tom and I went on to hear many wonderful R&B performers around town, at Club 888, the Beverly Hills Motor Hotel, the Peach, the Saphire, Club Bluenote, and Grossman's. We saw James Brown perform with Wilson Pickett, the Downchild Blues Band, Little Caesar and the Consuls, Chubby Checker, and B. B. King.

Elaine Gaber-Katz

How Jackie Shane Helped 'Satisfy My Soul'

Yet one of the most electrifying performers we saw was someone far less well-known – Jackie Shane, with Frank Motley and his band. Tom had first seen Jackie Shane perform at a dance club at Jackson's Point on Lake Simcoe. While he loved her energy and campiness, mostly he loved his vocals and the R&B music s/he played. (I use her and his interchangeably to signify that Jackie Shane presented as a gay man in the 1960s and now might be transgender and use the feminine pronoun.) When Tom introduced me to Jackie Shane, I was captivated by her colourful performance and sexually telling lyrics.

Like Tom, I too loved Jackie's soulful voice and the funky sounds of Frank Motley's crew. But most of all, I loved Jackie's sauciness. I didn't have words then to describe what I loved about her. After all, I didn't come out as queer for thirty more years. But I profoundly sensed, that first time I saw him perform, that Jackie's queer, in-your-face presentation expressed that part of me that would never fit well in the straight world. Jackie spoke to a side of me that I didn't yet understand and that my 'then' world wouldn't have easily accepted. To get it, I played her 1967 *Live* album repeatedly, until I simply wore down the grooves.

The most memorable performance of Jackie's that I got to see was at the Broom & Stone in Scarborough, a curling hall/dance hall. We went to this cavernous venue with my cousin, which allowed me to see Jackie Shane through his conservative eyes. That night, I sensed Jackie Shane represented the future, my future, even though I wouldn't put these feelings into words until much later, when I fell in love with other bodacious musicians like Ma Rainey, Big Mama Thornton, and Gaye Adegbalola.

With his flamboyant dress, evocative lyrics, and prophetic performances, Jackie Shane provided satisfaction to my soul at a time when I didn't even know why I needed it.

The first thing Hanna and Saied noticed about the gay community in Canada was the normal lives its members led. The Syrian couple, who arrived in Toronto in June 2016, thought it remarkable that some gay couples had been in committed relationships for twenty-five or more years; that they hosted dinner parties where they invited guests of all sexual orientations, including family members; that both single and partnered members of the community held steady jobs, owned homes, and even raised children. Everything the LGBTQ community now takes for granted felt, to them, like a trip to a parallel universe.

Kamal Al-Solaylee
Hanna and Saied's Story

Thanks to the generosity of ten predominately gay male sponsors who partnered with the Canadian government to bring Hanna and Saied from Malaysia, where they had waited out the Syrian civil war, the two men have a shot at following in their hosts' footsteps.

To Hanna, twenty-eight, and Saied, thirty-seven (names have been changed at their request), the transition to gay Canadian citizenship is the latest stop on a journey that started long before the civil war. It's a path that many queers from around the world have taken: fleeing sexual and political oppression for the freedoms of liberal democracies. Cities like Montreal and Vancouver, but particularly Toronto, have acted as sanctuaries for gay men and women for decades.

George Hislop, the late Toronto-based gay activist, led the way in making Canada a more welcoming destination in the 1970s by pressuring federal immigration officials to reconsider a ban that put LGBTQ newcomers in the same categories as 'pimps' and 'prostitutes.' The ban was lifted in 1977, 'effectively turning Toronto into a sanctuary for gay refugees,' noted *Toronto Life* in a July 2016 article.

The 519 in downtown Toronto, Canada's foremost community centre with an LGBTQ mandate, has continued Hislop's mission by running Settling In, a program that provides hundreds of refugees and newcomers to Toronto with contacts and emotional support.

The significance of this kind of service can't be emphasized enough. Other charitable or volunteer-based organizations in Toronto, such as the Rainbow Railroad and the Iranian Railroad for Queer Refugees, have given the city a leading global role in helping queers and trans people escape persecution and violence in countries like Russia, Mexico, Uganda, Trinidad and Tobago, Brazil, and South Korea.

Yet the journeys made by refugees like Hanna and Saied don't always come with clean breaks. Finding a community of like-minded queers in Toronto is one thing; finding work that allows you to make the most of this new life is another.

Settlement Services for Lesbian, Gay, Bisexual & Transgender Newcomers who are Black, African, or Caribbean

A Program of the Black Coalition for AIDS Prevention
www.blackcap.ca
BLACK C·A·P

Despite their differences in age and religious backgrounds – Hanna is Christian; Saied, Muslim – the two men shared the experience of growing up gay in a society that considered homosexuality a deviation and ostracized (or severely punished) those who exhibited any hints of it. One human rights advocate recently suggested that honour killings of gay men in Syria remain common, and the civil war has intensified the targeting and murder of those who, according to the country's penal code, exhibit 'carnal knowledge against the order of nature.' The long-haired, slim-built, 'arty' Hanna, who liked to wear colourful shirts when strutting down the streets of Homa with his four sisters, knew that sting from a very young age.

'I felt different from all the other people around me,' Hanna tells me over tea in the basement apartment he shares with Saied. At one point he even asked a friend to videotape how he walks in order to change his gait. It didn't help that Hanna decided to study interior design in Damascus, a field – like hairdressing or dancing – that practically screams effete homosexual. By comparison, the bearded and sturdy Saied studied mechanical engineering, owned property, and led a relatively hassle-free life. 'But,' he adds, 'I lived a secret life in my gay side.'

The two met on a popular gay dating site in 2011, just as the war was revving up. It took five months before Hanna felt comfortable enough to send a photograph. Even after they first met, he couldn't trust Saied completely. Syrian intelligence and morality police were known to visit dating sites and entrap gay men. Because Saied could pass for straight, Hanna feared he was being set up.

Other problems surfaced. 'He looks so much younger than me,' Saied recalls. 'To walk down the street with a younger guy who is not your colleague is not normal.'

By 2012 both men faced bigger challenges as the Syrian war escalated, threatening even the relative safety of Damascus. Hanna left for Kuala Lumpur in October of that year, a move that provided a way out of war and the closet. Saied joined him the following year, first on a ninety-day visitor's visa and then illegally. Hanna registered with the UN refugee agency and had the foresight to include Saied as his partner, qualifying both as a family unit for refugee applications.

What followed was almost three years of waiting and wading through a molten bureaucratic process. Saied worked illegally in clothing stores or restaurants, pretending to be a customer during Malaysian police raids. In late 2014, the United Nations High Commissioner for Refugees informed them of three possible countries that might accept their applications: Switzerland, Australia, and the U.S. Canada, then still under the Harper government's anti-Muslim and anti-refugee grip, was not even a possibility.

But in April 2015, they received two simultaneous life-changing phone calls. On one call, Hanna received news that his father had just died. Saied, on another, found himself talking to a UNHCR official. 'Canada took your files,' he was told.

As he processed the news of his father's passing, Hanna joined Saied, and they began checking out Canada on Google, looking up the names of provinces and territories they had never heard of before. They watched YouTube videos of Pride celebrations in Vancouver and Toronto. One of their Canadian sponsors even suggested they listen to CBC Radio online.

The two arrived at Lester B. Pearson International Airport on June 8, 2016.

They insist that I make a note of the date. 'It was our new birthday,' says Hanna. All ten sponsors showed up with banners declaring, 'Welcome to Canada.' The summer consisted of parties and celebrations and moving into the first apartment they've shared as a couple.

Months after the euphoria of arrival, however, both men were still looking for paid work in their fields. Hanna gave up a part-time coffee-shop job for an unpaid design internship, while Saied's best offer was also as an unpaid helping hand in an engineering start-up. 'This is the difficult part of this story,' an anxious Saied tells me. 'It's hard to find a job with my qualifications. I already lost four years of my life in Kuala Lumpur.'

In an ideal world, refugees and immigrants don't need to choose between a safe, welcoming place and one that recognizes the importance of meaningful work in their integration and happiness. Toronto's scorecard on the former may not be perfect, but an array of queer community and advocacy groups have worked hard over decades to make transitions into full Canadian citizenship less stressful for newcomers. The Toronto I love doubles as the largest city in Canada and one that remains livable and community-minded. As someone who was once a newcomer, I can testify that the space in between a metropolis and a (queer-friendly) neighbourhood is what made this city home.

For Hanna and Saied, the involvement with resettlement services is receding as they weave their lives into the community they've found in Toronto. Later on the same Sunday we met, in fact, they were planning to host a small dinner party.

How mundane and how perfectly marvellous for them.

Postcard from AIDS committee of Toronto's 1992 safer sex campaign. Illustrated by Maurice Vellekoop. 'Summer in the City' was a three-city educational project between Vancouver, Montreal, and Toronto.

SPACES

Natalie Wood

Kiss and Tell (2013):
Church Street Mural Project

In creating my mural 'Kiss and Tell,' I was inspired by NYC-based AIDS activist artists' collective Gran Fury's 'Kissing Doesn't Kill' poster that educated people about HIV/AIDS. 'Kiss and Tell' is located in an alleyway on an unpainted wall. The location denotes that even as we were being marginalized, we still created spaces for ourselves and were an integral part of the environment and space of Church and Wellesley.

I created 'Kiss and Tell' using digital silhouettes that consist of the texts, anthologies, novels, and magazines that make visible the lives of queers of colour.

To collect the titles of the texts, I asked queers of colour to share any print material they had read and that sustained and fed them when they were coming out. I sought texts that were seminal to understanding their lives and experiences as queers. In particular, I was interested in highlighting the kind of politicized culture that queers of colour created in the 1980s after the bathhouse raids and the first Pride march, especially since there was often very little space for the kind of culture that we, as queers of colour, wanted to create. I sought to represent organizations such as Lesbians of Colour, Zami, and Punani Posse in the mural.

In essence, this mural is an opportunity for me to thank many of the activists working at the time to make my lifestyle safe and possible. I attended many meetings and parties that helped me become proud to be queer. I was finally given a chance to find love and happiness.

T he park was never as silent as it was when filled with thousands of people the evening after the Pulse nightclub massacre in Orlando, Florida, on June 12, 2016. Then, not yet twenty-four hours into history, a vigil hastily organized that morning saw the park jammed with people, filling up every available space, many holding candles aloft.

Barbara Hall Park was the only place this could happen, the town square of Toronto's queer community, perhaps even its spiritual heart, too. 'Perhaps,' because the latter is certainly decentralized geographically around the city in various local communities and niches, an ephemeral spirit that is individual as well as collective.

Shawn Micallef

Town Squares and Spiritual Hearts

The park, too, is still becoming comfortable with its town-square role. Toronto is a city where the embrace of public space as a public living room has been slow and sometimes reluctant. The community comes to the park on occasion, but it doesn't always hang out, nor do all members of the community embrace it equally, if at all. It used to be much more reliably easy to pinpoint the heart of the Church and Wellesley neighbourhood.

Certainly not representative of the wide diversity of queer Toronto, the Steps, just a half block from the park, once served as the visual focal point of the gaybourhood (see pages 61–63). For a spell in the late 1980s and early 1990s, nearly every city in Canada had a downtown Second Cup coffee shop that was a haunt for various subcultures, but the franchise on Church Street was *the* gathering place in the Village, day and night.

Located just south of the corner, the coffee shop sat half a dozen brown-tiled steps up from the sidewalk, an incline that turned this short stretch of Church into a parade ground of sorts: permanent bleachers from which to watch an endless line of humans, mostly men, though not exclusively, many of whom would make numerous passes. In a period when gay bars were just beginning to have sidewalk presences rather than remain hidden behind tavern walls or up stairs, it was a very public, conspicuous, and sexy high-jeaned kind of cruising. We're here, we're queer, and the sidewalk is ours.

Crucial to many Toronto-area gays of the 1980s and 1990s, the Steps were also the place visitors from cities and towns that didn't have any public gay life or spaces would come to see first when visiting Toronto. So important

Monteith Street and Church, 1971: the future site of Barbara Hall Park.

and well-known, they became a recurring Kids in the Hall sketch, but the gathering place outlived the show's run by more than half a decade, until the early 2000s, when building management bricked up the Steps because of the loiterers. Cities try so hard for this kind of organic community, but then when it exists, there's a contradictory urge to move it along down the sidewalk.

After the eradication of the Steps, a diluted version of the ambulatory pageantry migrated two blocks south, to Church and Alexander and the couple of steps up to retail shops on the main floor of the Alexus condo building and to the adjacent benches by the statue of Alexander Wood, Toronto's controversial gay icon. This spot never really took off – perhaps these steps are too low and people have to look up rather than across or down at passersby. The City also removed the benches after complaints from condo owners: people were actually sitting on them, it seemed.

Barbara Hall Park, then, remains the only public space in the Village where lingering without buying a beverage is permitted, but even there, it isn't without tension. Until 2014, the space was named Cawthra Park, after William Cawthra, an early Toronto millionaire who was twice elected alderman before his death in 1880. After receiving a $1.4 million renovation in time for 2014 World Pride, the City renamed the park for former mayor Hall who, as a lawyer, defended people arrested in the bathhouse raids and has been supportive of the LGBT community throughout her public life.

As city parks go, it's a good one, almost European in its connectivity. Parks in the Toronto street grid tend to be deliberate things, entire blocks or tracts of land given over to the City by some benefactor. But there isn't always a master plan. Barbara Hall is midblock and doesn't touch an intersection, a medieval-style pedestrian passage between Church and Cawthra Square, a short dead-end thoroughfare that leads out to Jarvis Street.

Even after the renovations that saw multicoloured LED lights, new plantings, retaining walls, and a platform that doubles as a temporary performance stage, the park has managed to keep a bit of ruins about it, something rare in Toronto. Along a portion of the park's north side, bordering late-nineteenth-century Second Empire row houses on Monteith Street (one of which was the birthplace of Lord Thomson of Fleet in 1894), are remnants of the foundation of the original Granite Club. It lends the park an even more European feel – think Scottish castle ruins – and partially frames a grassy knoll that hosts impromptu picnics and summertime naps.

There has long been leisure activity here. Early Toronto maps from the nineteenth century show lacrosse grounds on the Jarvis side of the block, though there's no trace of those now. However, leisure pursuits have left an even stronger legacy here with the 519 Community Centre, a building that dates back to 1906, when it was built as the annex to the original Granite Club. The club was destroyed by fire in 1913, leaving only that foundation wall behind. The original club grounds ran from Wellesley up to Gloucester Street, and from Church to Jarvis. Some of it was developed over time, and the club itself moved up to St. Clair and Yonge in 1928, and later to Bayview Avenue in North York.

Over the decades, the building at 519 Church Street, with its second-floor ballroom, has housed the German Harmony Club, the Ulster Athletic Club, and, from 1945 to 1975, the headquarters of the 48th Highlanders. In 1975, the old 519 building was on demolition death row, soon to be replaced by a proposed high-rise apartment that was to bookend the existing one at the Jarvis end of the park. However, four hundred people turned up at a 1975 open house meant to gauge interest in turning the building into a community centre. Not long after, 'the 519' was born. Much of the present-day park was used for parking for decades. A Loblaw Groceteria, which squatted just north of the 519, was later demolished and converted to parkland, along with the rest of the open space we have today.

From the beginning, the 519 was a little different from other community centres in that it was the first in Toronto to have a community-elected management board. The original Yuk Yuk's comedy club was located in the basement 'Pine Room,' but within a year, it had to find a new home to accommodate large audiences.

gay toronto

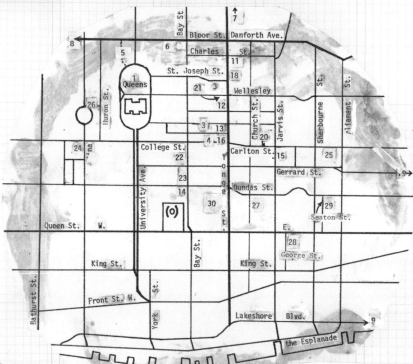

cruising spots

1. Queen's Park
2. Yonge St. from Bloor to Dundas
3. Grosvenor and Grenville Sts.
4. In front of the YMCA, and east to the corner at Yonge
5. *Philosopher's Walk -- the walkway behind the Museum from Bloor to Hoskins
6. Inside the Colonnade on Bloor
7. David Balfour Park -- just north of this map, but still downtown. From the St. Clair subway, walk east to Avoca, then south to the park.
8. *High Park -- in the west end. Take the Bloor subway to the High Park stop, or drive west on Bloor to just past Keele.
9. Woodbine Beach -- in the east end. Take the Queen St. car to Woodbine, and walk south to the beach.
10. Hanlan's Point -- take the Bay St. bus to the docks, then the Hanlan's ferry. The beach may be difficult to find; follow the pavement walkway, keeping to the right. The beach is on the lake side, at the west end.

 * Watch for police in these areas.

bars & restaurants

11. Quest -- Yonge just south of Charles
12. Parkside -- Yonge at Breadalbane. The lounge is often mixed, but the beverage room is men only.
13. St. Charles -- Yonge north of College
14. Charley O's -- Bay south of Dundas. Mainly leather and denim. Upstairs Friday and Saturday nights.
15. Carriage House Hotel -- two downstairs beverage rooms, and an upstairs lounge with dancing, where evening meals are served. The hotel is gay, as well.
16. Fran's Restaurants are predominantly gay at night. Locations: Yonge @ College, Yonge @ St.Clair, Yonge @ Eglinton.

clubs

17. Manatee -- St. Joseph St. Toronto's most popular gay spot for dancing. Opens at 10 PM, Friday to Sunday. Men only.
18. Sugar's -- Yonge at St. Joseph, above "The Market". Opens July 18.

 Milk Bar -- for bi's and trendies. Located upstairs from Parkside (12)

 Maygay -- upstairs from St. Charles (13). Men only, and licensed.
19. The "Club" -- women's gay club. Pape just south of Gerrard, east of the Don Valley. Open Thursday, Friday and Saturday nights.

baths

20. Club Baths -- Carlton at Mutual.
21. Library -- Wellesley, just west of Yonge, upstairs.
22. Roman -- Bay south of College.
23. Terminus -- 600 Bay north of Dundas.
24. International -- Spadina south of College.

gay organisations

25. The Body Politic -- 193 Carlton, at Ontario. 961-9389.
26. Gay Alliance Toward Equality (GATE) A gay civil rights group meeting Wednesdays in the Graduate Student Union Bldg. on Bancroft St. (U. of T. Campus). Office at 193 Carlton, Call 961-9389.
27. Community Homophile Assoc. of Toronto (CHAT) -- 201 Church, south of Dundas. Dances Friday, Saturday and Sunday nights. General Meeting Tuesdays at 8 PM. Women's night · Thursdays at 8 PM. Call 862-1544 (office) or 862-1169 (CHAT Centre).
28. Women's Place -- 137 George St. A lesbian collective meets Fridays at 8 PM. Call 363-8021.
29. Glad Day Bookstore -- 139 Seaton. Gay books and periodicals. Open evenings during the week, and all day Saturday. Call 364-6731.
30. Metropolitan Community Church (MCC) Services Sundays at 8 PM, at Holy Trinity Church, on Trinity Squnre, off Yonge, south of Dundas. 364-9799.

Though providing many of the functions of a standard community centre – seniors' meetings, gardening clubs, and the like – the 519 in 1976 allowed Huntley Youth Services to organize a weekly gay youth meeting, a move that came with some controversy initially. That youth group was the first in the queer community to find a home at the 519. By 1981, a gay community choir met there, and soon the 519 became a centre for the dissemination of HIV/AIDS information, on the vanguard in the days before higher levels of government even acknowledged the plague.

A bursting cardboard file box at the nearby Canadian Lesbian and Gay Archives contains years of paraphernalia produced by the 519. A chilling amount is anti-bashing material from the 1980s and 1990s and beyond; the 519 has operated a bashing hotline for years. There are notices of meetings addressing gay-bashing, guides on to how to avoid gay-bashing, what to do when you're gay-bashed, how to go on a date and avoid being gay-bashed. How to attack. How to defend. The Toronto the Good enjoyed by some of the city seemed like another country from the very violent and precarious one described by these outreach activities.

In this cultural storm, the 519 was a place of safety but also of resistance, such as a 1984 meeting held there to discuss the public response to Pope John Paul II's Toronto visit. In the days after the Orlando vigil, the steps leading to the 519's restaurant were covered in flowers and candles, a shrine where people would stop and read the cards and messages.

Today, the 519 offers a range of services, including newcomer and refugee settlement, older LGBT services, queer parenting programs, trans community services, and community drop-in programs. The ballroom hosts meetings of all kinds, as well as the occasional dance and wedding. Out back, a daycare playground means there's often the sound of children playing alongside the adjacent dog park. The park has life, but like Pride, the 519's role in the wider community is often debated; still, it remains a busy place and an important part of making the surrounding park an essential civic space.

The 519 also oversees the AIDS Memorial just beyond the playground, updating it each year before the Pride candlelight vigil with new names requested by lovers, family, and friends. More than 2,700 names are now on plaques that curve through a rose garden, providing privacy for those who grieve, a place to leave flowers, and the occasional make-out session. Life goes on, even here.

The memorial began as a temporary installation in the late 1980s, led by long-time activist, writer, and academic Michael Lynch, himself a victim of AIDS in 1991. The permanent monument today dates to 1993. Similarly, in 2014, a chalk memorial to the trans community, experiencing its own plague of disappearances, violence, and murder, was drawn on the old Granite Club foundations. A city crew caused some controversy when

Previous page: Layout board from an early issue of *The Body Politic*.

they later accidentally spray-washed it away. But the memorial was reinstalled quickly and a permanent one has been proposed.

The contested nature of the place remains visible in how the park is used. Church Street, despite its downtown location and million-dollar homes nearby, remains an urban place where the well-heeled and dispossessed exist together. The benches under the ever-changing LED lights sometimes echo the vibe at the Steps. During Pride, the entire park becomes a massive outdoor discotheque. Homeless and street-involved youth often make use of the park, too, and sometimes spend the day on the grass or on the stage area. Neighbourhood residents and businesses have complained of drug use and anti-social behaviour, prompting the local BIA to begin a music series as a way to 'take back' the public space and, once again, discourage loitering. Town halls are places where ideas and ideologies are hashed out and compromises made, but also where different community uses clash, meaning not everybody feels welcome all the time.

At Barbara Hall Park, the town hall is there, but the spiritual heart remains elusive – sometimes present, like after Orlando, but sometimes lost in community tension. Like so many things in this city, it remains a work in progress.

'I was in charge of kitty litter, and we had seven cats, so that was a lot.'

'The vegetarians had a separate set of pots and pans, but I used them for meat anyway.'

'We'd crank up Janis Joplin's "Piece of My Heart," everyone screaming along. OMG the poor neighbours.'

'The parties were important, and hilarious. We had the gynecologist table in the living room and I remember a guy sitting on it and somebody from across the room said, "Now you're gonna feel a little pressure … Don't worry, just a little pressure."'

Jane Farrow
I Was in Charge of Kitty Litter

You know you're getting old when you can barely walk down a street without having some kind of flashback that turns the grey-brown bricks instantly technicolour. Of course, LGBTQ people live everywhere in Toronto, but there's a special place in my heart for the queer houses, as I call them, where we did much more than sleep and eat. These are the houses, almost all of them rental, that were passed down through successive rounds of friends and lovers, the places where many of us learned how to be a family and how to make a home, through trial and error, or just error and error.

'The chore list was massive, but what bothered me is I had the smallest room and had to participate in cleaning the whole house even though I was never there.'

'You did your bit to clean up, and you didn't drink the last beer.'

'It got complicated when I was sleeping with two roommates at the same time.'

'Potlucks were all about mac and cheese and tuna casserole. No one gave a shit about vegans or gluten at that point.'

'The biggest issues were dishes and people leaving mess around, but considering the different and varied people who lived there, we got along very well.'

A quick call-out on Facebook netted dozens of addresses and recollections of queer houses. In the 1970s and 1980s, shared homes, like those on Browning Avenue, Palmerston Square, Seaton Street, Boswell Avenue, D'Arcy Street, Washington Avenue, Dewson Street, Walnut Street, and Simpson Avenue, functioned as political hothouses. Within their walls germinated the seeds and leadership of organizations like International Women's Day, Glad Day

Bookshop, Right to Privacy Committee, Lesbian Mothers' Defence Fund, *The Body Politic*, and AIDS ACTION NOW! Some houses were quite explicit in their desire to put an end to patriarchy and figure out new, more equitable arrangements for child-rearing and families.

'We all pitched in making meals for the kids, getting them to and from school. We were instant aunties to the kids who came and went.'

'We had Lesbian Mothers Defence Fund meetings in the living room, that turned into afternoon dance parties with the kids.'

'For our daughter it was wonderful, there were always lots of young women for her to talk to who were doing their master's, being political. She took part in all the discussions and really benefited from that.'

The 1980s and 1990s brought new ideas and configurations, like the pan-sexual anarchist-tinged Cathedral A and B on Crawford Street, the artsy mayhem of Gore Vale, musician central on Baldwin, the backyard bonfires and kiddie pool on Jersey, the spontaneous Girlco parties and cavorting on Peter and Huron streets. Most of the houses that popped up at this time consciously eschewed communalism, a post-chore wheel posture that marked the utopic bloom falling off the communal-living rose. We didn't need to coordinate our groceries so much as create spaces where you could fully explore your queer self at home. And you didn't have to explain your jokes or how you dressed or why you didn't want to go 'home' for the holidays. Living in these spaces was an extension of coming out, making the personal political, finding self-acceptance, having nothing to hide. Feeling like you belonged.

'I was living in an apartment with straight friends when I was starting to come out, and they would sit around analyzing Joan Armatrading lyrics and insisting she was straight. And I just thought, OMG, I can't even begin to come out here.'

'My favourite memories as a "baby queer" happened in that home. One of the most loving spaces I've ever lived in.'

'For Thanksgiving dinner, anyone who didn't have a place to go would end up there. Weirdly enough, welcoming other people made it feel like a home; it was a safe place to come.'

'People who just broke up and needed to go somewhere would end up there. We called the middle bedroom Heartbreak Hotel.'

The queer houses of Toronto are a crucial substrate of connection and creativity that we all share, whether we lived in one or not. It's what makes a city feel like a hometown – a glittering sedimentary layer of formative fun and chosen family.

And, thankfully, it seems to be a housing form that has staying power. To wit, Kaleb Robertson's recent 'roommate wanted' Facebook posting for the Parkdale Gem, whose alumni include novelists Zoe Whittall and Mariko Tamaki.

Must love cats
2nd floor (up stairs) of a house in the heart of Parkdale
Old house, has some quirks, but is a really great space
Tons of other great things
$1000 inclusive
Me: mostly vegan + cooks at home a lot, cat lover, queer, likes a chill house, watches bad tv, works mostly nights
* Besides the usual list of respect in a potential roommate, also NO #notallmen, police belong in the pride parade, #alllivesmatter kind of people.

In researching this article, I chatted with and received comments from many people, including Mary Louise Adams, Laurie Bryson, Karen Chapelle, Feral Fae, Elinor Rose Galbraith, Pam Gawn, Shelley Hobbs, Kate Lazier, Nina Levitt, Jackie O'Keefe, Tori Smith, Chelsey Lichtman, Ed McDonnell, Lisa Pottie, Jax Ruggiero, Mariko Tamaki, Freddie Towe, David Walberg, Ruth Wilford.

In late 2016, two buildings at the northeast corner of Church and Carlton disappeared, demolished for a thirty-eight-storey condo tower. For many years before its demolition, 72 Carlton had been home to Zipperz and the Cellblock, a gay piano bar/dance club combo that was a stalwart of the southern end of the Church-Wellesley neighbourhood. And 70 Carlton had housed the Maple Leaf Medical Clinic, which has a focus on the treatment of patients with HIV.

The demolition was just one example of how development pressure in the Church-Wellesley neighbourhood has continued to transform it. But this incremental change pales against the wholesale razing of the Carlton-Church-Yonge-Wellesley precinct that was actively planned over a five-year period in the 1950s.

Mark Osbaldeston

Wood-Wellesley and the 'Mystery Block'

Eaton's and the 'Mystery Block'

The condo tower that was approved to replace 70-72 Carlton is called Stanley. The name evokes the Stanley Cup, and Maple Leaf Gardens across the street. The presence of the Gardens at Church and Carlton is linked to abandoned plans of the Eaton's department store chain. In the period before World War I, Eaton's believed Toronto's suburban growth would draw the city's major retail focus northward from Queen Street, the site of the company's flagship store. Determined to lead and anchor the shift, Eaton's arranged for the purchase of land in the two blocks bounded by Carlton, Alexander, Yonge, and Church, acquiring 75 per cent of the area over one three-day period in 1910.

Eaton's role in the assembly remained unconfirmed, even as, behind the scenes, it hired Chicago architect Daniel Burnham to draw up plans for a grand Carlton Street store. But within a few years, Eaton's focus moved to the west side of Yonge Street. In 1928, Eaton's started constructing a thirty-two-storey tower whose base on College Street would stretch from Yonge to Bay. It wasn't until October 1930, when the first phase of the Eaton's complex was about to open (as Eaton's College Street store, the current College Park), that the Toronto *Telegram* confirmed Eaton's' interest in what it called the 'mystery block' to the east.

With the College Street store open, Eaton's was keen to see compatible redevelopment in the surplus mystery block. Eaton's felt that the presence of Simpson's department store across the street from its Queen Street location had benefited both retailers. Hoping to recreate that synergy, it offered the mystery block to Simpson's. After Simpson's took a pass, the Leafs stepped in, in 1930. An arena wasn't part of Eaton's high-end vision for the area, however. It first tried to interest the Leafs in land tucked back between Alexander and

Wood streets, but the Leafs wanted a Carlton Street presence. The retailer capitulated on the condition that it would retain design control. As a result, Ross and Macdonald, the architects of Eaton's College Street store, would also design Maple Leaf Gardens.

Wood-Wellesley Revelopment Area

After World War II, Eaton's abandoned its plans for a College Street tower, but remained vigilant in ensuring appropriate redevelopment in the mystery block. In 1952, it agreed to let a Swiss developer, Hubert Durrenberger, construct the City Park apartment buildings on the eastern two-thirds of the block between Wood and Alexander streets. That same year, the province amended the Planning Act to allow municipalities to designate 'redevelopment areas' for the purposes of urban renewal. With the encouragement of Eaton's and Durrenberger, the City created the Wood-Wellesley redevelopment area in October 1952. It comprised some fifteen acres bounded by Wood, Wellesley, Church, and the right-of-way for the new Yonge subway line.

The idea was that the City would acquire land in the redevelopment area north of the mystery block, and sell or lease it to a developer who would construct high-rise apartment buildings. The idea outraged area residents, who formed the Bloor-Carlton Ratepayers' Association, led by future mayor William Dennison.

By 1954, the ratepayers group argued that the lingering spectre of expropriation with no firm action on the City's part was, perversely, discouraging investment in the redevelopment area. The next year, the City entered discussions with Ridout Real Estate Limited, acting on behalf of an unnamed principal. Reflecting the City's preferred approach of closing Maitland Street and treating the entire redevelopment area as a tabula rasa, Ridout proposed eight seventeen-storey slab towers aligned alternately north-south and east-west, in a pinwheel configuration around a central open space containing tennis courts and a pool.

By the end of 1955, the City decided it would be appropriate to issue a formal request for proposals. Five respondents produced various takes on the 'towers in the park' that had been proposed by Ridout. In 1956, the City once again commenced discussions with Ridout, who acted as agent for Consolidated Building Corp. Talks continued into 1957 before ultimately fizzling over financing concerns. The City repealed the Wood-Wellesley redevelopment bylaw in June 1957. The towers were never built.

Tall Buildings and the Future of Church-Wellesley

City Park had opened in 1954. The three International Style towers were Toronto's first high-rise apartment complex. A decade later, tenants moved into the three towers of the Village Green apartment complex across the street, between Alexander and Maitland.

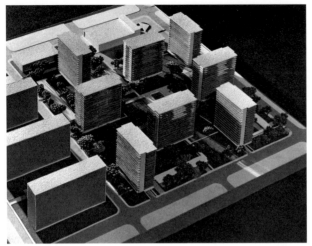

A model of the 1955 proposal submitted by Ridout Real Estate Limited for the Wood-Wellesley redevelopment area. Church Street is in the foreground, Wellesley Street to the right. At the bottom left is the City Park apartment complex, between Wood and Alexander streets.

High-rise developments like Village Green were dramatically transforming the city's core in the 1960s and early 1970s. In December 1973, while it awaited central area planning studies, Toronto city council passed a 'holding' bylaw prohibiting any new buildings in the core greater than forty-five feet in height or 40,000 square feet in area.

In the decades since, Torontonians have re-embraced height in a big way. But current planning practice rejects the other defining features of the 1950s Wood-Wellesley proposals, namely, the lack of relationship to the historic street grid and the strict separation of uses, with no retail or commercial at grade. Village Green and City Park are both products of this earlier era in planning. And although the popularity of those complexes with gay men contributed to the rise of Church-Wellesley as Toronto's gay neighbourhood, it seems unlikely that would have been the case had they not been inserted into an historic neighbourhood with a mix of building types: old and new, large and small, residential and commercial.

In particular, had the Wood-Wellesley redevelopment gone ahead, Church Street would not have been as attractive as a neighbourhood 'main street' once its west side had been stripped of any potential for commercial uses south of Wellesley. Certainly, the street life that has typified that stretch would have been diminished – had it arisen at all.

New, individual building projects will not have the power to instantly refashion the Church-Wellesley area as the Wood-Wellesley or Eaton's redevelopments would have. But as the area redevelops incrementally, its character will inevitably change.

In the future, Church-Wellesley might be associated with an LGBTQ presence only in the way that Yorkville is now associated with hippies – that is, historically. For some people, that might be hard to imagine — like Toronto without Eaton's, or Maple Leaf Gardens without the Leafs.

O n a snowy day in downtown Toronto, defiant palm trees fill the glass dome of the Allan Gardens Conservatory. Clusters of visitors, as diverse as the city itself, follow the park's axial paths to wander its greenhouses, basking among fiery bromeliads and plump barrel cacti.

Allan Gardens has been an urban oasis for over 150 years. Former mayor George William Allan gifted the land, part of his Homewood estate, to the Toronto Horticultural Society in 1858. Later named Allan Gardens, it opened as a free public botanical garden in 1863, making it one of Toronto's oldest designed landscapes. But it is also one of the city's oldest contested sexualized spaces, where tensions between public and private, social liberalism and civic constraint, have played out on City-owned land for generations. Hidden in Allan Gardens' carefully coiffed shrubbery is a queer history that dates back to Oscar Wilde.

Tatum Taylor

Wilde and Urban Wilderness:
Defining Public Space in Allan Gardens

'A bright little town' was Wilde's impression of Toronto, a stop on his North American tour of 1882. The press went wild covering the quintessential aesthete's lecture series, particularly savouring the sartorial details – from his 'cobweb-coloured velveteen coat' to his 'black felt hat of unusual proportions.'

On the afternoon of his arrival, Wilde attended a lacrosse match, where he didn't shy away from revealing certain preferences: 'On being asked by a *Globe* representative how he enjoyed the match, Mr. Wilde said, "Oh, I was delighted with it. It is a charming game. That was the first opportunity I ever had of witnessing your national game, and I enjoyed it so much – but can you tell me who that tall, finely built man, that played defence for the Torontos, is?" broke off Mr. Wilde.'

After a two-day visit, he delivered his farewell lecture to Toronto amidst thousands of flowers in the Horticultural Pavilion at Allan Gardens. The *Globe* reported that his talk on 'The House Beautiful' was well attended.

However, Wilde's warm reception was not universal. Reporting on one of the twenty-seven-year-old dandy's lectures, the conservative *Evening Telegram* observed, 'Miss Oscar Wilde seems to be a charming young lady, although her costume is rather unfeminine.' Another *Telegram* piece elaborated: 'He wears his hair long – just like a woman; when he crosses over a muddy street he has been seen to put his hand on the back part of his overcoat and swing it round in the front so as to keep it out of the mud – just like a woman; and on two occasions when he sat down his left foot disappeared in the mysterious manner characteristic of the gentler sex.'

The author then suggested that Wilde be arrested for fraud – tabloid prattle that anticipated the British media's attack on him during his 1895 trial and conviction for gross indecency – effectively, for his crime of homosexuality. In a spectacular and public fall from grace, Wilde spent two years in prison, an experience that would lead to his premature death in 1900. Although the grand Horticultural Pavilion where he lectured burned down in 1902, and was replaced in 1910 with the current iconic domed building, Wilde's presence in Allan Gardens remains part of the mythology of this storied park.

Since the era of Wilde's visit, Allan Gardens has been a setting for clandestine but perilous sex. Based on his exploration of court records of gross indecency trials, queer historian Steven Maynard has found that Allan Gardens was a popular cruising ground for men seeking encounters with other men as early as the 1890s. The park's hundreds of trees provided cover for homosexual trysts that were otherwise impossible in Toronto's spaces, either public or private.

But as such intimate activity increased, so did the risk of police surveillance in defence of public morality. Maynard uncovered documentation of two men's trials for having sex in an Allan Gardens washroom cubicle in 1922. When the arresting officers were asked how they were able to catch the pair in the act, they testified that the police had a ladder and a platform allowing them to spy through a hole in the lavatory wall.

Although Allan Gardens fell out of favour among cruisers by the mid-twentieth century, the local magazine *Tab* declared in 1968 that 'Allan Gardens has become an "in" spot again. Indeed, with Philosopher's Walk defoliated and Queen's Park full of hippies, the gardens may become "the spot" for outdoor cruising.' *Tab*'s regular column 'Gay Set,' written by the dubiously named Duke Gaylord, included salacious tidbits on the gay 'mating season' in Allan Gardens. Of 190 arrests for public sex between men in 1979 in Toronto, twenty-one were in Allan Gardens – a tally exceeded only by nearby Greenwin Square, Philosopher's Walk, and the Parkside Tavern.

The Body Politic published the account of one such arrest that year. Andrew Britton, a film professor visiting Toronto from England, wrote of his encounter with a man he had found attractive and followed into the bushes, many metres from a public footpath or lamppost. 'It was, in effect,' he observed, 'a private place and, if we'd been a straight couple, it would almost certainly have been treated as such.'

Having only kissed in the shadows, Andrew and his companion, Alan McMurray, were soon accosted by two plainclothes policemen staked out nearby: 'We were simply two of the night's quota of faggots.' After booking and fingerprinting at the Morality Squad offices, Andrew and Alan pleaded not guilty to a charge that had not even been described to them. Ultimately, a judge acquitted the pair on the basis of reasonable doubt (the surveillance occurred at night, in darkness). Still, Andrew observed, 'Unfortunately, there will continue to be lots of gay men who will not be so lucky … unless we begin to challenge an arrangement that allows

Several men, including a police officer, stand by the central fountain in Allan Gardens, c. 1910.

policemen to earn Hawaiian vacations by skulking in the shrubbery to arrest harmless victims.'

A few years later, in June 1982, a twenty-three-year-old man named Lawrence Perrault – described in the mainstream press as a 'homosexual prostitute' and a 'native Indian' – was arrested in Allan Gardens for the murder of George Roach, 'a homosexual known as Peaches.' Perrault claimed he had been soliciting in the park when the prospective customer, much larger and twice his age, approached him but refused to pay. Perrault claimed the man began to sexually assault him with a knife, which Perrault seized and used to stab Roach to death in self-defence. The Ontario Supreme Court found Perrault guilty of manslaughter, with the judge reportedly censuring him for soliciting. But in a move the judge called unprecedented, one of the jurors, an elementary school teacher, defended Perrault: 'Just because he is a male prostitute doesn't mean he can't be raped.' Crown counsel insisted her sympathy was 'misplaced,' and Perrault received an eight-year prison sentence.

In the same month as Perrault's trial, and exactly a century after Wilde's lectures in Toronto, the Canadian Gay Archives (now the Canadian Lesbian and Gay Archives) organized the Wilde '82 Lesbian and Gay History Conference to commemorate his visit. Held a few blocks from Allan Gardens at the Ryerson Polytechnic Institute, Wilde '82 was North America's first conference for gay and lesbian historians. Twenty-two attendees shared eight slideshows, nine papers, a panel discussion, and a dramatic reading of 'Wildflower,' a poem by Richard Howard imagining an encounter between Oscar Wilde and Walt Whitman. *The Body Politic* reported that the conference's participants, including such pioneering historians as New York's Jonathan Ned Katz, 'could be identified by their bright yellow buttons of Oscar – sporting a very modern pink triangle on his lapel in place of his usual carnation.'

Given the park's history of surveilled sex, it is both ironic and fitting that Allan Gardens has been the location of countless protests against sexual violence and persecution, and for sex workers' rights and LGBT liberation. Allan Gardens has long served as a stage for social liberalism and civic engagement, from the founding meeting of the National Council of Women in Canada (1893), to a protest of poets that resulted in a city-wide bylaw allowing free speech in parks (1962). In August 1974, only two years after Toronto's first Gay Pride Week, the Gay Alliance Toward Equality held a pride march from Allan Gardens to Queen's Park and back. The 1976 pride rally began at Allan Gardens and ended in Nathan Phillips Square. The park saw demonstrations against Anita Bryant's anti-gay Save Our Children campaign and rallies for the threatened constitutional rights of sex workers. Since the Dyke March first became part of Toronto's Pride festivities in 1996, it has either begun or ended at Allan Gardens. In 2014, World Pride featured a ten-day licensed arts venue there.

In Allan Gardens, perhaps more than anywhere else in the city, covert queer uses have occupied the same space as overt demonstrations of queer presence. This history should inform a future for Allan Gardens that commemorates and continues its social legacy as a place where Torontonians negotiate the meaning of public space.

The intersection of Church and Wellesley streets has long been known as the heart of Toronto's gay neighbourhood, a focal point for queer businesses, bars, and community services. For twenty years, this corner also marked the location of 'the Steps' – a set of stairs on the southwest corner leading up to a Second Cup cafe.

From 1984, when the stairs were first built, until 2004, when they were bricked in, this stoop became a local gay landmark and informal gathering place for coffee drinking, chatting, flirting, and cruising. 'Meet me at the Steps' became an iconic phrase, and the Kids in the Hall brought the site to national television.

'To most,' Alan Vernon observed in *Eye Weekly* in 1997, 'the Steps are the summer stomping ground where a motley crew holds court after last call. Drag queens way past their expiry date, leathermen, dykes, moustached clones, jocks and fags-in-training alike, pig out on hot dogs and pizza slices as drive-by cowards yell out homophobic remarks when the lights change to green. It's really quite a seedy scene – and the seedier the better.'

Allison Burgess

Steps to Gentrification

Nostalgic media accounts of the Steps reinforce that importance. 'The Steps meant a lot to me,' *Toronto Star* reporter Bruce DeMara wrote in 2004. 'It was the in spot to be, it was where everything was going on.' 'For so many years,' added Joseph Couture in *Eye Weekly* in 2005, 'the Steps were always the place to go to see and be seen.'

These memories present an interesting image of what some people imagined the space to have once been. The writers evince a longing here for an informal gathering place where people could meet up with friends and be a part of the gay scene.

The story of the removal of the Steps begins in 2001, when the Second Cup and its neighbouring businesses began to receive complaints from patrons about the increasing numbers of people described as drug dealers, the homeless, street youth, and sex workers occupying the space on the stairs. These complaints continued as the Second Cup managers tried unsuccessfully to get rid of the 'unwanted' people.

Media reports suggested the change in occupancy on the Steps resulted from a cleanup on Yonge Street – after police forced out sex workers, homeless people, and street-involved youth there, they shifted east, toward Church Street. The Yonge Street sweep was related in part to the development of Dundas Square, a so-called public square on the southeast corner of Yonge and Dundas.

The term community enters the newspaper discourse when the 'other' seems to be threatening this community. 'People are standing around blocking the businesses,' Rachel Ross wrote in 2003 in the *Toronto Star*. 'At a high point, there will be 30 of them blocking the Steps. These aren't members of the community. It's street people and kids.' She continues: '[T]he feeling in the community is that the status of the Steps has waned in recent years.'

The nostalgia in these quotes articulates a sense of loss for a community that once was. The notion of community becomes connected to the efforts by some in the Church/Wellesley neighbourhood to collaborate with the Church and Wellesley Business Improvement Association, a group highly motivated by the desire for respectability. There are constant tensions around the definition of community, between those who work to construct a gentrified gay neighbourhood with its implicit whiteness and those who criticize the Church and Wellesley area as a space dominated by gay white men.

What was going on in this process of creating respectability and what does respectability look like in Toronto's Gay Village? Who gets access to it, and who embodies it? How is it marked racially, by gender, by sexuality?

The attempts by the Second Cup managers to remove the unwanted occupants from the Steps involved a number of tactics to encourage them to leave. For example, while the cafe had previously been open 24/7, the store moved to more restricted hours, installed extra bright lights, and hosed down the Steps to keep people from sitting on them. They installed black lights in the washrooms to prevent intravenous drug dealers from finding their veins, and played classical music through an outdoor sound system.

There were clear implications around the choice of classical music, which spoke to whiteness, elitism, and assumptions about who does and does not appreciate this musical form. The Second Cup chose these pieces of music, instead of other types, as a deterrent. The music served to simultaneously drive away a particular group based on derogatory assumptions about race, class, and sexuality. But it also was an attempt to appeal to another group, likewise subject to elitist assumptions about race, class, and sexuality.

In 2004, the landlord bricked in the stairs and extended the storefronts of the Second Cup and neighbouring businesses more than a metre toward the Church Street sidewalk. These actions – the Yonge Street sweeps and the bricking in of the Steps – raise the question of how certain bodies are excluded from public spaces generally, and the particular issue of how 'undesirables' came to be excluded from the space in front of the Second Cup.

Spaces are regulated by assumptions and discussions about who does and does not belong in them. While some might assume that public spaces are open to everyone, the experiences of marginalized communities tell a different story: it becomes quickly evident that public spaces are not, in fact, open to all. Bodies are variously racialized, gendered, sexualized, classed, aged, and abled/disabled; some are understood to belong in particular places, while others are 'out of place.' The boundaries and limitations of public space are always being contested and redefined. Those who are marginalized continue to make claims on space, disrupting assumptions about who belongs.

There is an interesting history of how queer people have made claims to particular spaces in order to create gay or queer spaces. The establishment of the Gay Village at Church and Wellesley is one example. Catherine Jean Nash argues that in the 1960s and early 1970s, gay activists resisted the creation of gay neighbourhood spaces, seeing them as both potentially segregating and a reinforcement of a conservative business-oriented identity. However, in the aftermath of the Emanuel Jaques murder and the raid on *The Body Politic*, both in 1977, and the bathhouse raids in 1981, perceptions changed, and a dedicated gay space in Toronto was seen as essential to organizing. The neighbourhood just off of Yonge Street emerged as a gay space, and the Steps became a central meeting place.

At work in the contestation of the space of the Steps is the functioning of homonormativity, accompanied by white privilege and the privatization of space. Male homonormative spaces such as Church Street, writes Rinaldo Walcott, are 'always potentially hegemonic white queer space[s].' The publicness of the Steps was bricked in, removing unwanted occupants to ensure the sanctity of a particular formation of community, as well as to ensure good business. In the process, business space was expanded, literally and figuratively privatizing what was once imagined to be public space.

While the Steps have been gone from the Church and Wellesley neighbourhood in Toronto since 2004, the sense of 'community on a step' moved two blocks south to the corner of Church and Alexander, where there is a short step up from the sidewalk leading to another coffee chain, Timothy's. But it was never the same. As for the Second Cup on the corner of Church and Wellesley, it closed up not long after the Steps were eliminated.

Fifteen-year-old tomboy Pam Gawn got the itch to go downtown in 1975, coaxed by her schoolmate Julie and stories of gay nightlife and the club scene around Yonge and Wellesley. Pam snuck out one night to meet Julie at David's Discotheque and was instantly captivated by the demimonde of drag queens, dykes, dancers, hustlers, working girls, pimps, and dealers.

'Everyone hung out together dancing and doing Quaaludes, bennies, or downers till dawn, then we'd head over to Fran's or HoJo's for breakfast,' Pam recalls. 'Back then it was more dangerous to be "out" – we couldn't go just anywhere. So sticking together provided a certain safety. Clubs like David's, the Carriage House, and Studio 2 were our sanctuaries.'

Jane Farrow
Downtown
Friends:
Photos by
Pam Gawn

Pam's circle of friends included Hattie, Noni, and Shirley, pictured here. 'They were cool and tough,' she says. 'Some of them were gay, but boundaries and categories could be pretty vague back then.' Pam eventually got into Ryerson to study photo arts. One of her first projects was to return to her circle of friends and document the downtown demimonde she'd encountered as a teenager – a scene that, by 1983, was dispersing and fragmenting into separate and distinct enclaves around Toronto.

Noni with weights.

Hattie sitting at bar.

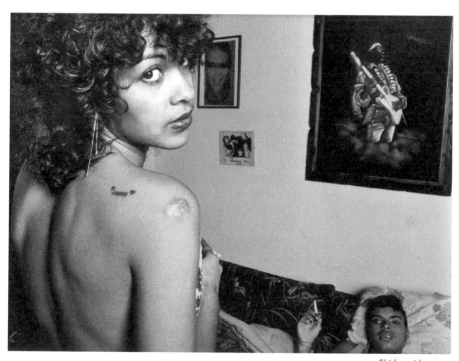

Shirley with tattoo.

Gay ghetto, Gay Village, Boystown, gaybourhood – the area east of Yonge to Jarvis, and south of Bloor to Carlton – has gone by many names. The Church Street corridor is synonymous with all things gay, and the intersection of Church and Wellesley has been ground zero for thirty years of Pride celebrations. The surrounding ward elected the first out gay city councillor in 1991 and the first out lesbian councillor in 2010. The area even has its own creation myth (see page 91–2).

Michael Ornstein and Tim McCaskell

The Evolving Demographics of Toronto's Gay Village

While mere counting cannot capture the spirit of the community, a study of the population can tell us a lot. Statistics Canada census tracts 63.01 and 63.02 capture the core of the Village along Church, between Yonge and Sherbourne and from Bloor to Carlton. In what follows, comparisons to the city refer to its 1998 post-amalgamation boundaries.

Accelerated by the 1954 opening of the Yonge subway line, the area's distinctive demography made it a candidate for a new gay enclave. The 1961 census shows that 'families' accounted for 86 per cent of all Toronto households, but in the Village-to-be, the figure was only 40 per cent. There were almost five times as many one-person households along Church as in the rest of Toronto, 44 per cent versus 9 per cent. Less than one-third of Toronto dwellings were apartments, compared to 86 per cent along Church; and 66 per cent of people in Toronto lived in family-owned dwellings, whereas 92 per cent of Church Street residents rented. A neighbourhood with fewer families and more people living alone in apartments can change much more rapidly than a family-dominated residential area.

The Sixties

Between 1961 and 1971, the number of households along Church nearly doubled, from 3,040 to 5,745. But this increase was not in traditional families. The proportion of people living alone nearly doubled to 35.1 per cent in 1971 – compared to just 4.6 per cent for the city overall. Children under fifteen fell from 7.8 to just 3.5 per cent of the Village population, compared to 25.3 per cent in Toronto. A buoyant economy and labour market, plus low rents, made this a time when young singles were drawn to the area. Young adults twenty to twenty-four increased from 8.8 to 19.2 per cent of the Village population.

Between 1961 and 1971 there was no change in the gender balance in the Village. The population age twenty and older was 49 per cent male and 51 per cent female. The thirty-five to forty-four age group, however, went from 53 per cent men in 1961 to 59 per cent in 1971, and the forty-five to fifty-four age group increased from 45 to 54 per cent men. How many, we wonder, were patrons of gay bars like the St. Charles and the Parkside?

The 1960s expansion of higher education in Canada is visible in the increase in university graduates in the area, from 8.1 per cent in 1961 to 18.6 per cent in 1971, three times the Toronto average. The even larger drop in those without a high school diploma, from 68.0 to 24.6 per cent between 1961 and 1971, represents generational change, but also hints at a transformation of the Village from a mixed area with a substantial working-class population to an area differentiated by youth, the absence of families, and, increasingly, sexual orientation.

Earnings, however, were not particularly high. Despite high inflation, average wages of $3,928 in 1961 increased to average annual *earnings* (the census measure changed) of $6,298 in 1971, compared to $3,816 and $5,869 for all of Toronto. These figures likely reflect the lower pay of younger workers, and perhaps job and pay discrimination against gays and lesbians.

In terms of immigration, the Village did not stand out, with roughly the same representation of immigrants, 36.2 per cent in 1961 and 38.4 per cent in 1971, as the rest of the city.

The Seventies

In the 1970s, the Village, now a recognizable neighbourhood, became more distinctive demographically. By 1981, just 1.5 per cent of the population was under fifteen, compared to 18.5 per cent in the city. Adults age twenty-five to thirty-four jumped from 28.0 to 36.7 per cent of the population, more than twice the city average. But as the economy tightened, the surge of young people from the 1960s began to recede. The twenty to twenty-four age group fell from 19.6 to 16.1 per cent of the population. At the same time, the Village was becoming decisively more male. From 1971 to 1981, the twenty-five to thirty-four age group increased from 53 to 57 per cent men, and by 1981, 60 per cent of the thirty-five to forty-four age group and 57 per cent of the forty-five to fifty-four age group were men. In 1981, just over half the Village lived alone. This reflected an overall trend in the city, even though the corresponding figure for all of Toronto was still only 9.3 per cent.

The expansion in higher education accelerated in the 1970s. By 1981, 28.7 per cent of Village residents age fifteen and older were university graduates, and 17.8 per cent had completed some university, roughly twice the figures for the city. The relative income in the Village, however, did not budge, averaging $15,340, only a bit higher than the city average.

While Toronto saw an influx of immigrants between 1971 and 1981, the Village trend was in the opposite direction, down from 38.4 per cent to 33.8 per cent immigrants.

The Eighties and Beyond

Though its population grew steadily, from 9,520 in 1981 to 15,225 in 2011, the dramatic demographic changes of the 1960s and 1970s gave way to consolidation. The neighbourhood remained largely child- and adolescent-free, with children under fifteen accounting for just 2.7 per cent of the 2011 population, compared to 15.3 per cent for Toronto overall. The Village was also aging. Young adults twenty to twenty-four fell from 16.1 per cent in 1981 to 9.1 per cent by 1996, before increasing somewhat to 12.7 per cent in 2011.

The twenty-five to thirty-four age cohort remained dominant, accounting for 36.7 per cent of the Village population in 1981 and 32.6 per cent in 2011. The next two ten-year age groups were only about half as large. In 2011, 16.6 per cent of the population was thirty-five to forty-four and 14.5 per cent was forty-five to fifty-four. Less than a tenth of 2011 residents were over sixty-five.

A continuing imbalance in the sizes of the twenty-five to thirty-four and thirty-five to forty-four age groups is possible only if some members of the younger group leave. In 2001, for example, there are 2,235 men and 1,595 women age twenty-five to thirty-four; but ten years later, in 2011, there were only 1,670 men and 875 women age thirty-five to forty-four – despite a 23 per cent increase in the total Village population in the same ten years. There is a similar exodus of the thirty-five to forty-four age group over a ten-year period. People in late middle age, fifty-five to sixty-four, in contrast, do not leave the Village.

The Village's gay male community was aging. By 2011, just 43 per cent of young adults age twenty to twenty-four were men. The twenty-five to thirty-four age group, which peaked at 62 per cent men in 1996, declined to 53 per cent men in 2011. At the same time, the older age groups became predominantly male. In 2011, the thirty-five to forty-four group was 66 per cent men, the forty-five to fifty-four group 70 per cent, and the fifty-five to sixty-four group 64 per cent and the sixty-five-plus group 56 per cent men.

The distributions of household size and composition changed only slightly after 1981. Most marked, in comparison to Toronto overall, is the extraordinarily high proportion of Village residents living alone – 55.2 per cent in 2011, compared to 12.9 per cent for the city.

Changes to Statistics Canada's definition of 'non-family persons *not* living alone' tell an interesting story about the Village. As the number of rooming houses and shared apartments declined, this group falls from 34.5 per cent in 1961 to 10.1 per cent in 1986. Then, likely because of the growing numbers of same-sex couples, it rises to 14.9 per cent in 1991 and 15.3 per cent in 1996, before falling mysteriously to 8.3 per cent in 2001. As it happens, Statistics Canada first recognized and tabulated same-sex partnerships in 2001. This accounts for an increase in the persons over fifteen 'living in a family' – from 26.8 per cent in 1996 to 37.7 per cent in 2001. Therefore, a good guess is that same-sex couples account for a minimum of 11 per cent of the Village population in 2001, with slightly smaller figures in 2006 and 2011.

The Village's high levels of education also persist. By 2011, 52.4 per cent of the population age fifteen-plus were university graduates, compared to 32.9 per cent for Toronto overall. Only 5.6 per cent of Village residents were not high school graduates. Another continuity: the high level of education in the Village does not translate into higher incomes. Until 1991, Village incomes were slightly above the city's average. From 1996, Village incomes lagged slightly behind the city average. In 2011, the average was $43,120, versus $44,517 for the city. Interestingly, the *median* income – the figure exactly at the halfway point in the distribution – is considerably higher in the Village than the city, $33,759 versus $27,781. Thus, compared to the city overall, there is less inequality in the Village, both fewer poor people *and* fewer very high earners.

The decline in immigrants continued. By 2011, 31.8 per cent of Village residents were immigrants, compared to 47.9 per cent for the city. There was, however, little difference in recent immigrants, who arrived between 2006 and 2011 – they account for 8.1 per cent of the Village population versus 8.3 per cent for the city overall. Immigrants arriving between 1996 and 2005, in contrast, account for 19.5 per cent of the city population, compared to 12.2 per cent for the Village.

Only from 1996 did the censuses measure racialization. In that year, the Village had 0.9 per cent Aboriginals versus 0.4 per cent for the city; and 27.7 per cent of Village residents belonged to a visible minority, compared to 37.2 per cent for the city. By 2011, Aboriginals more than doubled to 2.6 per cent of the Village population, while visible minorities increased to 31.9 per cent. The Village remains less diverse than the city overall, which in 2011 had 49.8 per cent Aboriginals and visible minorities. While representation of Arab, Korean, and Japanese groups is greater in the Village than the city overall, the area has fewer South Asians, accounting for 16.6 per cent of all visible minority residents in the Village, versus 25.1 per cent in the city. Blacks are 9.5 per cent of the visible minority group members in the Village versus 17.3 per cent in the city.

The nascent Village of the 1960s, marked by a concentration of rental housing and few family households, was transformed first by an influx of young adults, and then in the 1970s by gay men. The Village *is* differentiated by its housing stock and by the demographic characteristics, but it owes its existence to social and political struggles for gay rights. Toronto is not unique. Gay villages around the world developed in the same period and typically in older working-class and industrial areas of cities. Other areas of Toronto might have become the Village, but once it became a gay focus, the trajectory of Church Street was established.

As with other gay villages, gentrification is changing and perhaps threatening the community. Until 2011, however, the censuses reveal a remarkable continuity from the 1980s, marked more by aging than by income mobility. This durability reflects the community's strength. The housing and social conditions that allowed the Village to emerge persist, but they also allow for rapid change in a different direction. Perhaps the visible effects of gentrification in the retail environment will seep into the surrounding residential areas with the mid-2010s' explosion of real estate values. Time will tell.

My day begins in Toronto with someone else's hands all over me. Touching me. Moving me.

Before you get too flustered and excited, these are unfortunately not the hands of a new lover, at least not usually. They are the hands of my personal care worker helping me get ready for the day. They dress me and help me get into my wheelchair, making sure I look presentable for a lecture, or that I look handsome and devilish enough for a night out on the prowl.

On the rare occasions when I do make it down to the Village at Church and Wellesley, it's always an interesting experience. As I get loaded onto the Wheel-Trans bus from my home in the Distillery District, I am full of an indescribable sense of hope and excitement: soon I will be in the iconic rainbow district. Almost every time I go, I am imbued with a giddiness that perhaps this time things will be different. Maybe I will meet someone, and maybe I won't feel so out of place.

Andrew Gurza

Queer and Cripple in the 6ix

As I get closer and see the welcoming rainbow flags peeking out of some of the establishments, my excitement around the possibilities grows that much stronger. The chance that maybe I'll get lucky, along with a mixture of excitement, fear, and trepidation, are some of the thoughts and feelings that race through my mind as I inch toward my destination.

Once I arrive, though, all that excitement begins to fade.

As I get off the bus and begin to navigate the Village as a wheelchair user, my feelings shift. I pass all the bars, pubs, and kinky clubs with their back rooms, looking at them longingly. I know I can't get my wheelchair inside these sacred spaces where my community comes (pun intended). I imagine what it would be like if I could enter these long-standing institutions, these palaces of possibility and playfulness. I picture each club with no stairs or tiny doors that I can't access, and envision myself rolling through the front door with a smile on my face and a good-looking guy on each armrest of my wheelchair. Those images fall away as I continue down the street.

When I glance at all the posters and event pop-ups plastered on signposts along the way, I can see that nearly every type of queer man is represented on these posters: muscle hunks, leathermen, bears, otters, club kids, twinks, drag queens. Each of these iconic staples has a place in our Village. The one figure I don't see is the Queer Cripple, the Bear in the Chair, the guy in his wheelchair inviting you to sit on his lap. He is nowhere to be found. He has no poster or place among all the rest, for he is invisible. Out of sight and out of mind.

While that's a shame, it isn't at all surprising, nor is it new. I found an archived article from the 1980s in *The Body Politic* entitled 'Blind, Dead or in a Wheelchair – and Gay.' It was both exciting and dismaying to see those who had come before, linking me to my past and my Queer Cripple history. As I read the article, I realized sadly that even some thirty years on, not much had changed. Queer Cripples are still fighting to be seen in our LGBTQ+ communities. As I read this, I started to cry a little (okay, I blubbered like a baby); knowing we'll probably never be able to stop fighting broke my heart a little.

As a 'Disability Awareness Consultant,' my role is to ensure that Queers with Disabilities get recognition, attention, and the resources they need when they arrive in this city, alone and not knowing where to turn. Through my brand, DisabilityAfterDark, I shed light on what being a Queer Cripple really feels like. With my work and podcasts, I share, candidly, my experiences hooking up as a Queer Cripple, what it's like getting intimate with me, and how sex for me carries so much more weight than people likely realize. DisabilityAfterDark allows me to claim my existence and place in Toronto, and to say, 'I'm here. I am going to make you notice me, and if you stick around, I guarantee you will like it.'

My work invites you into my village instead of my having to ask permission to enter yours.

I am a Two Spirit, mixed race, butch dyke from the Cree Nation. I have been queer all of my life, and out since the late 1970s, when I was eighteen. I've spent most of my adult life finding and making spaces safe for me and other Two Spirit folks.

In 2016, I had the honour, along with five other queers, of helping to organize a memorial service for a good friend and community member, the writer Beth Brant (Tyendinaga Mohawk). I really wanted the event, In the Spirit of Beth, to be culturally representative, not just queer-identified – something that would pay tribute to her life, her writing, and her queerness. It is hard enough to find inclusive spaces for memorial services; I can count them on one hand. It is even harder when you are Indigenous and need to burn sage or tobacco for a smudge or pipe ceremony.

Nicole Tanguay

In the Spirit of Beth:
Queering Indigenous Space

The first place proposed by a couple of the white members of the planning committee was the traditionally queer-friendly 519 Community Centre. It houses many programs that support and provide services for the LGBTQ2 community. Yet the committee members who proposed the 519 had no idea that some Indigenous people did not feel comfortable or safe there, nor did they consider this before suggesting the venue. I groaned inwardly, thinking, 'Yet again, I am forced (because I can't keep quiet) to ensure that cultural safety supersedes a white idea of being queer. I have to educate those from the dominant society that being Two Spirit is not just about being queer/lesbian/trans/ bi/gay/butch. It is about a lot more.'

I explained to them that, over the years, there have been some Indigenous trans and queer people who have not been treated well at the 519. I have heard personal stories where street people and trans people have felt unwelcome or unsafe there. I myself have been spoken to aggressively and dismissed. Once, outside in front of the building, I was verbally attacked by a non-queer person. When I asked for help, I was ignored. When I went inside to seek assistance, I was also ignored, and then finally told that the 519 has no security for outside the building and maybe I should call the police. Right! A butch, mixed-race dyke is going to call the police and face more discrimination due to being Indigenous!

In short, a venue dilemma for the memorial was brewing: what to do? Do we go ahead and have it in a place that is queer, because it is queer, and forget our cultural roots? Or do we bite the bullet and have it in a place that is more culturally appropriate and hope there will be no queer-bashing or queer-shaming?

In the Spirit of Beth

You are invited to a public gathering to pay tribute to Beth Brant (Degonwadonti) - her life and her groundbreaking work. Folks will be reading from some of her incredible writings, and we will be honouring Beth in the spirit that she honoured us.

Friday, October 23rd, 6 to 8 pm

Native Canadian Centre of Toronto, 16 Spadina Road, Toronto
Barrier Free Space. For more information, visit Facebook (facebook.com/Event - In the Spirit of Beth).
With support from the Native Canadian Centre of Toronto; NishDish Aboriginal Catering; Aboriginal Studies, The Mark S. Bonham Centre for Sexual Diversity Studies, The Women and Gender Studies Institute, University of Toronto

Beth Brant - Mohawk feminist writer, organizer, freedom fighter, two spirit, lesbian mother and grandmother, healer, teacher, author of these influential books:

Mohawk writer and poet Beth Brant, 1941–2015.

Fortunately, another Two Spirit *kwe – woman* in Ojbway – was part of the planning committee. I did not have to explain why culture was more important; she knew what I was talking about. There was also a Black woman who also did not have to be educated. She understood the importance of honouring the spirit as well as the person. That woman just smiled, and I knew things would happen in a good way.

After much deliberation, we decided to celebrate Beth Brant's life in an Indigenous space. Now came the real work. Finding an Indigenous place that was a) big enough; b) a cultural space everyone could feel comfortable with; and c) inclusive and a queer-friendly safe space. Most Indigenous agencies in Toronto, except one or two, are very inclusive. Just like mainstream agencies, they have their good and bad sides. But all recognize that in our traditional teachings, going to the spirit world is sacred, and therefore each person deserves to be honoured in a good way. That means if people are keeping to the traditional teachings, Indigenous agencies will not turn someone away due to how they look and what gender they are. Especially when a memorial is involved.

Luckily, the Black co-organizer had a connection to the Native Canadian Centre. The space held many attendees and was well located and accessible. In fact, a number of Two Spirit people had had their celebrations of life there, including the dancer René Highway, brother of the writer Tomson Highway.

The event came together with queers who gave testimonials on the impact of Beth's writing. Her daughter and grandson travelled from Michigan and talked about her life and her passing. My favourite part was the presence of Beth's moccasins and the shirt she wore when she wrote. Indigenous Two Spirit elder Aiyyana Maracle, who at the end of her life made one of her lasts trips to Toronto to honour Beth's spirit, spoke about how Beth had inspired her to continue to write and be who she is. Folks from Press Gang Publishing, Women's Press, and McGilligan Books, who had all published Beth in Canada, gave out her books to those who attended. There were straight, trans, and Two Spirit people, along with different generations of supporters.

Without the support of both the queer and Indigenous communities, I am not sure the celebration of Beth Brant's life would have been so spectacular. Each person who came arrived with an open heart, and gave more love and respect and joy to Beth's family because the space felt inclusive.

That is what we in the organizing group had wanted: when someone dies, we wish them to be remembered and to celebrate their life in a good way. Getting to that place can take time, and may involve holding one's ground, always remembering that the event is about the loved one who has passed.

Since I began to write this piece, there have been more people who have passed in my immediate circle. I have found it hard to just get by, as I have been filled with the grief of four more folks who have passed into the spirit world – two were elders who became my brothers. It never gets easier when dealing with death, but what I have learned these past few months is that no matter if they are queer, there needs to be a place of safety for all. We need to come together, even if we are from marginalized communities. We need to make it safe for all to be out and queer, especially at the end of our journeys.

I never know which option to select on the treadmill, but I follow my gut and push 'Weight Loss,' hoping no one around me notices. I have no idea what gays do at the gym, but it seems they stream out of these places like exact replicas of one another. I go to the west-end YMCA a couple of times a week. When I'm really keen, I can do up to four times a week, but then I revert back to once biweekly during my recovery periods. My goal: look like the boys I see on Pride floats and at circuit parties. If that fails, I can settle for cruising in the sauna at the gym.

Rahim Thawer

Cardio-Highs:

Winning and Running Away All at Once

Running on the treadmill is good fun (once you finally get to the gym). My eyes naturally start checking out the boys, and then I turn up the house music on my headphones to refocus: Micky Friedmann, Offer Nissim, Alain Jackinsky, Isaac Escalante – just scrolling through these circuit DJs on my iPod gets me energized. My twenty-minute jog (which is actually fifteen) is like getting mentally ready for the next big party at Fly 2.0 or the Phoenix. When the music starts, I'm basically there, feeling euphoric and imagining myself taking over the dance floor. I can already see myself in a tank top that I paid way too much for, pulling out a gigantic fan (that I don't yet own) while dishing out the moves like I'm onstage and everyone is watching.

The chemical release from the bass, beats, and my sprint allow me to imagine myself as sexy and desirable. For just a few fleeting moments, I'm my best self and want to be seen. I feel like I'm winning a race. But what is winning in this community?

Halfway into my jogging routine, I forward the SoundCloud track to something more intense to keep me going. Then I think, all I really want are bigger pecs, broader shoulders, a bubble butt, and sculpted arms. I don't care too much for a six-pack, but I wouldn't turn it away if it felt like an option. I should dream big but not too big, I tell myself. My own sarcasm reminds me that these desires are objectively seen as defining factors for what it means to be fit and healthy among the gays. Why am I buying into this garbage? Time to refocus and tap into my inner circuit queen: turn up Rauhofer (1965–2013) and reimagine the treadmill as an all-night dance party for my final five minutes on the inclined belt.

Between workouts, when the high has faded and the guilt of eating real food seeps in, I'm left with the reality that these cycles of feeling bad aren't sustainable ways to be in the world. I wonder again why I want my body to be different, and what I hope will change in my life if I successfully morph into a millennial gay clone. And the most daunting question: why did all gay men agree to this uphill battle? Wasn't coming out enough?

Some gym-goers are committed because sculpting is a hobby that comes with personal rewards. I have no doubt. What about the rest of us? I surely can't be the only one feeling pressured to experience someone else's idea of fun. But here I am … jogging away. This is why we are a gay city and not a queer one. There's a queer scene, but in a gay city. We're normative and binary in all the ways you can imagine.

Queerness would be celebrating all bodies, because we would recognize that we're not just fighting for the right to love the person we want. We're also fighting against the regulation of our lives and the very sources that cause us to experience shame. Many of us gays – being out for over a decade or two – still experience shame when we have casual sex, live outside the realm of monogamous relationships, consider PrEP a valid form of HIV prevention, act 'too feminine,' or don't go to the gym enough. Somewhere along the way, we've decided on body ideals that distance us from the weakness of AIDS and illness, and we've taken on sculpting targets to entice straight men to want to be bisexual for one night when they see how masculine we can be (if they focus on the pecs, not the sassy walk). That's what winning the race in this community means.

Some people will look at me and, despite my own body dysmorphia, think I look normative enough to make it in the scene. And really, what about those *other* bodies? How do other racialized guys, fat guys, disabled guys, trans guys, and poz guys deal it with it? Do they want the same body I want? Perhaps they want different things, but I'm guessing we all self-loathe the same.

Even this train of thought makes me feel bad. I'm reminded I have a hard time desiring other bodies and that I barely see myself as a sexual person. In some ways, I was much better before I came out. I imagine that being *queer* – in its politicized glory – means being attracted to people who don't simply bring me closer to the Adonis ideal by association. Maybe being queer also means liking myself, and feeling liberated as I intentionally (not guiltily) chomp down those greasy french fries.

I also realize I'm not *that* queer, and neither is Toronto. I'm just a gay man in a gay city, inducing that cardio-high while running away from the possibility of being rejected ever again.

I'm fairly certain I had never actually held a football before the first day. My friend Roberta took me to the game: pickup football in Trinity-Bellwoods Park on a Saturday afternoon. She was my best friend's new girlfriend, a jock who knew her way around a football. 'Why?' I ask her now, as I try to remember how it started. 'Why take *me*?'

'I was trying to get you laid,' Roberta replies. Kidding. Kind of.

The games began on one of those first weekends in spring barely warmed by weak sun, and lasted into the autumn, when the yellow leaves stayed late on the maple trees. A bunch of queer women meeting up at midday to play football in the park. The football calibre was not high. But so much else was happening on that field in 1999.

Stephanie Nolen

This Space Is Taken

We took up space. We *took* space: this wasn't a place that was designated ours for an afternoon, or a tiny part of the city carved off for us. Not Pride, not the Church Street ghetto. This was popular, premium Toronto real estate, and we biked up, skated up, walked up, a group of visibly queer women in their twenties who claimed it, boisterous and confident, unconcerned. We owned a chunk of the park each Saturday, for a few hours, and if we made anyone uncomfortable, it was on them to hurry past.

Roberta remembers that the game grew out of a casual desire to throw a ball around – something many of us had not had the chance to do growing up. Not like this, in a group, where the sight of us together made it obvious who we were. The fact that we had enough players to field two sides for football, assembled just by word of mouth – no texts, no Facebook back then – makes me realize now: there were a *lot* of us. By 1999, we felt safe enough to gather like this.

Some of the women knew each other through Savoy Howe's women's boxing club — the one that today is Toronto Newsgirls. A few played Pink Turf soccer together. But most of the people who became regulars were connected in an L-word kind of a way: everyone was somebody's ex and somebody else's current lover.

But it became a place to make friends. It's tough, in the city, my friend Steph pointed out, to make actual friends – you could go to a dozen dyke bars, you might hook up, but you wouldn't make friends. I met Steph at football; today she and her wife are the fairy godmothers of my children. 'It was the first group of dykes I'd ever hung out with,' Steph says. Me, too, if you don't count Take Back the Night.

In hindsight, that game marked the beginning of a westward shift for the community, particularly of women. We all lived west of Spadina; our social pole was not Church and Wellesley but Queen and Bathurst. We went to Vazaleen, and we packed out Ciao Edie on Sunday nights.

After the games, we went to La Hacienda or Squirly's on Queen West for beer on the patio. We picked up more than football, obviously. On one of those first Saturdays, I developed a wicked crush on a girl with a near-black brush cut and lean, strong arms. I wangled to sit next to her at La Ha, and then that night the beers carried on to a party in someone's tiny apartment in the Annex, and by midnight we had a date lined up. We were together for the next couple of years. That first summer, we did whatever we did late on Friday night, but we still made it out of the house for football on Saturday.

Most of the people who played were stylish butch girls like Roberta. There were three or four of us femmes. We wore our hair in braids, and shorter shorts than the butch women. It was broadly true that we were less adept with the football. But we were stroppy. One afternoon Beth, her lipstick as red as the bandana that held back her curls, plucked the ball from the hands of the broad-shouldered woman who held it and announced, 'I'm QB,' daring anyone to disagree.

Now, looking at the pictures from those Saturdays, I see several trans men who were pre-transition. There is one, Liam, who has passed away. The game had a whole separate value, I suspect, for the players who were living as 'bois,' as they identified then, beginning to feel out something new, beyond butch dyke identity. Over the course of the season that we played, several people changed the name they used. No one changed pronouns — not yet. The public conversation about the difference between butch and boi and trans was just beginning.

The boy-girls knew they belonged, though, while we femmes had to justify our presence. When I start asking around about who remembers what, trying to capture this sliver of history, one butch friend observes that a few femmes always showed up. 'I guess they liked the social aspect,' she says. Because she still couldn't quite conceive that we liked the sport, liked the hitting and the shouting and the occasional play that came together.

I ask Roberta why we stopped going; I can't remember. 'Because it stopped being fun for you,' she says, 'because of that stuff.' And then I recall the bitter tinge of exclusion, the in-jokes among the bois, the sense that I wasn't the right kind of queer, even there, in the park.

I kept the friends, though, and for a while, the girlfriend. And I kept the sense of myself as a person in a community rooted in the city, with borders that were slowly growing wider.

What is likely the world's largest lesbian hockey league started with an idea cooked up in 1992 by a handful of dykes meeting to play shinny at a Toronto outdoor rink. Some had participated in organized hockey; others were playing for the first time.

Despite the range of skill levels, what knit them together was the thrilling freedom of playing hockey in the glorious outdoors while being gloriously *out*. Making passes while passing. Teasing each other for loutish lesbian behaviour – encouragingly, rather than the shunning, gender-policing ways of het-girl change rooms. And then going for beers after the game, just like the boys, only blissfully with the girls.

Margaret Webb

The World's Largest Lesbian Hockey League

The seven regulars put out a call to friends and entered a team in an LGBT tournament in Montreal. That experience led to this idea: create a league where it would be safe, accepting, and fun to be who they were while playing the game they loved. Where they could meet other hockey-loving dykes for friendships and maybe more.

Early organizers of what would become the Women's Hockey Club of Toronto (WHCT) hailed from a range of careers: pet-shop owner, social worker, massage therapist, lawyer, nurse, banker. Like those in many lesbian sports leagues, they rejected the hierarchical executive structure preferred by gay men's leagues, instead forming a volunteer collective that made decisions by consensus. Their goal was to create a fun, inexpensive, and inclusive space for all skill levels and all manner of diversity. In this league, doctors and lawyers rub shoulder pads with truck drivers and carpenters, and often become best friends and lovers. The league even welcomes lesbian-positive straight women – as long as they can handle an off-ice pass as a compliment.

The collective secured Saturday-night ice time at the decrepit, undersized Moss Park, at Queen and Sherbourne, which is wedged between a men's homeless shelter and an underlit park. The location didn't deter new WHCT players. When the WHCT launched in 1993, enough signed up to form five teams, with a waiting list. By 2014, the league boasted twelve teams and more than two hundred players.

I joined in 1995, a few years after coming out. Saturday hockey gave me a community to be out in. Though I played varsity at the University of Toronto, I made some of my closest friends in the WHCT. The collective juggled the teams each fall, partly to balance skill levels but also to put ice distance between exes. But the practice of rotating teams had the wonderful effect of widening friendship circles and dating pools.

The weekly ritual came to be about so much more than hockey. It was a standing date on everyone's calendar. After each game, we congregated at the same pub to get to know new teammates and reconnect with old ones. By the time the 10 p.m. game finished, the pub was packed with hockey-mad lesbians high on the game and likely a little drunk.

During the decade I played, I befriended an entire league of teammates, which transformed Toronto from an often-alienating big city into a friendly village. I was constantly running into someone I knew from the rink. I once walked into an art show and was hailed across the gallery by the artist, shouting not my name nor a greeting, but rather the hallowed ice where we had met: 'Saturday-night hockey!'

While I was growing up and playing pond hockey on the family farm near Barrie, Ontario, my sports hero should have been Bobbie Rosenfeld – a trophy in her name is awarded to Canada's best female athlete every year. She was a 1928 Olympics medallist and a star in the half-dozen or so sports she played. But she loved hockey best. She graduated from the same high school I did, moved to Toronto, and also happened to be a lesbian. We also shared a passion for writing about sports, Rosenfeld as a sports columnist for the *Globe and Mail* from 1937 to 1957. But at a time when I really needed Rosenfeld as a role model, she'd vanished from view. Her accomplishments were hidden in dusty archives, along with those of so many other female athletes, and the fact of her being a lesbian had been all but expunged from the public record.

Saturday night hockey at the WHCT, Moss Park.

The Cabbagetown Group Softball League (CGSL), playing here in Riverdale Park, was formed in 1975.

In a piece for *Chatelaine*, Rosenfeld took her male colleagues to task for depicting women athletes as 'Amazons and ugly ducklings' and suggesting that sport made women 'quite Frankensteinish,' 'leathery-legged,' and 'flat-chested muscle molls.' Such caricatures dissuaded many girls from taking up sports (and their parents from letting them play) and kept many lesbian athletes deeply closeted. Those who came out risked a hostile reception from straight teammates who feared being thought guilty by association.

Rather than challenging me to discover my full potential, sport became an increasingly repressive force. What should have been the pinnacle of my career – playing hockey for U of T and winning the Ontario championships – was a deeply lonely experience. Years later, I discovered I had lesbian teammates all around me. But many of us had been so shamed we could not come out to ourselves, let alone to each other.

And so the lesbian-positive WHCT arrived in my life like a slapshot that blasted out the shame of change rooms past and replaced it with, well, a dressing room that finally felt normal – accepting, positive, supportive, *fun*.

The WHCT history does not stretch as far back as the earliest queer sports organizations in Toronto, but most followed similar humble trajectories: a few folks started meeting up for informal pickup games; in the gender-bending, shame-free playing field that is queer sports, they rekindled their love of athletics and discovered a healthier alternative to the bar scene. These nascent leagues booked time at arenas, golf courses, swimming pools, and gyms, extending Toronto's Gay

Village far beyond Church Street and queered playing facilities and after-game watering holes across the city.

In the 1970s, a few gay bowlers met at the old Olympia Bowl, just west of Church, and soon launched the Judy Garland Memorial Bowling League. Gay guys playing pickup in the Riverdale Park established the Cabbagetown Group Softball League in 1975. And Pink Turf women's soccer kicked off in the mid-1980s at Withrow Park.

LGBTQ sports leagues also helped forge a queer identity for Toronto internationally as they formed alliances with leagues in cities across North America and beyond. I played hockey in the 2000 Sydney Gay Games and 2004 Montreal Out Games with teammates I met through the WHCT. Toronto has hosted major queer sporting events, including the twenty-fifth anniversary of the Gay Softball World Series in 2000, which attracted 125 teams; the 2001 International Gay and Lesbian Aquatics Championships; and the Sports Inclusion Summit during the 2015 Toronto Pan Am Games.

U of T political science professor David Rayside noted in a 1985 article for *The Body Politic* that sports leagues had become 'the most active organizations in the gay and lesbian communities,' celebrating their 'wonderfully public assertion of our right to "social space."' Initially, some were eager to create a space for sport outside the heated arena of gay politics, crafting apolitical clauses in their constitutions. But Rayside asked those organizations to consider using their power to play a more political role in advancing queer rights.

That has happened, as leagues held fundraisers and advocated for queer organizations across the city. Organizing sports, says 519 Church executive director Maura Lawless, is about building queer communities and civic leadership. For example, members of the WHCT volunteer collective stepped up to defend the league's Saturday-night ice time before a city committee. 'If people feel good about themselves and they have a place to belong,' said lawyer and collective member Karen Decker, 'that makes them better people and makes them better citizens.' The WHCT kept its ice time. And the city started crafting a policy to get more underrepresented groups using its sports and recreational facilities across the city.

After a half century of queer sports organizing in Toronto, plans are in the works for a $100 million LGBTQ-focused sports and recreation complex based on a proposal developed by the 519. The facility will have gyms, a pool, a track, a community kitchen, and meeting spaces, plus a new arena to replace Moss Park.

Of course, the centre will serve not only the LGBTQ community, but diverse local groups. You could say the WHCT and Toronto's other queer sports leagues wrote the playbook on inclusion.

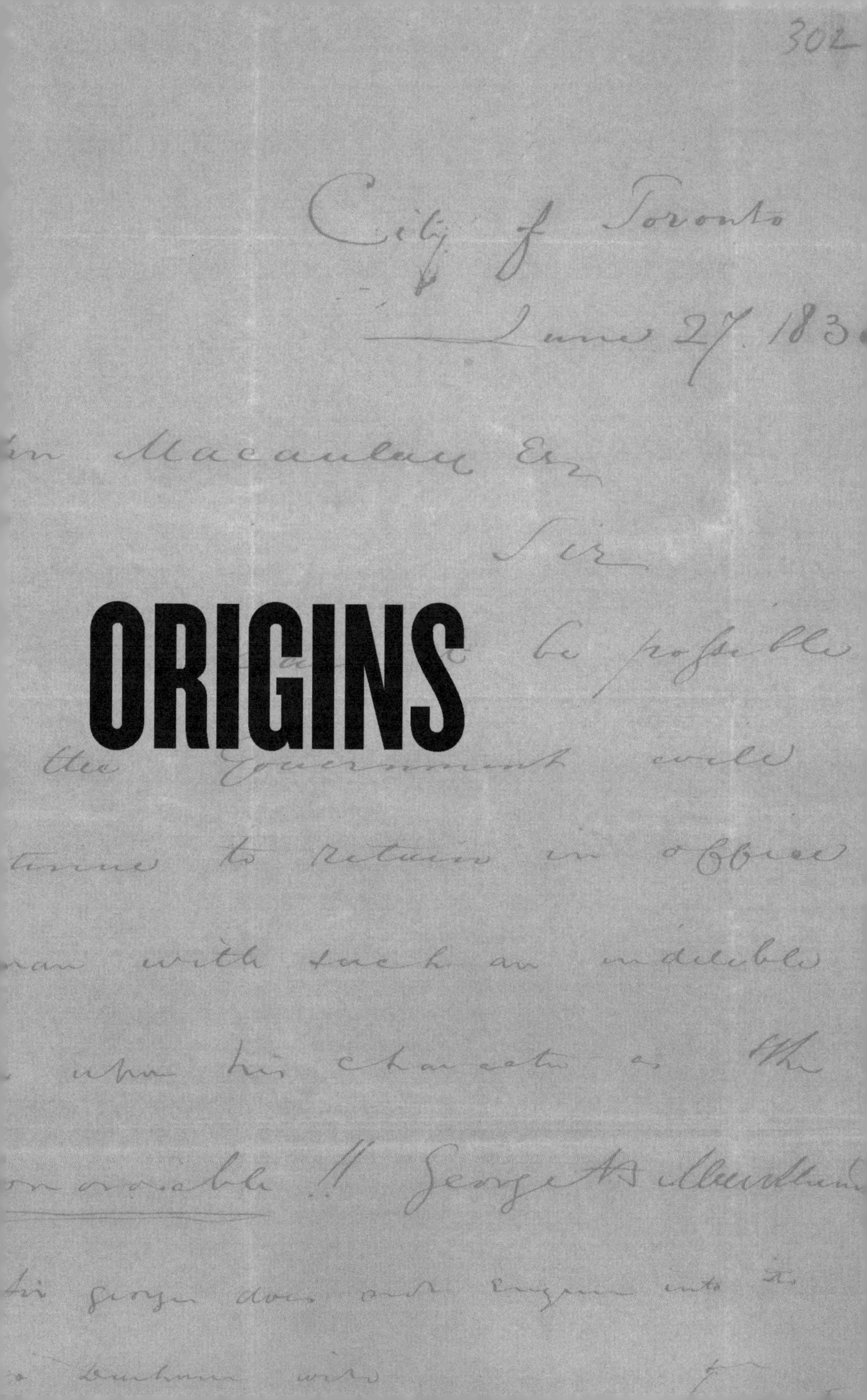

302

City of Toronto
June 27. 183_

_n Macaulay Esq

Sir

_ be possible

the Government will

_nue to retain in office

_ with such an indilible

_ upon his character as the

_ honorable !! George A Macaulay

_ir George does not enquire into its

_ Durham will

T hese are the stories of George Markland and Richard Yeo, two men whose lives emerge from the scanty archival records of nineteenth-century Toronto to shed some light on the ways a colonial city responded to same-sex desire between men. British laws in place in Upper Canada at the time made same-sex behaviour risky business. On the books, sodomy and buggery were punishable by death. Even though it appears this extreme penalty was rarely if ever applied, it meant the threat of disgrace and prison was real, and it has left great silences in the archive.

**Ed Jackson and
Jarett Henderson**

Sex, Scandal, and Punishment in Early Toronto

'Queer Doings': George Markland

George Markland was a leading member of Upper Canada's colonial elite. Born and educated in Kingston, he had risen quickly to the positions of inspector general and member of the Executive Council. When Markland was twenty years old, the future chief justice of Upper Canada, John Beverley Robinson, apparently described him as 'a good fellow, and very friendly,' but added, 'I prefer seeing a person at his age rather more manly and not quite so *feminine* either in speech or action.' Markland married in 1812. Little is known of his wife, but it appears Anna Markland remained in Kingston when her husband moved to Toronto at the age of thirty to become part of the colonial administration.

A bustling mercantile centre of 10,000, Toronto in 1836 was very much a garrison town, with large numbers of soldiers quartered at Fort York. Wealthy loyalists known as the Family Compact controlled Upper Canada's political and mercantile affairs. Markland had been a reliable member of the Executive Council. But in 1836 he suddenly resigned along with its other members, apparently breaking rank with the elite to side with a growing movement of reformers resentful of the Compact's arbitrary behaviour. Their resistance finally boiled over into open rebellion in 1837, and although the uprising was quickly suppressed, political animosities remained alive and visceral in Toronto. A year later, Markland's career as a colonial bureaucrat came to a sudden end.

The primary evidence of Markland's fate as a civil servant lies in File M, a collection of records of Upper Canada's Executive Council held at Library and Archives Canada in Ottawa. (The 1838 Markland Inquiry is transcribed here: http://blogs.mtroyal.ca/markland1838/.) During the summer of 1838, the council held a secret inquiry to investigate rumours of Markland's suspicious familiarity with garrison soldiers. While File M focuses primarily on evidence of inappropriate physical conduct with men, the rare newspaper coverage from that period suggests that Markland's shifting political allegiance might have also played a factor.

The first hint that the colonial public knew something was afoot came from two anonymous notes signed by 'Toronto' and expressing political outrage and moral disgust that 'an everlasting stigma and disgrace' would fall upon a government that allowed Markland – someone 'with such an indelible stain upon his character' – to remain in office.

Markland himself initially learned of the looming allegations through a veiled warning from Margaret Powell, the housekeeper at the parliament buildings, where he had an office and she lived. His movements, she wrote to him, were being watched and had 'become the subject of conjecture.' Powell later testified that Markland frequently visited his office or walked around the grounds in the evening accompanied by young soldiers. The behaviour, she said, suggested a kind of 'intimacy' she thought was 'extraordinary considering the relative rank of the parties.'

Once, she listened outside the locked door of Markland's office, hearing the murmuring of voices, and 'such movements as convinced me that there was a female in the room, with whom some person was in connection. No doubt remains as to the nature of the noise I heard.' Later, she saw a male army drummer, not a female, leave 'in great haste.' Though she also testified she could not be sure that this person was not a 'woman in disguise,' Markland departed a few minutes later and she accosted him in passing to make it clear he knew she was watching. 'Well, sir,' she declared, 'these are queer doings from the bottom to the top.'

At the inquiry, four young men, either clerks or members of the army band, confirmed they had spent time with Markland, either strolling on the waterfront or having dinner in his home. While they all reported that Markland took physical liberties with them in a way that made them uncomfortable, most continued to enjoy his company.

'He laid his hand on my arm as if he knew me, and leaned on my arm,' testified John Brown. 'I was quite alarmed. I did not understand his behaviour. I thought Mr. Markland must have been out of his mind from the familiar manner of his walks and with leaning on my arm.' But, clearly conscious of the danger to their own reputations, all the young witnesses insisted 'nothing improper happened.'

In his defence, Markland claimed to be acting in goodwill. 'I am suspected of what I declare myself wholly incapable of even imagining, and I unhesitatingly assert my innocence, which I can prove,' he wrote in a letter to the lieutenant governor. 'I can show … that mine were acts of beneficence, not of wrong.' According to testimony given at the inquiry, Markland did in fact help a number of soldiers by buying their discharge from the army.

Frederick Creighton Muttlebury, a young law student, testified in 1838 that this pattern of behaviour was long-standing. He had met Markland in 1833 and had frequently dined with him at his home. Over time, he testified, Markland grew more familiar, at one point taking Muttlebury's hand and 'keeping it in his own for several minutes, when I would allow him.' Muttlebury came to dislike 'the kind of smirking way' Markland looked at him. 'Do you know you have the most perfect figure of anyone in town?' Markland once told him. 'Several people have remarked on it.' This comment crossed the line, Muttlebury claimed. He abruptly ended the relationship.

Muttlebury also testified that Markland's behaviour had been common knowledge to colonial authorities for several years. He claimed to possess incriminating letters from Markland, which he had shown as early as 1833 to Lieutenant-Governor John Colborne, who advised him to hang on to the missives. These letters have since disappeared, if they ever existed.

Mackenzie's Gazette, a colonial newspaper published in New York State, charged that the inquiry sought to 'destroy a political opponent.' 'Finding all their schemes to oust him from office unavailing, what do they think they are now attempting?' wrote a commentator who signed as 'A Spy in Toronto.' 'Mrs Major Powell, the servant of the Legislative Council, has been got to swear a crime against Mr. Markland, of no less magnitude than that committed by the Bishop of Clogher. What fiends in human shape surround us! Bribing a woman to prove such a charge.' (Clogher was caught having sex with a soldier in London in 1822. Disgraced, he fled the country, his life ruined. The scandal became a source of popular ribaldry, with newspapers in England and the colonies reporting on the case.)

The inquiry's most damning testimony came from Toronto merchant Henry Stewart, who seemed to have brought the proceedings to an abrupt halt. Stewart, who had never met Markland, recounted his brother John's experience: 'That he had met Mr. Markland, who asked him to walk with him. That they walked up towards the Garrison. On the dusk of the evening that Mr. Markland had leaned upon his shoulder and had put his hand in an indecent manner on my brother's person. And that he, my brother, immediately kicked Mr. Markland on the body and immediately ran away.'

If the goal of the inquiry was to get rid of a political turncoat, it appears to have been successful. Six weeks after Stewart's testimony, on September 30, 1838, George Markland suddenly resigned as inspector general, without recorded explanation, and eventually returned to Kingston. Details of his later private life are scant. He never again held public office.

'Horrible, Indecent Liberties': Richard Yeo

Richard Yeo was a 'dancing master' who gave dance-step instructions to the town's ladies and gentlemen. Dancing was a popular social diversion during the long Toronto winter evenings.

Original Parliament, Upper Canada, Front Street, Toronto. Now the location of cbc Broadcast Centre.

In December 1840, Yeo was arraigned on a charge of assault with intent to commit buggery. In its coverage of his trial, the Toronto *Mirror* hinted at details but avoided naming the alleged misdemeanour, calling it only an 'abominable charge' and an 'unnatural crime.' Yeo was reported to have approached Private William White while White was standing guard outside the King Street barracks, and invited him for a drink at a nearby pub. When White refused, Yeo 'seized the soldier around the waist and took the most horrible, indecent liberties.' If he didn't leave at once, White told Yeo, he would 'give him an inch or two of steel.' After Yeo persisted, he was arrested and thrown in the guardroom.

In court, seven other soldiers testified that Yeo had made similar overtures. 'The examinations were most disgusting, and sufficient to strike horror in the breasts of the auditors,' reported the *Mirror*. The judge ordered Yeo to pay £200 bail or remain in jail until his trial the following year. No records remain to confirm this, but it is likely Yeo could not afford the large fine and languished in Toronto's jail for six months, until his trial in June 1841.

Covering the trial, the Toronto *Commercial Herald* called Yeo 'a fellow resembling less a man than a monkey' and hoped he would be subjected to hard labour and years in prison. But Chief Justice Robinson pronounced a more lenient sentence: one year in the recently constructed Kingston Penitentiary. Release records describe Yeo as a thirty-year-old man with 'florid complexion and light blue eyes.' Prison officials gave him a travelling allowance of fifteen shillings, six pence, for 'carrying him back to his starting place.' Was this England or Scotland?

We simply don't know. At this point, dancing master Richard Yeo disappears completely from the public record.

Privilege saved Markland from criminal charges and jail, while Yeo ended up in court, the newspapers, and prison. Their different fates tell us something about the advantages of class privilege, the effective use of sexual scandal to discredit political opponents, and the limits of acceptable masculine behaviour. Yet these accounts only hint at the fraught world of same-sex desire in nineteenth-century Toronto.

The colonial elite may not have approved of a gentleman consorting with soldiers in such a familiar way, but it was willing to turn a blind eye until the evidence could be used politically. Certainly, soldiers figure prominently in both stories. Yeo's abortive groping and Markland's strolls between Fort York and the Front Street parliament buildings suggest the waterfront may have been Toronto's first cruising ground.

Young men benefited from their relationships with Markland, either through financial assistance or through purchase of their military discharge. Pulled from their families and conscripted into the rough male environment of the army, soldiers could rarely afford to buy their way out. We do not know if they had sex with Markland or, if they did, whether they did so as willing participants or in return for his favours. Yet their testimony suggests they were keenly aware not only of the danger of self-incrimination, but also of male same-sex intimacy in early Toronto.

I n 2005, a local business association erected a statue of a nineteenth-century Scottish plutocrat, Alexander Wood, at the end of a downtown street that bears his name. From the front, the statue presents the image of a dashing young man in a swirling greatcoat, brandishing a sword and hat. But a small bas-relief at the rear of the plinth winks at the reason Wood has become celebrated as an early gay pioneer, a.k.a. Toronto's 'Great Fag.' It shows a bewigged older man kneeling in front of another man whose pants are dropped to reveal a bare ass, his brass buttocks shiny from playful rubbing by passersby.

It seems Alexander Wood, a wealthy Toronto merchant, magistrate, and the Inspector-General of Public Accounts for Upper Canada, found himself facing a potential sex scandal in 1810. After rumours had begun to spread around town, a man laid a complaint that Wood had abused his position as magistrate by pressuring him (and other men) to drop their trousers for a closer look at their genitals. Wood tried to defend himself by saying he was just trying to avoid embarrassment for the men. He claimed to be doing preliminary investigation into the rape of a

Ed Jackson
Alexander Wood:
The Invention of a Legend

woman who said she used scissors to wound her attacker in the crotch.

Alexander Wood statue: Church Street at Alexander, west side. Sculptor: Del Newbigging.

A judge who was a friend warned Wood that his behaviour, if true, represented a gross abuse of his authority and urged him to leave town or face criminal charges. Wood fled back to Scotland. But two years later, he returned to Toronto, where he remained a respected citizen for thirty years, with no hint of further scandal for the rest of his life. Wood owned twenty hectares of undeveloped land northeast of what is today the Yonge-Carlton intersection. The current Alexander and Wood streets, later carved out of this piece of land, are named after him.

The popular contemporary story is that after this incident, Wood was derisively called 'Molly Wood' – *molly* being a disparaging nineteenth-century term for homosexual. The area north of Carlton was dubbed 'Molly Wood's Bush.'

Were these aspersions early examples of colonial homophobia? Not exactly: historical evidence for this homophobic name-calling can't be found. Nor can we know for sure if Wood was sexually attracted to men.

Sadly, this queer hero story is built on a rather shaky foundation. Alexander Wood likely did abuse his position as magistrate, but he managed to escape without penalty because of his privileged place among the town's elite. Perhaps this inscription should be added to Wood's statue: The Invention of a Legend.

The photo below was taken just west of Yonge Street, midway between Queen and Dundas, north from Albert Street, looking up a narrow service lane. The brick wall of the T. Eaton Co. warehouse towers to the left. On the right is a small, recessed space at the rear of 230 Yonge, the Mason & Risch building, piano manufacturers. Police testimony given in court documents the arrests made there on six nights.

March, 30, 1917: 'In a lane off Yonge St., John P. came in and took out his penis and after he got it stiff, Frank H. came in and held the penis and pulled it back and forwards. Frank H. put his arm around defendant's neck.' John – guilty: $50 fine or one month in jail. Frank – guilty: four months in jail.

Steven Maynard
Six Nights in the Albert Lane, 1917

April 3: 'In a lane in this city Harry I. came in followed by a man named James B. They each got their penis out and each rubbed the penis of the other man.' Harry and James – guilty: six months in jail.

April 9: 'About 8:50 p.m. Robert C. came into lane rear of Yonge St. … and Charles V. came in and caught hold of Robert C.'s privates and

rubbed them. Defendant got his mouth towards Robert C.'s privates and a man came and defendant jumped and then rubbed Robert C.'s privates again.' Robert and Charles – guilty: six months in jail.

April 13: 'Robert M. came into Albert Street lane … and so did Austin C. and defendant masturbated Austin C.' Robert and Austin – guilty: one month in jail.

April 16: 'In a lane rear of Yonge St., Thompson C. had his penis out and a man named Wallace G. came in and rubbed it for him.' Thompson – guilty: sixty days in jail. Wallace – guilty: eighteen months in the Ontario Reformatory.

April 28: 'At rear of 230 Yonge St. in this city I saw John H. masturbating a man who was also masturbating him.' John – guilty: six months in the jail farm.

April 29: 'In rear of 230 Yonge St. I saw James D. with Earl B.'s penis in his mouth. I saw him take it into his mouth … I saw him do this twice.' James – guilty: six months in the Ontario Reformatory. Earl – guilty: six months in the jail farm.

Fourteen men. Some single, more than half married. Their ages range from twenty-four to fifty-nine. Ordinary workingmen, including two cooks, a sorter, a shipper, two butchers, and one barber, along with a few more middle-class types – a book-keeper and an optician. Anglos and 'foreigners,' with some of the Anglos foreign-born, too. Almost all lived and worked in either the west or east end of the city. They met in the middle, downtown, at night, away from home and family.

Maybe like John or Thompson, you first enter the lane alone. Despite the damp and cold – it hovered just a few degrees above freezing most of the month – you unbutton your trousers, take your cock out, get it hard, and wait. No words necessary; your desire is boldly on display.

Or maybe one of you is leaving the Rialto Theatre, on the southeast corner of Yonge and Shuter, and the other is coming up from Karry's Billiard Hall across the street in the basement of the Ryrie Building. You catch each other's eye in the crowd on Yonge and together duck into the darkness of the Albert Lane. Be quick. You reach for the stranger's cock and stroke, your arm, we're told, around his neck; a cloak of privacy, a way to remain steady when the knees buckle. Sometimes the

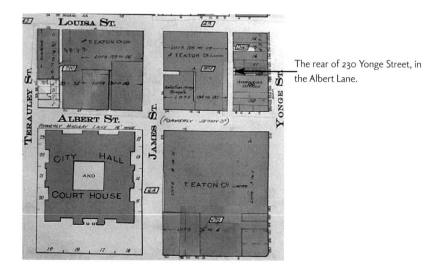

The rear of 230 Yonge Street, in the Albert Lane.

masturbation is more mutual. Other times, unable to resist, you bend down and take it into your mouth, so long as you're spry enough to quickly jump up when somebody else enters the lane, which is what happened to Robert and Charles.

The reports offer clues and questions. Charles, listed as a married Salvation Army superintendant. Did Charles, before returning to his High Park home, try to squeeze in a moment of pleasure after an evening meeting at the Salvation Army Temple, located just around the corner from the Albert Lane? Harry: a tailor, married, born in Russia, his religion 'Hebrew.' Given the lane's proximity to the sweatshops, synagogues, and junk dealers of the Ward, did Harry risk it all pursuing his pleasure so perilously close to his community? And what about the men's families? Surely these men had to tell their wives about being arrested, or did the women read their husbands' names in the paper?

Even closer and more dangerous: the Morality Department of the Toronto Police, headquartered in city hall, just steps away. Constables waiting (but where – the fire escape, a rooftop?), watching as men rubbed and pulled and put it in their mouths. The newspaper called the police testimony 'a disgusting recital,' but the police weren't so squeamish. They, more than most, were familiar with how 'perverts' took advantage of the city's maze of lanes and back alleys.

Much more could be said about these men. But I've already told too much. I've given names to men who, given a choice (and they weren't), would have preferred to remain nameless. I've revealed ages, occupations, religions – all details unknown to these men as they groped and grabbed in the dark. I've stripped them of the very thing, either by necessity or desire, they sought out: anonymity. For men who moved so surreptitiously through the city, searching for sex, I've pinned them down, traced their addresses, and tracked their movements. This is the work of historian as cop. Yet I do not let the police off lightly, their prurience and persecuting here for all to judge.

I have misgivings about this project of historical reclamation, which can't help but also be about the apprehension of men who tried unsuccessfully to evade detection, then and, in a different way, now. Yet it remains the only way I know to appreciate undomesticated desire, always-shifting sexual spaces (the Albert Lane is long gone, buried beneath the Eaton Centre), the power of policing, and the heavy price paid by so many men (and their families).

They all played their part in how Toronto got queer.

I f saintly Canadians run away with the idea that there are no sinners of Oscar Wilde's type in Canada, my regard for truth impels me to undeceive them. Consult some of the bell boys of the large hotels in Canada's leading cities, as I did, and find out what they can tell from their own experiences. A youth of eighteen once informed me that he had blackmailed one of Canada's esteemed judiciary out of a modest sum of money, by catching him in the act of indecently assaulting one of the bell boys connected with a hotel in that city.

The judge, with unblushing effrontery, had arranged with the boy to meet him outside that night, and the boy had told the blackmailer when and where they were to meet. His honour was highly indignant and threatened every possible punishment, but it would not do. He had to pay the money. This is one case only, but they are countless. Some of Canada's leading citizens could be implicated just as Oscar Wilde was implicated, if some of these bell boys chose to make public what they knew ... [T]his fact serves to demonstrate how little is actually known to the police of what is taking place almost under their very noses, while these very men and their acts of indecency are the talk of the boys all over the city.

C. S. Clark

Oscar Wilde's Type (in Toronto)

Excerpted from *Of Toronto the Good: A Social Study: The Queen City of Canada as It Is*, 1898

DEMIMONDE

At the corner of Dundas and Elizabeth streets stood the longest-running lesbian bar in Canadian history. Kitty-corner to the Bay Street bus terminal, the Continental started out as a modest twelve-room hotel whose guests included new arrivals in search of work, rural farmers in town to sell produce, and long-distance travellers stopping over for the night. Classified as a lowly 'beverage room' by the Liquor Control Board of Ontario (LCBO), its beer-only bar attracted a mostly poor and working-class clientele. The Continental, in short, was just the kind of place where lesbians, sex workers, and local male residents could find someone with whom to have sex and a few laughs.

Elise Chenier

A Place Like The Continental

The hotel's bar was one of many drinking establishments serving a growing lesbian clientele. These venues, recognizable only by the butch and femme women found inside, were a distinctly post–World War II phenomenon. Femmes styled themselves according to conventional women's fashions. Butches, on the other hand, were the offspring of middle- and upper-class 'mannish' women of the early twentieth century whose adoption of masculine style signalled a rejection of conventional female roles and, sometimes, same-sex desire. Butches adopted the 1950s style of disaffected youth popularized by James Dean: blue jeans, black leather boots, white T-shirts, and windbreakers, the hair short and slicked back. Whether a butch or a femme identity resonated or not, women who went to lesbian bars were expected to adopt one or the other. They could swap identities, but usually not more than once. Those who understood this basic rule could visit a lesbian bar in Los Angeles, Chicago, Vancouver, or Toronto and fit right in.

Yet Toronto's lesbian bar was distinct in several ways. Ontario's temperance history continued to influence LCBO regulations and social attitudes about drinking in public spaces, especially when those doing the drinking were women. Middle-class fears persisted that alcohol consumption, particularly among the poor and working class, encouraged promiscuity, which undermined social stability.

When Ontario resumed regulated alcohol sales in 1927, it required that public-house owners provide a 'Ladies and Escorts' room for women and the men who accompanied them. By partitioning space from areas occupied by males, women would ostensibly be protected from unwanted sexual attention, and sex workers would be prevented from soliciting male customers. After the war, the LCBO loosened its moral stranglehold and began licensing a wider variety of venues, but the prohibition against the mixing of the sexes in 'beverage rooms' remained. Ironically, this regulation mandated the availability of

The Continental House, Dundas Street at Elizabeth, northwest corner.

female-dominated public spaces for working-class women and aided the emergence of a lesbian bar community.

Bars already colonized by sex workers tolerated illicit sexual activity. The first known lesbian hangout was the Rideau, a public house in the city's red-light district. But in the mid-1950s, lesbians abandoned the Rideau. Local tabloids offered a theory: Montreal mayor Jean Drapeau's cleanup campaign drove pimps to Toronto, where they were getting into fisticuffs with some of the butches. Whatever the cause, lesbians reconvened in Chinatown at the Continental.

The mostly white lesbians and local residents of Asian heritage had two things in common: they were feared and loathed by most Torontonians, and they benefited from the existence of the sex trade.

Several factors drove demand for sex workers in Chinatown. Asian men who came to Toronto to work tended not to get into long-term relationships with local white women because of prevailing racist attitudes. After decades of settlement in Toronto, Chinese-Canadian residents and business owners developed a moral register different from that of both non-Asian Torontonians and also of their communities of origin. These men did not regard sex workers and lesbians as a blight on the landscape; they were part of the community. And because these women spent money in their shops and restaurants, they were good for business, too.

The Continental, of course, had a Ladies and Escorts room, as well as a solid sex-worker clientele. But it could only become a comfortable space for lesbians if the bartender was willing to serve lesbians, who were seen as social pariahs in the 1950s and 1960s. They were easy targets for physical and sexual assault by the police and male civilians, and few bar owners would tolerate their disruptive presence.

In American cities, a lesbian bartender could attract and keep a lesbian crowd. In post-war Ontario, however, women were legally prohibited from tending bar. But at the Continental, a bar manager named Johnny Russo did more than tolerate a lesbian clientele – he actively defended them whenever a physical confrontation erupted, even when male patrons complained they had been 'rolled' (had their wallet stolen) by one of the women. Russo's supportive presence made it possible for lesbians to secure and enjoy the space.

We'll never know what made Russo so willing to support his lesbian clientele. Perhaps he admired their nascent feminism: 'A butch is nature's way of saying that she has almost given up on the human race but is trying one last-ditch stand,' one Continental patron explained in 'What Is a Downtown Butch?' a short article published in 1962 in *TWO*, Toronto's first gay periodical. 'She is a piece of skin stretched over a rebellion. A war on two legs … She is a confused situation to be cuddled, fed, liquored, and loved at all times: a boy forever, a policeman's nemesis, the offspring of our times, the scourge of a nation. Every one molded is a taunt that woman can equal man.'

This article also hinted that the Continental's women comprised 'downtowners,' who went to the bar on a regular basis, and 'uptowners,' who came only on weekends. The former prided themselves on living 'the gay life' full-time, as opposed to the latter, who held normal jobs and generally passed as straight.

Living the gay life full-time was a source of pride, but it came at a cost. A bar-based culture encouraged excessive alcohol consumption, which made it hard to hold a normal job. Many women supported themselves through petty theft and sex work, and ultimately served time in prison. Illicit drug use, particularly heroin, was also a chronic problem.

The impact of alcohol and drugs was immense. Continental regular Lynn Crush recalls sitting at a bar with three friends in the late 1960s and drawing up a very long list of those whom they had lost. In 1965, St. Michael's Hospital emergency room nurse Peggy Ann Walpole, who had triaged many of them, opened Street Haven, the city's first women's hostel. By 1969, it had grown into a ten-bed, overnight crisis shelter. Many of its clients were downtowners.

By that time, the Continental had deteriorated beyond repair. Its beverage room was dark and dirty, the wallpaper indistinguishable behind the grime. Beer glasses stuck to tabletops, and ashtrays were emptied on the floor. The downtowners had become more violent due to years of poverty and addiction. Lesbians started looking for alternatives, for example, in the nearby Ford Hotel, at Bay and Dundas, which had a thriving sex trade. By the mid-1960s, the gay male-dominated Parkside had grown popular, likely because Sara Dunlop, the probable author of

'What Is a Downtown Butch?', opened an unlicensed club, the Music Room, across the street. She hired a doorwoman to keep out the rougher members of the Continental crowd.

When the Continental closed in 1972, its heyday as a lesbian bar was well behind it. Nevertheless, the bar's passing marked the end of a distinctive era in Toronto's – and North America's – queer history. By 1970 a new generation of feminist lesbians had burst onto the scene. Androgyny and a commitment to radical liberationist politics displaced butch and femme culture – but did not completely eliminate it. That scene had thrived during two of the most homophobic decades in North American history. It would not be so easily quashed.

Those with even a passing familiarity of Toronto's history are likely aware of the 'Halloween Hate' phenomenon – the annual queer-bashing ritual that took place outside the St. Charles Tavern on Yonge Street every October 31 throughout the 1970s. 'Ugly Toronto' put in its annual appearance, wrote one journalist in the *Globe and Mail*, referring to an angry mob made up, largely, of jeering suburban teens who would pelt drag queens and the front facade of the bar with eggs and tomatoes, all the while shouting, 'Kill the Queers.'[1]

Christine Sismondo

Halloween Balls:

From Letros to the St. Charles

Less well-known, however, is the fact that the annual St. Charles event was not Toronto's first Halloween drag ball. 'Charlie's' took over hosting duties from Letros's Nile Room, a bar at the intersection of King and Toronto streets. Throughout the 1950s and 1960s, it was home to the annual Miss Letros pageant, a drag event that challenged the era's rigid codes of masculinity and femininity by satirizing Canada's Cold War beauty pageants – spectacles designed to produce a standard, heteronormative notion of sexuality and gender.

The most striking thing about the Halloween ball, which dates back at least as far as the late 1940s, was that it was an open secret. Although it was never mentioned in the mainstream dailies, Toronto's tabloid newspapers – *Flash*, *True News Times*, and *Tab* – often reported on the 'poddy,' at which 'lavender lads' made 'woo-woo.'[2] Obviously, the tone that tabloid reporters used when writing about the event was steeped in homophobia and relied heavily on negative stereotypes of queer characters. For the most part, however, it was not hateful.

Neither was the crowd of curious gawkers and onlookers that assembled to catch a glimpse of the 'mink-stoled,' 'bejeweled' and 'begowned' contestants dressed as showgirls, flappers, and starlets, as they made their grand descent into the basement bar at Letros. Unlike the threatening Yonge Street mob, there is no record of hateful jeers or the egging of participants. Writing for *Tab*, Joe Tensee described the denouement of the 1959 event as the 'gala mob' made its exit:

> And drag it did to the delight of the massed spectators. Using busy, car-swollen King Street as a stage, the belles walked from one curb to the other. To and fro the pretty things went, mincing, camping, hamming it up, weaving between cars, casting admiring, come-hither looks at the cops trying to unravel the traffic snafu. Every now and then, a peel of ribald applause would drift down from some high windows in the King Edward Hotel, whereupon the she-men would

register acknowledgement by dainty bows and the throwing of kisses! Ole!![3]

Inside the packed-to-the-rafters bar, patrons were cheering for 'Billy' who performed the Charleston; a 'femme fatale gowned in a floor-length, gold lamé sheath' doing a 'seductive mannequin' routine and a 'red-hot mama Sophie Tucker type.' Presiding over all this subversive fun was George Letros, owner of the eponymous bar that hosted the city's pre-eminent drag ball for nearly two decades. Unlike the owners of the St. Charles, the staff and management at Letros didn't have a reputation for being contemptuous of (or abusive to) the clientele – at least not *after* 1953, when George inherited the

Contestants in the Miss Letros Pageant parade in front of Letros bar, King at Victoria, Halloween 1967.

business outright and became sole proprietor. Prior to that, he and his father, Christopher Letros, appear to have had a difference of opinion as to how the business was to be run.

At the highly successful 1951 Halloween ball, for example, one columnist reported that there was no conflict, except at one point when an 'elderly gentleman' descended from the upstairs restaurant and into the 'lower BELLEROOM and repeatedly swooned.' Later, it was 'whispered' that the swooning elderly gentleman was, in fact, the owner, Christopher Letros.[4] Tabloid columnists made frequent complaints about 'Poppa' and the Letros management (most of which disappeared after George was fully in charge), and it became the only bar we know of that consistently had a queer clientele, staff, and owner.[5]

As such, Toronto's 'gay bar' of record was the obvious place to host the ball throughout the 1950s and 1960s (the last one was in 1969). For the final six years, though, it had competition from the St. Charles, which hosted its first rival ball in 1963, an event that was said to have 'swung, swung, swung.'[6] For a while, this addition was a boon to community. Options are good to have, after all. Partiers, contestants, and their entourage hired taxis so they could hit both parties in a night. In time, however, Letros closed, and the action moved up to Yonge Street, which the younger generation was beginning to treat as a year-round midway – the city's new entertainment district. There, the crowds began to turn from non-violent gawkers into angry mobs acting out an annual queer-bashing ritual, to the point that, by the late 1970s, it had devolved into a menacing and serious safety issue.

Activists pushed back against Ugly Toronto, though – and eventually won. A massive effort that involved leafletting crowds, media outreach, safety patrol groups, political advocacy, and several meetings with the police finally resulted in a plan to keep the Halloween revellers safe. It was remarkably simple, too: police stopped the mob from forming in the first place by erecting a few barricades and directing foot traffic to move along.

It took a decade of hard work to make this solution a reality, but the results were well worth it. In 1981, following the February bathraids, journalist Gerald Hannon reported in *The Body Politic* that the police were doing their job for the second year in a row and had managed to keep the streets safe. The result, Hannon said, was almost a 'carnival atmosphere.'[7]

Now, many years later, that carnival atmosphere is upheld in the Church-Wellesley Village, which sees the street shut to vehicles and turned into a pedestrian zone for the annual Halloween Block Party. Costumes range from political satire to cartoon characters, from day-of-the-dead outfits to superhero costumes – and everything in between. Including, on occasion, a red-hot mama Sophie Tucker type.

1. 'Yonge Street Mob Shells Out Eggs,' *Globe and Mail*, November 1, 1979, p. 5.

2. 'Lavender Lads Make Woo! Woo! Hallowe'en Eve,' *Flash*, November 15, 1949, p. 5.

3. 'Confidential Diary: Choose Miss Letros,' *Tab*, November 21, 1959, p. 12.

4. 'A Study in Lavender,' *True News Times*, November 19, 1951, p. 14.

5. 'A Study in Lavender,' *True News Times*, April 7, 1952, p. 14. (One of several examples.)

6. 'The Gay Set,' Tab, November 30, 1963, p. 16.

7. Gerald Hannon, 'Controlled Crowd a Hallowe'en treat,' *The Body Politic*, December 1981, p. 11.

Although only one tavern was identified as a Gay Bar in this study, other taverns were observed or reported in the course of fieldwork to have Gay patrons ... However, in these the Gays were always a minority – usually a small minority – of the regular patrons, and often not entirely welcome in the tavern. Moreover, such patronage appeared to be transitory, persisting for a year or two in a given tavern and moving to another ... In contrast, the single tavern classed as a Gay Bar had almost exclusively Gay patronage ... Located within the central business section, close to the largest hotels, it clearly functioned as a Neighbourhood tavern for the local Gay community and as a Downtown bar for Gays on short visits to the city.

Robert Popham

Notes on the Gay Bar

Initial Visit to the Gay Bar with a 'Straight' Male Friend

The tavern consists of a long narrow basement room, attractively decorated ... Tables are arranged along each of the long walls and across the back. A bar is located about halfway down the room on one side and near it, a piano. The only vacant table was at the back, so that one had to walk the length of the room ... The stares, whispered comments and tittering which followed us on this journey made it clear that we were quickly spotted as neither 'regulars' nor Gay. We were made to run a psychological gauntlet. The experience was repeated more explicitly on the way out ... Then, several patrons stood up as we passed and 'bowed us out' to the merriment of all.

Nevertheless, once seated, we were served without difficulty ... Most of the patrons were male although there were several girls ... It was abundantly evident that the majority of patrons were known to each other. Considerable movement from one table to another occurred, and a great deal of clowning and pantomiming accompanied by general laughter. A male patron from a nearby table moved over and sat with the girls next to us. He put his arm around the shoulders of one and began to stroke her arm. This brought roars of laughter ...

One had the impression – later confirmed by Gay informants – that the male patrons fell into two groups: couples, and unattached individuals in search of romantic alliances or, at any rate, an evening's sexual pleasure. In the case of the former, the behaviour and conversation seemed that to be expected of a married couple with one in the role of husband and the other of wife ... Role differentiation seemed to extend to choice of drinks. The 'husband' was having a scotch and soda; his 'wife' a pink gin.

A unique aspect of social interaction in the Gay Bar ... is the distinctive language of its patrons: 'she' is consistently used for 'he' and 'her' for 'his.'

There are also many special terms and usages … as follows:

Bitch – n. a particularly effeminate person
Bitching – v.i. a game of insult
Butch – n. a person [with] hyper-masculine mannerisms (syn. Stomper)
Camping – v.i. act of seeking to gain attention
Cruising – v.i. act of looking for a homosexual partner
Drag-queen – n. a queen (see below) dressed in female clothing
Gutter-gay – n. unattractive, old or indigent homosexual (syn. For old
    homosexuals – auntie)
Queen – n. a homosexual with haughty or regal mannerisms, usually a
    focus point of a Gay group
Trade – n. male prostitution
Turn-a-trick – v.i. to have intercourse with a male prostitute

During the visit, no instance of drunkenness was observed.

Data from Informants
Below are selected quotes from interviews with … two regular patrons …

'In the area at the rear, especially, is to be found those engaged in cruising
and quieter men sitting along the wall. The queens occupy the centre.
After 9:00 p.m., the activities of the queens become increasingly fractious.
Sometimes it culminates in a session of bitching, a uniquely gay diversion,
which is considered a variety of camping. Bitching is essentially an exchange
or insult for the purpose of amusement. A session may involve up to four
persons, though two is the usual number; it rarely lasts beyond five minutes.
As in debating there is a definite protocol. The range of insult in the first
place is strictly delimited: it may pertain only to the appearance or to the
imagined sexual misadventures of one's opponent … A tactless remark will
prompt a rejoinder of maximum viciousness … Contests are waged in
high, arched tones … so that customers at surrounding tables are alerted.
They constitute the audience. Approval is awarded for speed and poise of
delivery and for the fancifulness of the content … Some queens have earned
a reputation for acerbity and cleverness and their entry into a bitching
bout is cause for general excitement. Since participation is governed by an
informant rank-order, the most respected queens keep themselves aloof
under most circumstances … '

'On Hallowe'en, the bar becomes the focal point of the Gay community.
Hallowe'en in general is the occasion for the transformation of attire into

costume, and the severance of the bonds between dress and role. Celebrants everywhere take up disguise … The restaurant area above the bar is taken over for a fashion show. By 9:30 p.m., the room is packed. There may be 40 or more queens present. To design and prepare gowns for this number would try the resources of the community, as there are only three designers in Toronto willing to work for queens. For this reason many wear their own creations. Celebrations like this are known as "drag balls."

Excerpted from *Working Papers on the Tavern: Notes on the Contemporary Tavern*, Sub-study 1982, Robert E. Popham, 1976, vol. 3, *Notes on the Gay Bar*, pp. 37-41.

The document was part of a larger participant observation study of 156 Toronto bars, with fieldwork carried out in 1955–56. Only one gay bar was studied. Other kinds of taverns classified in the study: neighbourhood taverns, skid-row taverns, downtown bars, and brothel bars.

Sensationalist reports on morality offences, particularly the old charge of 'gross indecency,' often appeared in Toronto's tabloids from the 1940s to the 1970s. But in the midst of all this negativity, tabloid coverage of the queer community began to change in the early 1950s. For the first time, explicitly gay material started to appear in gossip columns written from a gay perspective. These articles used a camp code to inform readers of local lesbian and gay activities.

Donald W. McLeod
Tabloid Journalism and the Rise of a Gay Press in Toronto

One of the earliest was by a contributor known as Masque, published in the weekly *True News Times* (TNT) throughout 1950. Mother Goose, another columnist, took over the renamed 'A Study in Lavender' in 1952 and simultaneously published 'Fairy Tales Are Retold' for *The Rocket* and 'Fairy Tales from Mother Goose' for *The Comet*.

Mother Goose's successor, Bettina, appeared in *Tab* under the title 'Toronto Fairy-Go-Round' from 1956 to 1959; the column was reborn as 'The Gay Set,' under Lady Bessborough in 1963. Bessborough's tenure at *Tab* marked the beginning of a long stretch of gay content there. Their byline was taken over in 1967 by Duke Gaylord, who wrote the column through at least May 1975. The identities of the persons responsible for these columns are uncertain and their publication histories remain incomplete.

These tabloid columns contained thousands of words offering hints of the details of Toronto's clandestine gay life. The accounts, in fact, sometimes provide the only extant written evidence of gay events and personalities of the time. They are an essential, if sometimes difficult and unpredictable, historical resource. For example, names were typically mentioned only in part, and sometimes feminized (Brianna for Brian) or presented as nicknames (such as the Duchess, or Our Lady of the Vapours).

The columns were particularly important because they introduced a gay voice into Canadian journalism, if only in the much-maligned tabloids. They attracted an avid audience, but also raised protest within the gay community. Some saw the columns as shoddy and inconsequential. While sexual minorities still faced discrimination, these columnists focused on gossip, fashion, and 'cruising.' Some showed the queer community at its most inane:

> Toronto's queer set are having mock weddings like CRAZY! Now that spring is here, gay romances are thriving just too-too much. We know of at least three recent weddings that have been modeled on Grace Kelly's recent smash hit. The trouble is – both of the partners want to be the Grace Kelly, and very few of the fairies want to be the Prince Charming. (Bettina, 'Toronto Fairy-Go-Round,' *Tab*, June 2, 1956)

A few entries hinted at the challenges of running a mixed gay club in Toronto, such as the Music Room (575 Yonge Street), operated by Richard Kerr and Sara Ellen Dunlop:

> Without Mr. Kerr's careful eye on the Music Room front-desk, there has been a marked increase in the number of butch girls at the club, including some of Sara's old girl friends from Chinatown. Even the notorious Tarzan has been allowed to become a regular. Better spend some time at the Music Room, Mr. Kerr, or you may end up discovering that you own a 'peg' club. And for goodness' sake, check the show: five numbers featuring butch lezzies, a lezzie MC, and two sick drag queens. Really! (Lady Bessborough, 'The Gay Set,' *Tab*, July 25, 1964)

And on occasion, the commentary could be nasty, or simply hurtful:

> A relic from days gone by turned up recently in the Parkside. Historians don't consider it much of a find though; it was only Jamie D. [Jamie Durette, a noted female impersonator]. You can figure out her age by counting the rings around her eyes. (Duke Gaylord, 'Gay Set,' *Tab International*, October 16, 1971)

Jim Egan abhorred this sort of fluff, and began publishing serious articles on homosexuality in the Toronto tabloids in 1951 (see pages 136–139). Egan also enabled the publication of a flood of reprinted gay material in *Justice Weekly* when he suggested to publisher Philip Daniels that foreign gay publications might be willing to allow republication of content for an exchange subscription. An examination of *Justice Weekly* issues published from 1954 to 1960 reveals 240 reprinted items, mostly from *ONE Magazine* and *The Mattachine Review*.

While Toronto lesbians and gays in the 1950s could keep abreast of both gossip and current gay political issues by reading tabloids, the formation of an independent Toronto-based gay press came later, in 1964, with the launch of Toronto's first two gay magazines, *GAY* and *TWO: The Homosexual Viewpoint in Canada*.

Founded by a group of middle-aged white men known as Miss Muffett Enterprises, *GAY* was doomed from the start. Although it was Canada's first gay tabloid, printed on pink newsprint, it never developed a clear identity. *GAY* aspired to be a light, general interest, non-political publication for the 'mainstream' gay population. But its articles and cartoons never caught on. The publication's purchase in August 1964 by Pennsylvania-based Robert Mish Marsden injected new energy. He rebranded it as *GAY International*, in digest format, included physique photos (many taken by himself), and distributed it in the U.S. But *GAY International* collapsed in 1966 when Marsden was convicted on morals charges involving underage youths.

TWO: The Homosexual Viewpoint in Canada was more professionally produced, but issued only eleven numbers between July 1964 and July–August 1966. It was in the traditional physique digest style, featuring quality physique photographs, fiction, commentary, and local news. A 'Cameo' section featured local drag performers (with photographs), which helped publicize the Melody Room, at 457 Church Street, where the magazine was published. Richard Kerr owned the club and the magazine, and supplied many of the physique photos through his enterprises R.A. (Rik Art) Studios and Can-art Photographers. Both the Melody Room and *TWO* closed in 1966.

Kerr was quoted in William Johnson's article 'The Gay World' (*Globe Magazine*, January 13, 1968) saying that *TWO* ceased publication because it had made its point: '[T]he field was adequately covered by American magazines.' Yet Toronto news certainly received no coverage in the American gay press. The collapse of *TWO* meant readers had to return to tabloid columns.

It wasn't until fall 1971 when a stable gay liberationist press arrived in Toronto with the appearance of the newsmagazine *The Body Politic*, which published regularly through 1987.

During the Cold War, Toronto's daily newspapers – the *Toronto Star*, the *Globe and Mail*, and the *Toronto Evening Telegram* – had what was, essentially, a news blackout on the LGBTQ community. The only stories that confronted 'homosexuality' were those that dealt with hysteria over 'criminal sexual psychopaths,' potential 'cures,' and the occasional theatre or book review that critiqued a piece of fiction featuring a queer character. The papers were silent on the actual lived lives of Toronto's queer residents.

Fortunately, there were alternative news outlets in the 1950s, 1960s, and early 1970s – namely, the tabloid newspapers, such as *Flash*, *Hush*, *True News Times*, *Justice Weekly*, and *Tab*, that *did* devote space to the 'lavender set,' to use their words. Some articles were textbook examples of yellow journalism, and used offensive tropes and militaristic metaphors. Others were merely offensively homophobic. Many likely originated with police-beat reporters who hyped up their stories with ironic and inflammatory language.

Christine Sismondo

Headline Homophobia Tops Tabloid Treatments!

But these tabloids also featured regular columns devoted to civil rights penned by Jim Egan, as well as queer social columns, including 'A Study in Lavender' and 'The Gay Set,' which chronicled the scene at Toronto's queer bars, such as the Continental and the Municipal Hotel, at Bay and Queen.

Regardless of whether they were friendly, condescending, or homophobic, there's a good chance that even the worst of these streams of discourse were used by readers in a different way than they were intended. A story such as 'Homos Bloom in Spring,' detailing sting operations at public bathrooms, could be read as a warning to men familiar with these places as cruising sites to stay away. Similarly, isolated men might learn for the first time about the existence of a new place to meet other men for companionship when they came across *Tab*'s December 2, 1961, piece, 'King Edward Hotel Declares War on Letros Queers.'

Here is a small sampling of the many headlines the tabloids churned out during that era:

"GAY-BOYS" NABBED IN BOWLES LUNCH

"Respected" Citizen Falls Foul of | Harvey's boss and Mrs. Ripley, his | in front of the Oshawa bookkeeper

DECEMBER 11, 1950   FLASH   PAGE FIVE

Cops Burst In On Mass Carnival Of Homo Lust!

Simpering Creatures Dress Like Girls; Lipstick Too!

during the evening decided to don women's clothing as a "surprise." The witness then described how he

Said "he": "I was upstairs in charge of dressing the boys. My friend was going to put on a show.

PAGE SIXTEEN   FLASH   OCTOBER, 15, 1951

Toronto Man Described As Abnormal Love Mate!

Homosexual Passion Related By Youthful Married Waiter!

Jolly Time

Questioned further in defence, he insisted Blair got undressed first. "He wanted to have his party, as we call it. He was quite strong in his desire. He told me he liked me

LOVE CONQUERS COURT!

A petulant blonde named Lorraine

SOCIALITE DOCTOR FOUND WITH PANSY

LESBIAN VERMIN PLAGUES TORONTO!

King Edward Hotel Declares WAR ON LETROS QUEERS!

Homos Bloom In Spring!

— See Page 2

TORONTO BUS TERMINAL STILL MALE SEX MART!

PITIFUL PLIGHT OF THE LESBIAN

QUEER YOUTH SPANKED YOUNG BOYS AFTER TAKING DOWN THEIR PANTS

I s your daughter safe? Safe from what? Safe from the Lesbian.

Not many months ago *Hush* warned its readers against the Pansy-Men that haunt Toronto's parks and streets.

Only two weeks ago Grant Graeme, one of the most notorious of these pests of society, killed himself rather than face a criminal charge in the police court.[1]

We have done the best we can in these pages – and without furtive thought of sensationalism – to drive home the fact that Miss Lesbia, also, is a social menace of the most shameful and scandalous character.

Is Your Daughter Safe?: Reactionary Reflections on the Suicide of a Pansy

We are trying to make it clear that, unlike the Pansy, the Lesbian is a professional seducer. And that her prey are virginal girls – and that once in her clutches all hope of decency, of wedlock, of happiness, of a normal existence is snuffed out of them. Not only so, but the Lesbian is more cunning than a snake, more relentless than a panther. Versed in all the arts of flattery peculiar to her degraded tribes, she seldom fails of conquest once she stalks her prey. Most pitiful of all, once she has established her amorous relationship, the victim becomes tied to her by an erotic infatuation so powerful as to be indestructible. It's not so long before she hates the male sex with the same megalomaniac hatred of her jailor.

Excerpted from *Hush*, December 31, 1930

1. The *Toronto Daily Star* on December 15, 1930, published a short item about this death. 'Cyrus Grant Graeme, age 38, of 22 Belvidere Ave., was found dead in his garage late Saturday afternoon, the victim of carbon monoxide fumes from his car which was still running. The deceased was dressed in his pyjamas with his overcoat, slippers and gloves and was lying in the back seat of his car.' The article cites police and coroner's office officials who deemed his death a suicide. 'The motive for this tragic act is thought to be that a charge had been laid against him by the city police upon which he was to have appeared in court Saturday morning. To S. Davis, a friend who saw him Friday night, the deceased is said to have confided that he would end his life rather than appear in police court.'

I was an undergraduate student in philosophy at Toronto's University of St. Michael's College from 1962 to 1966. I was also a deeply closeted, eighteen-year-old homosexual when I began my studies and a deeply closeted, twenty-two-year-old homosexual when I graduated.

There was no 'gay' back then. There was only 'queer' (but not in its modern, reclaimed sense). I began to hear about queer from the boisterous straight boys I'd befriended. They discovered that St. Joseph Street – which runs between Bay Street and Queen's Park and forms the southern border of St. Mike's – was a cruising area. If you walked that block slowly late at night, cars would slow down, and the drivers, always men, would catch your eye and smile. If you smiled back, the car would stop, and the driver would open the door for you.

Gerald Hannon

Piss in a Bag

My friends had figured out the scene, and gamed it. They'd get together, party, drink a lot of beer, and then piss into plastic bags. When it was time, they'd head out to St. Joseph, each surreptitiously carrying their piss bags, and stand somewhere along that block, waiting.

When a car would come by and slow down, the boys would smile. The car would stop, the door would open, and my friends would lean in. But instead of entering, they would swing the bag full force into the interior, drenching the driver and the whole front seat. Screaming 'Faggot!' they slammed the door shut and sauntered off.

There was no need to run. No faggot, in those days, went to the police, not with a story like that, not when it might seem clear you were trying to pick up boys. Homosexual acts were illegal, and would be until 1969. So those men drove home, and if they were married, they would have to explain why everything smelled of urine.

Queenie and Ted were together for forty-seven years.

I happened upon their photos at the Canadian Lesbian and Gay Archives (CLGA) some years ago and developed an immediate fascination, as well as a bit of a retro-crush. Like many younger queers, my impression of mid-century lesbian life was shaped primarily by the old pulp novels that inevitably ended in shame, madness, desolation, and/or death. However, this rare collection of snapshots spoke to a reality in which the pain of marginalization was leavened by love and community.

The photos were donated to the CLGA in 2000 by a long-time friend of the couple – Queenie had recently died, and presumably this bequest was part of the process of dealing with her effects. Beyond the few details included in the donation agreement or scrawled on the backs of the photos, the CLGA had no biographical information about the subjects. Hoping to remedy this absence, I sent a letter to the donor, but she had moved and it was returned to me, unopened. Later, however, I discovered we had a mutual acquaintance and I was able to meet with her in late 2016.

Kate Zieman

Queenie and Ted

Although she prefers to remain anonymous, the donor is a fabulous octogenarian who generously shared her memories with me. Armed with the context she provided, I was able to piece together a few more details about Queenie and Ted through old voters' lists, city directories, and newspapers. I discovered they had lived in my Broadview/Danforth neighbourhood for nearly five decades, and our shared geography drew me even closer to them. However, it is no easy task to find information about working-class lesbians, and each new detail I've been able to uncover somehow just underscores how much I'll never know.

Queenie, so named as she was the youngest and only girl in a family of many boys, hailed from Kapuskasing in northern Ontario. What brought her to Toronto is a mystery, but by 1957, she was working as a teletype operator for CN and living with Ted in an apartment house at 1022 Broadview Avenue. That building is long gone, but it was situated just above Todmorden Mills, and would have had an incredible view of the Don Valley.

Ted (her legal given name was Thelma) came from Mactaquac, New Brunswick. She spent the early 1940s in the army, and many of her photos from that time are included in the CLGA collection. She seems to have worked as an assembler at a factory in Downsview for a short time in the late 1940s before moving to the Don Valley Paper Co., a mill built in 1825 that routinely made the news for negligently dyeing the Don River a multitude of different colours. Ted spent most of her working life in that ramshackle old building at the foot of Beechwood Drive, banned from working in the front office with the rest of the women because she refused to wear a dress.

In November 2016, I traipsed down into the valley with my wife and our son, hoping to find the remains of the paper factory. As we scrambled over slabs of concrete on the banks of the murky Don, I pondered the changes that have occurred since Ted walked those paths, and wished, for the hundredth time, that I could talk to her. Would she and Queenie have wanted to marry if they'd had the opportunity? Did they feel restricted or liberated by their queerness? Would they recognize this city in which my family (usually) does not raise eyebrows?

From what I've been told, their social group consisted mainly of other gay women.

'Ted (left) and I on fountain in Moncton, NB, July 1953.'

When they went out, they frequented house parties or the one bar in which they felt comfortable: the Commodore Hotel on Danforth Avenue, just east of Broadview (it's now the Black Swan). While they were reportedly able to drink at the supers-ketchy Commodore in relative peace, Ted still ran into trouble when she tried to use the washroom and was taken to be a man.

Despite their struggles, their friend affirmed that their relationship was a good one. Ted was gentle, sweet, and caring toward Queenie. Queenie, in turn, was quiet and loved crosswords. True to lesbian form, they kept cats, including one with an insatiable taste for underwear elastic. By 1974, they had moved to the first floor of the low-rise building at 852 Broadview, where they would remain for the rest of their lives. Photos from the mid-1990s show them sitting on lawn chairs behind this building, two weathered old-timers smiling at some private joke.

Their remarkable romance ended a few years later with Queenie's death at Toronto East General Hospital on Christmas Day, 1999. In the *Toronto Star* obituary, her spouse is listed as 'Thelma (Ted).' I have not been able to find any information about Ted's death.

Queenie and Ted were here, together, for half a century. The *fact* of their relationship is undeniable. Yet so soon after their deaths, they have all but disappeared. To have seen their photos and learned a little about them has been a privilege for me, but it feels like the beginning of a much larger and more difficult project. Like the lost rivers that still flow beneath Toronto's streets, the lives of these women, and so many like them, still feel just beyond reach, their traces visible only to those who know where to look.

For underage dykes in the 1970s, it was practically impossible to find a girl. You'd go looking anywhere there was a hint or rumour the girls were – shared houses, warehouse parties, or the back rooms of old restaurants that had been seconded for the night. But I found what I was looking for at the Blue Jay, a dingy, one-storey legion hall at Gerrard and Carlaw that the dykes rented out for weekend dances. The exterior was pocked beige stucco with a faded Canadian flag hanging over the door. Inside, the Jay was decorated with flickering hurricane lamps, tables with red-and-white-checkered cloths, and rickety stackable chairs armed with tiny slivers of wood that pierced your butt if you weren't careful.

Cathi Bond

Dyke Fight at the Blue Jay

The dykes themselves were either butch or femme, and there was little nuance or androgyny. The butches mostly wore men's three-piece pastel polyester suits, taped their tits, and worked in construction trades, factory shop floors, welding shops, or as long-haul truckers or mechanics. They also knew how to fight. I saw a lot of these sprawling punch-ups, usually sparked by the distinct clarion call 'You've been fucking my old lady.'

When those butches fought, they fought for real, like the men they'd seen in westerns, gangs, or biker fights. One moment peace; the next, flash violence. It seemed to me the dyke fight was key to impressing a girl, or at least keeping the one you found.

One night, I rolled into the Jay and started to cruise, when I saw her in the lineup for beer tickets. Her name was Kim and she was oh so beautiful, wearing a creamy silk dress and high-heeled shoes. Me, I had on cowboy boots, Levi's 501s, and my lucky red shirt with polished pearl-snap buttons. One look at Kim and I'd spent every penny I had on beer tickets. Within two hours, we were smashed out of our minds, but Kim still wanted more.

I staggered up to the bar, clutching my final ticket, and was ordering one last Blue when the bartender tapped me on the arm and pointed. 'Bitch moving in.'

I turned to see Kim slow dancing with one of the stone butches. The bartender looked at me. The others at the bar looked at me. I had no choice. I had to defend my old lady's honour.

Without even thinking, I whipped my beer bottle across the room as hard as I could. A high school pitcher, I had excellent aim. The bottle struck the butch in the back of the head, and she hit the floor with a bang.

I barely recall being thrown out the front door, but I do remember lying on the asphalt, with my beautiful Kim standing over me, hands on her curvy hips, screaming that jealousy was the ultimate turnoff and then – *poof* – she was gone.

And so was any chance I ever had of getting into the Blue Jay again.

Lucky for me, the times were changing. Homos were emerging from the shadows, wanting the right to party in the light of day. More and more, we were going glam, following andro David Bowie and the Spiders from Mars.

Gay-disco visionary Janko Naglic sensed 'Jackpot!' and opened Jo-Jo's, a dance club on the second floor of what would eventually become the Barn. Jo-Jo's was a snazzy, upscale disco with mirrored walls, a flashing dance floor, leather banquets, and the vegetation of the day – bushy ferns!

I loved the place. No more Blue Jay bad taste for me. Now it was class all the way.

Janko wisely gambled that by creating a space for both dykes and fags, he could up his revenues significantly. But if we wanted to party in a nice place, we had to learn to get along. For the most part, this formula worked. But Janko hadn't bargained on the fabulously exciting, terrifying tsunami of violence the butches dragged in with them: the dyke fight.

The first one happened during a particularly hot night in June. I was perched on a bar stool, cruising with a couple of my gay boys, when a gigantic butch leapt up onto the flickering dance floor, bellowing, 'You've been fucking my old lady!'

The butch sprinted through the gyrating bodies, flinging them out of her way like dolls. She stopped in front of the accused 'old lady fucker' and grabbed a beer bottle by the neck. She smashed it on the edge of the table and sprang at her sexual competitor, leading with broad swipes of ragged glass.

As the bartenders hit the deck, the other dyke flipped the table up for protection and charged at her attacker. Within moments, some of the other dykes began to roar like buffalo.

The women who weren't fighting dove under the tables and banquettes, while stampeding fags, screaming, '*Dyke fight! Dyke fight!*' blocked the exits. Anyone who was too scared or simply didn't want to fight shoved through pelting bottles and the odd connecting fist, and ran for the shelter of the women's can.

The cubicles were already packed tight. Some of the girls tried to clamber over the cubicle tops and jump in, while others desperately attempted to crawl under the doors, only to be greeted with frantic kicks.

'Get out of here!'

'Fuck off!'

'Find your own place to hide!'

Bug-eyed girls cowered under the counter. Smears of blood decorated every surface. My dad had been a country doctor, so I began rapidly yanking paper towels out of stainless-steel containers with this black-haired chick. We soaked them with water to clean the wounds, searching for cuts that might need to be stitched.

I flashed back to the time when I had whipped that beer bottle and started my own dyke fight at the Blue Jay. It had felt like lobbing a bomb containing all the pent-up rage of my young gay life – one of rawest, most thrilling things I'd ever done. But this time, as I cowered with that gorgeous black-haired babe, I suddenly realized something about that deliciously primal sensation of throwing a bottle. If I ever wanted to land a real girl, one who wasn't turned off by old stone violence, I'd better hang up my boxing mitts and leap into the quickly changing new gay world that surrounded me.

There are places in a city that don't register in the public imagination, places we aren't aware of when we think of communities. One was an old filing cabinet in the former offices of *The Globe and Mail* at 444 Front Street West, an anti-quated object full of old #9 regular-size envelopes stuffed with yellowing paper and microfiche sheets of newsprint. These mostly unseen envelopes played a large role in how the public viewed homosexuality in the pre– and post–Pierre Trudeau period.

A newspaper library used to be known as a morgue, because the clipping files contained dead stories the paper's researchers and reporters would, with coroner-like scrutiny, inspect for clues in prior news coverage. At *The Globe*, the clippings were stored in three carousel filing cabi-nets, which I could activate with the flick of a button. The carousel of clipping trays rotated to the requested row, allowing the researcher to pull out a tray (think morgue slab) with a comprehensive packet of every story on a given subject or person clipped by *Globe* librarians between 1936 to 1987 (when digital storage replaced clipping).

Stephanie Chambers
See: Sex Perverts

In early 2016, *Globe* national affairs columnist John Ibbitson contacted me to request assistance with a story re-examining the incredible case of Everett George Klippert. In 1967, the Supreme Court of Canada upheld a lower-court ruling mandating life in prison for Klippert. He became the only Canadian ever to be sentenced and jailed as a 'dangerous sex offender' because he was gay; Klippert spent a decade behind bars.

Ibbitson wanted to know if we could track down relatives and original court files, and provide an overview of public perception of homosexuality in the 1960s. Could we find out what became of Klippert after he was released in 1971?

I couldn't have been more excited by a research request. This is one of those queries that come in that my colleague Rick Cash and I don't flip a coin for; he knew I should be handling this.

My first thought was to grab our clipping files for KLIPPERT, EVERETT GEORGE and HOMOSEXUALS. I'd been working for the paper for several years and had previously consulted the HOMOSEXUALS envelopes. I turned the switch on the old mid-century carousel. It shuddered to life, clipping trays creaking up into the ceiling, each row labelled and cranking into view: HANSARD, HAWKER, HELIUM, HIKES, HOCKEY HALL ... HOMOSEXUALS. I thumbed through the tray: each file bore a simple title: HOMOSEXUALS 1971 OCT–1984 OCT, HOMO-SEXUALS 1984 OCT–1985 JUN, and so on, until I noticed one I hadn't seen previously: an envelope marked HOMOSEXUALS – EDITORIALS. It had a message that stung like a blow to the solar plexus: PREVIOUS TO 1969 SEPT SEE: SEX PERVERTS.

That those long-forgotten colleagues classified queerness in this way reveals much about their era. The tragedy of George Klippert's story is that he was a victim of prejudice at the precise moment when gay liberation was gaining momentum and public consciousness was shifting. Reading the SEX PERVERTS and HOMOSEXUALS clipping files is like watching a sped-up version of the evolution of public and editorial opinion about LGBT rights, beginning with the decriminalization of homosexuality. The authority control change from SEX PERVERTS to HOMOSEXUALS in the clipping files is directly a result of George Klippert's experience of injustice. A sampling of some of the contents of both files bears this out.

Long-time *Globe* columnist John Verner McAree's February 21, 1947, story, 'Scientific Treatment for Sex Perverts,' begins, 'What are called sex crimes are increasing in Canada and the United States, and confronted with them the lynching spirit stirs itself.' McAree, considered a progressive voice, moves from this unnerving lede to classify various types of sex perverts: homosexual, indecent exposure, alcoholic degenerate, rapist, and monsters that ship dismembered women in trunks, with the homosexual morally compared to tuberculosis patients not responsible for their lot. 'Unless they commit public indecencies,' he wrote, 'we doubt if they are fit subjects for legal punishment at all.'

An April 13, 1966, news story headlined 'Drunks, Deviates Also Attracted to Parks in Spring' cautions women to avoid Toronto parks at night, particularly Allan Gardens, High Park, and Riverdale Park. 'But the parks will also be the gathering place for some of the most undesirable persons in the community – exhibitionists, homosexuals, drunks, vandals and thugs.' While Alderwoman June Marks said she was afraid to go in any of the downtown parks after dark, police inspectors and the parks commissioner all stated there was little crime or vandalism in these places. 'Queen's Park in the heart of Metro has a bad reputation, but Inspector William Henderson said he couldn't remember the last arrest there. He described it as one of the most crime-free places in Metro.'

Following numerous other stories in the SEX PERVERTS clipping file that conflate homosexuality with perversion and moral degeneracy, public opinion seemed to swing quickly. On December 12, 1967, *The Globe* published a landmark editorial supporting the Lester B. Pearson government's bill decriminalizing homosexual acts; this is the editorial that then-justice minister Pierre Trudeau paraphrases in his famous quote, 'The state has no place in the bedrooms of the nation.'

The rapid shift in opinion revealed by the succession of articles is a bit dissonant. From today's perspective, the change is moderate in that it focuses on adult men (lesbians were omitted from the law and the discourse), left to go about their mutually consenting business in the privacy of their bedrooms. Topics like parks, bathhouses, and age of consent are left for later consideration. Looking through the HOMOSEXUALS editorial clipping files in the 1970s, it's interesting to see *The Globe*'s cautious acceptance and encouragement of the mainstreaming of gay rights – with some exceptions.

After the 1977 murder of twelve-year-old Emanuel Jaques (see p. 167–70), *The Globe* editorial cautions demonstrators to be peaceful and not undermine the presumption of innocence, but there is no direct mention of the homophobia that accompanied the protest and calls to clean up Yonge Street. In another editorial, Ontario horse-racing steward John Damien's 1975 dismissal is viewed as an injustice. 'Why should Mr. Damien's homosexuality be regarded as a special case of conflicting – or potentially conflicting – interests?' But the paper was much more cautious in its support of amending federal and provincial human rights codes. 'Should not protection of homosexual rights be dependent on a reciprocal right of minors to be free from efforts at conversion?' asked a 1977 editorial.

It's also worth noting that for *The Globe* librarians and their methodical classification system, Klippert et al. were SEXUAL PERVERTS prior to September 1969, and then they were HOMOSEXUALS. What happened that month to prompt the librarians to alter subject authority control? The Stonewall riots? No, that occurred on June 28, 1969. The first Canadian Pride celebrations? They took place in 1971.

Rather, the turning point was the amendments to the Criminal Code decriminalizing homosexuality, which came into force at the end of August 1969. The librarian part of me grudgingly admires this punctiliousness. Parliament passed the law in June, but the language on the clipping file shifted only after the law came into force, in August. It was a greater authority – the Government of Canada – that altered *The Globe and Mail*'s classification system.

But the dyke part of me feels the decades of effort made by LGBT activists and artists who directly influenced that change, including Klippert's own experience and growing advocacy behind bars. Though the law changed in 1969, he wasn't released from prison until 1971.

The clipping files for SEX PERVERTS and HOMOSEXUALS – EDITORIALS with its PREVIOUS TO 1969 SEPT SEE: SEX PERVERTS cross-reference, are still active. I never considered updating the headings. A newspaper is a permanent record, and the language of the subject headings should remain faithful to the language contained in the stories, whatever the discomfort. Besides, it's a reminder of where we were, and provides a way to reflect on those turning-point moments when our language skips a beat.

Jennifer Coffey

And the Stars Look Very Different Today

Ziggy Stardust is everywhere in the early 1970s, but dressing in drag is still illegal. And yet remnants of the trade are always in evidence. Muddy lipstick, smudged mascara, hollow cheekbones made even more hollow with small pots of creamy rose blush they share for economy.

They – a band of sexual outcasts – roll in from the Parkside and St. Charles taverns, no farther than three blocks from Fran's at College and Yonge, and take up residence, occupying the carrot-orange leatherette booths in my section from midnight until dawn. The diner is their twenty-four-hour beacon, its garish fluorescence highlighting display-case pies and triple layer cakes, the puddings, and toppling bowls of colourful, whipped-cream Jell-O. The taunting aroma of fresh eggs, bacon, and hickory-smoked ham teases its way through wafts of freshly brewed coffee.

I am nineteen and new to the city, a Port Credit exile who has run from my mother's sad and intransigent life in the Lakeshore Psychiatric Hospital. They show me a Polaroid snapshot of themselves. In it, all but one are thin and decked out in boas, fishnet stockings, and the shiny material my mother once loved. Makeshift costumes, provocative and sheer. They lean at long-legged angles in metal chairs and against high-back stools, earnest, fierce, dignified, their painted lips slightly parted. Their wigs remind me of movie stars – Gina Lollobrigida, Candice Bergen, Brigitte Bardot – and they are thrilled when I tell them so. Only one pair of eyes stares back into the camera, her gaze penetrating and sad, a jumble of questions and answers.

They like me, not only because I take care of their immediate needs and don't complain, but perhaps because they see me as one of their tribe, an outsider living in a rooming house, adrift in a city rife with rejection. They call me 'Girl' and, looking past my tired orange-beige uniform and pantyhose, compliment me on my style. My pale face and coal-black hair prompt cries of 'Morticia' and 'Sally Bowles.'

Weaving my way through the cigarette smoke, I worry about how I will pay my rent working the graveyard shift. Tips on toasted Danish and coffee are paltry, and refills are free. In any event, these after-hours diners don't have much money.

But the girls offer me every other manner of sustenance, their advice wide-ranging and firm. How to stand upright in platform boots. Must-see movies (*Blonde Cobra*, *Flaming Creatures*, *Funeral Parade of Roses*, *Something for Everyone*, and *The Boys in the Band*, a sentimental favourite). The simplest and safest technique for unrolling a condom. The tidiest way to hand-roll a cigarette. How to turn on a lover. When to move on.

They tell me about their role model, their matriarch, Michelle DuBarry. In their voices I hear a protective savagery. I listen to their stories of laneways and parks, the places where they go looking for men, not merely for sex but also for connection. The hot spots where they gather. Spadina Avenue, the Quest, the Manatee, Cherry Beach. They talk about CHAT, which I later discover is the Community Homophile Association of Toronto. I remember the acronym because I like to talk.

They share other stories, too – stories that cast shadows. I hear about Christmases and Thanksgivings, and sons who, if they are invited home at all, are advised to behave. They tell me about missed funerals of fathers and brothers and beloved grandmothers. About cruel lovers, and loving johns who hold them until dawn.

One night, a willowy young man named Jimmy comes in looking haunted. He has been battered in Queen's Park. Two cops, he says, thrashed the shit out of him, but you can't see the marks on account of the hoses. And then he laughs, and doesn't stop laughing until everyone joins him, his eyes a milky blue, the tears barely visible as they cluster and slide down his face.

Every shift, I watch police on the beat stroll up to the cash to collect free cups of coffee and pastry, a guarantee of protection for the all-night restaurant. Here, the officers pay no mind to my section, either oblivious or intentional, much in the way most customers are blind to the occasional cockroach that scurries up the wall out by the kitchen.

During holiday season, and sometimes for no reason at all, I am bestowed with trinkets and treats – dangly earrings from a Yonge Street kiosk, a carton of Kent cigarettes, a packet of matches, its cover painted with dancing hula girls. Once, on my birthday, they bought me a heavenly piece of Fran's mile-high lemon meringue pie. And when they sing 'Happy Birthday,' they harmonize, their voices melodic and tender, their serenade followed by hugging and kissing.

I haven't felt this loved since I last saw my mother.

Many memories endure from those long-ago night shifts. Hands clasped over mouths, aghast or in playful hysteria. Heads huddled together in conspiratorial whisper. Sugar dispensers turned upside down over half-empty coffee cups, contents pouring out at length for comic effect. Voices raised in debate, sometimes in anger or resignation, and always a coming together.

And I wonder – what became of them? Did they stay in the city? Who found love? After I had moved on, did they like the new waitress as much as they had liked me? Do they miss the old days? Who survived? Do they remember me in the way that I remember them?

The very last shift I worked at Fran's was a cold one, the snow blowing and bereft. I had switched for an earlier time slot, a farewell drink waiting for me at the

Colonial Tavern, a new life in the offing in Fredericton, New Brunswick. I felt compelled to find relatives who barely knew me, longing to shake off a tumbleweed future. My shift ended well before midnight. As I walked out into the darkness, I heard their siren song call out from the restaurant radio.

'Ground Control to Major Tom ... '

In the mid-sixties, the Music Room was located above the King Koin Laundromat on Yonge Street slightly north of Wellesley.

Upstairs, you entered through a red-flocked foyer. Sara sat at the top of the stairs and quickly sized you up. If you were okay (say, a queen, or a butch, a fem lady, or with a gaggle of gay friends), you got in. If you were clearly some tiresome straight man bent on coming on to the gay women, or hassling the campier queens, you were quickly turned away at the front desk. And Sara thought nothing of knocking those creeps ass-over-tea-kettle down the stairs if any of them proved persistent, belligerent, or shifty.

The club itself consisted of a large open room, bathed in romantic red lighting, with pastel wall drawings, on powder-blue ground, of groupings of males and of females, wispily dancing with each other. (Or at least as I recall; I was seventeen or eighteen at the time, too young-looking for the bars and taverns.)

John Forbes
Sara Ellen Dunlop and the Music Room:
A Memory

Gossip had it there was one memorable night where a gang of motorcycle hoods tried to trash their way into the club. Sara responded by orchestrating a few heads with the aid of a baseball bat, joined by a tympani section of nelly queens brandishing ashtrays. Gangs rarely bothered the club again.

You couldn't club the morality squad though. Detective Belcher tried to close the Music Room on a gross indecency charge when two men were accused of fondling each other's asses immorally (dancing to a more exciting take on 'Cheek to Cheek'). Sara became the principal organizer of a fundraising benefit to help pay the lawyer who finally won the case in court. She had my complete respect from that point on – I saw her as a fighter for civil rights, on 'our side,' as I would have said back then, in those pre-liberation days of them (the straights) versus us (the outcast dykes and queens).

Well over a decade passed and I hadn't seen Sara – now Sara Ellen – for years, until one afternoon in June 1976, when we met at a rehearsal at the Community Homophile Association of Toronto Centre. There was to be a coffee-house evening during the National Gay Conference, with Sara Ellen as featured entertainer.

By then she was completely bald – a result of the chemotherapy fighting the cancer that would eventually kill her. It was a shock, but somehow the baldness added to her strength and presence; she was androgynous, a blue-eyed Buddha.

I said hello and received a familiar welcoming affirmation from Sara; for a second I felt transported back to the Music Room, circa 1963, gliding past queens in their puffy mohair sweaters, skin-tight white Levi's, and poufy bouffant hair; butches in men's trousers, sporting Elvis ducktails; drag shows with Alberta, Riki-Tik, Toni Seven, Jamie Durette, Johnnie Day, and the ever 'lovely' Anita, camping

On stage at the
MUSIC ROOM,
TORONTO's -
Alain Adams
Robbie Willows
Noel Barri
Jami Durette
Toni Seven

it up to the Ronettes, the Supremes, Martha and the Vandellas, Babs Streisand, Lainie Kazan, and Shirley Bassey.

The Music Room was our club, a focus for our community. None of us ever dreamed that one day there would be gay pride or gay liberation, or that what I recall of those days would so often be called sexist. But the club was still a centre, a rallying point, part of a community on which to build the gay groups that we have today. Women and men mixed freely in those days, something that sadly disappeared during the separatist 1970s.

Perhaps it is impossible to explain the past to a new generation. At the cabaret that summer night, lesbians and gay men from every part of Canada jammed into the community centre, as Sara's music took over completely, erasing factions and divisions. We were captured, all of us, blended into one unified song whose spirit was sown in the Music Room, when Sara, and others, had the courage to carve out a small part of the universe and call it ours. It was happening again. Now.

The last time I saw Sara Ellen was on Yonge Street. She was in saffron robes, and I slowly realized that this was Sara, not some Krishna figure. I smiled as I went by, but didn't stop to talk. She was deep in conversation. It was a beautiful, clear day, and my final vivid memory of Sara Ellen.

The Music Room (previously the Maison des Lys) was an unlicenced club that opened in 1962 at 575 Yonge Street and closed in 1966.

FOR THOSE WHO ARE HAPPY AND

GAY

INTERNATIONAL

50 Cents

LITHO'D IN CANADA   ADULTS ONLY

Vol 2 No. 1

EMERGENCE

Toronto Island beaches have been weekend destination sites for queers for many years. Among the first public events organized by early gay activists in 1971 and 1972 were community picnics on Ward's and Hanlan's Point beaches, although queer friends found pleasure in relaxing at Hanlan's Point as early as the 1950s. Its appeal is due partly to its remote location close to the island airport and the proximity of nearby trees and shrubbery for amorous encounters. Encouraged by the secluded location, swimming trunks began to come off, and soon this stretch of rare sand had morphed into a nude beach, to the disapproval of the local police, who swept through periodically to make arrests, even lurking offshore occasionally in a surveillance marine police boat.

Ed Jackson

Hanlan's Point

In 2002, through the lobbying efforts of Councillor Kyle Rae, Toronto City Council agreed to designate Hanlan's Point an official 'clothing-optional' beach, the only such designation recognized by a city bylaw and the only nude beach in Canada beyond the more famous Wreck Beach in Vancouver.

Hanlan's Point Beach circa mid-1950s. Philip McLeod (front centre) relaxing with a group of friends.

Four dykes walk into a bar …

It was 'amateur night' at the Brunswick House, January 5, 1974. By the end of the evening, four self-identified 'dykes' had been harassed, ejected by police from the pub – twice – and charged with various offences.

Five days later, a well-attended meeting at Holy Trinity Church initiated a defence committee and fund. In February, the committee organized a fundraising dance at the Community Homophile Association of Toronto Centre (CHAT) on Church Street.

'The community response to the police action and charges against the 'Brunswick Four' indicated a radical change in the consciousness of gays, lesbians, and bisexuals, and a hardening resolve to fight back,' observed former Ontario Human Rights Commissioner Tom Warner in his queer history, Never Going Back *(University of Toronto Press, 2002).*

Pat Murphy
The Brunswick Four:
An Oral History

Judy LaMarsh, former Liberal MP and cabinet minister, defended (pro bono) the Brunswick Four in court in March 1974. Two years later, the incident was one of several examined by the Royal Commission into Metropolitan Toronto Police Practices.

The following is from an oral history of Pat Murphy (1941–2003), one of the Brunswick Four, recorded by the Lesbians Making History Collective in July 1986 and edited by Maureen FitzGerald in January 2016. The audio and written transcript of the complete interview are available at the Canadian Lesbian and Gay Archives.

[Sue Wells, Heather Elizabeth, and I] were going out for dinner to the Blue Cellar, because that's where all the radio women used to hang out. Then we decided we'd go to the Brunswick for a few beers. So we called Adrienne [Potts] to join us.

We were just, you know, basically girls having a good time. Somebody was singing that song 'I Enjoy Being a Girl,' and Adrienne said, 'Oh, I know other lyrics.' She wrote them down on a napkin. When Heather went to the washroom, some guy sat down at our table, which we really didn't want. [We said], Heather will be back in a minute, and he'll give her her chair and he'll be gone. [But] he happened to see the napkin [and] he got a little feisty and a little weird. When she came back, he wouldn't give Heather her chair, and he asked her to sit on his knee. I told him he could sit right here on my knee if he could handle it – or leave.

He left, and something happened between him and Adrienne. I don't know if she [threw] some beer at him or something. He sneaked back and put a beer over her head, and another beer went over somebody else's head. [W]e decided, well the hell with this, we'll get up and sing this song because this guy had been such a jerk. So we asked if they'd play that song again. Adrienne and I were going to go up onstage and sing 'I Enjoy Being a Girl.'

[Instead], we got up and sang 'I Enjoy Being a Dyke': 'When I see a man who's sexist/Who does something I don't like/I just tell him he can fuck off/I enjoy being a dyke.' That's how the song goes. Everybody loved it and clapped and cheered.

And then we were cut off suddenly. They wouldn't serve us. The woman waiting on us said she didn't know why. People in the bar started passing us the beers off their order because nobody could figure out why we weren't getting served, because we were delightful all night.

The next thing you know, there's ten cops walking toward the table. They had been called and said we had broken a glass or something. The cops had really been set up, but we didn't know that, so they told us we had to leave, and we said we wanted a reason before we would leave. We hadn't done anything. Didn't it look all right? You see any problem here? Ask the people, is there a problem? No.

'You're going!'

They were obviously ready and had the wagon outside. Two of them grabbed Heather. I started hopping tables. Sue started going in that direction. I jumped up onstage to ask people to watch and witness what was going down here, because it didn't look too good to me. [A woman] was up there singing and just dropped me into the arms of a cop. We got taken away and held for about four-and-a-half hours in a garage and taunted and teased and not allowed to make phone calls. They were trying to figure out what to arrest us for, and they couldn't come up with a charge.

As we were being thrown into the paddy wagon, Heather's ankle was all twisted [and] my arm felt like it was dislocated. This guy came up as the door closed and said he was from the Attorney General's office and had watched the whole thing. We had been falsely arrested and he'd be willing to be a witness. Which turned out to be what he did do, and he was a witness at the eventual trial.

When they finally did let us go, one of the cops hit Adrienne on the way out. By the time we got out, her chin was bleeding. We were just fucking roaring by then. So we went back to the Brunswick to pick up the witnesses. As soon as we walked in, of course, it was filled with plainclothes cops. We were immediately arrested again and taken to 14 Division for another three hours.

We had to really protect each other. [They] threw a bag of heroin in my lap and said they'd found it on me when I was picked up. Adrienne says, 'Oh yeah? Want fingerprints?' And [we] started playing catch with this bag of heroin across the room. 'You've got them all now.' We all started singing 'I Am a Union Maid,' and we wouldn't talk anymore. We just kept singing and singing and singing and said, we'll see them in court.

We did.

The second time, they charged us with causing a disturbance, obstructing an officer, and some sort of obscenity [violation]. Judy LaMarsh took our case. That was a really good time for the community. There were fundraising dances, and the courtroom was packed every day with women. There wasn't a day they weren't there to support [us]. Every single day, it was just packed.

The charges did not hold [except] one [against] Adrienne. I think that's because she'd been arrested three times for obstructing justice, jumping on a policeman when he was manhandling a woman.

[The case] pulled together people who hadn't been together for a while. I think it also sort of got the message through that you can just be out any night of the week and something like this could happen.

I think it was politicizing for some of the people I worked with [at Thistletown Regional Centre, in Etobicoke] because they liked working with me and they liked the work I did. But [the case] affected one promotion that I didn't get. Well, not a promotion but a job that I really wanted to get, and I didn't find out until later.

People who hung out in the bars thought I was nuts. 'What's the point?' they would say. 'You're fighting against nothing. You have to win something, and twenty-five, thirty years from now, you'll be starting all over again. Leave it alone. Don't draw too much attention.'

Some people like to be involved politically and some don't. I don't know: if we all look back, maybe [that] has a whole lot to do with how we were brought up.

Pat Murphy was sentenced to thirty days in jail for contempt of court.

T he Parkside Tavern wasn't classy. It was a beer parlour, and though it was right on Toronto's main drag, it looked exactly like the legion hall in any small town across the country. It was owned and run by the Bolters, a resolutely heterosexual family who employed, over the years, equally resolute, usually middle-aged family-type staff to serve what was, for a long time, one of the larger gatherings of gay men in Toronto.

When you entered the Parkside, you knew where to sit, though 'neighbourhood' barriers might break down when the place was busy. The leather/denim crowd more or less took over the south wall under the windows. The tables along the north wall under the TV became known as 'the Drugstore.' The gay activists (I was one of them) might push two or three tables together in the centre of the room and continue the heated discussions begun at some gay liberation meeting. The staff were long-time regulars, too – Big Frank, with his surly geniality, had been slinging draft beer there for nineteen years when I interviewed him in 1980. It was a loud, grubbily cheerful, brightly lit, basic Ontario beer parlour that happened to be full of homosexual men (women were not allowed in a men's beverage room, and the owners had closed the 'Ladies and Escorts' side). It was, though not by design, something of a community centre. It was also, and in this case quite by design, a trap.

Gerald Hannon
Closing the Spy Holes at the Parkside Tavern

For years, the Bolters, with the co-operation of the police morality bureau, ran the equivalent of a backroom sex bar. Everyone knew it was possible to get it off in the basement washroom, and that was doubtless one of the Parkside's attractions. The Bolters got paying customers. The Morality Bureau kept its arrest statistics up with little trouble – management provided the officers with a spy hole from an adjoining utility room (from the washroom, it looked like a ventilation grille). It worked – in 1979 alone there were twenty-eight arrests. On October 3 that year, police arrested four men, having observed them 'reaching out and manipulating' each other's penises. One of the men, Derek George Grant, forty-four, panicked and was kept in a headlock until he was handcuffed. He died in custody, choking to death on his own vomit.

On February 25, 1980, I and three other activists met with Norman Bolter in his dingy, skylit office above the St. Charles Tavern. He was wearing a loud plaid suit and loosely knotted tie, and projected both indignation and a patronizing sympathy. 'It's a bloody disgrace what goes on in that washroom,' he said. 'The kids I could care less about, but some of the old guys, good customers, I don't want them locked up. I've got a lot of good gay friends and I don't even mind some kissing in the bar, but none of that soul kissing. No way.' He

The Parkside Tavern, 530 Yonge Street at Breadalbane, opened c. 1964 and closed in 1986.

told us the police had recently requested two more spy holes, to be focused on activity in the toilet stalls.

We talked him out of it, and talked him into sealing up the current one, by threatening to take a complaint to the liquor licencing commission. We also pointed out that the stink we could raise in the community, with pamphlets and picketing, would be really bad for business. Now we were speaking his language. We also asked him to abandon police surveillance and hire a gay man to monitor the washroom. He agreed. Suddenly, it seemed, we had clout.

I continued to go to the Parkside, and when I used the washroom I couldn't help but notice the five shiny new tiles, high up on the wall across from the urinals. They covered what had been the police spy hole and were, in a modest way, an epitaph for our powerlessness.

I n 1949, Jim Egan, a lab technician, began a campaign to combat the homophobia appearing in Toronto's newspapers. At that time, entrapment of gay
men by the police was still rampant, especially in traditional cruising
grounds, including parks, theatres, and public washrooms. Local yellow-press
papers such as *Flash*, *Hush*, *Justice Weekly*, and *True News Times* (TNT) delighted
in reporting these arrests, which were usually made on the charge of gross
indecency. The papers denounced the 'limp-wrist set' for their 'sex crimes'
and published details, including the accuseds' names, ages, addresses, and
occupations. This exposure often led to catastrophic results for
the men involved.

Donald W. McLeod

Jim Egan,
Gay Warrior

Egan felt personal outrage against unfair and sensational media
coverage of homosexuality, and decried what he saw as a conspiracy
of silence that obscured the true nature of homosexuality. As he
recalled later, 'I simply let [the press] know that there was at least
one person out there who was not going to sit by and let them get
away with what I considered to be gross inaccuracies and libels.'

Beginning with letters to the editors of publications great and
small, Egan denounced the media degradation of gay people – a
brave and unusual thing to do. His campaign predated the 1950 founding of
the Mattachine Society, the pioneering homophile rights organization in the
United States, and began twenty years before the decriminalization of gay sex
between consenting adults in private in Canada.

How did Jim Egan find the courage to become Toronto's first public gay
activist? He had a conventional childhood, born into a Roman Catholic
working-class family in Toronto and attending Holy Name School. Egan was
not successful as a student and dropped out by age sixteen. His father died
around that time, and Egan remained close to his mother for the rest of her
life. She came to accept his homosexuality, as did Charles, his only sibling,
who also later came out as gay.

Although not a good student, Egan was an intellectual autodidact and
book collector well acquainted with the works of the touchstone gay icons:
Walt Whitman, Oscar Wilde, André Gide. He worked on farms during the
late 1930s, and that experience opened up other opportunities, including a
position as a technician in the Department of Zoology at the University of
Toronto, and later at Connaught Laboratories.

From 1943 to 1947, Egan served in the merchant navy, seeing the world
and visiting gay bars overseas. By the end of the war, he had a circle of gay
friends, and in 1948 he met a loving partner, Jack Nesbit, at the bar at the
Savarin Hotel at 336 Bay Street. Egan ran his own biological specimen-supply
business and so he never had to worry about getting fired for being gay.

In 1948, Alfred C. Kinsey published *Sexual Behavior in the Human Male*. Its suggestion – that homosexuality was more common in men than previously believed – was much discussed in the mainstream press, and gave hope to gays everywhere.

Egan's independence, intelligence, wide reading, and simmering outrage propelled him into activism. As he recalled in his memoir, *Challenging the Conspiracy of Silence*, published by the Canadian Lesbian and Gay Archives in 1998:

> In October 1950, a letter of mine was published for the first time in *True News Times*. TNT published a ridiculous gay gossip or tid-bit column written by someone who called himself Masque. My letter complained about some of the stupid, nasty remarks that appeared there. These gay columns were filled with innuendo, such as 'What well-known bartender had been out with what well-known queen?' I never approved of this kind of gay trivia.

No longer content just to write letters of protest, Egan, in November 1951, persuaded the editor of TNT to give him a platform. For the next seven weeks, his unsigned series, 'Aspects of Homosexuality,' appeared in the paper. This was a watershed moment in the history of gay journalism in Canada: the first long articles written from a positive gay point of view. The content was heavily flavoured by Egan's reading, and included overviews of same-sex desire through history, legal and scientific aspects of homosexuality, and the need for more tolerance. The prose was highly readable, relentlessly logical, and blunt in its conclusions:

Jim Egan (left) and Jack Nesbit, 1954.

> Under the present anti-homosexual laws of Canada, Great Britain and the U.S., all of which are almost identical in scope and severity, it is a crime, punishable in some cases by life imprisonment, to engage in homosexual intercourse under any circumstances whatsoever. This

means, in effect, that literally millions of men are asked to forgo all sexual expression in deference to a law set up by Society, not for its protection, but rather in an effort to elevate its ignorance and prejudice to the dignity of brute force. ('Aspects of Homosexuality: Discussion of the Legal Aspects in the Life of a Homosexual. Part II,' *True News Times*, November 26, 1951)

Egan's crusade expanded in December 1953, when 'Homosexual Concepts' first appeared in *Justice Weekly*. These columns, now signed 'J.L.E.' (James Leo Egan), included important insights into debates about the cause and cure of homosexuality, as well as reports on current events, such as the ongoing purge, led by Senator Joseph McCarthy, of hundreds of U.S. government employees because of their sexuality. On this last point, Egan was particularly scathing:

The ferreting out and subsequent firing of several hundred homosexuals from various government offices [beginning in 1950] violated every single canon of justice, democracy, fair-play, common human decency and Christian charity. The tenets of the International Declaration of Human Rights were violated right and left, the very Constitution of the U.S. was ignored … ('Most Fantastic Witch-hunt since Inquisition Was Followed by Dismissal of Homosexuals by the Hundreds from U.S. Government Offices,' *Justice Weekly*, March 13, 1954)

Egan published twenty-seven columns by June 1954, when he took a hiatus to buy and run a farm with Jack in rural Ontario.

A highlight of Jim Egan's activism occurred in 1964, when he helped journalist Sidney Katz research 'The Homosexual Next Door: A Sober Appraisal of a New Social Phenomenon,' published in *Maclean's* that year. Egan – and his library – served as essential sources for Katz's research, and he also provided the writer with a tour of local gay haunts. (See excerpt from Katz's article, pages 140–141.)

Egan's collaboration with Katz was a triumph, but it also strained his relationship with Jack, who was apprehensive about Egan's increasingly public gay activism. Jack finally delivered an ultimatum: activism or their relationship. Egan chose to stay with Jack, and in July 1964, they fled to British Columbia, where they started a marine-specimen biological supply business, settling into the laid-back atmosphere of Vancouver Island.

But Egan soon developed an interest in environmentalism and became involved with the Society for the Prevention of Environmental Collapse and the Save Our Straits Committee. In November 1981, he was elected regional director of Electoral Area B of the Regional District of Comox-Strathcona. He was one of the first openly gay men to attain public office in Canada, and was re-elected twice before deciding to stand down in 1993.

Over the years, Jack became more comfortable with being openly gay, and in 1985 he and Egan started the Comox Valley branch of the Island Gay Society, hosting a monthly drop-in at their home in Courtenay until 1996.

In February 1987, Egan and Nesbit initiated a new era in activism when they applied on Jack's behalf for the spousal allowance benefit provided under the Old Age Security Act. Health and Welfare Canada denied their claim, which set in motion a series of court challenges that went to the Supreme Court of Canada. In May 1995, they lost their final appeal, but the court ruled that 'sexual orientation' would have to be read into the Charter as a protected ground of discrimination – a monumental finding in support of gay rights in Canada.

In June 1995, Egan and Nesbit were made honorary grand marshals of Toronto's Pride parade. As they rode in an open car, dressed in identical pink shirts, hundreds of thousands of people cheered them on. When the car reached the intersection of Yonge and Wellesley, the couple broke down and wept in each other's arms. They really had come full circle.

Both Jim Egan and Jack Nesbit died in 2000, at the ages of seventy-nine and seventy-two, respectively.

I have tried to make a realistic appraisal of the homosexual as a person by getting to know large numbers of them at the Toronto Club and elsewhere. I have learned that the homosexual is rarely the weird sex monster so often depicted in psychiatric case histories, police records, and lurid fiction. A surprisingly high proportion of homosexuals are indistinguishable from heterosexuals. Only a small proportion of homosexual men affect effeminate dress or mannerisms. The vast majority are industrious, law-abiding citizens with regular jobs – some of them positions of great responsibility. Like most heterosexuals, most homosexuals are outraged by adults who molest children or seduce adolescents.

Sidney Katz

The Homosexual Next Door (1964)

I spent an evening at the apartment of another couple who had been together for seventeen years. Verne Baldwin,[1] forty-three, runs his own business; George Galbraith, thirty-six, is a hairdresser. As Verne and I sat talking in the comfortable library, George brought in a tray of cold beer, glasses, and salted nuts. Later, he set an attractive table in the dining room and served coffee and refreshments. George, I was told, does the cooking, washing, and ironing; chooses the furniture and decides on the colour scheme for decorating the apartment. The actual painting is done by Verne, who also handles all the repairs and heavy chores. As in the case of other 'married' couples, a good deal of this pair's social life revolves about their home. As will be explained in a later article, maintaining a homosexual marriage is a formidable task because of male promiscuity, the absence of children, and the censure of the law, church, and society.

A 'single' homosexual, who has decided that he belongs to the gay world, is apt to spend considerable time at one or another of the city's high spots. High on his list is the Homosexual Club, which charges an annual membership fee of $7.50. On nights when the members stage their own entertainment, the Club stays open till 3 a.m. As many as two hundred people pack in on a single night, about one fifth of them female homosexuals and, usually, a few heterosexuals, friends of the members.

One of the Club's managers, John Deems, a thirty-seven-year-old bisexual with an infectious sense of humour, told me, 'Heterosexuals come here expecting to see terrible things – an orgy of perversion, perhaps. They're disappointed.' What they see is a clean, well-furnished establishment resembling a small nightclub. Members arrive singly, in couples, or parties. They sit around quietly chatting, sipping coffee, listening to music, or dancing. The only thing that might make heterosexuals uncomfortable is seeing members of the same sex dance together. The Club plays a definite role in educating at least some members of the public about homosexuals. More than one member of the Club told me, 'I've taken a relative or friend there with me to show them what nice friends I have.'

Members told me they liked the Club because it was one place away from home where they could relax and be themselves. 'In heterosexual places you have to be on guard so that you won't say or do the wrong thing,' one young homosexual told me. 'Constant concealment is a heavy burden.' Deems claims that the Club is maintained purely for social reasons and is not a place used by members to make pickups. 'Our members have a chance to meet nice, respectable people,' says Deems. 'We keep out drunks, hustlers, child molesters, seducers, and other kinds of riff-raff.' While the Toronto police tolerate the Club, they have misgivings. They believe that such clubs encourage young people to become homosexuals.

Deems denies it. 'By the time a young man joins our club his sexual orientation has been firmly determined. We don't manufacture homosexuals. We only give homosexuals a comfortable, dignified place to meet socially. They're better off here than they would be out on the street.' Deems and his co-manager Susie Coleman, a lesbian, hope to expand the Club program to include classes in arts and crafts and to publish a monthly magazine.

Before arriving at the Club late at night, the homosexual is likely to have spent several hours drinking with his companions in a gay bar. There are at least six in Toronto. The first one I visited is well-furnished and the drinks are expensive. One of the proprietors is a homosexual who carefully excludes 'tourists' (thrill-seeking heterosexuals) who might make his guests uncomfortable. A second bar, much larger, was filled with music, laughter, and friendly chatter. There was much gossip about mutual friends and talk about books, movies, plays, and politics as well as an exchange of gay jokes. The conversation was sprinkled with the lexicon of the homophile world.

On February 22, 1964, *Maclean's* magazine published 'The Homosexual Next Door: A Sober Appraisal of a New Social Phenomenon.'

1. Katz used pseudonyms. Verne Baldwin is Jim Egan; George Galbraith, Jack Nesbit; Homosexual Club, The Music Room; John Deems, Richard Kerr; Susie Coleman, Sara Dunlop.

B efore I enrolled at the Ontario College of Art, in 1974, I had imagined art school as a bohemian utopia and a paradise for homosexuals. Growing up in Trinidad and then Ireland, I'm not sure where I acquired these ideas (most likely the movies), but I was wrong: the Ontario College of Art in the 1970s was a bastion of heterosexual male privilege.

Gay liberation was relatively new in 1974, just five years after the Stonewall riots in New York City and Canada's decriminalization of homosexual behaviour between consenting adults in private. There was little discussion of, or sensitivity toward, homosexuality at the college, never mind courses or support groups. John Grube, who taught creative writing, was the only openly gay professor. For a student from the Caribbean, OCA to me looked very white. But so was Toronto: according to the 1971 census, over 95 per cent of the city's population was of European background.[1]

Richard Fung

A Bastion of Straight Male Privilege: OCA in the 1970s

I enrolled as a student in industrial design, which was about problem-solving and professionalism, and not at all countercultural. When I switched to photoelectric arts the next year, I finally met the type of students I'd hoped to encounter. In one particular clutch, Neil was English, Frederico came from Portugal, and Derek from Barbados. They were strikingly international and seemed unabashedly queer. I remember Derek swathed in a cloud of diaphanous fabric, but he would later return to the Caribbean and marry.

I thought of them as the very heart of OCA, but many students I met there saw themselves on the institution's margins. Neil Cochrane, a decade later, told me he always felt on the outside at OCA – a sense of not fitting in that I had thought was mine alone. Shalhevet Goldhar, who was heterosexual but lived in a lesbian/feminist co-op on Beverley Street, offers that she also felt alienated as a student: 'I didn't just feel like an outsider; I felt I was from outer space.' Shalhevet grew up in a small town in Israel, and perhaps we shared a sense of being other in that not-yet-multicultural Toronto.

Bruce Jones, who entered OCA ahead of me in 1971, came from Jamaica, and recalls flying up for a week to attend the admissions interview. He was already working in advertising and, wanting to appear professional, wore a tie and blazer, only to be greeted by 'a bunch of people in torn jeans.' As he walked down Yonge Street afterwards, he ran into an acquaintance from Kingston who invited him for a drink. That was his introduction to the St. Charles Tavern, one of Toronto's premier gay bars.

Bruce says there was nothing memorable about gay life at OCA. He would attend student parties where 'there were lots of undercurrents, but nothing ever happened.' Things were very underground at school. I remember John Goodwin as very friendly at the time. But, because he was an athlete, it didn't occur to me that he could be gay. He was on the national lightweight rowing team, and he says the coach used to tease him about being gay. Years after, he ran into his tormentor at the Club Baths. For Bruce and John, gay life happened outside OCA. But Neil recalls that he and I would hug and kiss whenever we saw each other at the college, 'because we felt it was our duty to be visible.' In fact, in my second year, I joined the Gay Liberation and Marxism course at the Marxist Institute on Bedford Street, and started the process of coming out.

The nearest thing to a gay-friendly course at OCA was Jacqueline Levitin's class, Women and Art. Fran Schechter, whom I met in the course, along with her then-girlfriend Trudy Cathcart, recalls the course as 'an oasis of feminist consciousness at OCA. Most of the students had emerged from suburban high schools, and the faculty was almost entirely male,' she recalls. 'The gay and women's movements hadn't made many inroads into the awareness of either group. It was common for male teachers to proposition and sleep with female students.'

Shalhevet adds, 'I remember the first year sitting in a classroom with some young straight white male student from Alberta suggesting that the fact that there were no great women artists was an indication that women were inferior. The teacher blurted out in response, "Well, Emily Carr!"'

Women and Art sparked my first experience with student activism. After OCA threatened to cut the course, we students protested at a department meeting. Jackie, a part-time teacher, recalls one administrator's sarcastic justification: that Levitin had taught the course so well that she had 'solved the women's problem.'

Nor was the curriculum 'diverse.' One of the few courses outside the Western canon was a class on Native Canadian art, with Selwyn Dewdney. I once approached Selwyn about a disturbing quote by Anishinaabe artist Norval Morrisseau, who claimed there was no homosexuality in Canada before colonization. Selwyn, who is credited with fostering Morrisseau's early career, replied by talking about the influence of Christianity on the artist's thinking. He didn't mention Morrisseau's own homosexuality, which I only learned about later.

Other teachers, however, had far more to offer than discretion. Morris Wolfe, who turned me on to cinema and sparked my defection to photoelectric arts, often invited students to his home, where once we met Margaret Gibson, whose short story 'Making It,' about her friendship with female impersonator Craig Russell, became the groundbreaking 1977 movie *Outrageous*.

Today, I'm a professor at OCAD University. Among my roster of courses is Making Gender: LGBT Studio, conceived by the late Wendy Coburn, an activist and artist who directed the 2014 video *Slut Nation: Anatomy of a Protest*. Many students who take this course are heterosexual and cisgendered, just as many of those who take my other classes identify as queer and trans. From my days as a student, the categories of identity have shifted: the last time I taught Making Gender, more than a third of the students identified as non-binary trans and bisexual. I now start my classes by asking students for their preferred gender pronouns.

Since the 1970s, most of the gay civil rights demands have been met in Canada. The urgency is now around gender identity and expression. Homophobia, trans-phobia, and misogyny probably still lurk in dank corners of OCADU, but there is institutional protection from discrimination. Yet while I am one of several openly queer faculty and senior administrators, there are only a handful of racialized or Indigenous professors. The OCADU faculty composition is out of sync with the city's demographics, which in the 2011 census put Toronto's white population at just 50 per cent.[2] Racialized faculty, staff, and students report a sense of alienation that reminds me of how I felt when I arrived in the mid-1970s.

In 2017, the university senate approved an ambitious Academic Plan, whose first principle is to 'transform the settler social relations that underpin knowledge production and what constitutes knowledge within the university context and beyond.' Building the utopia is still a work in progress.

1. Michael Ornstein, *Ethno-Racial Groups in Toronto, 1971-2001: A Demographic and Socio-Economic Profile* (Toronto: Institute for Social Research, York University, 2006), Table 1.1.

2. See Backgrounder, '2011 National Household Survey: Immigration, Citizenship, Place of Birth, Ethnicity, Visible Minorities, Religious and Aboriginal Peoples' (City of Toronto, Social Development Finance & Admin-istration, May 9, 2011).

was beside myself with excitement about the first Michigan Womyn's Music Festival, in 1977. To me it held out the thrilling promise of an uprising of female rockers. But when I arrived, my dreams were dashed. The music over three days – folksingers moaning about oppression or crooning about sisterhood – mostly sucked.

While bitching mightily throughout the weekend and at one point borrowing a guitar to sing Cream's 'Sunshine of Your Love,' a Toronto feminist tapped me on the shoulder: 'Why don't you just stop whinging and start a women's band?'

In the late 1970s, feminism was a fact, and there was a burgeoning scene of artists recording women-centred music (thank you, Olivia Records in America, who gave us Cris Williamson, Teresa Trull, and Meg Christian). But there had been no groundswell of women storming the stage with their amps and axes.

Susan G. Cole
Get Mad – Play Rock 'n' Roll

I had been thinking about doing just that since I was a teenager in the 1960s. I had some musical talent, I loved rock 'n' roll, and I really wanted to play it. Thing is, it was only the guys who were playing guitar and forming bands. Everyone of my gender was consigned to groupie status. It made me angry and ridiculously jealous – not of the sex, but of the power of the music. *Feminism* wasn't a word anyone was throwing around at that time, but I had the distinct sense that if women could play that brand of searing, fierce music, the world would change. Anyway, almost all the songs those boys were playing had only four chords. I mean, I could do that.

So when I returned to Toronto from Michigan, I wrangled musicians who played at the Lesbian Organization of Toronto (LOOT) Three of Cups coffee house, including sax player Linda Robitaille and acoustic guitarist and singer Donna Marchand, and we started to rehearse cover tunes.

We performed a few times as an acoustic combo and then reoriented with new musicians, including newbie electric guitarist Susan Sturman, who, like me, belonged to the *Broadside* magazine collective. But we couldn't find a drummer until Linda Jain said she'd simply learn how. She wasn't the only novice. To be clear, none of us was very good, except Robitaille. Amidst all those caveats, Mama Quilla II – named in honour of keyboardist and Music Room owner Sara Dunlop, who had a band called Mama Quilla in the early seventies – was born.

I believed that rock 'n' roll could be a vehicle for female empowerment, even though I had few role models to prove my point. Neither Heart nor Chrissie Hynde and the Pretenders yet existed. Except for a few very obscure American feminist bands we weren't aware of at the time, we were, more or less, on our own. But I knew that rock 'n' roll didn't have to be a boys' club, and that electric guitars didn't have to be played as if a man were stroking his penis.

Our first gig as the expanded Mama Quilla II was at a LOOT dance three months after the Michigan festival. With Ruth Dworin, of groundbreaking sound crew Womynly Way, handling the tech, we played a few tunes without percussion to an appreciative crowd. Then Linda sat down at the drums and we played a rewritten version of Jackson Brown's 'The Load-Out,' celebrating our experience at that Michigan festival. When Linda's snare finally kicked in, the place went bananas. I'd never seen hundreds of women so ecstatic; when we segued into 'Sherry (Won't You Come Out Tonight),' well, don't ask.

We weren't the only women's music going in town in the late seventies. Among the few trying to make some female inroads, pianist/writer Boo Watson played solo gigs, sometimes with Lorraine Segato, who already showed signs of the charismatic performer she'd become. And a trio called Hamburger Patty – Gwen Swick, Cathie McKay, and Sherry Shute – were playing clubs around the city.

That group was an essential part of this history. Performing mostly original material, their harmonies were dynamite and they had the nerve – and the chops – to play in legendary venues like the Horseshoe. (Swick still sings in Quartette with Sylvia Tyson, Cindy Church, and Caitlin Hanford.) Sherry, in particular, was a marvel, blond hair flying, grinning at the crowd as she got that guitar wailing in those intricate solos. An original, she never really got her due.

The first iteration of Mama Quilla II developed more fully when Cathie McKay joined the band to play bass, while Maxine Walsh and BJ Danylchuk added a conga percussion section. But I couldn't resist Sherry Shute, and when Cathie suggested we start a band of our own with Sherry, we and stellar keyboardist Evelyne Datl formed No Frills.

Segato then joined Mama Quilla II and helped turn the band into a viable outfit that released an excellent EP – the ironic cover featuring an old-school Tupperware party.

In the meantime, No Frills workshopped new material at Pat Murphy's dyke bar, the Fly By Night, at George and Jarvis. I had played a solo set there weekly for about a year, and Murphy was a huge supporter of women's music.

A drummer? Again, not so easy. We were so desperate that at one point we went through the entire list of female drummers active in the musicians' union. There were quite a few, but almost none had a drum kit; they played snares and brushes, accompanying singers in cocktail bars. Lovely women, but not what we were looking for.

Eventually, we gave up looking, but I don't want to give the impression that we settled for our male drummers, first Gord Skinner and then Ben Cleveland. Both were respectful, appreciative of the band's talent, and, I don't mind admitting, occasionally carried my heavy Yamaha electric grand piano.

In retrospect – and especially in the wake of the Riot Grrl movement – I realize that No Frills was a flat-out great band. We performed original songs and a few covers, like the Kinks' 'You Really Got Me,' long before grunge guys Pearl Jam ever thought of it. All the while, we waited for the miracle of a record deal that never came. I often imagine what it would have been like to have a band like No Frills now, when artists have more channels for sharing their art.

These days, a band plays a one-off set on a slate that usually contains at least two other bands. Back then, you played three sets every night for six days a week, Monday through Saturday. But still, it was difficult to make a living playing Toronto. Often, we made only a percentage of the bar, and our audience, mostly female, tended not to drink with the same gusto as other club crowds.

Nor were there that many clubs to play in T.O. We performed at the Horseshoe (including the night John Lennon was murdered), Grossman's, the Isabella, and the El Mocambo a few times a year; that was about it. But there was no question we transformed those grotty, male-centred joints. You could even say that for those weeks, we were queering the clubs.

Eventually, we had no choice but to play out of town, occasionally in a small Montreal club called the Rainbow, and in Ottawa. Audiences were friendly in the larger cities, but smaller towns were godawful. If women had ever played there at all, they performed as lead singers, expected to be scantily clad and heavily made up. We were neither. Hostile crowds screamed for us to take off our clothes. We eventually stopped touring smaller-town venues.

Back home, the scene had improved immensely as the eighties began. Queen West was bursting with new bars, bands, and political energy, and queer visual artists were making their own kind of noise. No Frills crossed over into both the queer and indie scenes: Blue Rodeo keyboardist Bobby Wiseman routinely lent me his piano – I don't think we could have managed without him.

Strangely, No Frills was not an overtly political band, not like Mama Quilla II under Segato's leadership and, later, the Parachute Club. We didn't play politically explicit or rage-driven material. We wrote mostly tunes about relationships; various band members were sleeping with each other, had slept with each other, or were about to sleep with each other. Even our most politically pointed tune, 'Kickback,' seemed to be less about resisting authority than encouragement for abuse survivors to stand up in the world.

Still, I had been an activist for years, and all our members were politically committed, leading activist orgs to engage us at their events, and we always said yes. We performed for Lesbians Against the Right and at Rock Against Racism, proving again the power of rock 'n' roll to galvanize community.

But my favourite political appearance was at the first 'official' Pride celebration after the bathhouse raids in 1981. As furious queer activists completed their march past 52 Division and arrived at Grange Park, they were greeted by No Frills playing 'Kickback.'

It didn't matter what the song's original inspiration was. The music had deep meaning in that moment as gays and lesbians stomped their feet and pumped their fists to the music of women rocking out.

New York's plus-size gender-fuck maverick Divine hit the stage at Massey Hall in a tiger-skin bikini and frazzled blond beehive. Riding shotgun, Carole Pope, in a black leather body stocking, crooned in a trench coat and flicked her whip over the thighs of a rapturous sidekick lying on the scarlet satin bed sheets.

It was December 19, 1977. The show was entitled 'Restless Underwear' – a kinky mash up of Rough Trade's catchy synth-pop and Divine's 'filthy trash' camp genius immortalized in John Waters's movies *Pink Flamingoes* and *Female Trouble*. A few weeks before the show, Massey Hall's board of governors had held an emergency session to determine if the show violated their decency standards.

It did.

Jane Farrow and John Lorinc

I Want Her So Much I Feel Sick:
An Interview with Rough Trade's Carole Pope

But, as Carole Pope explains, 'Restless Underwear' would go on there or elsewhere because Toronto was tired of being good. Rough Trade was hitting its stride with songs like 'Birds of a Feather' giving the peak-disco Bee Gees a run for their money on the charts. The band's club performances were the hottest ticket in town. Adoring Toronto audiences ate up every sultry detail of their proto-punk, glam, new-wave stage shows. Carole, trying to explain herself to the mainstream, would refer to herself as a 'female fag.' And then, in 1980, she purred the lyrics to the band's thumping break-out hit, 'High School Confidential':

She's a cool blonde scheming bitch,
She makes my body twitch,
Walking down the corridor
You can hear her stilettos click,
I want her so much I feel sick,
The girl can't help it, she really can't help it now ...
It makes me cream my jeans when she comes my way.

It was scorching-hot lesbian visibility to some, and pansexual catnip to others – a song about a guy lusting after a female schoolmate, or a girl with the hots for another chick. It didn't matter. Suddenly, Toronto had shot past the days of Helen Reddy's 'I Am Woman.' Everyone got in formation and saluted the dawn of an exciting, alternative, queer-positive future.

JANE FARROW: What you did, starting in the late 1970s, was really brave. Did you have a sense of yourself as presenting in an overt sexual manner or was it camp performance?

CAROLE POPE: [*Laughs*.]. There was this background of sexual repression in Toronto at that time. So to us, it was kind of like sexual parody, and titillating. The more we did it, and the more 'out' we were, the more people wanted it. People started to dress like me. I would sometimes wear a bondage suit. It was just like, 'How far can we push it?'

JOHN LORINC: Why do you think people were so eager to hear your music?

CP: We were doing original material, and those songs were overtly sexual and silly, and I don't think anyone else was doing that. There were other punk bands in that scene, but we were the first. People really responded to it.

JF: You were way more new wave than punk.

CP: Our music was influenced by all these different genres – some new wave-ish, some punkish, rock, funk, R&B. We were all over the map. We often played Grossman's on Spadina, and attracted a very diverse audience. General Idea. Celebrities. Famous actors showed up: we already knew Gilda Radner. Margaret Trudeau even came to Grossman's.

JF: What do you remember about Margaret Trudeau's response?

CP: We didn't meet her. I just remember watching her. That's when she was being scandalous and hanging out with the Rolling Stones. We were just trying to be cool – 'Oh, Trudeau's in the audience.'

JF: So along comes 'High School Confidential' in 1980, on the *Avoid Freud* album. It's a huge moment for so many people, queers or straight. The lyrics are so explicit, and there's really no denying what you're singing about. Yet it was on mainstream radio, and people are saying, 'I'm not really sure what she means by "she makes me want to cream in my jeans."'

CP: I actually wrote that song for the movie *Cruising*, and with [New York proto-punk dandy] Mink DeVille in mind.

JF: How did it feel to perform it?

CP: Oh, my god, it was very liberating. It was fun. Everyone – straight, gay – just totally related to it for whatever reason. Straight people were, like, 'Yeah, high school, yeah.' And gay people were like, 'Yeah, you're talking to me.'

JL: Were you surprised that it got as much rotation on the radio as it did?

CP: We were surprised in general at our success. The stations wanted to censor the lyrics. CHUM-FM actually paid us to just sing another line over 'cream my jeans.'

ROUGH TRADE
Avoid Freud

It's a Jungle / High School Confidential / Lie Back, Let Me Do Everything / Physical Violence / I Can't Take It
What's the Furor About the Fuhrer? / Fashion Victim / Emotional Blackmail / Hostage / Arcade B Movie

I really couldn't do it. A friend of mine who is no longer with us said, 'Just say, "She orders Chinese food."' [*Laughs.*].

JF: So you never did it?

CP: No. So they played the original and bleeped out the 'cream my jeans' part.

JF: What was going on in Toronto that informed your work?

CP: In the 1970s, all the arts supported each other. We would go to plays, we would go to see other people's art, to bands. We were a close-knit community. We played a lot in New York, but Toronto was our home. My father was really sexually Victorian. I remember having lesbian thoughts when I was eight and thinking, 'Something's wrong here, I'm attracted to girls.' I had this sense that if I went there, it wouldn't end well. When I started writing music, I knew I just couldn't go there.

JF: That was an issue for Lorraine Segato in the early days of the Parachute Club. She'd been effectively 'out' as the lead singer in Mama Quilla II. But when Parachute Club started up in 1982 and *NOW* Magazine raved about the band, proclaiming Lorraine a lesbian, there was major concern inside the band that this would limit their shot at mainstream success. I noted a reserve, too, in the coverage about you – that you were a little oblique. Were you being bisexual or were you just not that interested in explicitly declaring that you were queer?

CP: I just wanted to be mysterious. In public, you know, I was blatantly out. I was making out with women. But [Rough Trade guitarist and keyboard player] Kevan Staples and I were lovers, too, so I covered the sexual waterfront. Also, in the 1970s, I totally got into radical feminism and read a lot of books. I was just in a fury about women in society.

JF: You were a very sex-positive feminist. No Andrea Dworkin on your reading list. Correct?

CP: That's correct. Sexuality is beautiful. I always believed that. I was going to keep on pushing and pushing and pushing.

JF: What was Queen West like in the early 1980s?

CP: Trashier, funkier. No Gap. We'd go to the Fiesta on Yonge Street. All the bands used to hang there late and drink. My brother used to work there as a bus boy for a while. Just a real social scene. All these amazing people would show up and it would be like a salon.

JF: Is there anything else you want people now to know about Toronto in the 1970s?

CP: I just think that at that time, Toronto was magic, brilliant. Everyone was finding themselves … Everyone was so supportive, it was exciting. I want that again for Toronto.

RESISTING, SHARING, ORGANIZING

A gender-distressed teenager of nineteen, I transitioned from female to male in the Nation's Capital in 1971, three years after my parents died in a car crash. I was a Carleton University psychology student, and my academic career coincided with my gender transition and my trans activism. Blazing the trail for other transsexuals across Canada and the United States from then until now, I have seen a lot of shit go down in the transgender and cisgender (non-trans) worlds, and in straight and queer scenes alike. This essay will give you a glimpse of some safe and unsafe spaces, and some good and bad times, of trans and queer life in the early days of Toronto, the world's most diverse city – and one of the trans-/queer-friendliest.

Rupert Raj

Worlds in
Collision

Community Centres (58 Cecil Street and the 519)

Before the 519 Church Street Community Centre became the heart and soul of the Gay Village in 1975, there were no queer or trans community centres in Toronto, despite the efforts, in 1972, of the Canadian Homophile Association of Toronto to turn 58 Cecil Street into such a venue. Cecil Street was also home to the Association of Canadian Transsexuals, Canada's first trans group, formed in 1970 by three transsexual women: Diana LaMonte, Lynne Pellerin, and 'Louise' (a pseudonym). I first met Louise in the summer of 1972, driving down Highway 401 in my new, shiny-red Toyota Corolla. I'd recently started testosterone therapy ('T') and was raring to go, desperate to seek out other trans folks.

The 519, in those days and now, was a hub for the trans and queer communities – typically worlds in collision. I co-founded and led three trans groups: FACT Toronto (a local chapter of the Foundation for the Advancement of Canadian Transsexuals, 1979-86), Metamorphosis Medical Research Foundation (1982-88), and the Trans Men/FTM Peer-Support Group (1999–present). FACT Toronto became Transition Support, one of the longest-running trans groups in Canada. The Trans Men/FTM group petered out (pun intended!) not long after I left, but I'm working to persuade the 519 management to fund a group for older trans guys (forty-plus) and their loved ones and allies.

'Jurassic Clarke' (The Clarke Institute of Psychiatry)

Gendercide, a term I coined for the erasure of trans and gender non-binary people, generates trauma. In the 1970s and 1980s, Dr. Betty Steiner, the Clarke Institute of Psychiatry's Adult Gender Identity Clinic's chief psychiatrist, loftily claimed there was no such thing as female-to-male transvestites (although she conceded the existence of male-to-female cross-dressers). Tongue-in-cheek, I informed my three female cross-dressing friends that according to modern psychiatry, they were only figments of their 'self-deluded' imagination. 'Control queen' Steiner also put the kibosh on a potential extension of the Clarke's one-year pilot program to recommend Ontario Health Insurance Plan (OHIP) coverage of phalloplasty (penile surgery) for female-to-male transsexuals (trans males/trans men), categorically deciding this form of 'bottom' surgery was 'too experimental,' given the limited outcomes back then, and despite the stated relative satisfaction of many of the trans guys. So much for patients' 'informed choice.'

Betty also chose not to notify her trans-male patients of my gender-consulting service (Metamorphosis) because it wasn't OHIP-insured and she didn't want them to have to pay out-of-pocket. This was an unwarranted withholding of a valuable, unique resource, given that I was the only game in town for trans men at the time. Clarke psychologist Dr. Ray Blanchard was equally exclusionary, smugly informing Lou Sullivan, an 'out' gay trans man, that he didn't fit the classic typology of sexual or gender types for '(born) females,' meaning his identity couldn't be 'authenticated.' Blatant transqueerphobia! And if you happened to be a femmy T-boy, genderphobia ran rampant!

Our trans sisters were similarly pathologized. In the early days, T-girls were denied approval for sex hormones or genital surgery if they identified as lesbian or bisexual, thereby closeting trans dykes and trans bis for many years. (The Clarke clinicians reluctantly conceded the existence of trans lesbians and bisexuals in the 1990s, but it took them nearly another decade to similarly 'tolerate' trans gay men and bis. Reverse sexism!)

Male-to-female transsexuals (trans females/trans women) seeking sex-reassignment surgery (a.k.a. gender-confirming surgery) had to dress in über-femme attire (no butch or tomboy T-girls allowed!). Those married first had to get divorced because the Clarke feared potential lawsuits from wives resenting the (perceived) 'emasculation' of their husbands. Psychiatrists' paranoia or what? To add insult to injury, a number of these patients were (voluntarily) subjected to Dr. Kurt Freund's controversial phallometer (a.k.a. penile plethysmography), an electronic device measuring penile responses to photographs of children, gay men, and males dressed in female clothing, respectively. The goal: to determine if they were adult sex offenders, pedophiles, effeminate gay men, transvestites, or transsexual women. Righteously enraged, one trans woman exclaimed some years later, 'They fried my penis!'

Fortunately, I escaped the clutches of the Clarke's gender clinicians until 2011, when, approaching sixty, I applied for OHIP approval of metoidioplasty (another form of genital surgery for T-boys). Thankfully, I came through the screening process unscathed, due to a new transpositive clinical staff headed by Dr. Chris McIntosh, a psychiatrist, and Dr. Nicola Brown, a patient-friendly psychologist.

Rupert Raj, 1975.

Sex Clubs (Black Eagle, Tool Box, Spa Excess, Pussy Palace)

Although I rarely went to sex clubs, I did check out the Black Eagle and the Tool Box (bathhouses for queer men) on occasion, but never made it inside the Pussy Palace. There were no trans-specific sex clubs until trans sex worker/porno star Mandy Goodhandy and pro dom/porno producer Todd Klinck co-founded Good-handy's in 2006, at 120 Church Street. Alternatively called a 'pansexual playground' and a 'tranny bar,' it catered to 'tranny chasers' (mostly men turned on by trans-genderists and presurgical trans women). Most trans people, including me, disparage the trashy 'tranny' label as commodifying and offensive. Of course, before the 2000s, cis gay male bathhouses excluded known trans men; it's questionable, even now, if they're truly trans-male inclusive. 'Transqueerpositivity' is taking its sweet time!

Queer Churches (Metropolitan Community Church of Toronto)

Sexuality and spirituality are both important human needs. When I first arrived here in 1979, I asked Rev. Brent Hawkes, pastor of the Metropolitan Community Church of Toronto, if he thought I had a hope in hell of finding a cis gay male lover, given that I hadn't yet had 'bottom' surgery. I don't recall his exact words, but he was encouragingly transpositive (a rarity in cis gay men back then) and welcomed me into his Christian church for queers and our allies. Other gay, lesbian, bi, and trans-affirming ministries soon followed: Dignity and Christos (both Catholic), Integrity and the United Church (both Protestant), the Universalist Unitarian Church (non-denominational), Dharma Sitting (Buddhist), and later, in the 1990s, Queer Muslims, Trans Jews, neo-pagan covens (many trans women are witches, and some trans men warlocks, preferring the goddess religions), and interfaith groups.

These spiritual havens kept us somewhat safe from homophobic or transphobic fundamentalist religionists. I met a post-transitional trans woman who soon after 'detransitioned' to their natal (male) sex because of a rejecting Christian fundamentalist mother. He wanted to join my Metamorphosis group 'to learn how to be a man again.' Regretfully, I advised that the group was only for (female-born) trans males, so 'he' married a strict Christian and now lives the life of a God-fearing, straight, cis man. What a price to pay for the right to be who we are!

Then and Now ...

Nearly half a century after I transitioned, we're finally starting to move beyond societal genderphobia, community infighting, and gender policing, with promising examples of collaboration across all spheres in Toronto and Canada. Working together across cisgender and transgender, straight and queer spaces, and all of society's institutions, we must continue to bridge our diverse communities, forming sustainable partnerships, locally and globally. As effective allies, we must fight against all forms of violence (anti-indigeneity, racism, classism, sexism, genderism, ageism, ableism, homophobia, biphobia, transphobia, trans misogyny, trans misandry) to ensure a safer city and world where we can all live, work, and play together.

I n late January, 1969, I emigrated from the United States to Canada to take a research position at the University of Toronto's Faculty of Medicine. Eight months later, I founded Canada's first post-Stonewall gay organization: the U of T Homophile Association. Soon after, *The Globe and Mail* published a letter criticizing U of T for formally recognizing the UTHA. I wrote a letter in response, and was fired shortly after *The Globe* published it.

I travelled for several months and then returned to Toronto, immediately re-involving myself in the city's three gay organizations.

Jearld Moldenhauer

A Literary Breakthrough: Glad Day's Origins

The sheer number of new and used bookstores had always made me feel happy to be a Torontonian. Books had played a central role in my own life – not just those about the subjects that interested me, but also those that allowed me to overcome my own self-oppressed mentality about being gay. French writer André Gide and American sex researcher Alfred Kinsey were crucial to my developing a positive image of myself as a homosexual. I felt that the power of books offered the prospect of advancing social democracy, especially in literate but oppressively backward societies such as the U.S. and Canada.

After Stonewall, publishers started to issue books about gay and lesbian life, written by a generation of newly 'liberated' homosexuals. This literary breakthrough began to combat the traditionally negative images of homosexuality – often defined by disease and sickness – that dominated the literature of the time. While Toronto served as the centre of Canada's publishing industry and had an abundance of bookshops, I could never find copies of these new releases, even though most were being reviewed by the *New York Times* and *The Village Voice*.

As I learned, Censorship needn't be overt. Rather, I noticed widespread, internalized self-censorship, driven by forces seeking social conformity to community standards, insidiously reinforcing the status quo. Toronto's webs of power wanted to protect and thereby sustain the existing class structure.

Censorship – conscious and unconscious – was of utmost importance to those who might find their status altered by new ideas or new ways of looking at old ideas. The perception and experience of human sexuality is a culturally based reality that changes from one society to another, and from generation to generation. Queers were situated at the bottom of that pecking order, subjected to propaganda in every form of media, including the advertising of heterosexual status as it directly related to the purchase of consumer products. The sustenance of that order also depended on traditional state power, superstitious religious authority, and pseudo-scientific psychological theory.

My response to the backwardness of Toronto's bookstore scene began with a few phone calls to publishers to find out how one could order books at wholesale prices. I didn't aspire to become a businessman, but I wanted to make this new gay literature available to the Canadian public. From my inquiries, I realized that if existing bookshops were afraid to breach the barrier, then *I* could … and would. And so I started Glad Day late in 1970.

Gay books and periodicals were vital tools for communicating with individual gay men and lesbians who had not yet formed a community. As queers, we grow up isolated (even from each other) and often in hostile environments. Literature provided the path to raise the political and social awareness of our oppression and our common identities. By sharing our stories and ideas, we could emerge as a community determined to not only claim our rightful place in society but also take control of our future.

It was easy and inexpensive to enter the book trade in those days: minimum orders were low and you were given ninety days' credit. For all its aspirations, Glad Day began as a kind of mobile bookshop. For the first few months, I packed up the books that arrived at my apartment in my backpack and rode my bike to the meetings of Toronto's three gay groups: UTHA, the Community Homophile Association of Toronto, and Toronto Gay Action. The more catalogues I ordered from publishers and distributors, the more new titles I discovered, as well as older books of historical importance.

I then began to compile the titles and print copies of my own little catalogue. I also advertised my book service in a weekly scandal rag called *Tab*, a sensationalist newspaper full of mostly heterosexual titillation. It contained a few gay-oriented news stories and was the only cross-country print media that would accept an ad from a self-identified gay bookseller. (In 1974, Glad Day filed a complaint with the Ontario Press Council against the *Toronto Star* and, in 1985, another against the *Globe and Mail*, for refusing to accept our advertising. Glad Day won both cases, and those adjudications were among the first victories in the struggle for equality.)

My little classified ad brought inquiries and requests from all over Ontario and beyond. It also brought my first seriously supportive customer: Jean-Raymond St-Cyr, director of the French CBC Radio in Ontario, and the father of *Star* columnist Chantal Hébert. St-Cyr encouraged my efforts (especially when it came to French writers) and bought more books than any other long-term customer. (He remained supportive of Glad Day until his death in 2007.)

Late in 1971, my roommates bought a house in Kensington Market with a plan to create an art gallery on the ground level and use the second floor as our apartment. They agreed to let me occupy an unheated shed at the rear as both a bookshop and an office/workspace for *The Body Politic*, the gay newspaper I founded. During

those first few years, I considered Glad Day and *TBP* to be complementary projects. Book sales provided me with a subsistence living while allowing me to help run an alternative paper.

In the summer of 1972, *TBP* experienced its first crisis after we published Gerald Hannon's feature on intergenerational gay male relationships. It precipitated a nationwide newspaper editorial response that advocated criminal charges against the paper. No charges were laid. (But, in 1978, after the publication of a second piece by Hannon on the same topic, the directors of what had become Pink Triangle Press were charged with obscenity.)

However, what this first media-induced scandal did precipitate came as a surprise: our gay landlords evicted me, John Scythes (who in 1991 became Glad Day's second proprietor), and the local gay movement. This meant that *TBP*, Glad Day Bookshop, and the newly formed Gay Alliance Toward Equality – which had initially used the unfinished gallery space for its meetings – were left without a home.

John Scythes and I decided to try and buy another old house in the downtown core. We spent many hours in John's 1948 Packard driving up and down residential streets both east and west of Yonge Street until we found a house in the poor southern sector of Cabbagetown, at 139 Seaton Street. The owners offered it to us for about $39,000, and we had just enough savings for the down payment.

A decision was then made to not only shelter these recently founded gay organizations, but also to structure the house as a gay male commune shared by six or seven core occupants, as well as many short- and long-term guests. Our narrow hallway became the bookshop, while the front parlour served as the newspaper's office. A year or so later, the books, newspapers, and flyers I had been collecting seeded the Canadian Gay Archives (later CLGA), which was accorded its own cozy room in our basement.

The Australian writer Dennis Altman, the German gay publisher Egmont Fassbinder, and the British writer and physicist Andrew Hodges were among the high-profile gay men who stayed at the Seaton Street house. Our left-leaning mayor, John Sewell, lived around the corner, and we often exchanged polite hellos. Liberal MPP Margaret Campbell (St. George) was savvy enough to take a photo of me chatting with her in the front yard after many of us started attending all-candidates meetings. She later used the image for a campaign flyer, presumably aimed at gay voters.

In 1974, the paper was doing so well we decided to rent a storefront. I found a suitable location nearby on Carlton Street. Naively, I assumed Glad Day would occupy part of the space – the space was certainly large enough for both projects. The shop even had a nice window that I fantasized could be used as a new-releases display. But the collective that ran the newspaper had other ideas. The members voted and decided, to my shock, that Glad Day was not wanted on the voyage. Since no one had even mentioned a split prior to the vote, I concluded that the decision had been made behind my back. Devastated and feeling betrayed, I left the collective.

For the next three years, I continued to run the bookshop out of the house and networked with both gay organizations and international publishers. In August 1977, after travelling with my lover Michael from Europe to India and Nepal, I settled down and accepted my future role as a bookseller. I moved Glad Day into its first store, a second-floor space at Collier and Yonge, next to the new Toronto Reference Library. The volume of business was far greater than anything I had experienced while running the shop from the house. However, as I found out, we still had quite a ways to go before claiming our rightful place in Toronto's bookshop community. Publishers' sales reps, for example, rarely paid a visit to the store.

Despite its grassroots character, Glad Day now began to attract prominent writers and customers. Novelist Jane Rule always dropped by when she was in town. The British stage legend Sir John Gielgud came by twice during his stay as an actor in Harold Pinter's *No Man's Land*, and playwright Edward Albee happened by one afternoon and stayed to chat for a few hours. We did signings for the English writer Quentin Crisp (during his first North American visit), Mexican-American novelist John Rechy, and Christopher Isherwood, on tour following publication of his autobiography, *Christopher and His Kind*.

As difficult as it may be to believe, the rest of Toronto's booksellers just kept on stocking the evil pre-Stonewall homosexuality-as-disease literature throughout the 1970s.

By 1981, we needed more space and moved south, to 648a Yonge, at Irwin Street just north of Wellesley. I still felt that a second-floor retail space was the more viable plan. Despite the downsides to this decision, the move brought us several blocks south of Bloor Street, nearer to the heart of the city's gay neighbourhood. Business quadrupled overnight.

While this move marked Glad Day's maturation into a serious literary institution, many more challenges lay ahead: four censorship-related trials between Glad Day and the federal government, and the horrors of the AIDS epidemic. It soon became apparent that we had also begun, quite literally, to fight for our lives.

George Hislop told me my first dirty gay joke, and here it is: 'What's in the air in San Francisco that keeps the birth rate so low?' Punchline: 'Men's legs.' It wasn't wit, which I knew was gay. It was a real, old-fashioned dirty joke that asked for nothing more than a quick laugh, but somehow it made me aware that we didn't always have to be the butt of other people's nastiness. We could laugh at ourselves, on our own time, and in our own way, and for our own reasons. This was progress, back in the early seventies, when George was co-chair of the Community Homophile Association of Toronto (CHAT), and though he took very seriously the struggle for gay rights, there was always the air of the bon vivant about him, the raconteur with an apparently endless supply of anecdotes spiced with dirty jokes and self-deprecating humour.

Gerald Hannon

George Hislop:
The Unofficial
Gay Mayor

'I've been demoted,' he quipped when someone told him he'd been described in a news story as Toronto's unofficial gay mayor. 'I've been a queen for years.' He tuned his humour to his audience, of course. Police chiefs, members of the legislature, city councillors – the power brokers he met with in his capacity as an acknowledged voice of the gay community – got the buoyancy without the ribaldry, but got the message, too. Faced for the umpteenth time with the complaint that homosexuals had stolen the word *gay* and made it unusable in its old sense, he replied, 'You can have *gay* back, if you'll also take back *fag*, *queer*, and *deviate*.' He could be plainspoken, too. 'I didn't want ... to be tolerated' was the way he put it when he was inducted into the Canadian Lesbian and Gay Archives Portrait Collection in 1999. 'Nor did I want other lesbians and gay men to be merely tolerated. I wanted us, all of us, to be understood and acknowledged and, yes, loved in our sexual orientation.'

Though he spent some time working as an actor in London, England, he was a homeboy Torontonian, born in what was then Swansea (now a neighbourhood west of the Humber River) on June 3, 1927, and living, during all his years as gay activist, in an apartment near Avenue Road and St. Clair. He shared that space, and his life, with Ronnie Shearer, whom he'd met in 1958, and though it was clearly a love match, it was just as clear it wasn't monogamous – at least not for George.

I remember an early orgy we were both involved in, with George, pudgy and gleeful, lavishing his oral attentions on one young man after another. He made shameless, guiltless promiscuity seem the gay norm, and became both a frequent patron of gay bathhouses and a part owner of one of them, the Barracks. He spent his declining years in ill health, essentially living at the Spa Excess (a bathhouse on Carlton Street), watched over by concerned friends who didn't moralize (I snuck in bottles of vodka for him; another

George Hislop at the launch of Gay Pride Week, 1972, outside CHAT's building on Cecil Street.

friend supplied the orange juice, and voila: screwdrivers!). Hustler boys who respected his history as an activist were kind to him, helped pick him up when he fell in the hallways at the spa, let him blow them, and occasionally granted him the grace of a fuck.

His gay-activist history was a lot longer than those boys knew. He was involved with the University of Toronto Homophile Association, founded in 1969, and he went on to co-found, with lesbian activist Pat Murphy and others, CHAT. He helped organize and spoke at the August 28, 1971, rally at Parliament Hill, the one that presented a brief to the government called 'We Demand' (the ten reforms therein seemed almost ludicrously pie-in-the-sky at the time – almost all have since been enacted).

Convinced that working from inside the political system would give the gay movement extra traction, in 1980 he ran as a candidate for city council in downtown Ward 6, a district with a large gay population. He lost, as did gay-positive mayor John Sewell, running for re-election, both of them subjected to viciously homophobic propaganda from both the religious right and the police. That double loss emboldened the constabulary – many see it as having given the authorities a green light for the notorious bathhouse raids of February 5, 1981. (The Barracks, of which Hislop was a part owner, had been raided in 1978 and again as part of the larger assault in 1981.) He was charged as keeper of a common bawdy house in both raids, but was acquitted of the first charge and eventually had the second charge dropped. He famously quipped that, should he go to trial, he hoped it would be 'before a jury of my queers.')

George lost again the following year, when he ran provincially as an independent in the riding of St. George, though by then his speeches had a newfound vehemence. 'Send me up there,' he said at a 1,000-strong gay-freedom rally. 'Sit a faggot right in the middle of the legislature so they can't ever forget us again.' He never won an election, but he did, albeit posthumously, win an important battle.

When Ronnie, his partner of twenty-eight years, died in 1986, George applied for Canada Pension Plan survivor benefits. He was denied them – in the eyes of the law, he was not a spouse. That partially changed in 1999, when the Supreme Court ruled that the term applied to gays and lesbians in conjugal relationships whose partners died after January 1, 1988. But since Shearer had died in 1986, Hislop lent his name to a new class-action suit petitioning the government for partner benefits retroactive to before 1998. Prior to Hislop's death of esophageal cancer on October 8, 2005, he'd secured a partial-benefits cheque. His lawyer is quoted as saying Hislop was thrilled, and that 'he felt it was a tacit admission by the government that he was going to prevail in the Supreme Court.' Indeed he did. In 2007 the Supreme Court released a decision favouring Hislop and the class-action litigants.

In 2001, a park fronting on the gaybourhood's Isabella Street had been named in his honour. I turned up for the ceremony. George was there: frail, bolstered by an entourage of street hustlers, cracking jokes – clean ones this time, given that the crowd included the sitting federal MP and other notables. An acquaintance, gay but much younger, passed by, stopped, and asked me what was going on. I told him. 'Who's George Hislop?' he asked. I had my potted history ready. He listened, stayed for the entire ceremony, went up to George, introduced himself, and thanked him for everything he'd done. Nice of him, but he didn't know the half of it.

In February 1976, I rented a space in a rooming house at 78 McGill Street, between Church and Yonge, just south of Carlton. As with many rooming houses, its tenants included people with economic, alcohol, and personal life issues.

Each day, I never knew if I would be greeted with smiles or a hurled beer bottle and homophobic slurs. Three months later, I told Connie, the landlady, that I could find friends to fill the rooms. By June, she offered me the whole house, with the condition that if I did repairs, she would pay for paints and materials.

My dear friend John Scholtes and I ripped out the kitchen cupboards, stripped the wainscotting, and installed wall brackets with white boards to create open kitchen shelving. Soon, the kitchen was decorated with plants and mirrors, a large table, and standing cupboards, to create a lovely space for family meals. Other room improvements followed. John and I made a great team. Together, we returned this dowdy row house back to its beautiful Victorian roots.

Dennis Findlay

Co-operative Living Happens in the Kitchen!

Each new tenant was responsible for their own room, choice of colour, cleaning, and painting. By August, we had the house filled with five friends, and began working out the co-operative living principles.

A job wheel ruled the house, with its five-pointed star in the centre, and the occupants' names on each spoke. The tasks were printed on the outer wheel: food shopping (for two people), vacuuming, bathrooms, and garbage. Since the kitchen served as the central hub, there was an understanding that you left it cleaner than you found it. Each Sunday, the star rotated one spot.

Every week, the two designated shoppers would head to Kensington Market, starting with the European Meat Market, then adding coffee, beans, dried fruits, cheeses, veggies, fruit, and finally bread from various other market shops. For five, we could shop on $100 to $125 per week. We lived well and very affordably.

But back to the kitchen! In the early morning, this is where John would be found, having consumed his first pot of coffee, with a stack of joints rolled for the next sleepyhead to appear. He had brought into the house a tiny wooden car. He would slip a joint into one of the windows and matches into the other. While you were settling in with your first coffee, he would flick the car toward you, greeting you with 'Good morning, darling, something to start your day with?'

Because the members of the family loved to travel, the kitchen bulletin board always groaned with postcards and newspaper clippings from around the world. This was also the room where drag bags were brought out from under beds. People would get all dressed up and either party in-house or

Jack Herman, 78 McGill Avenue.

head out for a night on the town. Dresses, hats, shawls, heels, and all the needs of the radical drag queen were tried on and swapped as we played with gender fluidity.

While the kitchen served as the social centre of the house, a second one upstairs functioned as the bakery for my dessert business. But my bakery kitchen was often the place where heart-to-heart conversations would happen. A stool, which sat in the corner, was often brought close to the work table, and Mother Dennis was consulted for her opinion or advise. Most often, only listening was required.

Number 78 McGill was not particularly political, although most of the occupants had a strong sense of gay liberation, equal rights, and a respect for diversity. For those who were new to gay or community politics, it could be a bit of a crash course. John Sewell and George Hislop were candidates for city council, and we had their signs out front. Some of us volunteered at *The Body Politic*, while others were involved in other community groups. We were all swept up by the demonstrations protesting the bathhouse raids.

During that era, the many gay and lesbian communal or co-operative houses downtown became places where political organizing happened. But 78 McGill became a focal point for a community of our friends. Lovers came and went. Overnight guests were included in breakfast and sometimes became tenants when a relationship formed. Dinner parties happened spontaneously. In fact, I remember returning home late from an evening at the baths to find five people at the kitchen table, playing cards; not one actually lived there.

In the fall of 1981, the house sold for the third time, and the new landlord wanted to use it for himself. This shift happened at a good time, as some occupants were starting to move away. The house had served as a home in the centre of the city and the community, a place where many people found the space to discover themselves. I am so happy and proud to have been a catalyst for what the house at 78 McGill came to mean for so many of us.

The 1977 murder of Emanuel Jaques remains a bruising episode in Toronto's collective memory.

Jaques, the twelve-year-old son of recent immigrants from the Azores, worked as a shoeshine boy on Yonge Street. One day in late July, four men lured Jaques away from his stand to a nearby apartment, where he was sexually assaulted and brutally murdered. On August 1, his crumpled body was discovered under garbage bags on a Yonge Street rooftop, just south of Dundas Street.

The public's shock and the ensuing media uproar unleashed an unprecedented police clampdown, accelerating a backlash that would fundamentally change the relationship of Toronto's queer community to the city. Political and police assaults escalated over the next six years, setting back gay-rights progress in the short term, but eventually raising the visibility of LGBT issues and galvanizing community activists to respond and resist.

Ed Jackson

The Fallout

of a Murder

Impact on Yonge Street's Sin Strip

The Jaques murder should have been understood primarily as a wrenching personal tragedy for a vulnerable working-class immigrant family. Instead, the crime, characterized repeatedly by the media as a 'homosexual murder,' became a much larger social signifier. It gave local politicians permission to dramatically escalate a legal campaign to shutter popular heterosexual adult entertainment businesses on Toronto's 'Sin Strip,' a gritty but alluring cluster of strip clubs, adult movie houses, peep shows, porno bookstores, and body-rub parlours on Yonge between Dundas and Queen.

Citizen pressure to clean up Yonge began soon after David Crombie's 1972 victory as reformist mayor. In the years following his election, Crombie's office was inundated with irate calls and letters, orchestrated in part by the right-wing *Toronto Sun*, supported by evangelical churches, and animated by a sense of growing unease with the effects of sexual permissiveness.

The 1977 opening of the Eaton Centre, coupled with rumours of further redevelopment along Yonge, led to rent spikes and the disappearance of family-run retailers. Sex industry establishments, such as body-rub parlours, were among the few businesses willing to put up with the expensive short-term leases and deteriorating buildings.

Over the years, the municipality had tried unsuccessfully to curb the sex-trade businesses through increased bylaw and licencing powers. Despite Crombie's insistence that the city was not on a 'moral crusade,' it began to feel like one. The sense of moral panic after the discovery of Jaques's body in a building on the Strip silenced objections and dramatically accelerated the cleanup. The tragedy, although unrelated to body rub parlours, provided politicians with convenient cover to use extraordinary legal powers to achieve their ends.

The police and the legal system worked quickly. Metro Council appointed a special prosecutor in mid-August 1977, to fast-track the cleanup through a special court. City inspectors slapped sex-trade businesses with a blizzard of fire, health, and building code infraction citations. A beefed-up police force from 52 Division and the Morality Bureau stepped up efforts to lay bawdy-house charges, employing the little-used provincial Disorderly Houses Act (often called the 'Padlock Law') to force landlords to close tenant businesses convicted under the statute. By October 1977, two months after Jaques's body was found, only four of forty establishments remained open.

Impact on the LGBTQ Community

The convergence of several events following the boy's murder created a toxic atmosphere that felt threatening to Toronto's queer communities. Participants in a march on City Hall organized by some people in the Portuguese community clamoured for the return of the death penalty and included signs that read, 'Kill Sex Perverts – Jail's Too Good.' A petition circulated with the title 'Stamp Out Gays and Body Rubs.'

Just one week before the murder, the Ontario Human Rights Commission had released 'Life Together,' a report recommending the addition of sexual orientation as a prohibited ground for discrimination in housing and employment, a hopeful sign of social change. Sadly, the political response to the crime proved disastrous to the LGBTQ movement's rights-protection advocacy.

In November 1977, The Body Politic published 'Men Loving Boys Loving Men,' an article intended to confront the stereotype that equated all homosexuals with child molesters. The feature sought to spark a community discussion about inter-generational sex and youth sexuality. In different circumstances, the article might have led to a heated but short-lived internal community debate, particularly between gay men and lesbian feminists. Instead, this spectacularly ill-timed inter-vention prompted Sun columnist Claire Hoy to further inflame public opinion by pushing authorities to take legal action against the paper. The police responded by raiding the Body Politic offices in December 1977, an action clearly designed to discredit and close down the newspaper. The raid resulted in obscenity-related criminal charges and an expensive, protracted freedom-of-speech legal battle.

In March 1978, trials of the four men accused of murdering Jaques received sensational coverage. 'There is one feature in your case that disturbs me more than a little,' Justice Arthur William Maloney said during the sentencing of one man, echoing growing public hostility. 'It is your acknowledged tendency to seek out ever younger homosexual partners. I wonder how common that is among homosexuals. There are those who seek legal protection for homosexuals in the Human Rights Code. You make me wonder if they are misguided.' Community activists demanded an apology but were met with hostility and virtual press silence.

In the aftermath of this conflation of events, lesbian and gay rights became a third-rail topic among provincial politicians for years to come. All three parties feared losing votes and backtracked repeatedly on calls to include sexual orientation in the Ontario Human Rights Code. That reform would not occur for another nine years.

The Use of the Bawdy-House Laws

A strong link can be made between the political and legal response to the Jaques murder in 1977 and the infamous police raids on gay bathhouses in 1981.

During their clampdown on Sin Strip establishments, the police learned that bawdy-house laws were effective for securing convictions based on evidence of both prostitution and the law's ambiguous 'indecency' provisions. The Sin Strip operation allowed the influential Morality and Intelligence units to lobby for increased funding and, with these new resources, the units' officers were eager to flex their muscles. They extended their undercover surveillance operations to the LGBTQ community over the next five years. Police sources hinted to reporters how U.S. organized-crime operations were linked to increased male prostitution, particularly in the area further north on Yonge where gay bars had become established. Despite citing little evidence, Attorney-General Roy McMurtry fretted to the media that male prostitution had become a troublesome development in Toronto.

During the 1980 municipal election, the police focus on the LGBTQ community became a key issue. Mayor John Sewell had spoken out at a public rally in January 1979 in defence of *The Body Politic*, prompting a massive outcry (p. 194–6). Sewell continued to voice criticism of heavy-handed police actions, particularly against the black community, while gay activist and bathhouse owner George Hislop announced he would run for city council.

Coincidentally, a wildly distorted CBS television documentary called *Gay Power, Gay Politics* aired in April 1980, warning of the disproportionate role of the gay community in San Francisco politics. Toronto mayoral candidate Art Eggleton warned against 'facilitating San Francisco–style gay power politics in Toronto.' Evidence surfaced of a police-initiated political campaign against Hislop and Sewell, with a brochure entitled 'Queers Do Not Produce; They Seduce!' and produced by a group called the League Against Homosexuals. The document turned up on the counters of downtown police stations. The police association circulated a confidential memo announcing a special project to campaign in Hislop's ward, and police officers helped distribute posters supporting his opponent. The election became a kind of referendum on police accountability and attitudes toward minority communities. In the end, however, both Hislop and Sewell were defeated in November 1980.

The Intelligence and Morality police units started to step up their undercover surveillance of gay bathhouses, deploying increasingly large numbers of officers to launch their assaultive raids. They started with the Barracks, in December 1978, followed by the Hot Tub Club raid in October 1979. The campaign culminated in the massive multi-site campaign called Operation Soap, on February 5, 1981, which saw a platoon of two hundred police officers assembled to conduct raids on four bathhouses, laying a total of 286 bawdy-house charges. At the time, it was the largest mass arrest in Canada since the 1970 invocation of the War Measures Act.

With the outraged community response to this controversial misuse of police resources, a new chapter in the relationship between the police and Toronto's queer community had begun.

On December 30, 1977, a grey Friday afternoon before the New Year's Eve weekend, I was working late in the *Body Politic* office, a fifth-floor loft space at Adelaide and Duncan. Suddenly, five heavy-set men appeared at the door, displaying a practised menace straight out of central casting. They were plainclothes officers from Operation P, the police pornography unit, brandishing a search warrant. In a panic, I phoned lawyer Clayton Ruby for guidance; he advised me to refuse to help the cops in their search. 'All right,' they replied, 'we'll take this place apart!' And so they did, spending four hours sifting through filing cabinets. I watched in shock as boxes of seized material, including our subscription list, disappeared down the freight elevator.

At that moment, the future of *The Body Politic* changed forever.

Ed Jackson
The Raid on The Body Politic

The Body Politic, a cheeky tabloid newspaper, was a countercultural experiment that quickly became a key voice of Canadian lesbian and gay liberation, read by activists around the world. For fifteen years after its first issue in November 1971, its writers challenged sexual orthodoxies, documented community resistance, celebrated queer history and culture, and fought for freedom of the press in a famous court case.

For better or worse, TBP has acquired a privileged and visible place in Toronto's queer history, partly because it was a printed newspaper, self-consciously obsessed with documentation and its own role in that history, but also because it became a symbol of resistance to state oppression. TBP was produced by a core group of educated white middle-class cis-gendered gay men, of whom I was one. Talented white women like Chris Bearchell, Mariana Valverde, and Gillian Rodgerson eventually joined us, and a number of young women became active staffers, but they were always a minority. In retrospect, we had advantages we were not even aware of. It helped us in confronting the pervasive oppression of the wider world, but it made us less sensitive to race and gender inequalities within our own communities.

I was deeply involved in TBP for twelve of its fifteen years; it was the most passionate and galvanizing period of my life.

We 'Beepers,' as we called ourselves, knew that what we were doing was unprecedented. We were part of a larger historical movement around the Anglo-American world. That confidence in the inevitability – and rightness – of the changes we dreamed of was deeply exciting. We thought no queers in the past had ever been so upfront and confrontational.

We insisted on using our full names, and we photographed ourselves without fear, when many queer people were still afraid to be as public.

Visibility, being proudly out, was a key operating principle for TBP. We wrote about the joys of 'throat-ramming' and flaunted our queerness in print. The take-no-prisoners attitude inspired many readers, but frightened others.

A group of talented writers contributed to the paper throughout its lifetime, among them Gerald Hannon, Herb Spiers, Merv Walker, Rick Bébout, Ken Popert, Tim McCaskell, Michael Lynch, David Gibson, Chris Bearchell, David Rayside, Mariana Valverde, Gillian Rodgerson, Jane Rule, Robin Hardy, Michael Riordon, and Thomas Waugh. Hundreds of other volunteers came and went over the years, helping out in a myriad of tasks.

I was a political naïf when I got involved, having just spent a year backpacking around Europe with my friend Gerald Hannon. We nervously joined our first public gay liberation demonstration in the summer of 1971 – a march on London's Fleet Street protesting homophobia in British tabloids. The experience was enthralling, and I knew I had to return to Canada to get involved in the movement.

I went to my first meeting of the Community Homophile Association of Toronto at Holy Trinity Church in November 1971, where I ran into Jearld Mold-enhauer, who was selling queer books out of his knapsack and flogging the first issue of TBP. He invited Gerald and me to the next editorial meeting.

Moldenhauer, a bright, prickly, socially awkward guy, was the brains behind the early TBP. He conceived the idea of a newspaper as political project, particularly inspired after a local countercultural tabloid mangled his story about the first national gay demonstration in Canada. No one remembers exactly who came up with the name, but *The Body Politic*, a choice both inspired and clever, revealed the founders' intellectual pretensions.

We didn't know anything about creating a newspaper: paste-up, news and headline writing, editing, design, typesetting, printer instructions, subscriptions, distribution, advertising. We learned it all by doing. At first, we hawked the paper outside Toronto's gay bars, but not everyone welcomed us in those early years. One not uncommon reaction: 'I'm liberated. I don't need your newspaper.'

I shared a house with core members of the *Body Politic* editorial collective. I experienced the joys and irritations of living in a communal household. I fell in love with a handsome young man who arrived on our doorstep fresh from Saskatchewan; he became part of the editorial team and our household. We all lived and breathed gay liberation.

Initially, we put the paper together in the windowless basement of our rented Marchmount Road house. Outgrowing that space, we moved to a draughty shed behind a house on Kensington Avenue that we shared with Moldenhauer's Glad Day Bookshop. There was no welcoming Gay Village then.

We Beepers were a group obsessed with history. We were the first to expose English readers to the story of the Nazis' brutal erasure of the German homosexual

The Body Politic collective members (from left): Merv Walker, Ken Popert, and David Gibson, 1976.

emancipation movement in the 1930s. We published the first versions of John D'Emilio's pioneering book on the creation of the Mattachine Society in 1950s Cold War America. And we popularized the pink triangle (which marked homosexuals in Nazi concentration camps), calling our non-profit parent organization Pink Triangle Press.

Our news department documented incidents of discrimination, police harassment, and media homophobia. We recorded the endless efforts to pressure governments to change laws and regulations that curtailed and stunted our lives. The news we published over 135 issues remains a vital record for historians.

Because we had a public office, we also became the first-responder organizers of the protests following the notorious bathhouse raids in 1981. We covered the subsequent fallout in detail, and what we wrote became essential reading, giving voice to the community's rage.

Some years later, we sought to provide a calming voice during the hysteria about AIDS. The cover headline 'The Case Against Panic' in our November 1982 issue set the tone. Our commitment to sexual liberation ensured that Toronto's subsequent response to HIV/AIDS prevention remained sensible and sex-positive.

For all that, *TBP* may be best known for its legal battles, set in motion by that 1977 police raid and seizure. The intent of the raid was to close us down. We found ourselves fighting for our survival in a very hostile world, some of it coming from our frightened community. After the raid, the police charged three directors of Pink Triangle Press – Gerald Hannon, Ken Popert, and me – with an obscure obscenity-related statute in the Criminal Code: using the mails to transmit immoral, indecent, and scurrilous material. The charge led to six years of worry, two trials, one retrial, numerous Crown appeals, and endless fundraising efforts to cover legal costs. Over the years of our legal challenges, we raised $100,000 – all small sums from individuals. At the time, it was a huge amount for a queer legal case.

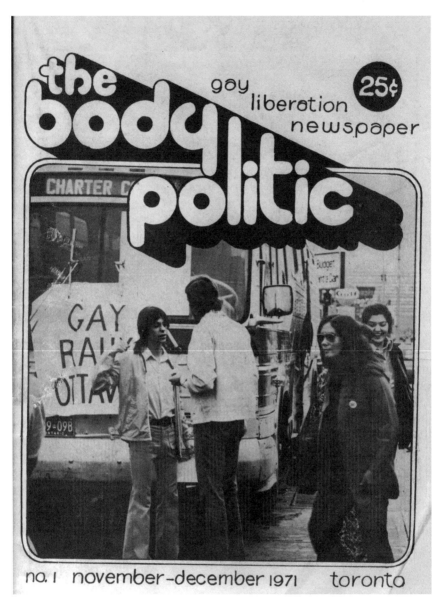

the **body** gay liberation newspaper 25¢

politic

no. 1 november-december 1971 toronto

Despite the support, the ordeal was endless and exhausting; I often wished it would just go away!

Early on, the mainstream media mostly ignored us. But in November 1977, this changed abruptly with the publication of Gerald Hannon's feature 'Men Loving Boys Loving Men' and the subsequent police raid. In the overheated atmosphere after the Emanuel Jaques murder (see pages 167–170), we were hoping to initiate a discussion on the issue of intergenerational sex (a.k.a. pedophilia) and the persistent shibboleth of the child-molesting homosexual. But we did not count on the virulence of the *Toronto Sun*'s response, nor the homophobic forces within the police force. And the timing turned out be spectacularly unlucky. (For a full chronology, visit hwww.clga.ca/Material/Records/docs/hannon/ox/chronos.htm.)

TBP became a legal cause rather than simply a newspaper – we turned the attack into an issue of press freedom. People began to rally to our defence, both straight allies and queer activists from around the world. Now we found ourselves in the media far more than we ever wanted. The first trial got daily coverage; each day, the three of us did the 'perp walk' out of the courthouse under the intrusive watch of the TV news cameras. What they saw were three young clean-cut middle-class guys rather than the filthy pornographer caricature created by the *Sun* and the cops. The *Sun* called *TBP* 'a dirty crummy publication without a redeeming feature.' We wore it as a badge of honour, and in the end we won, acquitted at each trial.

Of all the challenging topics *TBP* tackled, it was the issue of race itself that most illustrated the blinkers of our white privilege. That tension came to a head in 1984 with the publication of a classified ad by a white man looking for a black 'house boy' as part of a sexual fantasy. The ad prompted much discussion within the collective and elicited sharp protests from queer people of colour. We printed the differing perspectives in an effort to foster discussion. But in the end, the collective had opted to publish it. Though some of us were uneasy about that choice, we accepted the majority decision.

Queers of colour had already begun to challenge white privilege in the movement, particularly in lesbian-feminist organizations. But *TBP* stalwarts had become so caught up in our anti-censorship struggle against state regulation that we privileged the inviolability of sexual expression above all other considerations. Our response to the issues of the ad debate became our greatest political failure.

I believe the decision to publish it marked the beginning of the end of *TBP* as a central community voice. We had begun to lose touch with a diversifying community. It was around then that I resigned and went to work for the AIDS Committee of Toronto; HIV/AIDS had become the new battleground. Other *TBP* old-timers left, too, exhausted by our legal battles and uncertain how to respond to changing community needs. The paper began to flounder financially and ceased publishing in 1986, replaced by its spinoff publication *Xtra!*, which continued in print for another thirty years.

As for those boxes of seized office materials: in April 1985, seven years and four months after they had taken them away, the cops finally returned them.

Not a single document was ever entered in evidence during our trials.

When Stephanie Martin and Makeda Silvera bought a three-storey, turn-of-the-century house on Dewson Street, in a leafy, largely Portuguese immigrant part of town in the west end, they never imagined the place would become ground zero for black lesbian and gay organizing in the 1980s.

I was almost twenty-one in 1983 – completing my first year of university, just coming out, and needing a place to live with my three-year-old daughter – when some gay men I met at a Toronto Board of Education anti-racism program told me about a Jamaican lesbian couple who were looking for tenants.

I phoned them up, and moved into that rambling house.

Debbie Douglas

That Collective House on Dewson Street

Dewson was a house for gays and lesbians of colour – mostly lesbians. D. S. was the only guy who officially lived there. I remember the screening interview. The tenant collective asked questions about feminism, about being lesbian (including some very intrusive questions as a way of weeding out pretenders), about collective living, shared parenting, work, school, and my family and their attitude toward my sexual orientation. They especially wanted to know about my relationship with my husband and how he was reacting to my leaving and coming out as a lesbian. The house had been pelted with eggs before, and they were cautious and concerned about issues of safety.

It was an exciting and scary time for me, as I didn't really know what to expect. My daughter was missing her home and her dad. She refused to sleep without me at night, and we spent many nights in the basement of the house with her screaming at the top of her lungs that she wanted to go home. Within a few months, however, she was okay, enjoying the other three kids. On some level, it felt like home: the smells of Caribbean cooking (although mostly vegetarian), the sounds of reggae and calypso and soul and, what was new to me, women's music – Tracy Chapman, Sweet Honey in the Rock, Joan Armatrading, Toshi Reagon, Casselberry and Dupree. And the conversations – about politics in the Black community, feminisms, organizing, writing, music, identities, and, of course, gossip. I immersed myself in feminist and lesbian-feminist writing, searching out Black women writers, especially lesbians. It was a time of women's publishing houses, with women-of-colour presses like Sister Vision Press, started by Makeda and Stephanie at Dewson Street, Kitchen Table Press in the U.S., and feminist presses like Women's Press here in Toronto.

The house was traffic central, with folks dropping by to borrow a book, drop off flyers, attend late-night meetings about a protest or rally, or an editorial meeting for one of the many feminist publications at the time.

We talked about how to discuss gay and lesbian issues within the Black community – very serious conversations about how to open up spaces in organizations like the Congress of Black Women and other Black, women of colour, and immigrant women's organizations. Some of our politically active older folks doing Black community organizing were not open or tolerant of those of us who they saw as going against Black community values as they existed at the time.

Then we began thinking of other folks who didn't have a space like Dewson to hold these conversations. We decided the way to do that was to create a lesbian and gay Black and Caribbean group. We called it Zami, a West Indian Creole word for lesbian. Zami wasn't only a Black group – folks who weren't Black from the Caribbean were welcome – but the focus was the Black community. We wanted a group that could speak to gay and lesbian issues in the Black community and to issues of blackness and racism within the broader, primarily white, lesbian and gay community.

Although it was hatched at Dewson, Zami met regularly at 519 Church Street. It was a support group but also very much about visibility. We took part in the Pride Day marches, held social events, were the Black representative at the Inside Out film festival, and part of the protests against the *Body Politic* houseboy ad. We were the visible Black queer organization in the city.

Over time, Zami became a largely men's group. Although we Black women still helped out from time to time, we became more involved in organizing around feminist issues and particularly in Black feminist discussions. (Gender identity certainly wasn't on the table then in any central way.) Some of us were involved in the organizing of York University's Women's Centre. For many, that was our first time working across lines of race and sexual orientation.

In 1986, we created the Black Women's Collective. Again, this political group was formed around a kitchen table at the home of one of Canada's celebrated Black feminist poets and novelist, and her then musician partner. A large number of us were lesbians, but we didn't identify as a lesbian organization. We had begun to move away from the politics of sexual orientation and saw ourselves as Black feminists. The Black Women's Collective was where we came to check our political assumptions, to seek sustenance and validation, and to have our feminist and political selves challenged and called up when necessary. We did a lot of work within the International Women's Day Committee, testing the assumptions of white feminists and provoking discussions about issues of power and leadership, race and class, and published a newspaper called *Our Lives*.

Meanwhile, Douglas Stewart and others from Zami went on to help found the Black Coalition for AIDS Prevention in 1989, and later Aya, an important group for Black gay men in the 1990s. At the end of the decade, many of the same people helped start Blackness Yes (see p. 339–341).

If you trace back the histories of most of Toronto's Black queer and feminist organizing, you will find a common root: that collective house on Dewson Street.

St. Helens Avenue, 1981: Grandmother's House

When I overheard my grandmother downstairs in the kitchen whispering loudly into the phone, I turned my drinking glass upside-down on the floor of my room and listened. She was not a woman who whispered. Her voice boomed like a nyabinghi drum that could be heard from our house to Bloor and Lansdowne.

Makeda Silvera

From St. Helens Avenue to Dewson Street

'As God is mi witness a nearly fall out a mi chair when de gal – de one she call friend – ask mi if mi know say mi have a sodomite grand-daughter.' There was a slight pause; I imagined her catching her breath. 'Yes mi haffee talk some sense in her head, after all she have di two lovely pickney to tink 'bout.' She was silent awhile, then I heard, 'Hmm, hmm, hmm.' Then, 'Yes, mi going to talk to her right now. It too important – dis grease ago catch fire.' Finally, she said, 'God bless.' Then she slammed the phone down hard.

Her house slippers shuffled to her bedroom, two doors from the kitchen. I heard a kiss-teeth and a sigh. She shouted my name so hard I shook. In the kitchen, she ordered me to open the Bible in front of her. It was mid-morning: my children were at daycare.

'A hear from yuh good frien', de one wid de car, who yuh up and down wid all de time. She say you gone to 'oman, say yuh turn sodomite.' She was looking straight into my eyes. By then, tears were paddling in my eyes, mucus dripping from my nose. 'Yuh know dis is a serious ting, is hell, brimstone, and fire on yuh.' She paused, waiting for me to speak, but I had nothing to say. I was not ready to be out as a lesbian. As she read out Scriptures, I sat numb, looking out the kitchen window. At twenty-five, with two children and divorced, I felt like a child being scolded. She had on a yellow-flowered house-dress, and talked and talked, certain I could be saved. My grandmother had been a practical person, but a heart condition and other ailments had led her to frequently take up organized religion.

My 'friend' eventually called me but only to offer her condolences for my 'affliction.' She urged me to admit myself to the Clarke Institute of Psychiatry. I had no intention of going there. She also outed me to my fellow Rastafarians. Talk soon travelled to the wider Caribbean and Black communities.

The house on St. Helens had been a comfort during my teens, and I had come back to it after my divorce. I had taken a liking to the strip joint at the corner, the church right next to it, the immigrant shops at the top of our street, the ladies of the night, and the men doing a little hustle to get by. I remember how friends dropped in for some Jamaican comfort food: steam fish with okra, oxtail, red pea soup with pumpkin and dumplings. In the

1970s, my grandmother's passion for cooking and baking resulted in meals served up at African Liberation Day at Christie Pits.

But as I sat at the kitchen table, listening to her boom out her conviction that she could save me, it was as if I were eating a meal with too much salt, too much Scotch bonnet pepper. Then and there, I knew I had to find another home.

Dewson Street, 1983: Love at First Sight

When I first saw the house, it was a grande dame who showed her age. Paint had flaked and fallen from weathered wooden windows. A FOR SALE sign had been planted in the wilting grass. The front door opened onto a wide hall still smelling of the forty cats reportedly kept by the former owner. Downstairs, some walls had cracks and peeling paint, but the oak trim, the hardwood floors, the front room fireplace, and the high ceilings were beautiful. I convinced S. to join me in my crazy plan to meet with the realtor and convince him to lease instead of sell.

We spent Christmas and New Year's pulling 1935 newspapers off the walls of the rooms on the second and third floors. The basement shower reminded me of *Psycho*. S. painted many of the rooms and used her carpentry skills on the house. After a short stay with my grandmother, my two children came home to us.

For all, there was a feeling of liberation. There were also problems. Once a neighbour called 14 Division, complaining that a young Black woman was coming and going from a three-storey house. Two policemen arrived to question me about my relationship to the house.

Dewson Street, 1984: Lesbian and Gays of Colour

Since we had so much space, we put out the word to lesbians and gays of colour, with or without children, that we had rooms in a collective house where we would share chores, groceries, and meal preparation. In time, we settled in: five lesbians and two gay men, and four children all under eight years old. Dewson spawned many political groups: sometimes the house felt like a Ferris wheel; other times, a rollercoaster. We came from similar backgrounds, and had experienced rejection both by our families and many straight friends, as well as alienation from the white gay/lesbian community. But we were not alike in other ways. Some of us were mothers who had loved men, while others had not experienced the demands of parenting. This made for great debates. But at Dewson we belonged; we learned to appreciate each other's food: bannock, chapattis, ugale, doubles, cou-cou. At Dewson, it was safe to laugh, to cry, to argue, to look at the different ways a lesbian might represent herself. Lovers toyed with roles and relations: butch-femme, s&m, lipstick femme, interracial relationships, monogamy versus non-monogamy.

Holiday cheating was not unusual 'among the family.' Lovers would break up, which could have affected our solidarity within and without the house. But we worked hard to make sure that didn't happen. Sometimes there was bitterness, a first taste of lesbian and gay sexual betrayal. We were young, and most of us had never experienced the joys of lesbian sex, never felt our bones crashing against another woman's, never had a tender fuck, opening legs with mouth. Mostly, we reminded ourselves that our collective work was as important as the individual's needs.

Dewson Street, 1985: Sister Vision

Here, in 1985, in the basement of the house, Sister Vision: Black Women and Women of Color Press came into being. It was time we women of colour had a press, time we took control over what happened to our words, time we published works about our worlds, told our stories, collected our poems, met each other through our anthologies.

Forming the press was not easy. A few women we invited refused on the grounds that a women's press would go against men of colour. Neither established nor alternative publishers, nor arts councils, gave us encouragement. But we were determined to create a press that would make a difference to women of colour on the Canadian literary scene. We raised money through parties at the house. After the press formed, many women came together to volunteer their time.

Sister Vision published more than fifty titles over fifteen years. Undoubtedly significant was the anthology *Piece of My Heart*, the title taken from Janis Joplin's classic rock song. *Piece of My Heart* spoke directly to the women who called Dewson Street home and brought joy to lesbians of colour across Canada and the U.S. Published in 1991, the book was the first of its kind in Canada. The writers' voices made it unique in its anger, in its uncompromising stances, in its at times funny-as-hell takes on life, in its poetry, its personal essays, its short stories. But perhaps the most significant change it heralded was the voices of Caribbean women, aboriginal women, and Latin American women who shared their lives at a time when to do so was to run some risk. *Piece of My Heart* took four years to come together, but it was a joy to read the submissions, to edit, and finally to celebrate its publication and reception.

The press closed around 2000. A new generation has taken up the fight.

Dewson Street: 2016 Postscript

I wish I had asked my grandmother, before she died, why my choices caused so much fear in my family. What I did know was that in my community, being gay was seen as a 'white thing.' I had become an enigma. For queer and trans millennials, this narrative of my exit from my grandmother's house, and my journey at Dewson Street, might conjure both painful and liberated images of ancient times. It might also be a reflection of contemporary experience for Black LGBTQs struggling with family, leaving home, and creating new queer and trans communities of colour.

Following the police raids on four Toronto bathhouses on February 5, 1981, an impromptu demonstration was organized by activists for the corner of Yonge and Wellesley streets at midnight the following night. Although Philip McLeod (1923–2010) had been an enthusiastic supporter of the lesbian and gay movement, especially financially, he had always remained behind the scenes. Fifty-eight years old, a retired librarian and a World War II veteran, Philip was the product of a generation that had mostly avoided the public gay demonstrations of the seventies. However, the shock of the police raids prompted a different response to the February 6 protest demo and march. Here, Philip describes his impressions in a letter to friends in Ottawa.

February 8, 1981

Dear B. and R.,
What a weekend! This one started around 11 p.m. Thursday, although it was not until two hours later that one of my tenants knocked on my door to tell me that the baths had been raided. Throughout the next day, as people talked by phone, the story got spread through the community. By nightfall, leaflets were being passed through the bars announcing a mass demonstration at midnight at Yonge and Wellesley. 'What am I doing this for?' I asked myself as I started there on foot. I got there at 11:45 p.m. I haven't marched since the end of WWII! I hadn't expected to find myself marching in the middle of Yonge Street in the middle of the night with about 2,000 others. 'Lift me up; I want

Philip McLeod

Out of the Cold the Thousands Came

The third bath raid protest demonstration, June 20, 1981, was marred by violence and infiltrated by undercover cops who worked their way to the front to hold the lead banner.

Bathhouse raid aftermath: Richmond Street Health Emporium.

to see how many people are here,' one fellow said to his friend. We watched him hoisted. 'Jesus Christ!' he shrieked.

At Yonge and Wellesley, pairs of police stood in doorways along the west side of Yonge. I read a pamphlet entitled *Enough Is Enough!* before crossing the street to join the crowd on the steps of one of the office buildings. Some of them were thrilling the street with whistles, little plastic earsplitters. 'I'm a Fag,' one of the posters read. 'Stop the Cops!' read another. The whistles set up a chorus. I suddenly decided that we needed to say something. I faced the group on the steps. I spread my arms. Was I supposed to be Toscanini? Or did I look like Lawrence Welk? 'STOP THE COPS!' I shouted. 'Stop the cops,' came back. In a minute our oratorio of chants was in full throat: 'NO MORE RAIDS!' 'GAYS HAVE RIGHTS!'

Out of the cold the thousands came. They packed the pavement. They overflowed into the gutter. Cars began to slow down. One by one, in groups, trekking in from the bars, the gays came on. Within half an

'The Battle of Church Street,' June 20, 1981. Police violence at demonstrations following two steam bath raids on June 16.

hour all traffic was being rerouted. The intersection was packed, in smiling, shouting, laughing, hugging assembly.

And here at last was the sound truck, here the speakers, including Chris Bearchell, resident dyke at *The Body Politic* and the best speaker. (Her phrase 'No more shit!' became one of the recurring chants of the march.) Media lights flared on. One of the organizers told the crowd: 'We're going to march down Yonge to Dundas, along Dundas to 52 Division. And remember: this is a PEACEFUL demonstration. There is to be no violence.' The crowd shouted: 'MARCH, MARCH, MARCH ... ' 'Follow the marshal carrying the flag.' I turned around with the rest and faced south. We began to move like a mass of ice. The black flag fluttered. The chanting was incessant. Up ahead I could hear, 'No more raids!' Behind I could hear, 'Stop the cops!'

Scattered homophobes came out of their bars and taunted us. At least, their mouths were moving. You couldn't hear them in the rhythmic roar. Policemen kept abreast of the march. At Dundas, they placed their cruisers at odd angles across the road. It forced the mass to file between the cars. We slowed and moved past their obstruction. I saw one unmarked automobile being rocked. Two of the marshals rushed forward and shouted down the attack on the car, and the offenders rejoined the march. A streetcar halted and we flowed around it. One fellow climbed up and spread his placard for the driver and the riders to read. Our 'rampage' may have produced the broken streetcar window the *Toronto Star* so faithfully described

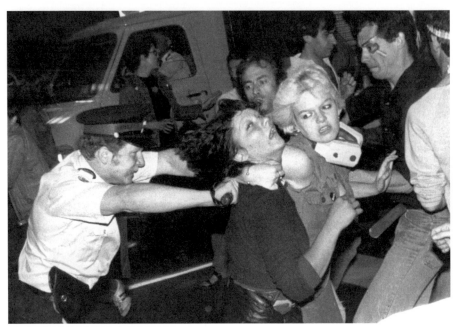

'The Battle of Church Street,' June 20, 1981.

to its readers the next day. A line of adolescent homophobes obstructed the march by linking arms across Dundas at University. They collided with the front edge of the march. A skirmish broke out. The mass rolled them to one side and went on.

I left the march a block before at Elizabeth Street. It was there that we were halted for a moment. Suddenly from a second-floor window in what is Chinatown, hands began to applaud and continued to clap. Just shadows in the frame of the window showering us with a little blessing.

I hadn't come for a march. I had thought I was going to praise speakers and make a donation and go home. I was trembling with the cold. I walked up Bay, a little soothed by the quiet that now surrounded me. I reached the Roman Sauna; twenty-four hours, before it had been vandalized by hooligan-like members of the Morality Squad. 'Hi, I don't want a room,' I said to the attendant. 'Can you sell me a coffee? I'll drink it here in the lobby. I've just left the march.' Naturally, I was studied with wariness. 'It's okay,' I said. 'I'm glad you're open.' 'Well, not right now. They're still fixing the doors,' he said. 'Sugar?'

I lay awake most of Friday night …

Love,

Philip

C hris Bearchell was a brilliant political organizer, a skilled builder of coalitions, and an articulate, radical thinker, writer, and speaker. And for a long time in the 1970s and 1980s, she was the public face of Canadian lesbians, loudly and proudly 'out' and willing to take the risks that came with claiming that identity.

Ken Popert, a fellow member of the *Body Politic* collective, remembers Chris as 'an unsurpassed rabble-rouser.' 'On the occasion of Anita Bryant's appearance in Toronto [in 1978], I recall participating on a dark and rainy evening in a decidedly dispirited demonstration. When Chris arrived, she produced a stepladder, climbed up, and began to work her magic. In about sixty seconds, she transformed that timid, quiet crowd into a screaming, raging mob. The picture of her atop the ladder, a conductor goading us to a crescendo of anger, has stuck with me ever since.'

Gillian Rodgerson

An Unsurpassed Rabble-Rouser: Chris Bearchell

A survey of Chris Bearchell's political work offers a picture of Canada's late-twentieth-century feminist, socialist, and gay liberation movements, which she always encouraged to work together where possible. In 1972, at just eighteen, she had already spoken publicly against the war in Vietnam and co-founded the Alberta Women for Abortion Law Repeal. She was also there at the beginning of the Coalition for Gay Rights in Ontario, the Lesbian Organization of Toronto, Lesbians Against the Right, the Committee to Defend John Damien (a racing steward fired simply for being gay), the Canadian Organization for the Rights of Prostitutes, and Maggie's, the drop-in centre for Toronto street prostitutes.

Chris also served as a long-time member of the *Body Politic* collective (initially its only lesbian member) and worked as the paper's news editor. In 1981, she presented a brief to Ontario MPPs, detailing the discrimination lesbians and gay men faced in areas such as housing and employment. After leaving *TBP*, she joined the board of the Canadian AIDS Treatment Information Exchange and worked in AIDS education for street-involved youth.

Far from simply wanting to achieve equal rights or legal equality, Chris was committed to the transformation of society itself into a more liberated, less constricted place for everyone.

Chris had tremendous energy, courage, and confidence, which she shared with others, inspiring less experienced activists to take on bigger challenges. When I turned up to volunteer at *TBP* as a fairly naive young lesbian looking for a way into the community, Chris didn't dismiss or ignore me, but instead suggested I could work with Tim McCaskell on writing international news. I worked out a lot of my politics and my lesbian identity through talking with Chris, wanting her friendship but also hoping to earn her respect.

Chris Bearchall, centre, with microphone, at February 6, 1981, demonstration: '*No more shit!*'

Ottawa activist Marie Robertson worked with Chris when they were both young lesbians in the early gay liberation movement. '[Chris] and I were two of the very small but dedicated group of lesbians amidst a large group of gay men … all of us trying to organize in the early days of gay liberation in Ontario. People need to remember that in the "olden days" lesbians were almost totally invisible. Dykes like Chris and I had our work cut out for us! Fortunately, both of us were loud, insistent, and persistent!'

One of Chris's finest hours as an activist took place on that frigid February evening in 1981 when Toronto's gay community rose up in protest against the police raids on the baths the night before. Speaking from atop a bus shelter at Yonge and Wellesley (Chris stood about five-three), she used her beautiful, powerful speaking voice to galvanize the crowd.

'Chris Bearchell had a voice clear as a bell, sometimes melodious, explaining her socialist feminist analysis, sometime pealing urgently, a call for action,' recalls Tim McCaskell. 'On the platform at the February 6 demonstration, the night after the bath raids, it was her voice that echoed out over Yonge Street. "We're not going to take this shit anymore: *no more shit!*" Her iconic phrase reverberated in the throats of 3,000 people as we marched on 52 Division.'

While Chris presented a fierce presence on the political frontlines, her friends knew her as a warm and loving individual with an unforgettable laugh – someone constantly expanding the circle of people who felt welcome and included at her house on Walnut Avenue in Toronto.

Chris also loved sex and wasn't squeamish about lesbian porn. Indeed, she was one of the first to analyze it from an anti-censorship perspective and literally 'put her ass on the line,' making a sex film with a group of friends and enthusiastically supporting others producing grassroots 'lezzie smut.'

Of course, not everyone agreed with Chris. She passionately defended her convictions, and some of them set her at odds with other lesbian feminists at the time. (Although Chris believed it was important to make alliances with gay men, she would always claim the term *lesbian feminist*, refusing to let others define what that identity might mean.)

In a 1996 interview with Miriam Smith, published in *Journal of Canadian Studies/Revue d'études canadiennes*, Chris discussed the changes she'd seen in the gay and feminist movements. 'While gay liberation has gone on this peculiar trajectory from sexual freedom to equal families, feminism has gone on this peculiar trajectory from control of our bodies to save our daughters,' she observed.

Susan G. Cole, *NOW* Magazine's arts editor, says, 'Chris Bearchell and I were both lesbian activists in the late seventies. We were both involved in journalism. Though her political orientation was more toward gay liberation and mine was explicitly feminist, we were both in the umbrella group the Lesbian Organization of Toronto. It was a time of intense activism.'

Cole continues: 'Though there were hundreds of lesbians out on the streets at the relevant demos, there was exactly one woman who would speak to the press as an out lesbian – and that was Chris Bearchell. She was the only one courageous enough at the time to be articulate about our political missions, passionate about them, and be out and proud. Every dyke celebrating our visibility and our rights in this day and age owes her a debt of gratitude.'

When Chris left Toronto in 1995, headed for Lasqueti Island off the coast of B.C., she found another close community in her house at 'Camp Swampy,' helping her neighbours organize against threatened RCMP raids.

In 1999, Chris was diagnosed with breast cancer. It would kill her eight years later, but she faced her illness with the same brave and open spirit she embodied to deal with earlier injustices.

As her lover Irit Shimrat said after Chris's death, 'Wherever she was, and regardless of what was happening in her own life, she always made it her first priority to feed the hungry, house the homeless, caffeinate the weary, comfort the lonely, welcome with open arms the marginalized and oppressed.'

Dennis Findlay was a baker, not a lawyer. But in April 1982, in a Scarborough courtroom, he encountered a gay man who faced a Criminal Code charge of being 'found in a common bawdy house.' The man had no lawyer and, with no other option, pleaded guilty. Findlay held back tears and rage, as he knew exactly how the man could have won his case. Although he had no formal legal training, he had attended many trials as an activist with the Right to Privacy Committee. Seeing Findlay's frustration, a lawyer advised him that he could offer to represent the accused men as a 'friend of the court.'

Tom Hooper

'Friend of the Court':

Legal Resistance at Old City Hall

The RTPC, created in 1978, was best known for organizing protests, fundraising, political lobbying, and legal coordination in the wake of the February 5, 1981, mass bathhouse raids, dubbed Operation Soap. After the raids, owners and managers were charged as 'keepers' and patrons were charged as 'found-ins' in a common bawdy house (defined as a place used for prostitution or 'acts of indecency'). Findlay was a key volunteer of the RTPC's Legal Coordinating Committee (LCC), along with fellow activists Elan Rosenquist, Paul Rapsey, and Philip McLeod. More than $200,000 was raised to cover legal fees, and their courtroom tactics resulted in a more than 85 per cent success rate for the 286 men charged as found-ins. In effect, the LCC turned the courtroom into a space of political resistance against the bath raids.

Findlay went on to represent twelve men, and two of the trials included a full cross-examination of police witnesses. He won all of them. 'Acting on behalf of those men was the most frightening thing I have ever done, and yet the most empowering experience of my life,' he reflected thirty years later. 'Standing up for a stranger does make a difference.'

The first task of the LCC was to identify the men who were charged in Operation Soap by attending court in the weeks following the raids to review the posted dockets. These contained the names and charges for those scheduled to appear on any given day. Using this information, volunteers contacted many of the found-ins to convince them to fight their charges by pleading not guilty, and matched them with queer-friendly lawyers. Crown prosecutors tempted those who were charged with a quick and easy plea deal, promising a swift trial, a light sentence, and no media attention. However, found-ins were often pleasantly surprised to find they had the option to fight.

Because of the sheer number of charges, the burdened court delayed the bathhouse trials until winter 1982, with most cases being heard at Old City Hall. The legal committee diligently attended these trials and took notes. Defence lawyers' strategies varied – in some cases, they argued that the found-in was in the bathhouse not for indecent acts, but for a lawful excuse. This included using the steam room or sauna to treat bronchitis, or to use the hot tub for back pain. The primary defence tactic was to question whether the Crown could properly establish the identity of the accused at trial. The police had assumed most found-ins would plead guilty, and raiding officers had not been diligent in keeping notes or gathering other evidence to present at trial. Under cross-examination, the officer who issued the citation to the found-in could often only identify the accused by name; this was insufficient to warrant a conviction.

The key defence tactic was to request that the found-ins be allowed to sit in the body of the court and enter their plea of not guilty from there, instead of at the defence table. In addition, the defence requested that all prosecution witnesses be excluded from the courtroom prior to the accused entering his plea. The legal committee filled the court with RTPC members and other queers who might have a physical appearance similar to the man facing trial. The confused arresting officers surveyed the rows of upturned faces in the courtroom and in most instances were unable to identify the found-ins during cross-examination, establishing a precedent for the hundreds of cases to follow. This was galvanizing for the legal committee, but frustrating for police, prosecutors, and judges. 'The police saw fit to charge these people,' remarked a judge in one case. 'One would have thought they might have made enough of an observation that they can identify them later in court.'

Findlay and Philip McLeod, a retired librarian, became vital to this effort when cases were transferred from Old City Hall to a Scarborough courtroom. In some cases, this made it easier for the defence because many of the arresting officers called as Crown witnesses did not appear for trial. However, it also made it difficult for the legal committee to pair found-ins with lawyers and to fill the courtroom gallery. At one point, McLeod noticed that police officers excluded from the courtroom were peering through the window in the courtroom door to get a glimpse of defendants while they entered their plea. He quickly moved over to stand in front of the window to block their view, and RTPC lawyers requested that the court keep witnesses away from spaces where they might see the found-ins.

After the Operation Soap trials, Findlay and McLeod rebranded the LCC as Gay Court Watch. This group earned a reputation among the workers at Old City Hall as a respectable institution. In May 1982, when Findlay asked for office space, they were granted the use of room 337. Each day subsequently, photocopies of the court dockets were slipped under the door. In early 1983 they received a grant from the Gay Community Appeal to obtain a computer for keeping arrest data and statistics. For example, between September 1984 and May 1985, they tracked 253 charges laid against men for having consensual sex with other men in Toronto. Like the LCC, this rebranded group fluctuated in size, with anywhere from seven to twenty active volunteers at any given time. They held monthly meetings at

Findlay's bakery to discuss new issues, develop defence strategies, and update their legal resources.

Gay Court Watch remained affiliated with the RTPC, but their mandate expanded beyond bathhouses to include any charges against queer people for consensual sex. Their primary task remained the same as in 1981: to convince queers charged with morality offences to plead not guilty, and then provide legal assistance in resisting the state in the courts. After the failure to obtain significant convictions in the bath-raid trials, police forces began to refocus their efforts on the surveillance of public washrooms, a strategy utilized through the 1970s. In 1983, Gay Court Watch worked with alderman Jack Layton to resist police entrapment in the washroom at the Hudson's Bay department store on Bloor Street. Beyond Toronto, Gay Court Watch offered assistance to the thirty-one men who were charged at the Orillia Opera House that same year.

The group was similarly concerned about an increase in the number of charges laid in various public parks. In the 1970s, parks across the city were subject to this surveillance, including Cherry Beach, Philosopher's Walk, Queen's Park, David Balfour Park, Allan Gardens, and High Park. Charges stemming from park sex were initially not part of the RTPC mandate, but Gay Court Watch resolved to offer their assistance in these cases. By the mid-1980s, park operations expanded outward to the suburbs, including a 1982 sting in Marie Curtis Park on the boundary between Etobicoke and Mississauga, and a 1985 bust in Guelph that used new surveillance technology.

The strategies employed by Gay Court Watch left an enduring legacy for the community. In the fall of 2016, Toronto Police were back in Marie Curtis Park, where a six-week undercover operation netted the arrest of seventy-two people for engaging in sexual acts. Marcus McCann was one of the lawyers who worked alongside a new group of activists calling themselves Queers Crash the Beat to coordinate the legal strategy to resist this renewed police campaign. Citing the RTPC and Gay Court Watch, McCann looked on the bright side: 'At least we have a template for how to respond.'

I was a newly hatched dykeling when I moved onto Washington Avenue in 1981. The supportive women around me had known of a lesbian collective house in downtown Toronto that was looking for a new member. My interview meeting was toward the end of that summer – we sat around the kitchen table.

Maureen was dressed in khaki shorts and a white shirt, her legs and bare feet curled up against her on the kitchen chair. She was just back from a year in Vancouver and full of a languid sexuality. A lover in Vancouver and a lover in Toronto, and an openness about choosing an alternative way of having relationships.

Nancy didn't fit any of my ideas about lesbian feminists. She had a marvellous collection of frilly china teacups with no sense of irony. I didn't know you could be a dyke and still like domesticity. She was also in a non-monogamous relationship, though not by choice.

Sandy loved shopping, the movies, sci-fi, socialism, and union organizing.

Diana Meredith

An Experiment in Alternative Living:

Washington Avenue

They were all actively involved in feminism and constantly referred to an alphabet soup of organizations – IWD, RMG, LAR, OPSEU, CUPW.

When I moved in, I was still a student and wanted to store my cardboard moving boxes in the giant basement, just to be ready for the next moving day, which seemed to come often. Nancy and Sandy looked surprised when I said this. 'Oh, but we want you to stay and live here.' They didn't actually say 'forever' or 'happily ever after,' but that's what I heard. This was definitely going to be a different living experience. And it was. I had entered a new world.

The house itself was a large, rambling Victorian owned by the University of Toronto. The rent was cheap and the location superb: Spadina and Bloor, near to the subway and centrally located. All the placards and banners for International Women's Day were stored in piles in our basement. The sitting room was large and comfortable, spacious enough to hold political meetings many nights of the week. There were family photos on the wall – both from our families of origin and our new, constructed family of four plus Harold the cat – and sometimes a child.

We did have a child who lived with us one night a week, courtesy of Maureen, an anthropologist. We all benefited from her experience living in Africa, where the nuclear family wasn't necessarily the dominant social structure. Maureen was friends with an anthropologist couple who were also interested in alternative methods of child-raising. They lent us their child one night a week. We would pick Miriam up from daycare, bring her home for supper, keep her for the night, and return her to daycare in the morning.

Occasionally, we'd get her for a whole weekend. While we were all very busy, we did have house dinners four nights a week. We all tried hard to be home on Miriam nights, because she was such fun – there was a lightness in the air when she was around. I remember sitting at those dinners, feeling amazed that this was my life. I had love, laughter, family, children, and a community all in one, while at the same time feeling illicit, revolutionary, and even a little bit smug.

Nancy really wanted to have her own baby, so we decided to make one. I asked a close friend if he was willing to donate sperm. I made it clear that if he agreed, he was not going to be involved with the child, and the mother promised not to go after him for child support. He would do this for the sake of the emancipation of women.

Not that we put any of this down on paper. Nancy kept track of her cycle via basal thermometer. When the time was right, I'd give Jerry a call. He'd come over to the house and masturbate in my room at one end of the hall. He'd call out, and I'd carry a cup holding a blob of warm semen to Nancy at the other end of the hall. I saw more semen as a lesbian than I ever had as a straight woman. Sadly, no baby ever came about, though Nancy did get pregnant twice; both ended in miscarriage.

Of course, there were differences between us. One was class. At dinner one night, Sandy and Nancy challenged me about my sense of entitlement. Nancy pointed out that at these dinners, I often dominated the conversation. I'd hold forth and take a controlling hand in steering the discussion, bringing other people out. They proposed it was my sense of class privilege that gave me the confidence to occupy all that space. I was shocked and terribly hurt. I had witnessed men dominate space in classrooms, meetings, or dinner parties – as well as organizations and world politics – but I had never seen myself in that light. I had just come out as a lesbian feminist, so I was busy seeing how heterosexual privilege and patriarchy had shaped my choices. I preferred viewing myself as a victim rather than an oppressor. It was eye-opening and uncomfortable to see how class and, later, race intersected with these other social structures.

A steady stream of lovers, friends, comrades, workmates, and fellow students flowed through the house. One night, at one of our big, jolly house dinners, Maureen began to draw a network chart showing overlapping relationships of sex, love, work, and organizations. We had shared lovers, bonded with the same friends, worked in the same organizations, attended some of the same classes, and even shared the same therapist! I was amazed how this experiment in alternative living could be visually mapped into a web of community.

It lasted only five years, yet the ideology and vision of that period has stuck with me. Central to our domestic arrangement was the feminist rallying slogan 'The personal is political.' Now, some thirty years on, I'm a heterosexual woman married to, and living monogamously with, a cis-gendered man – the very social structures we were pushing against. And yet the idea that the experiences of my woman's body are relevant to the larger social discourse and to my work as an activist artist took hold in that house on Washington Avenue.

Two days after the inaugural city council meeting in December 1978, when I formally became mayor of Toronto, I received an invitation to speak at a rally called by the gay community for January in support of the *The Body Politic*, a local weekly.

I was generally aware of the issue involving the paper. In November 1977, *The Body Politic* published 'Men Loving Boys Loving Men,' an article arguing that men and youths could have non-exploitative relationships.

John Sewell

Speaking Up for the Gay Community, 1979

Toronto Sun columnist Claire Hoy wrote four articles attacking TBP and demanding police action on the article. The police raided the offices of the paper shortly after, seizing subscription lists, distribution and advertising records, corporate and financial records including the cheque book, classified ad records and addresses, and a number of books. A week later, criminal charges were laid for distribution of obscene material and possession of obscene material for the purpose of distribution.

At the time, I was not seen as a politician active on gay issues. Like most others on council, I endorsed a 1973 resolution that City employees could not be discriminated against on the basis of sexual orientation with regards to hiring, assignments, promotion, or dismissal. I felt comfortable with this policy and Toronto's leadership on the issue.

Generally my politics sided with those who felt under attack by powerful forces, and I had been active in trying to make the police more accountable. So when I was invited to this rally, it seemed reasonable that I would speak up on the issue. With my assistants Hugh Mackenzie and Lynn Spink, I talked to two friends much more involved in the issue: lawyers Lynn King and Clayton Ruby. Lynn King had chaired the fundraising committee in my mayoralty campaign and was now fundraising for the paper. I had known Clayton Ruby since the mid-1960s. As a prominent lawyer, he was representing the paper at the trial. Both strongly supported my acceptance of the invitation.

Their advice sealed the matter, and I agreed to speak. I wasn't aware the event would be held on the eve of the trial, nor did I expect the matter to be explosive. I simply saw this appearance as the sort of task that I, as mayor, should do – advocate in the cause of fairness and justice. That's what I had done as a member of council for nine years. The police laying charges was one thing, but seizing unrelated records they might use to intimidate members of the gay community was wrong.

Lynn King suggested I emphasize human rights and non-discrimination arguments. At this point, I didn't yet realize that when it came to addressing public issues, the mayor's voice was much more powerful than an alderman's voice.

Then the situation intensified. In December, a few weeks before the rally, police raided the Barracks, a club for homosexual men, and arrested thirty-five people on various charges relating to sexual behaviour. The gay community saw the raid as nothing short of intimidation prior to the trial, which was about to begin.

Some of those arrested feared their names would be disclosed, leading to the loss of their jobs, since that was a form of discrimination from which they were not protected. Others wondered why the Barracks had been raided when the activities there were allegedly no different from those at any other gay club.

Was this a new crackdown by the police?

As the new mayor, I took two actions: I met with Deputy Police Chief Jack Ackroyd to understand the police side of the story. I explored with him when the police might lay charges if they judged that a certain behaviour was deemed unacceptable and infringed community standards of behaviour. If police contemplated charges for activities that had been ongoing for some time – for example, gay clubs and bathhouses – shouldn't police give offenders a warning that they now considered such activities to be infringing community standards?

Then, at least, those involved would know that the rules were being interpreted differently and their acts now constituted criminal behaviour in the eyes of the police. If such notice had been given in the Barracks case, then law enforcement officials could argue that those charged had had fair warning and no one would be taken by surprise. Ackroyd was not amenable to such a process, but promised to give it further consideration. I confirmed our conversation by letter.

Second, I wrote to Attorney General Roy McMurtry, asking him to consider a ban on releasing the names of the men arrested. I repeated my concern that people had been charged with offences for which there were no clear rules. After all, the police had not deemed the behaviour unacceptable to the community in the past, and so those involved should not have to be subjected to embarrassing and perhaps harmful publicity because of a sudden change in enforcement.

McMurtry replied that he did not distinguish between this situation and any other involving a criminal charge, and he would not step in to prevent the names of those charged being made public.

These activities by the police, and the follow-up conversations I had, made it clear to me that this clampdown had become a significant political issue. But I did not doubt for a moment that my intervention was entirely appropriate.

As the January 3 rally approached, and media attention intensified, it was clear my attendance was becoming something of a cause célèbre. I would choose my words carefully, and reviewed the text of my speech with my assistants as well as with Lynn King and Clay Ruby.

The event took place in the evening at the University of Toronto Schools auditorium on Bloor Street. The room was crowded, with six to seven hundred people squeezing in. It was my first big performance as mayor. As I made my way to the stage, I noticed how bright the lights seemed around me, and how dark everything appeared beyond this pool of light.

I took my place behind the lectern, arranged my papers, and, in an even voice, began my speech.

At the end of June 1985, the Lesbian and Gay Pride Day Committee decided to occupy the street outside the 519 Church Street Community Centre. In previous years, no police officers had attended these events, and only showed up when the parade began. That year, however, we were confronted by Sgt. Daniel Quigley, 52 Division's obdurate bylaw-enforcement officer. He arrived early, demanding the stage and sound system be removed from the street, even though our street-occupation permit was in place. With the crowd on the verge of a riot, I quickly phoned 52 Division's duty sergeant to ask that Quigley be pulled out. The officer complied.

Over the next few years, as the 519's program coordinator and then its executive director, I noticed that officers rarely patrolled the streets of the Village, despite the area's commercial and residential density. It was as though the police had acknowledged that this was our safe territory or ghetto, where we looked after our own because the police would not, or could not, do the job.

Kyle Rae

Turning the Page

Some community members felt we should initiate an attempt at dialogue with the police, but the leaders of many local LGBT organizations disagreed. While a report commissioned in 1981 by the city council had recommended better relations, then-Chief Jack Ackroyd refused to acknowledge the legitimacy of the LGBT community. We had to wait until 1991, when Chief William McCormack finally took that step.

In the spring of 1991, I became aware of a wave of gay bashings. People were stopping me in the street to relate their own experiences or share stories they had heard. Then I had my own encounters: late one afternoon, as I walked down Church Street to an event at Woody's, I saw three louts verbally and physically abusing a slightly built gay man. After I intervened, they turned on me and chased me up the steps at Woody's. Somehow, I picked one guy up and hurled him down the stairs. Just two nights later, outside the Barn, a friend and I were surrounded on Granby Street by five homophobic thugs. Afterwards, I asked myself what was prompting this surge of violence.

I contacted 52 Division to alert the police. A day later, Sgt. Jim Sneep dropped by the 519 to discuss the situation. The division, he said, had no records of assaults occurring in the area. Sneep said he couldn't rectify the problem as long as the queer community, which had good reason not to trust the police, declined to report assaults. He left my office having agreed that we would try to resolve this problem.

It was clear to me the community needed a way to report assaults, but the victims had to believe the police would act on their information. For years, the police never attempted to understand that the lesbian and gay communities deserved protection under the law. (Indeed, at a high-profile social event

519 Community Centre executive director Kyle Rae (right), with NDP MPP Rosario Marchese, Pride 1990.

soon after the 1981 bathhouse raids, the head of the Intelligence Squad was heard to say that wherever you found the gay community, you found illicit sex, drugs, and pedophilia.)

A few days later, the 519 management team and I came up with the idea of a Gay Bashing Hotline, with calls coming in to a dedicated phone line at the community centre. The 519's staff would record all the details of the caller's experience. The victim could leave his or her name, or choose to be anonymous.

We then went a step further: to compel the police to act and keep records of gay bashing, we faxed copies of all the gay-bashing incident reports to 52 Division. Once a week, I would call to find out if the police were investigating, especially those reports with a named victim. The police responded: they investigated our reports. In some cases, the perpetrators were charged and eventually convicted.

Inspired by a new 1990 U.S. hate-crimes law that recognized gays and lesbians,[1] I asked Sgt. Sneep about collecting hate-crime statistics. We all knew perpetrators used pejorative terms while they assaulted queer people. But as Sneep confirmed, the police regarded 'gay' assault as merely assault. I pushed back. What, I asked, was domestic assault? Sneep couldn't easily answer that one.

1. On April 23, 1990, President George H. W. Bush signed into law the Hate Crime Statistics Act – the first federal statute of the United States to recognize gays and lesbians.

Perhaps the solution lay in the notion of sensitivity training for police. I pitched the idea to the 519's board of directors. One Wednesday evening in the spring of 1991, a swarm of police cars from 52 Division descended on the 519 for sensitivity training. We began with twelve officers. With Chris Phibbs, the 519's program coordinator, I walked them through a series of issues we felt needed to be addressed. We sought a visible police presence to serve and protect the lesbian and gay communities in response to escalating violence. We talked about appropriate language, and equality rights guaranteed by the Ontario Human Rights Code.

The dozen officers in the room had their own issues. Why, they asked, were the members of the community determined to be so visible and vocal? Several officers said they were fearful about HIV/AIDS. Some added that they felt unduly scorned because of the bathhouse raids a decade earlier.

I can't say the first event marked a breakthrough. The officers did not seem interested in the discussion and were very familiar with those parts of the Criminal Code reserved for queers: gross indecency, indecent acts, and the bawdy house laws.

Despite an inauspicious start, we held five more sessions, with the support of the superindendent of 52 Division, David Boothby (later the police chief). The sessions were eventually transferred up to Charles O. Bick College, the training school for Metro Police, and extended across the whole service.

Suddenly we were talking to sergeants from across the city, mostly men with little experience of the queer community. These officers demonstrated confirmed homophobic and sexist attitudes: disgust with male sexual practices, religious objections to homosexuality, resistance to the presence of female officers, and a lack of respect for the Ontario Human Rights Code.

During one particularly heated exchange, several officers demanded repeatedly that I appear in the queer media to ask gay men to stop having sex in parks. The men who participated in these activities were not necessarily local, I explained; they travelled long distances to avoid being recognized. Second, these men did not necessarily identify as gay, so they might not read gay newspapers. They were quite likely married with children but involved in this form of consensual male sex.

The officers didn't accept my answers.

I then asked if any of them had had heterosexual sex in their teens ... in a park. I could tell that some had. I asked if they ever arrested heterosexual couples for having sex in parks or if they just gave them a warning. They knew where I was going, and pushed back.

Chris Phibbs, in turn, had to deal not only with their sexism toward her but also with the way the officers referred to female co-workers. In 1991, the ranks of the police included only a few women. We'd emerge from these sessions feeling beaten up not so much by the officers' homophobia but by their sexism and aggressive male assumptions.

After I was elected to city council in 1992, I noticed that Sgt. Boothby had begun to actively engage with the queer community, establishing a foot patrol of twelve officers who volunteered to work in the area to establish a presence. They would introduce themselves to Village merchants and attend sessions of the Church-Wellesley Neighbourhood Police Advisory Committee.

The following year we asked the police to set up bike patrols, as was happening elsewhere in Toronto. When our contacts at 52 Division told us they didn't have the equipment, a remarkable thing happened: that neighbourhood advisory committee organized a fundraising event at Woody's to purchase five bikes.

It seemed like we had turned a page.

A s Toronto's queer community slowly moved out of a marginalized and hidden existence in the 1970s and 1980s, its members began to exert increasing pressure on the municipal political realm. Several key motions passed by city council highlight official Toronto's changing response to the community's growing visibility.

October 11, 1973

Toronto City Council in Motion:

Three Tentative Steps Toward Recognition

Motion: *'Employees of the City of Toronto are to be in no way discriminated against with regards to hiring, assignments, promotion, or dismissal, on the basis of their sexual orientation. 'Sexual orientation' is understood to include heterosexuality, homosexuality, and bisexuality.'*

The result of a lobbying effort by members of the Gay Alliance Toward Equality, this motion made Toronto the first legislative body in Canada to acknowledge the right of LGBT individuals to equal opportunity in employment. *The Body Politic* called it 'our first win.'

July 13, 1981

Motion: *'That Arnold Bruner be engaged by City Council to look into the disagreement and difficulties surrounding relations between the Police and the Homosexual Community and that he submit a report to His Worship The Mayor and City Council, recommending ways to bring about improved relations.'*

A response to the massive protests over the February 5 police bath raids, consultant Arnold Bruner's report, 'Out of the Closet: Study of the Homosexual Community and Relations with the Police,' acknowledged that the gay community was a legitimate community, identified significant homophobic attitudes within the Metro Toronto Police Service, made recommendations for improving police recruitment and training, and suggested the creation of a liaison mechanism between the police and the community. (Bruner's report is here: www.ncjrs.gov/pdffiles1/Photocopy/89100NCJRS.pdf.)

November 13, 1990

Motion: *'Recommends that the Council of the City of Toronto declare the last Sunday of June Lesbian and Gay Pride Day.'*

For five years, beginning in 1985, the Pride organizing committee tried unsuccessfully to persuade Mayor Art Eggleton to proclaim Lesbian and Gay Pride Day. Eggleton repeatedly rebuffed the requests, instead declaring a generic Equality Day in January 1990, to no one's satisfaction. Finally, in November 1990, council declared Pride Day, substituting 'City Council' in place of 'Mayor' to ensure passage. In 1992, June Rowlands became the first mayor to sign the proclamation.

I had two jobs at the end of 1985. During the day, I worked at Glad Day Books. In my nineteen-year-old baby-dyke mind, I was serving valiantly alongside my brothers on the front lines of our people's struggle against censorship. To a casual observer, I appeared to be dusting shelves.

At night, I worked at Rumours on Cumberland – a bar where, by some mysterious process, every evening between seven and eight, the straight, male, after-work drinkers would exit and be replaced by lesbians swaying on the dance floor, lesbians making out, and one recently transplanted Montreal lesbian – me – pretending to tend bar. I'd lied to get the job, telling people I could make the cocktail they wanted but only if they knew its name in French.

That year, the gay censorship wars in Canada had barely begun, but they would unfurl into a furious battle between the state and the gay community, serving as a rallying point that brought the lesbian community in closer contact with their gay brothers. But that fight also led to a deep rift that emerged in the late 1980s between anti-pornography feminists and the pro-sex lesbians looking for ways to express our desire. I stepped into this chasm early on.

Elle Flanders

Seized by the Cause:
Glad Day and the Canada Customs Battle

On my fifth day at Glad Day, November 12, 1985, I climbed the musty staircase to the still-mustier bookshop. It was a time of 'gay books.' They literally saved our lives. They shared intimate stories between lovers like us; they told us where we could find one another; they exhibited a history that allowed us a future. Except, as we would soon discover, that future was about to start dimming.

Four men were already waiting at the entrance as I rattled the keys in the locks. The door swung open, and they trailed in after me. We all knew where they were headed: the floor was especially worn in the porn corner beside the cash. These early customers were devotees of time-sensitive material, the newly unpacked porno mags: *In Touch, Mandate, Black Inches, Honcho*.

Not one man had spoken to me so far. After scanning and thumbing the magazines, they picked several at once, paid, and left. A stack of fresh porn in hand, they did not pause to discuss 'the struggle' with the teen-lez store clerk.

Had they asked, I could have told them that peeling back the white opaque plastic from the bundle of glossy men's porn magazines was as exciting for a young dyke like me as it was for them. The highly charged eroticism and the raw sexual energy was so at odds with Victorian Toronto mores. If these magazines made it past Canada Customs, we won collectively – and some, of course, won personally.

But on that day, a tall, moustachioed older man turned toward the desk and asked, 'Has *Bound and Gagged* shown up?'

'No,' I replied. 'Customs seized those with three other boxes yesterday.'

As the person who unpacked the boxes and came across those official notices, I had the most up-to-date information and was therefore, in my own mind, a deeply valuable resource to the community. I knew how many titles of *Drum* were taken, and which other books and magazines had been deemed obscene.

'Ha,' the man with the moustache said. 'They're probably jacking off to them right now in the back of Canada Customs House. Sons of bitches.'

The seizures weren't limited to porn. Canada Customs swiped *The Joy of Gay Sex* and *Damron Men's Travel Guide*, a benign publication about gay-friendly vacation spots, written exclusively by men, for men, and about men in places that often excluded women. Why did I care about this material? I had arrived from the fierce but claustrophobic Montreal Lesbian Feminist Separatist movement. Now I wanted to connect with gay men, whether they wanted me or not.

The censorship battle was something I could sink my teeth into – a salacious and sexy antidote to shouting 'Femmes sans peur!' on frozen Montreal streets. There was something aspirational about the relentless focus on sex in the censorship battle. I was not having much sex at the time, but I wanted to talk like these guys, leer openly, and thumb through magazines deemed obscene by the state. It was the edge.

We didn't know it on that winter morning, but within a few months, our political battles would reveal themselves to be more urgent than we could have imagined.

Rumours was less than a kilometre from Glad Day. But the lesbian bar and the gay bookstore stood worlds apart. A basement hangout on Cumberland, Rumours was located a few doors down from a rough-and-tumble straight tavern called the Pilot. Its heavy dark wooden bar, maroon leather booths, and tiny dance floor formed one planet in Toronto's tiny lesbian universe circa 1985.

I settled in as Rumours' bartender. Perhaps I couldn't make many drinks, but I happily talked to the customers – both the after-work men and the lesbians later on. The conversations didn't vary much: stories of infidelity, divorce, and unhappiness ran seamlessly across both shifts. At nineteen, I had little wisdom to offer women in their forties or fifties nursing broken hearts or looking for love. There was sometimes something desperate about the older dykes that made me pause. Would that be me someday, sitting on a stool, hoping the loneliness might abate with each new arrival? Today, people swipe through their phones to see who is around; then, the scene was in front of you – all of it. It was at once intimate and lonely.

People had until midnight to get their dancing in or find someone to go home with. My manager, Michael, who wore pink V-neck sweaters and a moustache comb on a gold chain, made sure that at exactly 12 a.m., all bottles were removed from the lit bar shelves and returned to a locked cupboard, in accordance with Ontario's liquor laws. Toronto in the 1980s felt like the 1950s – a potent mix of repressive Protestantism and its incumbent intolerances – racism, homophobia, and the rest.

Although Glad Day ran against Ontario's grain in some obvious ways, it also manifested the sexism of the time: men managed and women tidied. The men I worked with at Glad Day were not the political comrades I'd dreamed of, but they all captivated me, and I felt real affection for some.

On the day my picture appeared in *Xtra!*, the new Toronto gay newspaper, I showed the page to Don, who had worked at the bookshop for over a year. He suggested a different jacket would have benefited me, and the conversation turned to his weight loss. 'Fifty pounds in eight months!' he trilled, extending his arms with pride. He had bleached-blond hair tinted to a canary yellow that sat on his head like meringue. It curled in places that seemed impossible, and I wondered how he had survived without being gay-bashed. I had never met anyone that gay.

Don, from a small town in Ontario, took issue with my plaid shirt, which, he said, reminded him of the macho guys back home. I knew I had chosen the shirt to telegraph my committed dyke status but didn't have the vocabulary to explain – to myself or to him – that lesbians were appropriating and subverting hyper-masculine symbols. Don threw me: I fingered the soft flannel dejectedly and wondered if my lumberjack shirt was sending the right message.

If Don sometimes acted like the shop's mean girl, James was its sensitive intellectual. His straight light brown hair fell over his thin boyish face. The store's manager, he was only four years older than me but bookish and serious, exuding sagacity. James was kind, if a little peevish; I was sure he had read every volume in the shop.

I decided (unbeknownst to him) that he would become my gay literature and history mentor. His wire-framed round glasses and tweed jackets completed his librarian look, and his attenuated, somewhat shaky hands seemed out of place handling all the porn purchases. They were the store's lifeblood, while the literature on the shelves served as Glad Day's reason for being. To ensure customers understood that our mission was elevated and cerebral, even if our trade was in smut, we played classical music on the audio system.

Although Rumours had its regulars, the bar couldn't compete with the large, crowded, and frankly much more fun Chez Moi. In summer, the Chez had a patio with a crush of softball players from the newly formed Notso Amazon League. It was the first place in Toronto where I encountered dykes from all walks of life: sporty dykes, Notso political dykes, big-haired lesbians, rocker chicks.

The Chez's DJs stood high in their booths, out of reach of the sweaty, grinding lesbians below. It felt like the place to meet girls, with few other options beyond the occasional Gay Community Dance Committee parties at the Masonic Temple. I finally found a girl as Whitney Houston's 'How Will I Know' pounded through the dance-floor speakers. The Bronski Beat had brought us our anthem — 'Smalltown Boy' – and thereafter we convinced ourselves that every song had a hidden gay agenda. The DJ Elaine, the wise older dyke who every baby-dyke needed to help navigate new lesbian terrain, played Rumours, the Chez, and later Felines, another bar I tended with mediocrity. On the day my lover dumped popcorn over my head at Rumours (I did cheat on her), George Michael crooned to me that I shouldn't have wasted my chance, and I knew it was impossible I'd ever dance again the way I'd danced with my popcorn-dumping ex. And then Michael fired me.

While 1985 felt like a meteoric time for a community bursting at the seams, and a beginning for me, that moment marked the dawn of a catastrophe that was coming fast and furious. Not long after my stint at Glad Day, I heard that James had died, as had his partner six months earlier. Then Don died, and so did Michael. AIDS had replaced the censorship wars, and dykes and fags mourned and moved together.

W hen we moved Buddies in Bad Times Theatre to 12 Alexander Street in 1994, we saw ourselves, to some degree, as *settlers*, and we were not untinged by a passionate queer zealotry. We were staking out queer territory, and the stakes were high.

The *Oxford Dictionary* defines that loaded word as 'a person who settles in an area, typically one with no or few previous inhabitants.' The Palestinian territories under Israeli occupation are 'settlements.' The first West Bank settlers 'believed that Israel's victory the prior year was an act of G-d,' says the Jewish Virtual Library.

Indeed, extreme religious belief has often spurred settlement. Early New Englanders belonged to Protestant sects fleeing England. My own ancestors were Puritan settlers who hated their bodies with an ominous intensity. Zealotry is overpowering and can have murderous consequences, some of it directed at sexuality.

Sky Gilbert

Theatre as Settlement: Buddies in Bad Times

Peter Martyr's *Decades of the New World* tells us that the Spanish conquistador Vasco Núñez de Balboa, seeking to settle Panama in 1513, murdered forty effeminate, cross-dressed, sodomitical Indigenous men. 'He founde ... many other younge men in womens apparell, smoth & effeminately decked, which ... he commaunded to bee gyven for a pray to his dogges.' Passionate belief, sexuality, and the threat of violence: all have a special relationship to Buddies in Bad Times Theatre.

Buddies had only had one previous home – 142 George Street, an old gas station converted to a video studio by dance aficionados Lawrence and Miriam Adams before we rented it in 1991. Prior to that, we had been homeless – unless you count shared space with other companies in the early eighties on Danforth, King Street, and the old Poor Alex. We were then part of the Theatre Centre – founded by Buddies along with Necessary Angel, Autumn Leaf, Nightwood Theatre, and AKA Performance Art in 1979 – but that meant we didn't have our own identity. When the old City-owned Toronto Workshop Productions building on Alexander became available, we went for it.

I worked hard to secure that space with Buddies' general manager Tim Jones and board president Sue Golding. We were an unbeatable trio. Or at least we thought we were; in point of fact, our dynamite proposal came in second. At first the space went to Christopher Wooten and a dance/theatre producing 'consortium' (whatever that is!) that had promised to put on commercial runs of successful shows. But this nebulous project never materialized. So we applied to the City again, and the theatre was given to us. But not without a battle. Led by the right-wing Beach alderman Tom Jakobek, city council tried to stop our bid but didn't succeed.

Sky Gilbert at the naming of lane beside Buddies in Bad Times Theatre.

After we opened, the *Toronto Sun* attacked us in print. One letter to the editor said Buddies was not a theatre but a depraved sex club. A headline warned of 'Live Sex Acts.' 'A professional could probably tell you what kind of tortured soul sees as his worst enemy a middle-aged mommy,' wrote Christina Blizzard, the fundamentalist, right-wing, fiscally conservative columnist, on February 1, 1994. 'I suspect Mr. Gilbert wants me to smack him and tell him he's a naughty boy ... This is not art. This is a cry for help from a sad and twisted soul.' However, the *Sun*'s ploy to discredit Buddies didn't work either, because we actually were a legitimate theatre, buoyed by significant support from the arts community.

All this was mostly about art. But it was also more than a little bit about sex.

When Buddies was housed at the Theatre Centre on Danforth Avenue, a handsome, suave, young arts bureaucrat named Peter Caldwell came up to me and said, 'You know what I *really* like about Buddies? I like that I can kiss my boyfriend here.'

I was very moved.

Now, of course it's true that Peter could have kissed his boyfriend in a gay bar, or in the privacy of his own home. But that's the point, don't you see? Straight people can kiss their partners anywhere they want; we could only do it in bars or at home. The reason you need a gay 'ghetto' is so you have a place where you can hold your boyfriend's or girlfriend's hand or, let's face it, get nasty in an alley or a washroom while doing blow (the way straight people do in the clubs on Richmond) without getting harassed, arrested, or beaten up.

This, as I see it, is primarily the reason for the existence of urban gay ghettos from the 1960s on. In the 1980s, when Buddies was coming into its own with my plays *Drag Queens on Trial* and *Drag Queens in Outer Space*, the Church Street Village was thriving after the closure of gay haunts on Yonge Street like the Parkside Tavern, the St. Charles, and the leather bar Trax. By the mid-1990s, when we opened Buddies, we carefully crafted our neon sign to be visible from Yonge Street. It felt to some of us sex-positive renegades at Buddies like a land claim to make Yonge part of a newer, larger gay ghetto.

The very term *ghetto* is offensive to some because it evokes the Holocaust (though the word traces back to sixteenth-century Venice). But the truth is, the Nazis forced homosexuals to wear pink triangles and eventually rounded them up and murdered them. Many of us queers do feel – to this day – that we need a 'gay street' in order to be intimate in public. Thus we end up somewhat confined to that street, feeling like (but obviously not the same as) Jews when they were forcibly confined to the ghettos.

Frankly, today these views would be considered radical by most gay and lesbian people. For most have rejected the moniker *queer*. Gays and lesbians now are – many of them proudly, sometimes even aggressively – socially conservative. Some long for the good ol' days of Stephen Harper, faithfully attend church, and support our troops and local police. Like my father, who – when he saw my cousin Meg kissing her boyfriend at a Connecticut town fair in 1967 – would often say, 'There's no need for such displays in public!' But as a good old-fashioned sexual liberationist, I believe that sex should be public and religion should be private.

Or maybe sex is my religion: that's how crazy I am. Even when – as I get older and older – I spend less and less time actually *committing the act*, I still can't help nursing a nostalgia for it, and for the young who, I know, still like it (if perhaps more secretly and virtually than before). For that reason, it makes me sad to know that, even today, if LGBT folk take their same-sex dates to a straight Richmond Street bar and start necking, they might get more than disapproving looks: they might be kicked out or beaten up.

That's the way it was then, and (sigh!) that's still the way it is now. Which is why we at Buddies were so happy to occupy a space right next to Yonge Street back in 1994. We were transporting our religion to a new land and getting a little bit closer to taking over foreign territory where we knew that, frankly, we might not be welcome.

You may call us settlers if you like.

The term is certainly just as fraught, controversial, and paradoxical as queer culture itself.

Black Friday? by Audrey Butler premiered at the Actors' Lab on May 10, 1990, to much acclaim. It was shortlisted for the Governor General's Award for Drama and served as a signature work in Toronto's lesbian theatre scene at the time.

Play Synopsis: After six years away, Terry, the 'prodigal' daughter, motorbikes from Toronto back to Cape Breton with Spike, her Black lesbian lover. She wants to look through the papers of her father – a famous labour organizer blacklisted by the union – partly to write a celebratory magazine article about him. But she also wants to see whether he wrote to her when he left Cape Breton, her mother, and her twelve-year-old self following Black Friday, when the steel company closed after breaking the union. In the process, she learns other truths about her father and reveals truths about her lesbianism to her mother and grand- mother.

Alec Butler
Black Friday...
With and Without
the Question Mark

The first version of *Black Friday* – the one without the question mark – premiered in 1989 at the 4-play Festival of Lesbian and Gay Works at Buddies in Bad Times Theatre. It was the beginning of an intensive workshop process that led, a year later, to *Black Friday?* We spent most of that time writing grant applications as well as a production-ready script.

But the difference between the two productions is more than the matter of a question mark at the end of the title. The very process of working on the play from the first version to the second took place in the midst of the revo- lutionary fever that led to the dismantling of the Berlin Wall in early November 1989, and continued afterwards. The queer community in Toronto was full of revolutionary excitement, but at the same time, there was queer resistance to the backlash from the HIV/AIDS crisis.

The energy of 1989 had been first watered by the sweat of queer bodies on the gay dance floors in 1984, the year of the Eurythmics' song 'Sex Crimes,' from the soundtrack for the film version of George Orwell's seminal book. During the mid-to-late-1980s, we would meet up after midnight with other radical queer punks to spray-paint downtown Toronto with bright pink queer- culture graffiti. We were environmentally conscious queers, tagging the very cement sidewalks we strutted along during the day with shocking pink paint that washed away with the next rain. Some of us lived in queer communes. We found community, lovers, and inspiration for erotic poetry. We shared infor- mation about safe fisting and female ejaculation, cruised, and picked each other up at dance parties after the Take Back the Night and Women's Day marches.

Our uniform in all seasons was steel-toed boots, black leather motorcycle jackets with red-and-black homemade 'Question Authority' pins on the lapels,

Marcia Johnson as Spike in *Black Friday?*

and thick steel cock rings in the leather shoulder epaulets. We accessorized with black-and-white kafias around our throats – throats sore from shouting, 'We're here, we're queer, get used to it.' Same-sex queer kiss-ins were all the rage in homophobic spaces; all public spaces were fair game for our in-your-face queer politics. The 'Read My Lips' posters depicting hot punk lesbians kissing and posted along the light poles on College Street were a sight to behold.

The Pride March morphed into a parade. Although it always had a parade-like atmosphere, the march now had a sound system on the back of a rented half-ton truck blaring the Parachute Club's anthem, 'Rise Up.' It was led by amazon dykes in leather vests straddling motorcycles, with their beautiful fierce femmes sitting in 'bitch seats,' or sometimes reversed, with the butch in the bitch seat. Pride also featured a proud display of outrageous drag queens.

Queer artists emulated the artwork and activism of Keith Haring on the streets of New York City, as well as the new-wave feminist anthem, Carole Pope's 'High School Confidential.' We read Audre Lorde's book *Sister Outsider.*

In Toronto, all genders and orientations worked arm-in-arm with straight but not narrow allies; we shared alternative performance spaces with other fringe-theatre companies – not necessarily queer, but radical. At the Party Centre, on Church Street between Shuter and Dundas, Buddies in Bad Times' Dyke Committee launched 'Strange Sisters: A Lesbian Cabaret,' in 1986. It was a first.

By the time 1989 rocked and rolled around, we had written and produced two plays about lesbian lives. *Black Friday* was my fourth play, but my third to focus on lesbian characters. I started working on the first draft while a member of the Six

Playwrights Unit at Tarragon Theatre in 1988. The idea for a play about a working-class lesbian going back home to the Maritimes to come out to their family had been on the back burner while we wrote and produced our second and third plays, *Cradle Pin* and *Claposis*. The ideas had started to percolate during the summer of 1983, when we were (courtesy of Blythe Theatre Festival) playwright-in-residence for three weeks in southern Ontario farm country, with the smell of cow manure in the air.

It reminded us of home on Horne's Road, a country road leading to the Atlantic Ocean at Mira Gut, Cape Breton Island, where *Black Friday* was set. The play was produced as a public reading at Nightwood Theatre's Groundswell Festival in 1988.

There was so much alternative theatre being produced in Toronto in the late 1980s that it was a mad scramble to find a place to perform *Black Friday?* In early winter, we put a down payment on a six-week rental on Actors' Lab, with grant money raised through Temperamental Journey, a second theatre company we co-founded with fellow Cape Breton playwright and director Bryden MacDonald.

The company included all but one of the actors who had been involved in the earlier underfunded workshop production. It was a goddess-send that lesbian filmmaker Kate Johnston again played the main role of Terry. Another goddess-send was Marcia Johnson, who played Terry's lover Spike. Some elements that had developed from necessity in that bare-bones production remained in the 1990 version. For example, in the 1989 production, the actors sat beside each other in a church pew found in the Actors' Lab, where they watched the play when they were not onstage. This device gave the play a surreal aspect, even though the living room setting appeared realistic. The 1990 staging had a set and lighting design by Chris Plunkett that also subtlety enhanced the surreal/real script elements.

As well, in the revised script, Spike is answering a question asked by Roddy, Terry's straight white ex-boyfriend who was left in Cape Breton when Terry fled. Roddy asks the $64,000 question: 'Why it is important to be out, to be blatant about it. Is it just the sex?'

> SPIKE: *Oh Roddy, it's everything, it's the way they walk, the way they talk, the way they think. Their stories, their hands, their hearts. Their wise loving ways. The way they make me feel. Sooooo good. When I was little I didn't know what a 'girl' was, I didn't know I was a girl, not a 'boy' but not a 'girl' either. I was just me. A tweensy. Now I feel like a whole person. Naw, fucking is only part of it, Roddy. The idea of women having sex in a society that hates sex and women, not to mention lesbians, makes it dangerous. For me. For us. I hate the danger but I take it on. Because I'm a dyke. I love women. Does that answer your question?*

This declaration illustrates the difference between the two versions. Roddy's answer and the question did not exist in the version without the question mark produced in 1989.

But there is also another reason for the question mark. Through the process of developing the play, I had began to perceive Spike, Terry's lover, as Black. For me, there was a clear connection between homophobia, racism, and the system that destroyed Terry's father, a union organizer in a steel plant that was shut down on what became known as Black Friday.

> SPIKE: *It pisses me off, the way people abuse the word* black – *Black Friday, black Monday, black market, black clouds over your heads, blacklisted black, black, black…*

Black Friday? was inspired by the revolutionary times in which we lived, loving and creating lesbian theatre and community in Toronto.

David Rayside greets you with a kiss on the cheek, twice, and you have to be prepared. He seems to use this brief moment of intimacy, a rare gesture outside his home province of Quebec, to reassure you that he sees you. He knows who you are, even if you are an underdressed graduate student at a fundraising gala where he is the guest of honour. And there is a good chance he bought your ticket.

David's generosity is widely known, as is his academic work, which is the headwaters of an entire scholarship on the roots and meaning of equity in North America. Born in 1947 in Montreal, David came of age during the Quiet Revolution of the 1960s, a period marked by intense social change. As his hometown was welcoming the world at Expo '67, David was in Carleton University's Political Science program, where he completed an Honours BA in 1969.

That same year, Bill C-150 passed third reading in the House of Commons by a vote of 149 to 55, partially decriminalizing homosexuality in Canada. In September, the Official Languages Act came into force, making French and English official languages with equal status in the Government of Canada. These two legislative keystones are familiar characters in David's writing. In 1975, he finished a PhD at the University of Michigan, and his thesis focused on the politics of language difference in Canada and Belgium. Since then, he has written extensively on sexual diversity, gender, and religion, often bringing in graduate students as co-writers and collaborators.

Such rich scholarship is consuming, but David has always found time for activism. In 1974, he joined the University of Toronto, and immediately became interested in feminism and women's equality movements on campus. He helped develop sexual harassment policies as he worked on his first book about class, language, and gender politics in the small town of Alexandria, Ontario. Although the quads and grounds of the university were known cruising areas for young queers at that time, it took David a while to feel comfortable about his own sexuality. The gay liberation movement was unfolding around him, but it was not until 1979 that he turned his attention to gay activism. He was a member of the *Body Politic* collective and managed a legal defence fund following the arrest of several members on obscenity charges.

In 1981, David joined the Right to Privacy Committee, which formed in response to the bathhouse raids. It was through this activist work that he was introduced to Gerald Hunt, who was a member of the RTPC's Toronto Gay Street Patrol, a group of gay men and lesbians trained in self-defence who patrolled the Village and responded to queer-bashing incidents, which were

Rebecka Sheffield

Disengagement Is No Longer an Option:

David Rayside

on the rise at that time. After meeting through a mutual friend and having dinner together at Hart House in late 1984, they became partners in life and love.

Shortly after, David joined with a group of lawyers and activists on the campaign to add sexual orientation to the Ontario Human Rights Code. The debates pitted gay and lesbian activists against a mobilizing religious right, amidst a divisive political backdrop. The recently ousted Progressive Conservative Party, employing tactics of homophobia and rhetoric around religious freedoms, used the proposed amendments against the ruling Liberals and supporting NDP. The strategy, however, was unsuccessful and marked the beginning of a series of legislative changes in Ontario in favour of protections and rights for lesbian and gay people. (The Ontario Legislature finally approved the changes on December 2, 1986, by a vote of 64-45.)

David could surely be called an institution builder. He was co-founder of the Canadian Lesbian and Gay Studies Association/*Société canadienne des études lesbiennes et gaies*, which raised up queer scholarship to a legitimate field of research. He also helped develop the Positive Space Campaign at the University of Toronto, signalling a new willingness on behalf of the institution to recognize and respond to the marginalization of LGBTQ people on campus. Behind the scenes, David used every single encounter with university administrators, fellow faculty, and community partners to convince them of the need for a formal academic home for sexual diversity studies (SDS). His work finally came to fruition in 1998, with the establishment of the first undergraduate program.

The impact was profound. The program sparked interest from emerging and established scholars from around the world. David again put himself to the task of securing resources and financial security for the program. In 2004, David became the founding director of the newly established Centre for Sexual Diversity Studies, which was given substantial philanthropic support by Mark S. Bonham. The program has expanded to include graduate programs and a still growing roster of its own interdisciplinary courses.

The cornerstone of David's academic and activist work is his insistence that LGBTQ people belong in mainstream culture and politics. 'Disengagement from mainstream politics … is no longer an option,' he wrote in 1983 in *On the Fringe: Gays and Lesbians in Politics*. 'The opening up of opportunities in courts, parties and legislatures demands participation, even if only for preventing setbacks.' At the time, there were no openly gay politicians in Canada, although some elected officials were quietly out to their constituents. NDP MP Svend Robinson came out in 1988. In Toronto, Kyle Rae campaigned as an openly gay candidate and won a seat in the 1991 Ward 6 election; he was succeeded by Kristyn Wong-Tam. George Smitherman was Ontario's first openly gay cabinet minister. The 2014 election of Kathleen Wynne to the position of Ontario premier – a Canadian first – would suggest that sexuality may no longer affect LGBTQ politicians' electability.

Setbacks, however, are always a possibility, and David's work has taught us to be vigilant in our attention to the barriers that prevent LGBTQ people from fully participating in society. He retired from teaching at the University of Toronto in 2013 and was elected fellow of the Royal Society of Canada in 2014. Graduate students can still consider themselves lucky that David remains an active part of the Bonham Centre, working diligently to sustain its important programming. He knows who you are.

T oronto was the birthplace of the first queer women's sex bathhouse in North America – the Pussy Palace, later renamed the Pleasure Palace out of respect for the diversity of women's bodies.[1]

Notoriously, in 2000, Toronto police raided the Pussy/Pleasure Palace (PP) and pressed liquor licence charges against two volunteers. Two years later, an Ontario judge tossed out all the charges and rebuked the police officers involved. And in 2004, the organizers won a $350,000 settlement in a human rights complaint against the Toronto Police Service, which was then forced to change its policies on the search and detention of trans people.

I was one of the organizers of the PP. I saw what followed the raid as mostly a success: the charges against our friends were tossed, we won our human rights complaint, and great grassroots organizations received money from the human rights settlement. But I had doubts at the time, which have stayed with me and blossomed into larger questions. Were the successes of PP organizing part of a growing tolerance for police and law enforcement within LGBTQ politics? And did we unintentionally help bring ourselves to the place we're at now – where many queers believe strongly that the police have a place in our community?

At the time of the raid, Toronto police were ramping up their harassment of gay and lesbian businesses. In June and July 1999, the cops raided the Bijou, a men's bar in Toronto. Eighteen charges of indecency were laid against patrons, the bar was charged with liquor licence offences, and an employee was charged with obstruction of justice. Eventually all of the criminal charges were dropped. The bar was forced to close down but then reopened without its liquor licence. In March and April 2000, the cops raided the men's naked parties at the Barn and charged them with permitting disorderly conduct under the Liquor Licence Act. Then, at 12:45 a.m. on September 15, five hefty and intimidating male officers from 52 Division entered the Pussy Palace. When the woman at the door told them it was an all-women event, they told her that if she did not let them in she could be charged with obstructing justice. The officers split up and proceeded to search every nook and cranny of the space until 2:15 a.m. Although many women were naked or semi-naked, we were explicitly prevented from warning participants of the police presence. Many women were deeply angered and emotionally distressed by the police presence. During and immediately after the raid, many of the participants left.[2] Going back to the Stonewall rebellion and before, so much queer resistance begins with resistance to police abuse.

Chanelle Gallant

No-Cop Zone?
Reflections on the Pussy Palace Raid

A few details are important to understanding the meaning and impact of the PP raid on larger queer politics. The first is that the raid began with undercover women officers who surveilled the party extensively and took notes on the public queer sex they observed – notes that then became police property. (The Stonewall rebellion in June 1969 also began with women undercover officers collecting evidence on patrons at the Stonewall before they tipped off nearby uniformed male officers to begin arriving.) After the women officers had entered, the male officers barged past the security at the door. Both the undercover and uniformed police took evidence that suggested they intended to press sex-related charges against the patrons: the police confiscated signage for a 'porn room' and recorded surveillance notes on the BDSM sling room. Following the raid, police gave differing explanations for why they had conducted the inspection, none of which were credible to the LGBTQ community, the straight press, or the court.

The raid aroused anger among many LGBTQ folks, including those who'd been affected by the brutal 1981 raids on men's bathhouses. The bullying presence of straight male officers seemed like a particularly sexist twist in the ongoing history of police attacks on LGBTQ communities. After PP organizers held a community meeting to talk about and formulate a response, hundreds of people spontaneously poured out onto the streets and marched to the police headquarters, shouting, 'Pussies bite back.'

The Defence

The defence strategy of the lead legal counsel rested on the argument that all of the evidence was inadmissible because the male officers (but only the male officers) had violated the defendants' constitutional right to be protected from gender discrimination. Lawyers argued that the defendants – and all of those in attendance at the club that night – had been subjected to what was essentially a strip search by male officers. The defence spoke about the transgender people at the bathhouse in ways that obscured and invalidated their gender identities in order to uphold the defence's narrative of men doing a sexist 'panty raid.' Though it was never explicitly discussed, all of the male officers were presumed to be heterosexual. Commentators in queer media echoed this argument. Typical headlines about the raid had sentiments like 'Peeping Toms: Cops Disrupt Lesbian Bathhouse.'

Only a few observers raised the question of our right not to be policed at all. Instead, speaking from a popular perspective on the raid, Justice Peter Hryn characterized male officers as having committed 'visual rape' because men watched undressed women who had a reasonable expectation that (presumably straight) men were not going to be present.

The women officers, however, did more than just watch us while we were naked – the female cops watched and recorded us having sex, something the male officers did not. And because the female cops, unlike their male counterparts, were undercover, we had no way to protect ourselves from their gaze. A number of witnesses at the trial affirmed that the presence of women officers did not distress or concern them. The judge and the broader communities, both queer and straight, seemed to agree: the problem was one of predacious men, not that policing in and of itself is predatory.

As a member of the collective that organized the Pussy Palace from 2000 to 2003, I felt panic that night when I knew police officers were on-site. It does make a difference to me that (presumably) straight men were present, taking sexual pleasure in our nudity. They probably got off on our fear and distress, too. I don't wish to minimize the traumatizing effect that male cops had on women that night, many of whom – like myself – are survivors of male sexual violence.

The problem I have is that by focusing exclusively on the male officers' gender, we naturalized and legitimized the right of police to be in our space, as long as the cops were women. Women officers also brought with them the massive power of the state that night.

What about their illicit pleasures? (Their sexual orientations were never discussed and were presumed irrelevant.) What about the ways those police violated us? What about how, as agents of the state, they, too, carried the power of police to define us, to press charges; to strip-search and abuse us; and to report any of us to immigration enforcement or to the Children's Aid Society? What about their power to sexually abuse as police officers, who, for the most part, live above the law and are so rarely held accountable for sexual violence?

When I recently reread the human rights decision, I was shocked to see that in our complaint, we had demanded that the police actively recruit LGBTQ people into the service. At the time, I felt the police were a necessary evil, a terrible and mostly misapplied form of power that was necessary for the greater good. But a rainbow-coloured fist is still a fist. I didn't know we had other options. Since then, I've learned about the activist movement led by Black and Indigenous people to abolish prisons and police, and replace them with more effective, just, and humane alternatives.

The legal defence did their best to protect the PP defendants from sexist and homophobic police harassment and intimidation. But we missed an opportunity in our activism around the case to push for an agenda that went beyond putting a rainbow on the police force and instead call into question the right of police to police our communities at all.

Pursuing a legal argument of gender discrimination by male officers required us to make transphobic arguments about who is part of the queer community and forced us to accept a presumption that any policing can be just or fair. This concession provides the historical context for today, when many privileged members of the LGBTQ community want to be seen as 'the good gays' by distancing themselves from the trans, racialized, and criminalized people who sparked our movement.

A revolution that began with a three-day pitched battle against police oppression by trans women of colour, drag queens, and homeless hustling youth at the Stonewall Inn morphed into a movement where many privileged members of the LGBTQ community insist that police officers belong in our communities and our Pride marches.

LGBTQ existence is increasingly being drained of its potential to challenge structural inequities and to demand radical institutional change. So I want this to go on the record: some of us queers don't just want the cops out of our bedrooms, our Pride marches, and our bathhouses. Some us want to dismantle the cops entirely. I hope we keep fighting for that.

1. Janet Rowe, founding member of the Toronto Women's Bathhouse Committee, who was then the women's programs coordinator for the AIDS Committee of Toronto.

2. This section is adapted from an article I co-authored with Loralee Gillis entitled 'Pussies Bite Back: The Story of the Women's Bathhouse Raid,' in *Torquere*, Vol. 3, 2001.

On May 28, 2016, activists, scholars, and artists gathered at the University of Toronto for a daylong symposium entitled 'Paper Trail: The Legacies of *The Body Politic*,' marking the forty-fifth anniversary of the paper's founding.

White queer historians, activists, and some founders shared largely congratulatory reflections on *TBP*'s impact and historical importance, performing a distinctly white version of the public archive that has become recognizable as queer Toronto. Few speakers offered critical reflections on the ways that anti-Black racism repeatedly played out within *TBP*'s content and collective publishing process – for example, a 1985 advertisement in the paper by a white cis gay man calling for a Black 'houseboy.'

At the time, the ensuing controversy became a catalytic moment of consciousness-raising within both the *Body Politic* collective and Toronto's wider queer community about racism, classism, and the sexualization of Black and racialized bodies. As University of Manitoba queer historian David S. Churchill chronicles, the collective's members met for three hours with community groups, including Lesbians of Color, Zami, and Gay Asians of Toronto, to discuss why the ad was offensive and had no place in the paper.

Jin Haritaworn, Ghaida Moussa, and Syrus Marcus Ware, with Alvis Choi, Amandeep Kaur Panag, and Rio Rodriguez

Marvellous Grounds:
QTBIPOC Counter-Archiving against Imperfect Erasures

During the symposium, Rinaldo Walcott, Lali Mohamed, and Syrus Marcus Ware's papers contested the evening's familiar celebratory tone driven by what Jin Haritaworn has elsewhere called 'queer nostalgia.' Both Mohamed's and Ware's papers called the work and organizing of Black activists and ancestors (including that of Black trans women Sumaya Dalmar and Monica Forrester) into the room and into the conversation about what rises to the status of a queer archive. They highlighted how queer archives celebrate white queer subjects as the only historic subjects, and erase QTBIPOC, thereby treating us as perennial newcomers with little historical agency and oversight of our own.

In the question period following these papers, there was a dramatic backlash from white audience members who responded by explaining that *TBP* had been under pressure at the time, facing raids and homophobic backlash, and that there had simply not been time or energy to 'address everything.' These comments excused the lack of racialized content by imagining queer content as essentially white. They also ignored the very real issues facing racialized queer spaces, many of which already existed at the time.

For example, the Lesbian Organization of Toronto's main organizing site, home to many women-of-colour gatherings, also faced police raids, according to leZlie Lee Kam. In addition, the Black community was facing ongoing attacks by the police. Is it a coincidence that the alliances that Black queer organizers formed then gave rise to an abolitionist movement that outlived the brief period of white queer antagonism with the criminal legal system?

Around the same time as 'Paper Trail,' the distance of white queers from their anti-carceral history was brought home by their violent responses to Black Lives Matter Toronto actions against police racism and its pinkwashing. In the same tradition of Black queer revolt, BLMTO resisted the Toronto mayor's apology for the 1981 bathhouse raids, as well as the presence of uniformed police in the 2016 Pride parade. They enacted a very different queer genealogy, where Stonewall is remembered as an abolitionist movement led by transgender women who are Black and people of colour.[1]

The Marvellous Grounds (MG) collective, which was formed in 2013 and co-authored this chapter, seeks to document precisely these histories and unruly presents that serve as a counter-archive to the nostalgic, triumphant figure of 'queer Toronto.'[2] These histories differ from dominant accounts that figure white – and often cis – subjects as 'pioneers' of the places, periods, activisms, and artistic creations that become memorable and noteworthy as queer. Such a queer cartography and historiography reinforces a gay imperialist view of Toronto as a beacon of LGBT rights[3] while positioning queer and trans Black, Indigenous, and people of colour (QTBIPOC) as absent from, or newcomers to, queer spaces and histories.

This results in a colonial archive that is fetishistic in queer-of-colour theorist Sara Ahmed's sense: it is cut off from the violent processes that produced it. QTBIPOC counter-narratives take issue with these tellings, calling out the racial, sexual, and colonial constitution of the map and the archive. As Paola Bacchetta, Fatima El-Tayeb, and Jin Haritaworn write in their article in *Society & Space*, they bring to the fore how pivotal stories get told, which 'subjects, objects, conducts, events, and histories are heavily inscribed and remembered,' and which are 'forgotten, erased, or denied altogether.'

The MG project seeks to provide a counter-archive that overhauls the crucial question of how we remember. We ask what is the how, when, and why of queer archives and methods. Who is worthy of archiving and thus remembering?

In the QTBIPOC contributions we have gathered, storytelling, performance, and other creative practices repeatedly emerge as embodied and continuous acts of archiving – a means, as MG member Alvis Choi notes in their master's work, through which QTBIPOC ancestral memory is called upon to represent queer and racialized realities in the present while envisioning new futures.

From Colour Me Dragg to Asian Arts Freedom School, from the drag musical to the anti-conventional burlesque platform of Unapologetic Burlesque, QTBIPOC artists, performers, and organizers tell stories to not only honour and remember the past, but also to embody and prefigure alternatives, literally living the futures we dream of in the here and now. These QTBIPOC storytellers reveal our powerful capacity to reinvent our genders and sexualities beyond the narrow moulds of white cis-hetero-patriarchy.

These historic and spatial interventions are marvellous. They use art, as Afro-Surrealist Suzanne Césaire describes, to perform a 'permanent readiness for the marvellous.' In Syrus Marcus Ware's words, 'they dream up futures where we can all make it.'

The stories archived by MG thus challenge the colonial definition of the archive, one that is invested with permanence, stability, and legitimacy defined by authority. The works present a powerful counter-archive that meets memory where memory happens: in our kitchens and parks, on fiercely fought-for stages, on street corners, and on steps. This counter-archive also meets memory in a time of need. Younger folks hunger for elders, in a context where QTBIPOC art and activism QTBIPOC undergo erasure – where QTBIPOC experience generations of burnout and premature death. MG digs into the archive to point us toward new pasts, to make better sense of our present, and to envision different futures.

Inspired by Sherene Razack's concept of 'unmapping' – a methodology of mapping that challenges rather than reproduces racial and colonial logics of time and space – we understand counter-archiving not merely to be the search for the QTBIPOC subject in the unlikely spaces of the past and the global south, nor are we simply trying to add QTBIPOC to an existing archive, now more colourful – rather, we wish to lay open the terms that enable past and present erasures in the first place.

The MG counter-archive highlights that these violent erasures are imperfect and incomplete. We rework anti-colonial feminist critic Jacqui Alexander's concept of the 'palimpsest' – a parchment that has been inscribed two or three times, the previous text having been imperfectly erased and remaining party visible – in order to mark the collective power of QTBIPOC to resist complete erasures from Toronto's histories.

MG's contributors bear witness to these imperfect erasures, highlighting a history going back to at least the 1970s and 1980s and a Toronto brimming with QTBIPOC organizing around homelessness, LGBTQ activism, HIV/AIDS education, anti-apartheid activism, disability justice, and other forms of marginalization and oppression.

Community members were getting together to support anti-apartheid and other international struggles – for example, by writing letters to South African gay rights activist Simon Nkoli. Queer and trans people of colour were also centrally involved in the city's creative political arts initiatives, such as Desh Pardesh, Mayworks Festival of the Arts, and Counting Past Two. Mainstream LGBTQ and municipal archives have omitted these initiatives, which nevertheless persist in our oral traditions of telling and retelling. In the words of Black trans community leader Miss Major, we are 'still fucking here.'

One example of a palimpsest that is told and retold, written and overwritten, in this counter-archive, is 'the Steps' in front of the former twenty-four-hour Second Cup at Church and Wellesley streets. As retold by MG contributor Aemilius Ramirez, in their MG contribution, and Rio Rodriguez, in their master's portfolio at York University's Faculty of Environmental Studies, this story is a key part of local QTBIPOC lore that directly intervenes in whitewashed maps and archives of the Village – an area that is increasingly a site of policing and gentrification.[4]

The Steps served as a meeting place for scores of people at any given time. Most Village clubs and bathhouses were not accessible to people who were under-age, disabled, unable to afford cover charges, or could or would not go to gay bars. In contrast, the Steps was an outdoor place not oriented around admissible white gay consumer citizens: no one was turned away. Unsurprisingly, these gatherings, which included street-involved people, Black and Indigenous youth, substance users, and consumer survivors, were subsequently labelled as 'loitering.' In 2005, the Steps were removed, but they remain partly visible. More recently, they were recreated in front of the 519, a site of gentrification, policing, and eviction that is nevertheless continually being reclaimed by the transgender, sex-working, and homeless bodies who are the targets of displacement efforts.

In unmapping and counter-archiving queer Toronto, we repeatedly run into the collusion between whitened histories and whitening spaces. The violent archiving practices we discuss in this chapter are mirrored in the gentrification efforts of a neoliberal city. This occurs not just in homonormative spaces such as the Village, but also in west-end areas like Parkdale and Bloor/Lansdowne, later pink-branded 'Queer West' as part of the neoliberal city agenda of queer gentrification. What this rebranding conceals is that these areas had long been dismissed as 'degenerate spaces,' in Sherene Razack's words, and considered home by Black, Indigenous, and people of colour, including QTBIPOC, who have increasingly been displaced as white queer businesses and residents have moved in.

Around Bloor and Lansdowne, for instance, this population exchange has targeted 'undesirables' through both policing and planning. When gentrifiers formed a residents' association called Dig In, they lobbied the local police precinct to clear so-called 'undesirables' with increased street patrols, harsher sentences for minor crimes, and making it a condition of release to not return to the area. They pressured business owners to install high-wattage lighting and urged the City to remove public benches to clear 'loiterers,' i.e., those who use public space as social space in a low-income, immigrant community. As the area successively became hipster territory, these benches were tellingly reintroduced, highlighting how the streetscape itself is an archive that enshrines some while rendering others disposable and forgettable.

These imperfect erasures and palimpsestic rewritings are histories in and of themselves. They help us recognize how, despite relentless erasure, QTBIPOC continue to shine through, impossible to quiet or disappear. The contributions to MG that we have shared not only bear notice of these imperfect erasures, they invent new methods of rewriting the archive, of centring overlooked queer traces of brilliance that have been forced out but refuse to go away.

1. Several contributors to the Marvellous Grounds archive have produced important alternative historiographies about this time and its aftermath:

Tara Atluri, 'Black Picket Signs/[15] White Picket Fences: Racism, Space, and Solidarity' (working title), in J. Haritaworn, G. Moussa, R. Rodriguez, and S. M. Ware (eds.), *Queering Urban Justice: Queer of Colour Formations in Toronto* (working title) (Toronto: University of Toronto Press, forthcoming).
OmiSoore Dryden, 'Má-ka Juk Yuh: A Genealogy of Black Queer Liveability in Toronto' (working title), in *Queering Urban Justice.*
Richard Fung, 'Queer Artists Organizing: Remembering Creative Resistance and Activism in Toronto' (working title), in J. Haritaworn, G. Moussa, R. Rodriguez, and S. M. Ware (eds.), *Marvellous Grounds* (working title) (Toronto: Between the Lines, forthcoming).
IeZlie Lee Kam, 'Lesbians of Colour in Toronto' (working title), in *Marvellous Grounds.*
Janaya Khan and LeRoi Newbold, 'Black Lives Matter Teach-in,' in *Queering Urban Justice.*
Gloria Swain, '300 Hours: What I Learned about Black Queer and Trans Liberation at BLMTO Tent City,' *Marvellous Grounds* No. 1, 2016. Available online: marvellousgrounds.com/blog/300-hours/ (accessed 2 February 2016).
Syrus Marcus Ware, 'Church Street Mural Project,' *Marvellous Grounds* No. 1, 2016. Available online: marvellousgrounds.com/blog/interview-with-syrus-marcus-ware-on-church-street-mural-project-audio/ (accessed 2 February 2016).

2. This chapter is indebted to, and draws on, the knowledges co-produced by the contributors to Marvellous Grounds, a written archive that treats QTBIPOC community members as geographic and historical subjects and authors in their own right. This archive consists of a blog (marvellousgrounds.com) that is currently in its second issue, as well as two anthologies (with University of Toronto Press and Between the Lines).

3. Kusha Dadui, 'Queer Migration and Canadian Border Imperialism' (working title), in *Marvellous Grounds.*

4. Aemilius Ramirez, 'Colour Me Dragg,' in *Marvellous Grounds.*

Toronto might have gotten queer, yet even in 2017, being both queer and Asian can still be challenging. Some online dating profiles still state, 'No Asian Please!' We remain objectified as skinny, smooth, and submissive stereotypes. Younger generations of queer Asians continue to struggle when coming out, and continue to struggle to find spaces where we can fully embrace who we are. This is unfortunate because Toronto is a city that holds many rich histories of resistance by the racialized queer communities, such as Gay Asians of Toronto (GAT). But where can we find our communities' stories now?

Vince Ha and Mezart Daulet

The Invisible Visibles and CelebrAsian

On May 28, 1983, in the auditorium of the 519, a motley crew treated an audience of two hundred to an evening of music, fashion, ribbon dancing, and martial arts. It was the first *CelebrAsian*, an intimate, community-led cabaret organized by GAT to celebrate queer Asian identities. A slideshow entitled 'The Invisible Visibles,' by Jonas Ma, challenged the experiences of homophobia and racism through interwoven personal stories from ten gay Asian men with diverse backgrounds, while the Oriental Express, a group of fierce Asian drag queens, brought excitement and joy to the overenthused audience.

The success of *CelebrAsian* created momentum for Toronto's queer Asians to come together to create and showcase our talents. GAT's membership exploded to over three hundred within a year and became an active hub for diverse queer Asians to explore our identities, meet friends, find support, and build communities. Riding on the event's success, GAT developed CelebrAsian, a magazine in which the communities' stories and events could be captured in print.

GAY ASIANS TORONTO

NEWSLETTER

November 1983

Between 1983 and 1998, twenty-two issues were published. The *CelebrAsian* brand also generated an oral history entitled *CelebrAsian: Shared Lives*. This 1996 book featured stories of thirteen gay Asian men from their twenties to sixties. In recent years, *CelebrAsian*'s legacy is kept alive through the biannual fundraising event of the Asian Community AIDS Services.

CelebrAsian magazine through the years.

Since GAT disbanded in the 2000s, these printed documents preserve our history. Yet they collect dust in the shadow of mainstream movements. The stories of racialized queers are often excluded from the dominant narrative; our contributions toward fighting for gay rights and responding to the AIDS crisis are measured under a white-centric microscope, often overlooked or tokenized to paint a picture of diversity, detached from our context and historical importance. Our fight for visibility is far from over. It is time we reimagined how the queer community of colour and our histories are represented.

Immigrating to Canada, we are often asked to share our stories as immigrants, or as Asians, or as Queers on issues of belonging, fetishism, and so forth. But we are turned away when we try to bring our whole selves. So in 2016, we started Invisible Footprints, a project to collect and archive the verbal histories, printed materials, and artwork of Toronto's queer Asian communities. It is important for us to preserve our legacy.

At the same time, we appreciate learning and interacting with these resilient stories from our elders. Simply knowing that queer Asians have been actively fighting for visibility, claiming spaces, and supporting one another for decades makes being queer and Asian a little less challenging today.

We've been meeting in dreary community rooms in the heart of Mississauga, which is code for 'near the mall.' Every third Thursday of the
month, we gather to share space, eat food, and be slightly awkward in
the way of gatherings of people with shared identity but not necessarily shared
experiences. It's been thirteen months since my friend Berkha and I first sent
the emails around about a QTBIPOC Mississauga Meetup, and thirteen months
since we first sat in a cafe, waiting and wondering. In 2016, we met
every month, still keeping our location private for safety. We celebrated the summer with a picnic and the winter with a performance
night. This year, we're talking to arts organizations about mounting
events and panel discussions.

Anu Radha Verma

Mississauga

Meetup:

Queer Organizing

in the 905

This convening isn't a fluke, or some random happening
because QTBIPOC people in the suburbs finally got together. It is a
response to the trauma of losing community, plus the small everyday traumas of being in a place where reaching across the expanse
of the city, and of the region, is so hard.

I grew up in Mississauga, living a child-of-immigrant life punctuated with the hope of home ownership and the reality of being
the daughter of an alcoholic. Unlike the tropes of queer awakening, I can't
trace my way back to a singular moment. Sexuality and sexual abuse or molesta-
tion were intertwined in my youth. To survive, I've done community and anti-
violence work on queer and trans issues. But if I reach back in my experience
as an ugly, unpopular kid in a screwed-up family, I just believed that queerness
was totally all right – even if I didn't have the language to say so until I was
sixteen and asked Maude (the only friend who was sexually active) to come
with me to the Healthy Sexuality Clinic at Highway 10 and Dundas to talk
about my desire. A Peel Public Health staff person interpreted what I said and
taught me the word *bisexual*. It's important to note that the Internet was just a
few years old at this point. I mostly used it to email my friends or join random
chat rooms and develop likely unhealthy relationships with strangers.

I went to three elementary schools, one junior high, and two high schools.
There was no GSA or QSA at Applewood Heights Secondary, and certainly not
in my boarding school in India, the Lawrence School, Sanawar, where I was
sent as a response to my running away from home with my girlfriend. It
wouldn't be until I was away from the burbs, in the whitest place in Canada
(statistically speaking, Peterborough, Ontario), that I found community for
the first time, doing queer organizing while navigating the micro-aggressions
of white supremacy.

When I came back to Mississauga for work at a community health centre, I
felt a mix of excitement and uncertainty about doing anti-racist queer and

trans work in the city I'd sought to escape for so long. Between 2010 and 2015, a bunch of us queer and trans workers worked in Peel. We built intense personal relationships while running programs, planning Queer It Up! (and then Pride Week in Peel), applying for grants, and developing resources for trans folks. My friend Kevin joked that our lives would have made a good reality TV show. Once, when we all went to Crews for a night of debauchery, I ran into a straight brown girl from high school. As she drank to console a broken heart, she exoticized the beautiful queens and gay dudes. That would have brought in good ratings, for sure!

In 2011, we organized Queer It Up! in a parking lot at Dixie and Dundas, followed by a march on the sidewalk, past all the thrift stores and with Saturday traffic whizzing by. My group grew that event into the Pride Week in Peel March and Community Fair, and moved it to Port Credit in 2012, where against the backdrop of boutique stores, we saw confused stares and heard hate.

The next year, we moved to Mississauga Celebration Square to take up space in the city centre. Hundreds of people showed up for performances, free food, thirty-plus community booths, and, of course, the sidewalk march. Kevin led marchers along noisy Burnhamthorpe Road, around City Centre Drive, and back to the amphitheatre for a show featuring QTBIPOC performers and hosted by Mississauga's Ryan G. Hinds.

The final year I was involved, just before the municipal elections, candidates showed up to the Festival at Celebration Square, marking the first time politicians paid attention to us. The number of events held during Pride Week in Peel grew significantly, and, though it's cheesy to say so, my heart swelled. This was my community, and things were happening.

But like all good reality TV shows, things erode and ratings drop. The managers of our respective organizations never fully supported our work, and the implicit erasure turned to explicit hostility when a new crew took over.

With my permanent job, and a track record for advocating to management, I had been 'marked.' I was targeted by a new manager with no experience working with racialized, queer, or trans communities.

The team began to have hushed conversations with office doors closed, trying to strategize how to get through the next day, the next meeting, the next set of expectations. The stress level was palpable, the silence booming. With the support of my colleagues, I expressed my concerns to the executive director, who offered to facilitate a conversation and promised to be neutral. While the ED promised no reprisals, the meeting proved to be incredibly anxiety-provoking. I was fired one week later, with no reason given.

I spent most of the next year in bed. When I tell that to people, I read a hint of incredulity in the subtle raising of eyebrows, or squinting of eyes. But it's true. After defining myself primarily by my work, the experience of being targeted and losing my job (and not being able to access EI or sue) was traumatic and debilitating. I had given all of my energy to community work in Mississauga, building deep personal relationships through hours and months and years of pushing back against racism, homophobia, transphobia, and ageism. I had met my now-former partner through this work. Though I identify as a diasporic person, I felt at home in the work and in my role at the community health centre.

That period was marked by chronic fatigue, body pain, sleep disorders, grief. I shed too many tears, but rarely in front of others. I watched as all of my colleagues and my staff left the organization – eight people, all queer and trans – within a few months. I mourned the loss of programs and services. I heard from people who lost their doctor and felt astounded that they were left without a support space. All of the grant money I'd secured for the Pride Week in Peel festival went to a consulting firm; the event moved west to a less transit-accessible location with little community presence.

I had to confront the truth that when we do work in our communities, it means something different than 'just having a job.' I still find it difficult to drive by the neighbourhood where I worked, the toxicity polluting all my good professional and even personal memories (like spending time with my grandparents, working at the Timmy's, or volunteering at Goodwill). We collectively grieved, and we collectively agitated. There were open letters to community about Pride Week in Peel and about the organization. A few folks spoke at length to the *Mississauga News*, but the story was so complicated, it never reached print.

After a year of hiding out, Berkha and I resolved to carve out new space. We couldn't wait anymore; our communities and our friends couldn't wait anymore. So we decided to hang out in a cafe and if no one showed up, we would at least get to spend time together. I could not have predicted the ways in which our meetup has profoundly changed me, and has brought people together.

Since that first gathering in the cafe, we've been meeting in dreary community rooms in the heart of Mississauga every third Thursday. We remind ourselves (and others) that there is a long, complicated history of queer and trans organizing in the burbs. Much of it lives in the minds and bodies of individual people, so even this writing feels monumental and strange. We are making our possibilities, and building a living archive, and a new future for QTBIPOC communities, outside of the oppressive structures of non-profit organizations.

Across the expanse of the city, of the region, we are reaching out to one another.

EPIDEMIC

Stefan Lynch
Life with Dad and 'the Aunties'

My parents met in college in Iowa City, in grad school. Both of them had acknowledged to each other that they'd had same-sex attractions and, in my mom's case, had same-sex relationships.

Still, they married and moved to Toronto when I was born. Then my dad was in the big city and met other men who were like him. And he very quickly realized, 'Whoa, this nuclear heterosexual family life is not what I want.' But he and my mom stayed married. She was supportive of him exploring his real sexual orientation and sexuality. They eventually separated, but never divorced.

My dad was from a small town – a very family-oriented, conservative environment. After he ended up in Toronto, his coming-out process as a gay man began. He refused to lead a double life: a parent with a kid on one hand, and a gay activist partying on the other hand. And so, in the spirit of integration, I was part of all of that activism and community that he was building for himself as a gay man. There was no separation. I would fall asleep sometimes on the floor of the disco and I would hang out in the political-activist collective meetings that would go until three in the morning. While they were talking about important matters, I would make rubber-band balls and paper-clip chains.

There were these men I grew up with in the 1980s. They were mostly my dad's friends and lovers, whom I called my 'aunties.' A few of them were uncles, but mostly aunties, and they were men who were peers of my dad: out gay men, living out and proud gay lives. For all of these men, I was the one kid they got to have in their lives.

Some of them were just extremely uncomfortable because they were never around kids. But some of them were always engaged with me, whenever I was around and awake, and there are a few who are still in my life.

I think of Eddie, my auntie Edwina Jackson, who we called 'the ice queen' when I was a kid. He was just cool. He was from eastern Canada. Canadians are not always the most warm and forthcoming people, but he took it to a whole different level of coolness and coldness. He had white hair prematurely.

As the years went by, he stayed part of the family. Then, when AIDS really became the dominant feature in our lives, he changed. I think from going through so much death and getting very close to a lot of women – lesbians working in the same AIDS organization that he was working in, doing the same kind of work in the midst of death and dying that he was doing, but doing it from a political place that was really informed by their emotions, their anger, and their sadness – he really softened. So Ed became a muffin and he still is.

He was the person I called when my dad was dying. I was nineteen, on a break from college and taking care of my dad full-time. I wanted to go back to

Stefan (left) and Michael Lynch, 1979.

school and was really at my wit's end and exhausted from taking care of my dad. So I called him up and said, 'Ed, I can't take care of my dad anymore, I need a break. I've got to go back to college. Can you help?' And he did. Within a week, he'd organized forty people to do round-the-clock shifts, taking care of my dad, and kept it up for six months when my dad was dying at home. 'The Lynch Mob,' we called it, the support group for my dad while he was dying.

So I got to know Ed really differently that way, and then he was the executor for my dad's estate. I just took my twenty-month-old son to meet him for the first time a few years ago. It was really special to have this little person meet Ed, who had known me since I was just a couple of years old, and who was the only other person in the room with me and my mom when my dad died. He was someone I had stayed close to since then. To get to introduce him to my son and for my son to know him – one of the men who survived this era and one of my only aunties who survived – was more than special. It felt almost impossible, like: how did this happen, you survived!

Then there's Bill Lewis, who was sort of the love of my dad's life and then his friend. He moved in right after my mom moved out, when I was five or six. They weren't lovers that whole time, but they did buy a house together. Bill lived on the top floor and I lived on the bottom floor with my dad, until Bill died of AIDS when I was fifteen.

Bill was very healthy and then one day was very *not healthy*. At first, we thought it was just a cold, and then we thought it was the flu, and then it turned out to be Pneumocystis pneumonia, and within three weeks he was dead.

AIDS was horrific, but there are a lot of happy memories, too. One of the things that gay men did very well, and still do very well, along with other queers, is resist through joy. There was a lot of resistance through joy, both to heterosexism, homophobia, and, later on, AIDS, and now to transphobia, to the assimilationist culture of the gay community. There was a lot of joy when I was growing up, and of course this gay male culture in particular expressed joy through dress-up and drag.

Dress-up for me as a kid was not cowboys and Indians. It was finding just the right cigarette holder and just the right wig, and bottles and bottles of half-used Aqua Net and nylons, and figuring out whether that ratty feather boa was still going to work. And just exactly how could I get away with a Bette Davis voice at seven years old.

There were a lot of drag parties, and I dressed up a lot. I was usually the only kid, but not always. Sometimes my friends would come over and they had straight parents who would let them get dressed up, too. We would be schoolmarms, or fifties movie stars, or the Wicked Witch of the West.

One year, I won a prize. It was at my auntie Eddie's apartment for a clutch and earring party. I was really into tennis, and I made earrings by cutting a tennis ball in half, putting little ear hooks on the halves, and hanging them from my ears. And I made a purse out of my tennis racquet case, and of course came in with short white shorts and a tennis shirt. That stuff was just so fun. Who gets to go to grown-up dress-up parties all the time when they're kids?

That was the lesson I feel the gay culture taught me, and that I don't see a lot of other people getting, which was how to really have fun, even when life is not easy and even when people are dying and even when you're not allowed to work because you're gay, or you're fired from your job because you dared to put a picture of your boyfriend up in your cubicle.

So that happens, okay. Go out with your friends, dress up, have fun, and see who can do the best Bette Davis impersonation.

Edited from an oral history on *The Recollectors: Remembering Parents Lost to AIDS* (www.therecollectors.com).

The feeling of Church Street was imprinted in my being long before I first visited Toronto's Gay Village in the late 1970s. I ached for a place to feel whole, to belong, and to be of use. There's a French expression that suits: *Avoir le cul entre deux chaises* – having your ass between two chairs: never feeling entirely comfortable, belonging in two worlds at the same time, outsider/insider.

I describe myself as a long-term AIDS survivor who is HIV negative. I don't live with AIDS in my body, but there isn't a part of me that hasn't been changed by my experiences with the virus.

In 1985, I began a four-month counselling contract with the AIDS Committee of Toronto (ACT). Those four months grew to eight years, as director of support services. After thirty years, I still work in the sector doing loss and resiliency work. When people ask what brought me to AIDS work, I tell them that AIDS hit my community and I, like so many others, responded.

Yvette Perreault

'Avoir le cul entre deux chaises'

But it wasn't that straightforward.

Outsider/insider is part of my identity. I grew up a smart little French kid in English communities in Manitoba at a time when French kids were streamed into non-academic programs in school. I was born with a nurse's heart and went into psychiatric nursing in the 1970s. I was on the West Coast in the mid-seventies when I fell in love with a woman who brought me to my first feminist meeting. That world of feminist politics became my home. It helped me understand my life and gave me tools for organizing alternatives to oppressive structures.

I tried hard to fit into the lesbian cultural norms of the time: Birkenstocks, flannel shirts, blue jeans, no makeup. But I was miserable. I liked my long hair. I liked good lipstick, a sassy hat, and heels. I disliked lentils and potlucks. I was an old-style femme at heart looking for a good butch in a sea of androgyny. My lover introduced me to the gay bars. I adored that subculture. I learned to tune out the silly, bitchy banter of gay men. Bars were spaces to feel safe, free, and easy in our bodies.

I moved to Toronto to be with a new love, who shared my working-class francophone identity. She appreciated a good femme, good drugs, the bars, and understood the connection my soul had with gay men. I co-facilitated a Lesbian Coming Out Group at 519 and worked at a battered women's shelter in the west end.

When Karsten Kossman, ACT's first coordinator, asked me to take on that counselling contract, many lesbian feminists I knew asked why I was giving my energy to men who wouldn't be taking care of us if we were dying of some bizarre virus. I wasn't a separatist by nature. I understood their questions. And still I stepped in.

ACT's office at the time was at Church and Wellesley. You'd walk up a long set of shabby stairs to the second and third floors above the Kentucky Fried Chicken. After a shift, I'd go home with the KFC smell of fried food in my hair and clothes (I still can't eat the stuff). The ACT office provided a safe space in the heart of the Gay Village. Gay men didn't have to go far to find us. But there were mouse nests in our desks, and we hoped the clients wouldn't notice the cockroaches crawling up the walls when we did counselling sessions. One would never confuse our small location with a public health office or a clinic. Too small. No privacy. But a real organizing hub. I was finally bringing my lesbian self and my nurse's heart into one location, but now being a feminist was the challenge. I was surprised by how many gay men on Church Street did not seem politically aware, beyond living in a sexually liberated environment.

Jim Black was the first man with AIDS I met at ACT. A tall, frail, working-class guy with dirty-blond hair, Jim had bravely made a movie about living with AIDS. But the T-shirt he chose to promote the film read 'Choose Life' – the infamous anti-abortion slogan. Yet he was this sweet, naive, sexually active guy who happened to end up with AIDS and wanted to choose life as he moved toward death. He wasn't about changing the world for women. Whatever my political brain might have argued, I believed it was our job to care for Jim with tenderness, integrity, and compassion, and that's what we did until he died the following year.

While this community was fighting to live, I had to learn to embrace death and dying, and be comfortable with relentless waves of grief within myself, my team, my agency, and the community. In one year alone, we recorded the names of 147 people with whom we'd worked who had died of AIDS.

How do you make sense of that?

I remember my first death, on a sunny Sunday morning in October. I left my partner curled up in our comfy bed to visit Alan, a gay married man with three young children. In his bed in the old Wellesley Hospital, Alan's body bore the ravages of AIDS, his once-beautiful dancer's body now a sack of skin stretched over bones. His wife and ten-year-old son were in the private room, and we chatted quietly.

Alan was in a deep sleep, his eyes not quite closed, his mouth wide open. Then his breathing suddenly changed. There on that quiet sunny autumn morning, Alan took his last big difficult breaths, chest heaving, deep gurgling in his throat as his lungs filled with fluid. We breathed big with him until there were no more breaths. We closed his eyes, cleaned his body, put a new gown on him, and then called people to come in and say goodbye. My first encounter with the moment of death was profoundly beautiful yet achingly sad. There were many deaths to follow that came with much more anguish and suffering.

How could I convey any of what had just happened when I finally returned home late that Sunday? The trek from the Gay Village back to the west-end women's co-op seemed like travelling between two planets.

Over time, I learned I was really good at sitting with people who were dying, at being a solid presence with families, loved ones, and care teams. It's an odd role. My deal was this: I don't want you to be dying scared or alone, but rather to be surrounded by people who care about you and who will say your name and remember your story afterwards. I will do my grief work so I can tell your story proudly and clearly, so that others will come to know you, not the story of my pain. And in that role I felt like Major Margaret 'Hot Lips' Houlihan in the trenches of a MASH unit – in an unpopular war where the Gay Village had become at once a play place and a battlefield.

Leonard Cohen's lyrics – 'I ache in the places where I used to play' – were in my head the day the owner of Woody's and Chaps called to tell us that a popular DJ had died of AIDS. He wanted us to help their staff cope with this huge loss. ACT counsellors Wayne Fitton, Glen Pelshea, and I went down to the bar to meet with all the staff before the clubs opened. The meeting was raw and real and immediate. I listened to the conversation, knowing that in a few hours, their sorrow would be transformed into a gathering space with loud music, bitchy bar banter, and sexual play. Resilience. It was so important we understood the meaning of this space.

This work is emotional labour, often unrecognized, and I told ACT that it needed to acknowledge the distress in a structural way. If I broke my leg on the job, I told executive director Stephen Manning one day, you would treat it as an occupational health and safety issue. 'This is the same,' I said. 'My heart is breaking and I need you to treat it as an occupational health and safety matter. I am not burned out; I am suffering from a repetitive stress injury!'

That conversation became the seed of the Care for the Caregivers project Wayne Fitton and I developed. I loved Stephen for seeing me and hearing me in that moment of distress. He wasn't a touchy-feely kind of leader, but he created a structured agency-wide response to ongoing losses and community devastation.

But I still wonder: why did many of the guys not see it as important to mark International Women's Day? Or Take Back the Night? How hard would it have been to support the women on the staff after the December 6 Montreal Massacre in 1989? Why did we have to fight so long for a distinct Women and AIDS Project? It helps me when someone recognizes that, while I choose to sit in this space, I am also rooted in other places of identity and meaning.

It takes courage to have a soft heart in a hard world, especially for those who sit with our asses between two chairs.

Michael Lynch, the veteran activist, understood that when it came to HIV/AIDS in the early years of the epidemic, there *were* grave political issues around medicine. Treatment in hospitals depended on where you ended up. In many places, the conditions were deplorable – visitors banned, nurses and orderlies refusing to empty bedpans or serve food, and hazard signs on people's doors. Some hospitals did tests that others wouldn't. Treatment for opportunistic infections varied greatly.

Tim McCaskell

AIDS ACTION NOW!

and the Aerosolized Pentamidine Trial

In the fall of 1987, Lynch and an eclectic group of friends – old radicals, former politicians, gay doctors – came together to devise a strategy. At least half of us knew we were HIV positive. A few of us had already been hospitalized for Pneumocystis pneumonia (PCP) or other opportunistic infections.

By that point, AIDS politics and gay politics had become seamless. The government wouldn't establish standards of care, support research, or speed up access to new drugs. We felt we were being left to die because of homophobia.

The Tory federal health minister, Jake Epp, who had a history of circulating homophobic innuendo, resolutely refused to deal with AIDS. So as we plotted strategy, some members were adamant that whatever we became in terms of our advocacy, AIDS ACTION NOW! (AAN!), the name we chose, had to be a gay organization.

The main killer in those early days was PCP. It could come out of nowhere, and apparently healthy people could be dead within weeks. The drug pentamidine wiped out the parasite that caused PCP, but in Canada, it was only administered intravenously once people were sick, and could itself be highly toxic.

I had seen pentamidine's side effects first-hand in Akio, whom I had met in the baths in 1985. We had sex only once, but became friends. In the summer of 1988, he found himself with less and less energy. In the fall he was rushed to hospital with what turned out to be PCP. His hospital experience was horrible. He reacted terribly to intravenous pentamidine. Akio's partner Gerry tried to alleviate the side effects with various naturopathic medicines. The doctors didn't approve, and he had to sneak in his remedies.

In the U.S., meanwhile, small trials were showing that if the drug was mixed with water and turned into mist in a nebulizer, those who breathed it in every week or so could avoid coming down with PCP. Canada had lots of nebulizers and lots of pentamidine, but Health Canada had not approved an aerosolized version, meaning hospital physicians would not administer it. The problem wasn't the medicine; it was red tape, and that was political.

Indeed, when Akio asked for aerosolized pentamidine instead of IV, he was refused. The doctors were cold and arrogant; the nurses, fearful. The hospital had little experience with PCP or AIDS.

In February 1988, Ottawa finally approved a trial of aerosolized pentamidine. But as details came out, our relief changed to anger. Health Canada had agreed to a double-blind placebo trial, meaning half of those enrolled would not receive pentamidine, just a bitter water mist. Neither the participants nor the doctors would know who was getting the drug and who wasn't.

In order to enroll, participants had to have already survived one bout of PCP. Since about half of such people could be expected to come down with a second PCP attack within the duration of the trial, the results would show whether or not pentamidine affected the rate of recurrence by comparing the group that got the drug to the one that didn't. With three hundred people expected to enroll, that meant 150 would wait around for a second bout of PCP, untreated. Given the higher mortality rate for a recurrence of PCP, as many as a dozen of our friends might die to demonstrate something we already knew from U.S. trials.

We organized AAN!'s first demonstration on March 25, 1988. Five hundred people left 519 Church Street, carrying empty coffins to the Toronto General Hospital for a candlelight vigil. TGH was one of the sites of the trial, and I explained to the media that the purpose was to stop the trial and keep the coffins empty. On the way, we passed by the offices of David Crombie, the riding's Progressive Conservative MP. We sealed his doors with red tape, and Michael Lynch gave a passionate speech.

The demonstration prompted a response. A few weeks later, Fisons, the company conducting the trial, announced it would set up a 'compassionate arm,' i.e., provide the experimental treatment to people who didn't meet the specifications of the trial for reasons of compassion (those in the compassionate arm would not receive placebos). It was our first, small victory. At least people like Alan Dewar, an AAN! member who had already had two bouts of PCP, could now get the drug. For everybody else, however, Fisons held firm on the question of placebos.

Meanwhile, George Smith, another founding member, had immersed himself in the history of science and medicine. One day, with enormous excitement, he shared one of his discoveries: after the experimentation on concentration camp inmates in Nazi Germany, the Nuremberg Code (1947) developed ten ethical principles for medical experiments involving human subjects. The World Medical Association affirmed those principles in its 1964 declaration, Ethical Principles for Medical Research Involving Human Subjects (www.wma.net/en/30publications/10policies/b3/).

The first principle read: 'The *voluntary* consent of the human subject is absolutely essential.' In other words, if there was any coercion or duress involved in recruiting subjects, a trial was unethical and the results should not be published.

George argued that if the only way a dying person could access a possibly life-saving therapy was to enter a trial, they were being coerced. They weren't enrolling because they voluntarily wanted to contribute to science, but because if they didn't, they'd die. There had to be an alternative way to access the therapy for participants unwilling to risk getting the placebo.

I had seen how vulnerable people could be coerced. When I visited my friend Akio in Casey House, the new palliative-care hospice for PWAS, his partner introduced me to an Indigenous man recovering from a very serious bout of PCP. His doctor had enrolled him in the pentamidine trial. The man knew he only had a 50 per cent chance of actually getting the drug, and admitted he was terrified of coming down with PCP a second time. I told him we could arrange access, but he'd need to leave the trial. He shook his head. What if his doctor got mad? What if they threw him out of Casey House? He'd be homeless, on the street. He had no choice but to take his chances and do what his doctor said.

AAN!'s members knew that access to aerosolized pentamidine couldn't be merely a protest issue. We also needed an immediate solution. Every one of us who came down with PCP risked death. Only systemic change could get pentamidine to everybody. But until that elusive approval, we were embedded in a community in Toronto where it was needed immediately.

We found out that one of the doctors who worked with us had a licence to practise in New York and could write prescriptions valid there. Pentamidine was not terribly expensive and available in American pharmacies.

For $300, less than the cost of a day in hospital for one patient, we developed information packages and set up a phone line explaining how to get a prescription and where to purchase the drug in Buffalo, a two-hour drive. In April 1988, we distributed the packages to doctors' offices, AIDS service organizations, and hospitals across the city. We set up a car pool to shuttle people across the border. We liaised with ACT and the PWA Foundation to make sure there was funding for those who couldn't afford the treatment. Dr. Wayne Boone volunteered to supervise and, within a few months, forty people were attending a busy Thursday clinic to inhale the drug.

Later that year, the federal Tories called an election. AAN! held a rally October 22 and, this time, burned Prime Minister Brian Mulroney in effigy. We received national news coverage for calling out the government's refusal to permit the use of non-approved AIDS drugs through the Emergency Drug Release Program (EDRP). During the campaign, whenever Mulroney came to Toronto, we made sure he was greeted by angry AIDS activists. Local Tory candidates were repeatedly booed in all-candidates meetings when we brought up the government's AIDS record.

In the end, AIDS turned out to be a minor issue in the 'Free Trade Election.' The opposition split the vote, and the Tories returned to power. While AAN! had been little more than an irritant, we did catch the Tories' attention. In January 1989, Perrin Beatty, the new federal health minister, announced that the EDRP would be open to requests for unapproved AIDS treatments, including aerosolized pentamidine. The trial promptly collapsed as its subjects opted out of the placebo roulette and started taking the drug.

Six months later, Toronto had a provincially funded aerosolized pentamidine clinic serving hundreds of people with AIDS. We had closed down our first unethical trial.

Adapted from *Queer Progress*, by Tim McCaskell, Between the Lines Press, 2016.

Michael Lynch

Cry

Morning through a city garden widens
its swath. Shiny eyes of cinquefoil,
azure eyes of myosotis, bruised lobelia
refuse to blink. Intruders trapped in the cross-
stare harden, crumble into fine
dusting because our sympathies
will not adapt to sun and cinquefoil: our world
steel and concrete, oil and song.
We hoist our lives high over the drone
of traffic and screwing gulls, hoist bags
of soil to terraces at the setbacks; set out
cinquefoil, watch its leavings, count
its days. Some days we doze in the sun
and dream we too are cinquefoil or lobelia,
blowing and blanching without demur.
Then pneumocystis breaks.
We open our eyes to that skyline we incised
and know as a jet cuts through a cloud that
cities are our gardens, with their stench
and contagion and rage, our memory, our
sepals that will not endure
these waves of dying friends
without a cry.

From *These Waves of Dying Friends: Poems by Michael Lynch* (NYC: Contact II Publications, 1989).
Reprinted with permission, Estate of Michael Lynch.

Michael was the founder of the AIDS Memorial, situated in Barbara Hall Park behind the 519. 'Cry' is inscribed on the first plaque at the entrance to the memorial.

SCENES

ADMITS ONE $30
SAT. SEPT. 8TH
DEPARTS 8 PM SHARP
SPADINA QUEENS QUAY

ON THE EMPIRE
SANDY
MORE INFO @ 533-0236
VASELINE

Janis Cole and Holly Dale were a couple of working-class Toronto girls who decided to study art at Sheridan College in suburban Oakville in the mid-1970s. There, they made non-fiction 16 mm films together, works that were wildly different from those produced by their fellow students. Their subjects were their friends downtown: sex workers and entertainers of every conceivable gender and sexuality, and other young people who hustled and hung out on the legendary Yonge Street strip back when it was home to a smorgasbord of adult entertainment, from strip clubs to drag revues, body-rub parlours to gay bars.

Jon Davies

Our People:

Janis Cole and Holly Dale in the 1970s

Cole and Dale went on to make two landmark feminist-humanist documentary features: *P4W: Prison for Women* (1981), which ventured inside the notorious Kingston Prison for Women, and *Hookers on Davie* (1984), focusing on a diverse group of sex workers in Vancouver. Here, though, I want to focus on the first two shorts they made together as Sheridan students in their early twenties: *Cream Soda* (1975) and *Minimum Charge No Cover* (1976). (Both can be booked through the Canadian Filmmakers Distribution Centre.)

The intense identification, emotional intimacy, and political solidarity that Cole and Dale show in these films would be impossible without a deep concern and affection for 'our people' – an alternative family of folks: street kids and drug users, prostitutes and prisoners, women and queers of all kinds – who had essentially been cast away from their biological parents and cut loose from the safety net of mainstream Canadian society.

A materialist portrait of women working at the French Connection, an Elm Street body-rub parlour, Cole and Dale's first short film, *Cream Soda*, is about the fine art of the hustle. The filmmakers were given full access to the premises, as the owner owed Dale some money. The resulting film shows how, through body and talk, one can seduce a client into a sale. Beginning with hands counting twenty-dollar bills, the thirteen-minute film captures the private and public spaces of the bawdy house in great detail, all achieved via wiretaps in the rooms. The unvarnished, flesh-and-blood women we meet are a far cry from the gussied-up fantasy they represent to their johns. This distinction between backstage dressing room, where the women gossip while applying their makeup and donning their outfits, and the reception area, where they meet their clients (complete with an alcove of dirty magazines to get the men in the mood), is sharply delineated, a nod to all the labour that goes on behind the performance of gender and sexuality.

Cole and Dale's irreverence is tangible in their candid and matter-of-fact visual documentation of this sexual space and discussions with the women about how they work, what it's like, and how Canada's prostitution laws impact them. 'I put their sperm in a tissue,' one says, 'and throw it in the wastebasket.' But the film also includes witty details, like a man reciting the cloying children's song 'Jesus Loves

Victoria in *Cream Soda* (1975, 13 minutes).

Me' while being dominated to what would seem to be more fitting tunes like 'Big Spender.' As critic Kay Armatage has suggested, there is a claustrophobic quality to the film, too: its world is confined to this dark, mercantile establishment.

The fact that the conversations with the women in *Cream Soda* often aren't synced to the footage lends the film a dynamic energy and gritty, direct-cinema realism that is a far cry from the staid talking-head format favoured by institutional producers like the National Film Board of Canada. With words floating freely over images in Cole and Dale's work, the possibility of artifice and fabulation is left open, acknowledging the insufficiency of documentary authenticity, or 'truth,' in capturing an environment that is all about trafficking in a carefully stage-managed fantasy.

In their follow-up film, *Minimum Charge No Cover*, the friends Cole and Dale observe and interview are from all over the Yonge strip, from the Zanzibar to Le Coq d'Or, and we come to know them through a freewheeling collage of various opinions, lifestyles, genders, and sexualities. The eleven-minute film feels like a spontaneous 'these are the people in your neighbourhood' snapshot of the denizens of Yonge Street, most of whom were Cole's and Dale's friends, or friends of friends. This is the chosen family that supported them in making films and simply surviving. Street-involved themselves, Cole and Dale do not abide any trace of moralizing or sanctimony in their blissfully frank and open-hearted films.

Minimum Charge No Cover begins with an almost abstract shot of the lights of Yonge reflecting off a car door as a seductive woman gets out, the sounds of a prostitute and john arguing about money on the soundtrack. We first meet a familiar face from *Cream Soda* – Victoria, the beautiful pale woman in the bathtub, who we find out over the course of the film is trans.

We are also introduced to a sex worker dressed in businesswoman attire carving a giant roast beef for dinner with her young son; three black drag queens who appear both onstage and offstage; a man named Michael who identifies as a 'faggot' rather than as 'gay'; and myriad go-go boys, 'queens, dykes, and hookers' that you would likely have met on any given Yonge Street corner in the mid-1970s.

In *Minimum Charge No Cover*, the idea of 'normality' is playfully shredded in favour of complexity and nuance: trans Victoria looks every bit the 'normal' cis-gendered woman. Being nude in the bath adds to her authenticity, as if she's saying, 'I have nothing to hide, I'm coming clean.' The roast beef dinner, in turn, is highly stylized and stagy, much like every family dinner is a performance of an idealized image of domestic bliss. Already in 1976, homosexuality has come and gone as 'the next big thing' among Michael's sophisticated set, and all the subjects are in on the fact that other bodies, identities, practices, and affiliations are possible, if yet unnamed.

In addition to memorializing the lost era of public sexual self-performance that flourished on Yonge Street in the 1970s, Cole and Dale's short films also stand as monuments to subjects who died way too young: of AIDS, overdose, and suicide, of neglect and imprisonment. Cole noted that 'production is a privilege.' When they began making films about strangers, as opposed to their own social circle, they quickly became friends during the shoot. Or, as Dale said in 1984, 'In our first two films, our friends were our subjects; now our subjects become our friends.'

A rainbow vagina dentata ushers you into a full-throttle feminist hell-house featuring zombie lesbian folksingers, ball-busting butch dykes in plaid shirts hammering plaster truck nuts, a processing room replete with crocheted spiderwebs, and women's studies profs offering deep-listening therapy skills. KillJoy's Kastle was the brainchild of artist, filmmaker, and York University professor Allyson Mitchell, in collaboration with partner Deirdre Logue. The week-long performance-driven installation took place in a warehouse space off a back alleyway near College and Lansdowne in October 2013. It was an extension of Mitchell's ongoing aesthetic-political project Deep Lez, which seeks to mourn and celebrate the demise of utopic lesbian feminist herstories, culture, and critiques.

Jane Farrow

KillJoy's Kastle

Allyson Mitchell's

Vision

Suffice to say it hit Toronto like a stink-bomb tornado – crude, lewd, irreverent, and a much-needed opportunity for dialogue about the past and future of lesbian feminism. Predictably, the *Toronto Sun* decried it as an abomination funded in part by taxpayers. The arts community swooned. The blogosphere postings and Facebook threads were epic. Were the ball-busting butch dykes transphobic? Was the processing room cultivating or killing dissent and discussion? Was KillJoy's Kastle asking us to obliterate or resuscitate the 'sinking pit of identity politics'?

Mitchell responded to the comments by saying that the Kastle was intended to provoke strong feelings, ambivalence, and discourse. 'I am trying to play with stereotypes and realities of some of the greatest fears held about lesbians and feminists (as ball busters, carpet munchers, indoctrinators, collaborators,

and so on). I also chose to represent some of the more monstrous elements of lesbian feminist movements (such as racist cultural appropriators, gender-binary orthodoxy protectors, and self-righteous judgers).

'It is meant to be an apt and symbolic funeral for dead and dying lesbian feminist monsters as well as a place to cathartically face fears, self-critique, and contradictions. As the T-shirts in the gift shop read, "I'm with Problematic."'[1]

1. Since its inception, KillJoy's Kastle has happened in Los Angeles in 2015 and in London, U.K., in 2015. A book from UBC Press, the AGYU, and the ONE Lesbian and Gay Archive at the University of Southern California is forthcoming in 2018.

W e were shopping on College Street, and I bought a birthday cake and had the word *SHAME* written across it in green icing. Will Munro, my boyfriend at the time, bought a can of baked beans and some adult diapers. The plan was that later that night I would go onstage and sit in the cake dressed as my drag alter ego, Tawny Le Sabre. Meanwhile, Will would pretend to poop his diaper. It was a hot and sunny day in late June, and we were running around town preparing for the party. Pride Day was coming and Will was throwing his counterattack on normcore gays: the Vazaleen Shame party. The event flyer read, 'Toronto's nastiest queers fight for the Shame 2000 crown … Will Munro poops his diaper in shame.'

Will launched the Vazaleen party in January 2000. At the time, the event was a mix of scenes and subcultures historically siloed in Toronto's bar and club worlds. Vazaleen sought to break down those silos by bringing together a hodgepodge of punks, dykes, leather freaks, trans folk, fags, drag queens, nudists, cross-dressers, artists, and any other type of whacko person of any age.

Alexander McClelland

Vazaleen's Tawny Le Sabre

Will was the party's promoter and mastermind, but the event was realized and became legendary through a city-wide coalescence of personalities. Tawny belonged to a group of devoted Vazaleen members and performers from the art and music worlds, including Miss Margot, Andrew Harwood, Lorraine Hewitt, Charly, Zavisha, Joel Gibb, LadyFag, Lex Vaughn, John Caffery, Cecilia Berkovic, RM Vaughan, Luis Jacob, and resident DJs Robert and Miss Barbrafisch, among many others. The party brought in headliner sensations such as Beth Ditto and the Gossip, Lady Bunny, Jayne County, Cherie Currie of the Runaways, Jackie Beat, Joey Arias, and Kembra Pfahler and the Voluptuous Horror of Karen Black, which put Toronto on the international queer map. Will's brother Dave and his friends from the straightedge hardcore scene would do the door.

We all came together not at the intersection of a common identity category, the way so many lesbian and gay nights were organized. Instead, we came together because of how heterogeneously freaky deaky and different we all felt. We did not seek sameness. We sought community in our feeling of difference from the norm. Vazaleen marked a do-it-yourself shift in the orientation of queer nightlife in the city. The party was held outside the bounds of the Church Street Gay Village, under the iconic neon palm tree of the El Mocambo, the Spadina Avenue rock 'n' roll venue where the Rolling Stones once played.

With our shopping complete, Will and I got ready. Toronto alt-punk raunch queen Peaches was going to perform her new EP, later released as the now-legendary *Teaches of Peaches*. She'd just returned from Berlin to test new material. Scott Treleaven, of the queer zine *Salivation Army*, would do a film screening. Miss Guy of New York's Toilet Böys came to DJ. And resident DJ and dominatrix Miss Barbrafisch was set to play her mix of metal and hard rock.

I wore what was intended to be a top – a strip of hot pink leather dangling from a gold chain that went around my neck, along with skin-tight black rubber underwear, black platform stilettos, and a Bettie Page–style black wig.

Tawny's character was crafted to be the party's host and hood ornament. Will and I wanted someone androgynous, trashy, and punk rock to represent what the party was about. The Toronto drag scene at the time was limited, relegated solely to the Village and focused on boring and often misogynist tropes of female impersonation stuck in a rut of old-school pageant queenery. There was no one with edge who could represent what we were trying to create, so we came up with Tawny. I wouldn't wear fake breasts, or a bra or tuck. That was retrograde. I became known for revealing costumes, a bitchy punk-rock attitude, and the catch phrase 'Get off the stage,' which I would get partygoers to chant to the losers of onstage contests, such as bobbing for butt plugs. I first started using that saying later in the year 2000, when I kicked a guy offstage for dressing as a sexy police officer during the annual Halloween Vazaleen costume contest. Police were not our friends, and Vazaleen was a place where our politics were central.

In accordance with the party's queer punk do-it-yourself aesthetic, my looks for Tawny were primarily made by hand. Despite the outfits' small size, they often took hours of bedazzling and sewing. I also had custom outfits commissioned by Toronto artists Karen Azoulay and Sandy Plotnikoff, and I often performed in tandem with my 'twin sisters' Tanya, a.k.a. Miss Margot, and Vanité Vantié, a.k.a. Ladyfag, in matching drag looks.

On the night of Vazaleen's Shame 2000 party, when I took to the El

Tawny Le Sabre (a.k.a. Alexander McClelland) at the Vazaleen Shame party.

Mocambo's downstairs stage, Peaches was singing 'Fuck the Pain Away' for the first time. With its dark walls and dim lighting, the place was packed, sweaty, and dark. Will had hand-painted a giant, glittering silver sign that hung at the back of the stage. I teetered about in my seven-inch heels, carrying the birthday cake and showing it off to the crowd. I then placed it on a chair and proceeded to sit in the cake while Will revealed he had 'pooped' his diaper. We were gross and perverted as a way to intervene in mainstream gayness. Peaches wore pink spandex, and her powerhouse stage presence had the crowd entranced and freaking out. It was because of nights like this that Vazaleen came to be known as a paradigm shift in Toronto's party scene. We fucked with norms, created new aesthetics, and lived our own culture. We built our own community.

That night the party spilled into the city after the bar closed. In what became a summer tradition, a large group of us outrageously dressed, partygoing queers broke into the Alexandra Park pool, at Dundas and Bathurst, for an after-party cool-down. This tradition was forever memorialized by artist/songwriter Joel Gibb in the Hidden Cameras' video 'I Believe in the Good of Life.'

While there were many more wild, romantic, and ridiculous times, after one Vazaleen party that December, I was also bashed in front of the New Ho King Restaurant, just south of the El Mocambo. In flamboyant half drag, I was repeatedly kicked in the head until I was knocked unconscious, and a machete was pulled on my friends. This violent act marked us all and served as a reminder of how Toronto was not ready for our ways of being transgressive. The only one injured, I was rushed to the hospital by ambulance, in high heels and a bikini bathing suit, and with a full face of makeup. But friends had come to my aid, and we had each other's backs. For me, Vazaleen was more than just a party. It was a life-changing scene and support network, and one connected to my closest friends, my queer family, and my life story in Toronto.

Will's party, like most nightlife, is remembered only through the people who were there. Such scenes can be ephemeral, fleeting, even disposable, but Vazaleen deserves better. And while Will is no longer with us – he died in 2010 due to a freak brain tumour – his memory and impact live on through the stories we tell about the event that defined queer Toronto nightlife in the 2000s and opened up new ways to produce culture in our city, and new ways to be.

The images you see here feature artists competing for top honours in their respective dance categories. One performs on bended knee to show off his walk. Another poses for the camera and flaunts the intricate lace and pearl that could land them the award for best dressed, while a final candidate appears to take home the grand prize.

Captured by Toronto photographer Alejandro Santiago, this competition does not include bouquets or tiaras, and you can be sure that no one will be leaving with the title of Miss Congeniality.

This is Ball Culture.

Ball Culture, or the Ballroom community, is a subculture of performers who compete in various categories at events for cash prizes, trophies, and titles.

It may sound new or unfamiliar, but those in the know – the dancers, the dreamers, and the divas – will tell you it all began in the basement taverns and underground clubs (or 'Ballrooms') of 1980s Harlem, New York.

Kurt Mungal, with photos by Alejandro Santiago

Ball Culture

'New York is the headquarters of the main Ballroom scene,' I learn from Twysted Miyake-Mugler, a founding member of the House of Monroe in Toronto. 'When it began,' he adds, 'it was like our version of Hollywood.'

Created primarily by queer, Black, and trans communities, the Balls provide a stage not bordered by preferences for race, gender, sexuality, or body types, and their categories are as colourful as their competitors. They include 'Butch Queen Realness,' 'Vogue, Dips,' 'Sex Siren,' 'Runway,' and a slew of others. Each is designed so the participant can deliver a 'moment' – a performance so awesome it leaves judges and attendees gobsmacked and can potentially win you the grand prize.

But what binds the sequins, the jewels, and the people that give the Ballroom its radiance is the notion of belonging. 'Your house is like your family,' says Matthew Cuff, a member of the American house House of Icons. 'Some of us can't find support in our actual homes, so this community really becomes that family for us.'

He's not alone. Fellow Ballroom performer, and former member of the House of Pink Lady, SlimThick Monroe adds, 'Each house really is a family. Through the Ballroom, you can connect with so many resources that, as a Black queer youth, you may not even know exist.'

The concept isn't new. Queer people, people of colour, transpersons – all of us, at some point, have sought out or created spaces and communities where none have previously existed, or been allowed to exist. Ball Culture is one such space.

Despite Ball Culture's relatively underground status, its ferocity and confidence – and the unapologetic nature of its members – are what set this scene apart from other subcultures in Toronto's queer community.

You may not see the Legends and Icons of Ball Culture on the posters that blanket the Church-Wellesley corridor, but its designation as a space for the 'other,' and a platform for those who long to be seen, reverberates way beyond the Ballroom. So make room.

I n 1979, my yellow rubber boots traversed a two-block stretch of Duncan Street half a dozen times daily, as I ferried copy and galleys back and forth between our office on Richmond and our typesetter just north of Adelaide. A Garmin GPS runner's watch would have tracked these laps in a matching vivid yellow.

Our office housed *Centrefold*, the avant-garde arts mag consumed that year with Jamesonian questions, via Foucault, regarding how contemporary art and media practices might engage social-justice struggles in our evolving postmodern landscape. We rented space from Art Metropole, the artists' archive/bookstore/video distributor that was consumed by similar queries, but more through the filters of irony, camp, Barthes, and the dematerialized art object. Our typesetter was *The Body Politic* (*TBP*). We were all new to the neighbourhood, having arrived the previous year from other geographies, respectively Calgary, Yonge Street, and Carlton Street.

John Greyson
Yellow Boots
on Queer West

On the way out of the office, my yellow boots and I would chat with David Buchan (orange blouse, fitted green overalls, fez), the flamboyant performance artist from Grimsby who ran the bookstore and trafficked in fulsome art-world gossip, plus occasional sales of *FILE, Mounting*,[1] and the just-published translation of Deleuze and Guattari's *Anti-Oedipus*. On the way back, I'd check in with Ricky Bebout, *TBP*'s swishy designer (black T-shirt, crotch-faded 501s, 'stache, and glasses) and creator of campy subscription ads featuring faux quotes from Virginia Woolf.

Equally trim, wry, and fastidious, David and Ricky weren't friends per se, yet both had tangentially contributed to my securing a minimum-wage gig as *Centrefold*'s gofer and ad sales rep. Six months earlier, David had generously looked at my shabby shopping bag full of homemade artists' books and offered respectful advice about exhibition opportunities, as well as a crucial introduction to *Centrefold* editors Clive Robertson and Lisa Steele. Ricky had mentored me through a crash course in Franklin Gothic, Letraset, the creation of an utterly fictional ad sales rate sheet ('36% of our subscribers purchase photographic equipment annually'), and the authorship of *The Box Boys*, a likewise utterly fictional image-text piece consisting of fake newspaper clippings, published in *TBP*'s November issue, to the consternation of some collective members.

My partner Stephen[2] claims there are seven gay voices. David's was No. 3, a soft, purring stream (successfully burying his adolescent lisp) with occasional

1. A landmark feminist photo-text work concerning female circus riders by Rose English, Sally Potter, and Jacky Lansley.

2. I met artist Stephen Andrews this same year through Alex Wilson, his partner of the time and *TBP*'s editor of the 'Our Image' section. Two years later, Alex was purged from the collective.

3. They got busy with their Super-8 Labrys Rising takeoff on Kenneth Anger, and so *The Box Girls*

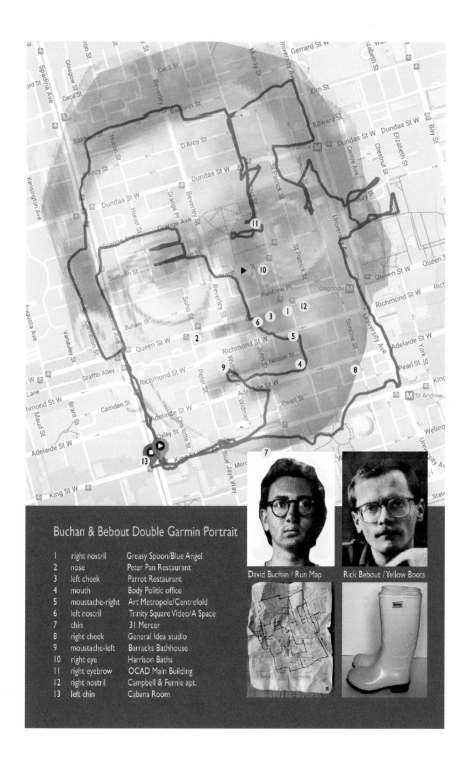

Buchan & Bebout Double Garmin Portrait

1	right nostril	Greasy Spoon/Blue Angel
2	nose	Peter Pan Restaurant
3	left cheek	Parrot Restaurant
4	mouth	Body Politic office
5	moustache-right	Art Metropole/Centrefold
6	left nostril	Trinity Square Video/A Space
7	chin	31 Mercer
8	right cheek	General Idea studio
9	moustache-left	Barracks Bathhouse
10	right eye	Harrison Baths
11	right eyebrow	OCAD Main Building
12	right nostril	Campbell & Fernie apt.
13	left chin	Cabana Room

David Buchan / Run Map

Rick Bebout / Yellow Boots

squeaks for sarcastic bite. Ricky's was No. 4, an earnest, queenly brook that slyly if shyly hid his childhood Massachusetts drawl. Thirty-seven years later, in memory of those two liquid voices (David died in 1993, Ricky in 2009, of the usual), I've pulled my yellow boots back on and used my Garmin to jog-sketch a crude GPS double portrait of them both, one headshot superimposed overtop the other, eye to eye and lip to lip, branching out from that two-block strip on Duncan that linked the two of them.

It's strange to jog in yellow boots, and perhaps stranger to claim that this map of their faces is an Etch A Sketch snapshot of that moment in 1979 when Queer West was inventing itself, long before the tsunami of brand-name logos and metrosexual *logos*. Go west, sang the Village People (Gay Voice No. 7), and so we did, creating a post-Yorkville, post-Church, postmodern hitching post from scraps of *Anti-Oedipus* and Letraset and yellow boots. Here are some autobiographical scraps of me and David and Ricky and this new neighbourhood – and some questions about processes of myth and memory.

1. *Their Right Nostrils*: Southwest corner of Queen and Duncan. Upstairs, a greasy spoon where OCAD/York U students and dykes Margaret Moores and Almerinda Travassos invite me for Scotch broth. They are keen to adapt *The Box Boys* into a short student film, but have just one small change to propose: it will become *The Box Girls*. Needless to say, I'm swooning with the glamour of it all, ready to sign anything.[3] Downstairs, a perennially broke club books feminist band Mama Quilla II[4] for that year's New Year's Eve party, and I dance till 3 a.m. in my yellow boots with Kenny Baird.[5]

2. *Their Left Cheeks*: Sandy Stagg[6] opens the restaurant Peter Pan in 1976, which is credited with being the first artsy anything in the hood. She is tight with General Idea (GI), the artist trio who founded Art Metropole, hired David, and published *FILE*, GI's elaborate parody of *LIFE*, devoted to ironically mythologizing this emerging Queen West scene.

3. *Their Noses*: The Parrot is No. 2 on the block, famous for chef Greg Coulliard's jump-up soup, as well as its bevy of illustrious artist-waiters, including Kenny and

---

was never made, but our friendship has been constant ever since, resulting in an extraordinary co-production (with Marg and her partner Pam): our daughters Maggie and Alice.

4. This iconic band was featured on the cover of a special *FUSE* music issue in 1980, and included Lorraine Segato on lead vocals and bassist Susan Sturman, by day a typesetter at *TBP*.

5. Artist and painter Kenny found fame in New York as the nightclub Area's production designer.

6. An occasional Miss General Idea muse and pageant contestant.

7. Fung, a Toronto video artist, did it as a gig for Rogers Cable. It's a crucial archival document in desperate need of restoration.

feminist performance artists the Clichettes (Louise Garfield, Janice Hladki, and Johanna Householder). General Idea, David, Clive, Lisa, and the Clichettes all perform at an extraordinary benefit for *TBP* on January 3, 1979, held at the Faculty of Education auditorium on Bloor. It is the first time Hogtown artists have collectively mobilized on behalf of queers, and the first time queers have collectively encountered this new generation of artistic esprit. If Queer West needs an official birthdate, this night gets my nom. Richard Fung films the proceedings.[7]

4. *Their Mouths*: *TBP* and its Compugraphic typesetting machine are located on the fourth floor of a warehouse. During press week, the offices become a frenzied, frothy, cruisy hub, with volunteers and collective members sharing the erotically manual tasks essential to distributing a pre-digital monthly non-profit mag: peeling labels, stuffing envelopes, licking stamps. Ricky is the eye of the hurricane, dispensing shoulder rubs and tart ripostes.

Gerald Hannon on Ricky: 'You were in awe, and you were irritated, for the same reasons: because he was smarter than you, better read, more thoughtful, more strategic. It probably made it worse that he didn't flaunt it. He wasn't a snob – he worshipped competence. You could be a Remington's dancer, a waiter, or a prof, but all that mattered to him was that you did your job well. If you did, he was yours.'

5. *Moustache (Right Side)*: Ricky's classic clone moustache speaks for itself. David doesn't have a moustache, but rather the scar from a harelip operation he's somewhat self-conscious about. He's the public face of the bookstore and possesses a librarian's encyclopaedic knowledge of Art Metropole's artists' publications, as well as an artist's disrespectful fascination for the art-historical canon. (His later photo series that reimagines classic paintings as po-mo adverts shilling consumer products includes a redo of Paul Peel's *After the Bath*.) Another bath scene: *Halo …* is an adaptation of Jacques-Louis David's famous painting *The Death of Marat*. Buchan lies slumped and inert in the tub. But while Marat's dead hand holds documents pertaining to the French Revolution, Buchan's flaccid hand holds his Visa bill.

6. *Their Left Nostrils*: AA Bronson, artist co-founder of GI and Art Metropole, is also central to the dematerialization of A Space, Toronto's foremost artist-run centre. Along with director Peggy Gale, he moves the gallery from St. Nicholas to an office on the fourth floor of the CHUM-City building, and from there launches a series of irreverent and ingenious satellite-art commissions.

8. Video and performance artist, voted Art Fag for Life by Images Film Festival.

9. Gillian also worked at *Centrefold* as a fellow gofer/distribution manager.

7. *Their Chins*: 31 Mercer is the showroom of a former glass factory, now rented out to motley artists as live/work space. Andy Paterson,[8] Gillian Robinson,[9] Paul Collins, and Gary Shilling live upstairs, and we all share a kitchen jerry-rigged in the former men's washroom, with a counter installed over the urinals. My bedroom is an office on the ground floor, notable for its glittering floor-to-ceiling glass and mirror samples. At 6 a.m. on New Year's Day, Kenny and I are awakened by a cop trying to crawl into the open casement window directly above my bed. The cop saw the open window, decided to investigate, and nearly fell in on top of us. Scenario for a Joe Gage porno romp, or eerie precursor to the bathhouse raids of 1981? You decide.

8. *Their Right Cheeks*: General Idea's studio is on the third floor of this warehouse on Simcoe, a spacious workspace that AA shares with his partners-in-art-and-life Jorge Saia (Jorge Zontal) and Ron Gabe (Felix Partz). I pose for a photo series by Jorge, wearing nothing but a cast-iron poker. While I'm dating AA a year later, he teaches me how to make perfect scrambled eggs on their gas stove.

9. *Moustache (Left Side)*: I don't know if David or Ricky regularly go to the Barracks bathhouse, which deserves credit for being the first gay outpost on Queer West until Will Munro's Beaver opened its doors in 1996. I run into Felix there one night. We note the Barracks' omnipresent trademark odour: poppers, dirty socks, mildew – or a terrifying redolence of all three, brought to you by ChromaZone perhaps?[10]

10. *Their Right Eyes*: The Harrison Baths, a swimming pool and public showers for waves of neighbourhood immigrants, is also an inevitable locus for Queer West cruising. The tiled dividers in the shower room only amplify the opportunities for hooking up, while the pool provides an overchlorinated winter oasis for earnest lengths. David and Ricky don't partake, but Jorge is a regular, initiating a petition when the pool is threatened with closure.[11]

10. ChromaZone, a loose collective of emerging artists resisting the siren call of the dematerialized art object, staged the collective art-fashion happening ChromaLiving of new post-punk design and painting in 1983. Andy Fabo, one of the driving forces and featured artists, paid his rent by working at the Barracks. In 1978, he was charged by police with being 'the keeper of a common bawdy house,' and responded with a series of life-size figurative oil paintings, reasserting the urgency and efficacy of this seemingly anachronistic medium. Fifteen years later, when the Paramount multiplex was being built, artist Michael Alstad curated a series of peephole installations in the construction hoarding. His own peephole, directly across from the Barracks on Widmer Street, afforded a view of a dollhouse replica circa 1979.

11. Half a block away was the site of the future Beaver Hall artists' co-op, where I lived through the 1990s, sharing an elevator and ground-floor studio with Colin, Margaret, Johanna (of the Clichettes), George Hawken, and Michael, among many others.

11. *Their Right Eyebrows*: OCAD in the late 1970s is crucial to the emergence of Queer West, training a generation of queer artists in tactics of pastiche, appropriation, and the pop mash-up, despite the almost utter absence of out queer faculty.

12. *Their Right Nostrils*: Video artist Colin Campbell and lyricist/filmmaker/painter/programmer Lynne Fernie will move to these legendary side-by-side second-floor apartments on Queen West a few years later. Colin has at various times before and after 1979 been lovers with David, Lisa, Kerri Kwinter, AA, George Hawken, and myself, among others. Ten years later, when he writes what stands as the first and still best chronicle of these turbulent times, Ricky dubs his blog-memoir *Promiscuous Affections*, a title that neatly sums up the elaborate rhizomatous roots that erotically entwined so many of us.

13. *Their Left Chins*: David as Monte Del Monte stars in Colin's *Bad Girls*, a multi-part melodramatic sequel to Campbell's *Modern Love* (part Waters, part Fassbinder), with each episode screening at the Cabana Room to SRO crowds through a desperately cold winter. The episodes revolve around the lives and loves of actual Cabana Room habitués, including a coke-snorting Miss Susan, a punk Sturm und Drang enigma Heidi, the clueless naïf Robin (Campbell), and Del Monte as the lip-synching, jet-setting, jizz-swizzling heartbreaker who ruins Robin's life.

If the *Body Politic* benefit was our Plymouth Rock, then *Bad Girls* was our Declaration of Independence. So many layers of artful irony and campy disavowal! Such a Dagwood sandwich of closets and costumes and crucial cranky critiques! With every recent television documentary[12] and retrospective exhibition[13] that attempts to capture this 1979 Queer West moment, we wonder anew: no matter how nuanced, relevatory, and idiosyncratic, can such nostalgia for a scene ever escape those processes of reification, mystification, and gentrification that inevitably overwhelm, pave, and pacify it? Rhetorical, of course, but I put the question to Ricky and David anyway, and their faces peer back at me from their streets, mute, linked by pavement, sketched by yellow boots.

Overlaid, perplexed, bemused, they are wise enough to be unconvinced by any claims made about their geography, their era, their stretch of pavement ... but passionate nevertheless about the processes (and necessity) of memory. Among their manifold talents, both were archivists of the first order, fetishizing the

12. For instance, Lorraine Segato's passionate *QSW: The Rebel Zone*, a TV doc about Queen West – and Lorraine, of course, spoke as the consummate insider: lead singer/songwriter of both Mama Quilla II and the Parachute Club, and Lynne Fernie's sometime partner/roommate.

13. Most recently, curator/artists Wanda Nanibush and Luis Jacob have presented their lush, imaginative versions of this history at the AGO and U of T's Art Museum. Curator Philip Monk in numerous exhibitions has likewise emerged as a crucial and passionate chronicler of this formative era.

catalogue and index, cherishing the mechanisms of storage and retrieval. Both in turn are remembered and celebrated, in ways that so many extraordinary others from Queer West are equally forgotten, footnotes fallen from the page, from the pavement. The former for his piquant blogs, regaling us with Jane Rule and Remington's gossip; the latter for his piquant photo collages, clutching a Visa bill. Such are the essential idiosyncracies of legacy, and the debt we owe both, helping us resist these mythologies of a halcyon underground, even as they aid us in troubling the Floridization[14] of our Queer West waters.

14. Richard Florida's theorization of the 'creative class' in part celebrates Queen West's gentrification as a triumph of LGBT upward mobility.

'It's hard to remember that being brown in the seventies and eighties sucked. It meant feeling like you were from another planet – one where your food stank, your parents were 'weird,' and you were trying to balance traditional culture with the realities of growing up second-generation. Things were even worse if you were a girl who wanted to avoid marriage, a boy who wanted other boys, a time-expired Indian from Trinidad, a desi bent on revolution. In the late-eighties Toronto onward, Desh Pardesh was the answer to that suckiness.' – Leah Piepzna-Samarasinha

Although the history of Desh Pardesh (1988–2001) has not yet been seriously documented, it lives on in the collective memory of those who participated in it. For these people (I count myself among them), Desh resonates with a vibrancy invoking a singular and treasured public platform that called into being a repository of cutting-edge cultural works amidst a heady mix of extravagant soirees, heated discussions, and avant-garde workshops. This was a risky and politically charged place where intersecting diversities and multiple identities collided for the first time; a place where racialized minorities who had until then hovered on the edges of progressive social and cultural scenes became groundbreakers, initiating self-determined interventions that resisted exclusion and negotiated social change in the arts – the kinds of interventions taken for granted in the Toronto of today.

Sharon Fernandez

Desh Pardesh: A Cultural Festival with Attitude

Desh Pardesh began in 1988 as a one-day cultural event entitled 'Salaam Toronto.' Organized by Khush: South Asian Gay Men of Toronto, Desh took place at the 519 as an informal celebration of South Asian fashion, food, and culture. This first incarnation of Desh was designed primarily to raise awareness about the South Asian gay and lesbian community. As Nelson Carvello of Khush recounts: 'We wanted to expose our families to our realities as queer South Asians and at the same time we wanted to expose the white gay and lesbian communities to our lives in more than a tokenistic fashion. There was so much creativity; we had a lot of fun, but the vision was always about outreach – outward and inward.'

In retrospect, it is not surprising Khush took on this task. In 1980s Toronto, gay South Asian men were more visible and organized around South Asianness than were South Asian lesbians and/or women activists. The handful of visible South Asian women activists tended to be involved with groups in which other collective identities took priority. Resonant with this is my own journey as a grassroots women's rights activist – a journey nurtured by the vibrant alternative social movements of the late 1980s, particularly those that emanated

SOUTH ASIAN *Desh Pardesh*

goddess woman girlfriend tit daughter Sri Lankan dyke bisexual slut ass paki

Exploring the Politics of South Asian Cultures in the West

out of Black feminist communities and flourished in women's cultural landscapes, such as the Toronto Women's Bookstore, the journal *Fireweed*, and Women's Press. That said, a few of us did attend Khush social events and participated in the launching of Desh.

From 1988 to 1995, Desh's popularity escalated. Responding to the obvious need it filled for young South Asian gays and lesbians, it grew from a one-day event with an audience of two hundred and an operating budget of $600 to an annual five-day conference/festival that, at its height, attracted 5,000 participants and had a budget of $150,000. In 1991, Desh became a non-profit dedicated to creating a public and civic space in which to develop a progressive South Asian identity.

By then, Desh was holding its main-space multimedia events at the Euclid Theatre – a former Orange Order hall at Euclid and College large enough to accommodate participants from across Canada, the U.S., the U.K., and India. In addition to these main-space events, locations such as artist-run centres, cafes, and repertory cinemas hosted a wide range of activities, including discussion groups, exhibitions, workshops, discipline-specific networking sessions, receptions, and huge dance parties. After being coordinated in church basements, apartments, and borrowed community spaces, Desh now shared an office with five other cultural organizations and the Toronto Arts Council in a building at Bathurst and Richmond. In 1992, the TAC took a lead role in supporting Desh, through a program called CultureWorks.

'We have made a conscious effort with this year's program to bring forward the views of South Asians who originate from all over the subcontinent, the Caribbean, and Africa,' Punam Khosla said in her opening address to the 1991 Desh festival. 'And I think what this speaks to is a real conscious movement toward unity for progressive social change in the world that we actually live in. It is moving away from romantic notions of nostalgia toward a forum within which we speak from our real memories, without any kind of shame or apology; within which we can begin to organize against racism, sexism, homophobia, and from which we can extend genuine solidarity to our other sisters and brothers, people-of-colour communities around us who also know in their bodies the experience of racism and, in North America in particular, the First Nations peoples.'

Racism in Toronto had been paramount when, in the summer of 1992, riots – precipitated by the Rodney King verdict in Los Angeles and a spate of Toronto police shootings of local Black men – broke out on Yonge Street. Following the shooting death of Michael Wade Lawson by police in Mississauga – making him the eighth Black youth to be shot in the Toronto area in a space of four years – and a rise of violent acts directed at Tamil immigrants by neo-Nazis, Desh Pardesh formed an alliance with the Toronto Coalition Against Racism. A coalition of fifty community-based anti-racist and social-justice organizations, TCAR formed after the near-fatal 1993 skinhead attack on Sivarajah Vinasithamby, a Sri Lankan Tamil refugee and restaurant worker.

In addition to joining this Toronto-wide campaign, Desh had by then become an invaluable resource and referral service for communities directly affected by racism. From regular features of the festival program, like the 'Brick by Brick Community Forum,' and conference panels with titles such as 'Breaking Down the Barricades' and 'Activism by Any Means Necessary,' several 'unity in adversity' coalitions across cultures were created, leading to greater solidarity across racialized communities.

While the plethora of activist concerns were important to Desh, what remained central was the group's commitment to lesbian and gay issues, enabling it to take on the broader social climate. At every festival, over half the programming was devoted to lesbian and gay artists and the community's concerns. Queer artists like Shyam Selvadurai, Pratibha Parmar, Sunil Gupta, Shani Mootoo, Atif Siddiqui, Kalpesh Oza, Urvashi Vaid, and Steve Pereira all participated at Desh.

Typical of the fare on offer was a video produced by Friday Night Productions entitled *Rewriting the Script: A Love Letter to Our Families* (2001), which originated in a 1998 festival workshop called 'So I Came Out to My Mom at the Dixie Mall Food Court.' The video (available on YouTube: www.youtube.com/watch?v=b2lMb-58MH4) sought to help South Asian families in their journeys toward understanding and accepting their lesbian, gay, bisexual, transsexual, and/or transgendered children, siblings, and other relatives. Sponsored by Supporting Our Youth, *Rewriting* was a good example of a cultural product that succeeded precisely because it had been collectively created by, for, and about South Asian queers and their families.

Four years after Desh closed its doors in 2001, Natasha Singh, an English teacher at the Collegiate School of New York, recalled the festival this way in a presentation in Ottawa:

> The throngs of people buzzing with anticipation, political squabbles, active debate on the floor between artists and community members, the excitement of seeing established and emerging artists, multiple genres, the numerous caucuses, the ever-present commitment to lesbian/gay roots/politics, the influx of new people year after year, the increase in representation from other countries both in programming and in audience. Desh politicized my generation; it was a place where many of us came of political age.
>
> It was a battleground as much as it was a refuge. Identities and acts of identifying were contested, corroborated, formed, checked and challenged, broke down, rebirthed ... It was a training ground for future activists and artists. Many artists were birthed here, or received tremendous support at Desh.

The gradual mainstreaming of the festival had meant it became progressively less radical – a pattern that, if ironic, characterizes what happens when marginalized groups start moving toward the centre. The complex histories of self-determination and resistance on the part of North America's feminist, civil rights, lesbian, gay, and Aboriginal movements created a climate in which Desh flourished. Riding on those waves of activism and progressive left politics that had shaken Toronto out of its white, middle-class complacency in the 1970s and 1980s, Desh made the most of the resulting ideological openness, climbing through this window of opportunity to fight for the inclusion of marginal communities in Canadian cultural life.

There was never a night it wasn't packed when I was there. It was part of why you went. Right there on Church Street, where there was still so much distance between our queer bodies and theirs, you could climb that narrow, steep staircase and be delivered into a crowd so giddy and over-flowing that it took you wherever you needed to go.

Maybe it was Clit Lit on a first Monday, with Beth on the mic, introducing nervous writers to a baby-doll-frocked and wallet-chained audience. Maybe it was Funkasia on a third Sunday, with Zahra and Vashti spinning Bollywood hits to a sweaty, diasporic dance floor. It might have been a Caribbean party *doux-doux*, all flags in the air, or papi, it might have been Latinx drag queen night, bringing Selena back one more time. Two blocks south of Wellesley, if you were brown or black in late 1990s Toronto, the Red Spot was the place to be.

We like to think of our gay bars as home, as welcoming sanctuaries where all LGBT people find refuge under the sparkling lights of a disco ball. This is one of those partial truths that adults tell each other so we can remain polite in each other's company. Deep down, we know different, but no one wants to ruin the party.

We know that some of us are always at the centre of the club, while some of us sit alone at the bar, and some wait in line all night and somehow never make it inside. We know that even in this city, where people never shut up about diversity, gayness equals whiteness, and when you are too brown or too black, too often you had to take what you could get or you stayed home.

Owned by Tamils, the Red Spot, a small club on the second floor of 459 Church, opened after the Black Eagle moved next door in 1997. Coming out in the mid-nineties meant that when you were feeling yourself, you were spoilt for choice: you could flirt with women at Buddies or Pope Joan or 52 inc., and at SHE Saturdays at 488 Yonge, or Ciao Edie on Sundays.

These were all places where you made recurring appointments with DJs, each bringing rhythm and regularity to your social calendar. These were all places where mostly you danced, mostly you smoked, and, if you were lucky, you yelled the perfect pickup line above the loudest music you'd ever heard. But the Red Spot was more than just a stop in my weekly bar rotation – it was a site of possibility, Muñoz's utopia made real.

The entry point was either a flyer someone would put in your hand, or a poster you would see at the Women's Bookstore, or you would call 967-SPOT to hear the listings for yourself. Dance nights and drag-queen performances, yes, but also feminist fundraisers for the Toronto Rape Crisis Centre and Pride floats and queer-people-of-colour support groups.

Michèle Pearson Clarke

Red Spot Nights

Cabaret nights, too, with the patience for both amateurs and professionals, and glory bestowed during the Miss Red Spot Competition and Talent Night. Latino Group Hola met there, and you could get help with your immigration case and real chile verde from Liselda, famous for her tiny Mexican kitchen. If you listened, you could hear soca, calypso, dancehall, reggae, bhangra, chutney, and salsa, but also the sound of so many people imagining futures different from anything they had ever known.

We know that Canadian multiculturalism makes us Black and South Asian and Latinx, but within those red walls, we made temporary peace with such erasure on our own terms. We ignored that our accents were different because we were different, and instead we screeched when DJ Nik Red or Verlia or Blackcat played that dancehall tune I used to wine to in Port of Spain, and you used to bogle to in Kingston. We ignored that our parents would probably have looked down on one another, and instead we taught each other dance moves from back home, my black skin rubbing up on your brown. We told each other how hot our dhotis and dashikis looked, even when they looked just okay. We could be cruel to each other, too, but even the hardest among us would melt when we showed them that woman in the corner dancing like their abuela.

Outside, there was always already winter and shitty jobs and the constant need to explain ourselves, but inside, DJs were saving our lives and drag queens were setting us free. Part tent revival, part community centre, and part basement jam, the Red Spot was no paradise, but we made the space that we needed in the Village, and we held each other's safety in our hands. We stared down what we had been told, and we showed each other how it could be otherwise. We all helped host that house party, and we never wanted to leave.

[Karleen] In May 2000, Lengua Latina, a creative writing group for Latinas in Toronto, was launched. At that time, Latina and Latino queers walked Church Street mostly unnoticed by the white men cruising one another. We went to the Second Cup for cafecitos and chisme, the Red Spot for enchiladas and salsa dancing, and the 519 for Hola and Lengua Latina.

janet romero-leiva and Karleen Pendleton Jiménez

Lengua Latina:
Queer Palabras en Toronto

[janet]
i arrive just after 8
not wanting to seem too eager
        too excited for   and about this new latina space
i look at the board and check the room number   three times
i have a habit of checking numbers repeatedly when going to unknown places
still today   i do this
double check
triple check
            sometimes more
and then there is this other thing
this other thing i do in translation   with numbers
i mix order   and sounds when going from spanish to english
                            y inglés a español
and though it is highly likely i am looking and seeing and reading the room
        number in english
it is also likely that this possibility of writing with other latinas is causing
        numbers to appear unfamiliar
and therefore needing of repetition

i begin climbing the creaky stairs
number 34   34   34
look down at my sandalled feet
the bottom of my jean legs brushing each other as I move further away from
        the entrance of the building
3 flights seem like a big climb to unfamiliarity
but the excited sickness of my belly keeps me moving
this familiar feeling has produced rewarding results for me in the past   mostly

finally   on the 3rd floor
most of the doors are open
making it hard to see the room number

but the space is small
it should not be hard to find a group of latinas
given this has probably likely rarely happened much in this building

and then I hear it
the quiet nervous chatter
the introduction of names
sense that awkward moment when you are trying to figure out if this is
a kiss-on-the-cheek latina
a hug latina
or
a gringa latina (= handshake)
and the chatter continues
until the next awkward moment
after a whole sentence has been spoken and you attempt to decipher where in the
    continent that accent is from
'eres del salvador?'
and if you can't be sure
'de dónde eres?'

i poke my head in
with as little movement as is possible when poking a head
      and i see them
         see me ...

[Karleen] I was 28, wore beige Dickies, dark T-shirts, and a gold Guadalupe medal around my neck. I wanted to write to save the world from colonization. I wanted to write about the death of my young mother. I wanted to write about when I was a tough little tomboy who couldn't always protect myself. I wanted to write about the lover who dumped me in San Diego and the lover who brought me to Toronto. I wanted to write with Latinas because I was schooled by Chicana activists.

I had learned to love writing in classes full of Chicano/as in Berkeley, California, spaces where queer voices dominated. I had learned Chicana identity as an ethnicity and politics that brought a community together to organize, debate, learn, love, dance, cry. There were not so many Chicana/os in Toronto when I arrived in the late 1990s. But a new Peruvian friend and I hoped that if we wrote 'Latina' on a flier, we could make such a room in Canada. We hoped the word might collect Latin Americans from across the city. We hoped to fill a room with the warm hugs and soothing Spanglish that sounded like home. We hoped that if we chose a space in the 519, the queers and only the coolest of straight women would come.

[janet]
we write
together
twice a month
together
in spanish and english and spanglish
together
we write
i write
i discover that writing is not just for other people
i realize this form of expression
            of creativity
                        nourishes my body in ways that wash away shame
and sadness
and confusion

i realize que sin estas mujeres
my authentic tongue would be forever trapped
unknowingly lashing out in frustration

sin estas mujeres
me tragaria palabras y sentimientos
too heavy to carry

[Karleen] Each mujer came with her own pressing words. There were the women
who came to Canada as children, as young refugees of dictatorships or immigrants
with parents who dreamt 'better' futures. There were the women who arrived as
adults, refugees fleeing violent homophobia and/or highly educated landed immigrants. We wrote both as settlers on First Nations land and as Mestiza children of
the Americas with continental critiques of colonial legacy. We wrote our yearning
for South American homelands and reunited families, healing of our childhood
bodies and memories, rage over unacknowledged Canadian racism, and lust for
queer sex.

[janet]
con estas mujeres
me recupero
lentamente recupero
my 6 year old self
who carefully and desperately gathered memories of home   antes de migración

fearing i'd never be allowed to return
a la casa de mi abuelita
al jardín de rosas and grapevines leaking through sunlight and warmth
a mi escuela
mis juguetes
mis primas

recupero
my 9 year old self
whose newly learned english words provided reprieve and possibility to parents
    too busy working to learn the language de este país
whose translated words were often coated in uncertainty
and the anxiety of feeling but not understanding discrimination and racism

recupero
my 11 year old hormone confused body
excited yet shamed
at my quiet noticing of the shape and size of breasts on other girls my age
how i wanted to touch and feel the gentleness of their lips   on mine
feel my own body   myself

[Karleen] Tender words were scribbled into our notebooks. Scary words were spoken aloud inside our circle. We listened and soothed one another. Even though we came from countries thousands of kilometres apart, our Latin American origins grouped in a Canadian community centre held us together for six years. Latinidad in the North was a special and secret club. Latinidad allowed us to drop our guard, and make way for queer confessions.

Several members told me that what they learned most was what it meant to be 'gay.' These answers came from queer and straight members alike. One woman said she didn't even like to write, just wanted the chance to hang out with 'gay' Latinas. It's ironic in that we never wrote anywhere that it was a 'gay' group. The leaders and location set the bar, regardless.

I'm not sure what 'gay' we taught. But we did learn about women desiring, touching, fucking each other. We learned about dildos and handcuffs. We learned about parents asking for Spanish translations of English euphemisms like 'gay' and 'bisexual' and 'queer.' We learned about siblings feeling threatened or underwhelmed. We learned about families loving their queer daughters.

'Gay' and 'Latina' gave us the excuse and opportunity for a group of women to share our most intimate stories with one another and to feel the pleasure of acceptance. It's not that there weren't Latina/o spaces in Canada; it's just that there were hardly any Latina/o queer spaces. The word 'gay' was both the sex and the idea of openness. If we could be so bold as to say 'gay,' and 'Latina,' then we could talk of any secret.

[janet]
and we write
together
twice a month
we write
write our queerness into this city
write our indigenidad/latinidad into queerness

Sarah Liss

The Hidden Cameras and Their Gay Church Folk

Y ou could always smell the kind of bar Clinton's was before you saw it: to walk in was to be immersed in the essence of archetypal pubness, a thick fug of dude sweat, ancient grease holding the memory of thousands of wings and fries, and innumerable draught beers spilled on the floors. That scent grounded you in the space, a drinking man's tavern dating back to the 1930s, a place Frank Sinatra was rumoured to have frequented.

The aroma wafted all the way into the back room, a dimly lit, linoleum-floored annex that felt like a time-capsule rec room. On a cool evening a few days before Christmas in 2001, however, that dingy afterthought of a venue felt like a pansexual Xanadu. Packed onto the pocket-sized stage, nearly a dozen beaming, bopping bodies held court, cajoling the swaying crowd to partic-ipate in choreographed moves to accompany a jubilant, melodic ruckus of guitar, xylophone, percussion, and voices.

This wasn't the first Hidden Cameras show. That one had taken place almost exactly a year earlier, an ad hoc performance curated by band mastermind, songwriter, and frontman Joel Gibb at the West Wing Art Space. But there was something elec-trifying about bearing witness to this explosion of queerness in the context of this quintessential drinking man's tavern – masked go-go dancing boys, tender allusions to BDSM, the candy-sweet camp of adults playing transgressive songs on little-kid instruments. As all this spilled into the most normative, unassuming space, it felt like the spark of a revolution.

At least it did to me, barely into my twenties, fixated, like so many other undergrads, on the deeper meanings of culture, and yearning to find that overlapping oasis in the Venn diagram that encompassed 'indie music' and 'queerness.' I'd been covering music for an alt-weekly for a year and was still enamoured of the job's novelty – listening to rock (and pop, and country, and folk, and so on) and getting paid! In the early 2000s, before social media became the dominant mode of reactive analysis, the opportunity to reflect on the significance of a pop song – especially as a young, queer, not especially femme woman – seemed like a Golden Ticket.

At the time, Toronto appeared stuck in a staid holding pattern, if not the Dark Ages. Local music acts were largely anchored by straightforward electric guitar riffs, played, more often than not, by straight white cis guys. There were some all-girl bands, and there were some female drummers, bassists, and vocalists in the boys' club of indie rock. And there were certainly other gay and lesbian and trans artists. But when writing about them, I was often left with the impression that, to most, their appeal had a niche-ness, and that the possibility of connecting with a broader audience was inversely propor-tional to the overt queerness of what came out of their mouths.

But then, suddenly, the Cameras arrived: though he'd been likened to Morrissey, Gibb resembled the enigmatic homo icon in cheekbones and onstage charisma alone – his songs exploded with gleeful perversity and gentle hedonism. He drew on the participatory tradition of euphoric praise he'd absorbed while attending a Baptist community church in Mississauga in his youth, swaying in front of a rapt congregation with eyes half-closed, hand raised as if to commune with a higher power. Gibb made weird sounds – not speaking in tongues, exactly, but elongating syllables until they sounded nonsensical, or shifting from a sweetly resonant melody into a harsh nasal drone. He'd be flanked by acolytes – boys in underwear and balaclavas, girls with tambourines, people of various genders grinning and waving and leading cheers and playing an impossible number of instruments with the gusto of preschoolers.

The audience responded in kind, and they – we – sang along to unabashedly pretty songs about sissies and cum and leather and pheromones, about the thrill of being dominated and the rapture of pissing on a partner. Gibb also wrote songs about things other than fucking: zine culture, for example, or overturning the assimilationist institution of marriage. But, though he pledged deep allegiance to an archetypically gay camp aesthetic – 'Oscar Wilde and Quentin Crisp, scarves and the seventies and more sexual liberation and great musicals with dancing,' he once said – Gibb's politic was deliciously and confrontationally queer.

So it was remarkable when the Cameras became cult heroes not just for the LGBTQ2SIA community, but the seemingly normative indie-rock fans who flocked to their live shows. Moving from chapel to chapel, Gibb and his mild-mannered army plied their so-called 'gay church folk music' to throngs of straight, cisgender disciples, who writhed in elation as yellow streamers meant to represent golden showers rained down from the balconies.

The precedents for this crossover queerness echoed in the bohemian rhapsodies along Queen West in the 1980s, where you could hear the punchy world-beat pop of the Parachute Club and the fractured feminist queercore punk of Fifth Column. Toronto had also witnessed the rise of Rough Trade, whose new-wave hits were propelled by Carole Pope's butch swagger and overtly lesbian lyrics. But the Hidden Cameras represented a new kind of cross-pollination – not coded homo content but a gender-fluid, sexually liberated, shame-free, inclusive ethos.

One could argue, in fact, that Gibb and his collaborators helped catalyze the movement that became known as Torontopia, a moment in the indie culture rooted in music and geared toward community, civic engagement, and DIY grit. Torontopia was far greater than the Hidden Cameras; it peaked more than a year after that show at Clinton's, in 2003, when the band released its transcendent breakthrough album, *The Smell of Our Own*. At its best, Torontopia was defined by many of the principles integral to the Cameras, and by the work of the band's principal members, too.

There was Gentleman Reg, the nom de guerre of Reg Vermue, a blond sylph who grew up as an army brat in Ontario and Germany and who, through the cosmic wizardry of the Cameras – with whom he frequently sang wraithlike harmony vocals – embraced his sexuality and used his foggy falsetto to sing songs about seeking out a boyfriend. (Years later, Vermue would find an exhilarating creative outlet in drag, transforming himself into Regina, an impossibly sleek dynamo with a penchant for synth-pop.)

There was Owen Pallett, a classically trained violinist and composer who helped buoy the Cameras' orchestral flourishes – until he broke away from Gibb's crew to pursue his own creative interests, first with the raucous art-noise dynamism of Les Mouches, and then, fatefully, through the glorious looped string-and-voice compositions he performed as Final Fantasy (later, dodging a lawsuit, he reverted to his own name). (Pallett would also find fame through his orchestral collaborations with the Montreal indie-rock heroes Arcade Fire.)

There was also Lex Vaughn, whose wry comic antics, pervy chutzpah, and steady drumming would serve her well in collaboration with Peaches – arguably Toronto's perviest, most in-your-face export; Will Munro, one of the city's greatest queer cultural heroes (see p. 247–250), who became the band's tour manager; and Maggie MacDonald, whose politics encompassed Marxism, speculative fiction, cyborg fetishism, and queer theory, and whose impassioned cheerleading as a long-time Camera translated into the kind of electrifying, multiform activism that defined Torontopia: city-building, environmental awareness, political organizing, dramatic productions, and numerous rock bands.

Hidden Cameras alumni would help establish and run Blocks Recording Club, a worker-run co-operative label/collective community. Blocks may not have been explicitly dedicated to non-normative gender and sexuality, but it was deeply queer in its anti-capitalist politics and devoutly DIY approach. Its commitment to craft translated into hand-assembled packages that cradled CDs in a maze of origami-like folds, impractical (but adorable) MiniDisc releases, and hand-stamped, screened, and lettered booklets.

Torontopia was far from a perfect fantasy – as many have noted, it was predominantly, uncomfortably white, and played into the segregation that plagues many indie scenes. Participants may have been conscious of and sensitive to trans experiences, but the movement remained mainly binary in its approach to gender. Even so, as a transformed vision of what a thriving indie culture could be, it was, for that handful of years when it thrived, an idyllic thrill. And there, in the early 2000s, in co-opted chapels, hole-in-the-wall galleries, and taverns reeking of fry grease, the Hidden Cameras sowed the flagrantly faggoty seeds of change.

The ceremonial Route of Heroes rolls through Toronto from the 401, down the Don Valley to Bloor, and then down Bay Street. It ends at the Ontario coroner's office on Grenville Street. It's an extension of the Highway of Heroes, a stretch of the 401 starting in CFB Trenton that the bodies of fallen soldiers ritually travel when brought home for burial.

My own private Route of Heroes are the streets just north of Grenville: Breadalbane, Grosvenor, Maitland, Elizabeth, and Surrey Place. Some would know this turf as Boystown. Though lacking any official recognition, a different kind of hero strolled this route. Men on foot, by car, on bicycle, and always under cover of night. These heroes are the largely forgotten, unknown sexual soldiers undignified by a ceremonial tomb or epitaph.

Keith Cole

Route of Heroes

And hard as it is to write about these times and this place, I remember the boys of those streets as muses, as chance encounters, as people. Between 1984 and 1989, Boystown was a magical place for nightly and early-morning trysts and taboo rendezvous. Swagger, sweat, and cigarettes. Sometimes I took precautions. But when you are treated as a human dildo, wearing a fresh condom each and every time was a little much to be expected. Some guys were into other guys' stenches, anyway. The customer is always right. Right?

The Germans have a word for outsiders writing history: *Alltagsgeschichte*, or *history from below*. History written by and for non-conformists and the disenfranchised – people of 'the everyday.' Boystown was a free outdoor stage where actions were exposed, raw, illegal, and on the front doorstep of Toronto Police headquarters. Likewise, a nighttime street market was situated in the shadow of a place of activism, politics, social justice, and injustice also known as the Legislative Assembly of Ontario (or Queen's Park).

Location, as they say, is everything. Perfectly situated geographically, Boystown and its ragtag crew could have been the stimulus for a sexual and political revolution. However, as with all fabulous ideas and grand dreams of an aesthetic and sexual utopia … a few things got in the way. Namely, Helmut Kohl, Margaret Thatcher, Ronald Reagan, Brian Mulroney, and AIDS.

An old lover accused me of embellishing Boystown, making it into something it wasn't. To him, it was dystopic, unfashionable, dull. A place so tawdry you would never confess, even to your closest confidante, that you frequented the area, either as a shopper, a seller, or a tourist.

I can only say that my own experience was different, and being promiscuous taught me life skills I still use to this very day. I learned to experiment, adapt, and be creative. These are problem-solving tools one needs as solutions to life's never-ending challenges. Plus, you get to see how other people live!

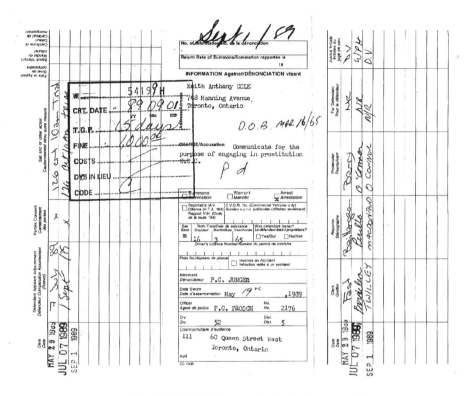

Keith Cole's citation for communicating for the purpose of engaging in prostitution.

How strangers live. You actually get in their car and go to their home! Taking it all in and checking it out, making mental notes, and uttering glib comments about how nice the place is and how great the view is, and being fake nice to whatever kind of pet they have:

'What's its name?'

'What kind of breed?'

'How old?'

'Ohhhh … so cute.'

All this small talk also serves to hide the fact that you're scared. You have been driven to some faraway location and are now in some strange man's home. Which way is south? Where is the subway? How do I get back downtown? Where am I? Did I remember to look for landmarks while in the car, or was I too busy giving the driver a hand job?

He has a nice car, so he can't live in a dump. Right?

The time you spend there is short, and you hope for a drive back downtown, to the safety of Boystown. And fifty bucks cash. And some cigarettes. Maybe some pot? The boys don't even think about crabs, syphilis, herpes, anal warts, scabies, and AIDS – they're far too young to worry about things that aren't on their radar just yet. The boy successfully dropped a load of cum in some dude's mouth, and was paid for it in cash. There was only one thing on his mind. Who would be next?

It was on Grenville Street – number 85, to be exact, right in front of the Ontario Nurses' Association building. A light brown, non-descript cargo van. Parked. Passenger-side window down.

The guy in the driver's seat asked me, 'How much for a blow job?'

'Fifty bucks.'

'Get in,' the driver said, and I did. He was extremely good-looking and young. This is great, I thought to myself. The final guy for the night was young and cute – such a sexy change from the others.

Then, BAM. From nowhere, someone appeared out of the darkness from the back of the van. And wouldn't you know it: he was good-looking, too. Of course, they were undercover cops. All the signs were there. Parked. Young. Good-looking. Too good-looking. Eager. Too eager. A dull brown van. But ultimately it was the definite and intentional *look 'em right in the eye* repetition of the 'money for service' question that should have given it away. And all I wanted out of the night was a little slutty action to top it off, but now you're being treated like a fifty-dollar whore.

Pickings are pretty slim in Boystown these days, what with all the new condos and a modern hospital. But you can still spot drivers slowing down, trolling the route. And not all the veterans are dead; old habits die hard. I don't blame AIDS, the City of Toronto, the military, the police, or everyone's current favourite killjoy, 'gentrification.' But I do blame the Internet for loss of income, loss of fun, loss of cloaked-in-darkness friendships, and loss of sexual encounters. All of which made my Route of Heroes a very beautiful place in this city.

T here are no easy answers. Nothing about the process is clear, and the ambiguity is always to the police's advantage, not yours. What follow are guidelines only, but they should help you in most situations.

- Ask for police ID.
- Ask whether you're under arrest and what the charge is.
- You're free until arrested.
- Do not resist arrest or use force against the police.
- Identify yourself.
- Say nothing else.
- Anything you say to the police will almost certainly be used against you at the trial.
- Ask to make a phone call.
- Don't give in to 'deals.'
- Ask to see a bail justice.
- You may be free in twenty-four hours.
- Do not plead guilty.
- You or someone else may have to put up bail.
- See a lawyer.
- Do not assume you are guilty just because the police say you are.
- Prepare for several visits to court.
- To find a gay-positive lawyer: in Toronto, call TAG (416-964-6600), LOOT (416-960-3249), or *The Body Politic* (416-863-6320). Elsewhere, call your local gay or lesbian organization, publication, or telephone information line.

Guess What ... That Hand on Your Shoulder Could Be a Cop's:
The Body Politic's Clip-and-Save Guide to Arrest and Trial

This is an abridged version of a pamphlet published in September 1979 by *The Body Politic*.

Walking through the Don Valley ravine on my way to a work event, I took a shortcut. I veered off the beaten track, following a pathway lined with dense foliage that created dark spaces even in the early-evening summer light. The tops of towers in Flemingdon Park were visible just beyond the trees. A man in his fifties walked toward me. He turned and headed into the bushes a few feet off the path. Our eyes met. I passed by, glancing over my shoulder. There was an intention behind that look. I had stumbled into one of Toronto's still-popular cruising areas.

Despite new technologies that allow people to connect easily, park cruising continues to hold its appeal for many. 'It's kinda retro, isn't it?' says Andrew, twenty-six, laughing. He's been having sex in parks

Jake Tobin Garrett

Desire Lines

since the age of fourteen and finds himself longing for it every winter. 'You reminisce about how nice it was to have the sun shining and get fucked on a picnic table.' But for him, choosing park cruising over popular hookup apps like Grindr and Scruff is also about efficiency. You can spend a lot of time arranging something on an app, he said, or you can just go to your local park.

Whether you're pressed against the dark side of a tree in Queen's Park or hidden in the grasses at Hanlan's Point, there's no shortage of Toronto green spaces to cruise. Websites like squirt.org combine the ease of smart-phone apps and GPS mapping with the thrill of cruising, telling you exactly where to go. But for many, the analogue spark that comes from a look that lasts just a little too long is what brings them back to the park.

'I think this is a whole other version of desire lines,' says Peter, forty-one, using the urban planning term for the informal beaten paths one finds in parks where people have blazed their own trails. The excitement of a chance encounter draws him to seek out sex in public spaces. But sometimes it's out of necessity. Once, living in a crowded house, Peter brought a guy to nearby Riverdale Park instead, for privacy. 'It was a summer evening and we just went down into the soccer field. It was one of these massive soccer fields. The lights aren't on. No one is going to see you if you're lying in the grass in this big field from up a far hill.

'There's probably a generation of guys who haven't had these experiences and who don't even know they're missing out,' Peter adds. For him, digital cruising is more utilitarian, like window-shopping. You can filter out what you don't want, but it lacks spontaneity. 'It's easy to default to your phone,' he says. If you put your phone away, however, you can just be at an experience. You can 'have that chance encounter, that eye contact, that cruising, that excitement that comes from being in the moment.' You hold a look. Follow someone down a path. Catch a glance over the shoulder. Yeah, okay, this person is actually interested. 'There's a discovery to it that's different in real life,' he says.

Of course, there is a danger to park cruising that includes a long history of police surveillance. This history resurfaced, painfully and publicly, in late 2016 when the Toronto Police charged dozens of men found cruising in Marie Curtis Park, on the border of Etobicoke and Mississauga. In an operation called Project Marie, police went undercover, positioning themselves to be approached by men for sex. Charges were laid. Some people swiftly condemned what they viewed as a regressive and disproportionate police entrapment operation, while others, from the surrounding community, supported this campaign to 'take back the park.'

Toronto politicians like Councillor Kristyn Wong-Tam urged the police to drop the charges, raising questions about the undercover tactics and police resources used (only one criminal charge was laid; the rest were simply bylaw infractions). Lawyer Marcus McCann offered to represent the accused free of charge. He argued that this prosecution could ruin lives, forcefully 'outing' men who decided to fight the charges in court, thus making their names public, rather than silently paying the fines. Not all men who cruise in parks are 'out' or even identify as gay. Park cruising provides a safe alternative for those who don't feel comfortable on Grindr or in a Church Street nightclub. It also offers an outlet for those still exploring the shifting sands of their sexuality.

JR, fifty-two, first learned about park cruising when he was a teenager listening to a CBC program about gay men. One, a concert pianist, said he would go to David Balfour Park to have sex with other men. 'The next day I went down to City Hall and said, "Where is David Balfour Park?"'

'This is before Internet,' JR says. 'This is before *Xtra!* magazine even. Even if I went to a store and looked at a magazine, I would always cover it with another magazine. There was no kids' help line or anything like that to go on, so you just had to do your own thing, right? I remember I used to have sex with this guy at school a little bit, and we'd go to Centre Island and we'd fool around there. It was really just discovering what you could find out on your own. I was thrilled.'

For JR, however, park cruising led to an arrest. 'I was splitting up with my boyfriend and we had a fight on the phone, and I thought, "Okay, I'm going to go out to the park." It was late. And I actually passed the cops on the way into the park – they were sitting there in plain clothes. I was with this guy and we both had our pants down. We hadn't really gotten to anything, and they arrested us. I remember they handcuffed us, put our hands behind our backs, and they said, "Don't say anything." We went up to the side of the hill. I think their police car was parked near Mount Pleasant. That was it. I got a ticket. I had to appear in court.' During the proceedings, it became clear that the judge lived above David Balfour Park. 'He wasn't too happy about what was going on.'

Public sex in parks is illegal, but as much as parks are governed by formal rules, there are also informal understandings about how public spaces can be used. One park becomes a spot where people can let their dogs run around freely, even though it's not an official off-leash park. Another becomes a hot spot for drinking beer and smoking weed. An area of dense trees and underbrush by the water's edge becomes a place where people seek out the touch of a stranger. We are constantly negotiating and renegotiating our use of parks and public spaces.

Chris, fifty-four, cruised parks when he was younger and recently started again. 'As a very young man, I cruised public toilets,' he tells me. 'That's like a gateway drug. Once you've done that, a park seems perfectly okay, I guess … Often public toilets are in parks, and so if you're there and you notice people are leaving there and going up a path, the path introduces you to the whole concept of park cruising.'

He now finds himself most often at Cherry Beach – a strip of sand and trees at the end of the Portlands, and a popular cruising spot. 'There are a thousand secret little places to misbehave in Cherry Beach,' Chris says. 'And because it's so big and so sprawling and so maze-like, it's an adventure. That's all I can say. It's an adventure. You just don't know what's around the next corner; you don't know whether you're going to meet someone or not. It has nothing to do with the beach or the lake. You have to fish where the fish are, and Cherry Beach is where the men are.'

Under a queer blue sky in this Kanien'kehá:ka-named city of Toronto, there is a not so ordinary, not so mundane, everyday life. Concrete walls scraping skies yield a life within life, a life beyond life. A place of lasciviousness dwells visibly, yet selectively, in the most public of spaces. In these cracks, hidden shadows, and open landscapes, gender roves, wanders, and explores the bodies inhabited within and beyond its boundaries. Same sex becomes different sex, and cis bodies and trans bodies ignite fire.

This city, ordinarily thought of as loaded with not-so-hidden gay male cruising spots and the odd women and trans bathhouse, becomes an active setting to displace manhood and womanhood as the sole possibilities sexually and viscerally.

Gender transforms with the help of alleyways, lush green trails, and hidden bushes to *bring your strange manhood a little bit closer to my strange manhood*. A friendly neighbourhood park can facilitate delightfully odd meetings where cis and trans bodies become compasses to one another. In places where bodies are assumed to have shapes that protrude in order to be seen as desirable to other bodies with shapes that protrude, a chasm erupts and opens up a realm of seduction no one knew was possible.

Sly Sarkisova
Under a Queer Blue Sky

On the secret naked beach nestled by the Bluffs, a space where gay men have played for the past thirty years becomes a site of unconventional education and desire. *The pebbles beneath your skin and mine make the same sound, as the waves gently lull while we study each other.* It is the place itself that facilitates a broadly obvious transgression of the norms of which bodies should be seen where, and to whom these bodies should be desirable.

Men with strange desires that fit nowhere mingle openly. Lurking and creeping and voyeuristic exhibitionism are at home here amidst foliage and fire ants. One man waits in the bushes, signalling for passersby to watch him shove and twirl a sizable zucchini up his ass. He gets bored when the audience sits still and expressionless, waving them away with mild disdain and a triumphant retreat into the hidden greenery.

Another, older man positions himself on the beach with shorts splayed open to reveal a semi-hard member to anyone who passes by. Later he can be seen naked, openly fellating himself in the same position while presumably cis straight bodies hover near the shoreline, cruising on Jet Skis. A few naked male bodies on the beach easily form into a voyeuristic masturbation circle that becomes transfixed and edified with my difference in size, shape, and form. All this happens as men chat idly while glancing by, not noticing anything is amiss here.

At the trails at Hanlan's, I learn this place, too, is not just for gay cis men. Dicks rain down like rays of sunshine, and smiles and curious steadfast looks unflinchingly indicate *there is nothing and everything to see here.* There used to be a thing called penis envy, but if one truly envies having a penis, there are many penises to be had at beaches like this. Penises, cocks, dicks, fucktoys, and surrogates rain joyously down on special occasions, making one feel amply abundant in the dick department. *Do I desire you for your dick, your body, as if it were my own?* Yes. It is near enough to my own, with a little something special on loan.

In the barely obscured hills of a Little Italy park, under cover of darkness, glistening stars, and alleyway lights a little too bright, I discover *it is possible to be desirable* to pansexual-leaning straight cis men. The risks involved in ordering a craigslist pizza paid off. Neither of us knew if we would be into each other until we got into each other. Maleness that was once dangerous and off-putting, reducing my gender to a submissive collection of feminine sexualized parts and roles, becomes transformed into my pleasure, power, and seduction. My body no longer is read and diminished by your body; it toys with, provokes, and overpowers your body. My masculinity is desirable to you now, and I am more masculine when we fuck.

Under cover of healthful sauna benefits at a local west-end community centre, I realize a revolving door exists in plain sight. There are not just men washing themselves here. They don't just have small dicks, not unlike mine, or average-sized dicks and giant dicks only thought to live in porn films. They have hips, too, pear shapes even. I discover the ideal male body is more of a myth than I thought my own possibility to be. I compare and contrast my body to theirs, openly gawking without them ever knowing a secret lies in their midst, until I decide to reveal it.

In the locker room of the Y lies a secret space of desire for cis straight married Portuguese men, bisexual men, effeminate gay men, queer men, old men, androgynous men, many varieties of men and people who appear to be all of the above. These men are surprised and delighted by bodies like mine that create our own beauty and our own strength through bravery. In spite of themselves, their bodies respond to my body, regardless of sexual leanings or identities.

In these low-key, open-secret spaces, trans bodies can have powers not many others would suspect we, nor anyone, should have. In these not-so-secret spaces, I achieve desire for myself in ways that would not otherwise be possible. My body transforms from a singular object of feminized desire to a cavern of possibility sheathed in a layer of the not so obvious. My body can inhabit you with a desire you never knew to question, and I no longer have to question my body. This is a place where I'm not your bro and I'm not your bitch, and neither are you. I am my own person who exists in that fairy-tale place only I invite you into.

In these spaces, I turn myself and the city into a playground that does not want for love, affection, intimacy, sexuality, or appetite. In these spaces, I do not desire you, but I achieve a vehicle to know the cohesion of all the separate aspects of myself at once, and this I desire greatly.

Prelude

Gay-bathhouse chalkboards archive important queer stories. Even after brushes or impatient fists smudge and smear to make way for new markings, there are layers of embedded storytelling that map and mobilize queer desire. Bathhouse chalkboards trace and tease fantasies, unlock codes and imperatives; some work like pop-song hooks, songs your ass intuitively likes. They refuse texting in favour of situated, material cruisings. I remember in particular the main-floor toilet-stall chalkboard at the Barracks, and the chalkboard in the back hall at Steamworks. Like graffiti, markings on these surfaces connect writers with readers in tactile, visceral, and practical ways.

Andrew Zealley

Chalking It Up to Experience

Movement I (Trauermarsch)

My first experience in a gay bathhouse was in 1980. I was pissed at a boyfriend and – seeking petty revenge – asked a close friend to take me to the Barracks. This friend had become familiar with bathhouse culture while I repeatedly locked myself into monogamous relationships. That night, he was my guide. The club was housed in adjoining Victorian row houses on Widmer Street, a location far enough from the Gay Village to warrant a distinguished and unconventionally attractive crowd. I lived on King Street West above a greasy spoon–styled diner at the foot of Widmer, next to Farb's Car Wash. Now defunct, the Barracks was swallowed whole by Toronto's straight entertainment district, but at the time it was frontier.

On that first visit, I did not give a moment's notice to the chalkboards. Sexual impulses are, after all, primal, and it's not unusual for bathhouse habitués to lose touch with their language skills. Some years later, I returned to 56 Widmer Street. Before long, I was engaging in full sentences and anonymous conversation like it was second nature. The chalkboards were, clearly, my next step.

Attending to the chalkboard in the main-floor toilet stall, my interest in visual culture transformed the board, and its bulletins and smudges, to a site of intense questioning and social traction. A second, located in the upstairs bathroom, continued and expanded the conversation, becoming a two-level, top-bottom, semiotic connect-the-dots. Visceral markings lingered on both slates: repetitive, abbreviated phrases and words, symbols, crude icons, directive gestures, and, most importantly, desire. At the foot of each chalkboard, a collection of little chalk sticks, slowly shrinking to nubs and dust piles along a shallow, ridged ledge, like deep-dish rails of coke.

Immersing myself in queer-sex culture at that pre-HIV/AIDS-treatment time felt, curiously, like a release from the violence of the pandemic. Some

guys developed fears of sex; I craved closeness and discovered the very different kinds of intimacies and relations that were possible during wartime. I particularly loved Saturday nights at the Barracks on lysergic acid diethylamide, walking the stars back home to Parkdale before daybreak.

Movement II (Stürmisch Bewegt, Mit Größter Vehemenz)

My familiarity with the Barracks turned, for a brief period in 1996, into a job. Working at the Barracks equated to doing bits of everything, minus bookkeeping. Working the front cage, where incoming clients signed in and settled up, employees also cleaned and prepared the rooms, did the laundry, washed the floors (on occasion), and kept an eye on the party. Barracks staff members were typically smart, sometimes tetchy, and intoxicatingly rough.

Working the cage, I performed as the 'towel hag,' a figure coined by Philip Hare, another toothsome local artist employed there. Hare would sketch his distinctive penis images, now found in galleries, in doodle fashion during slow periods. Harry, a lithe and adorable painter, also worked the cage. Harry lived – and painted – in a downtown storage unit. He would round up bottles of poppers left behind during room cleanings and sell them back, cheap, to clients, sardonically closing each deal with 'Pop away!'

Are you getting a picture of the Barracks? It was political, edgy, and artsy, though 'grungy' actually sounds more in tune with the themes and variations that played out there, twenty-four hours a day, all year long, and for over four decades. The Barracks was an excellent destination for lunch, and, accordingly, they offered noon-hour specials and coupons.

Movement III (Scherzo)

A repeated query when entering someone's room: 'What are you into?' Nine times out of ten, I still fumble on this one, though on occasion I offer 'Spontaneity' as a hopeful reply. The chalkboard provides the ideal space to clearly state your 'into.' In acts of resistance to the banality of expectation, I often scrawled 'Flowers' or

'Spontaneity' next to my room number on the Barracks' chalkboards. In this way, I could measure the outreach success of my memo in the facial expressions that passed by my door.

'300 I'm hot': The chalk veritably leaps from the well-used and smudged cubbyhole blackboard in the back hallway of Steamworks. This cubby formerly housed a public telephone with a hinged glass door, like a telephone booth set flush with the wall. So I go check room 300, to verify *how* hot. There is a toupée involved, and the individual has enhanced the room's atmosphere, towel draped over the wall light. He is spread out on the room's single bed, a rehearsed pose on belly, with head toward the back wall. He is propped up on elbows and in one-quarter profile to view passersby, his gentle shoulders graced with a soft layer of dark hair. His ass lifts ever so slightly. He's done this before. Each room at Steamworks is equipped with a mirror, installed horizontally, facing the bed: the ideal means to check your posture, the way the light (and your dimming of it) highlights certain body parts while obscuring others.

Movement IV (Adagietto)

Waking up at sunrise, Sunday morning. Not so much waking as coming to. The Barracks is, in this rare moment, almost silent. In the distance, I hear the shower area on the first floor, or specifically the sound of steadily dripping water on water that echoes off tile and concrete walls, floors. Dancing dust particles float in the air and catch the dawn light as it filters in through an open door at the back of the second floor. The particles follow air currents in choreographed movements that the chemicals in my body are assembling as loose vertical circles, miniature Ferris wheels made of light beams and silver dust. Saturday night was expansive.

Movement V (Rondo-Finale)

At the end of 2008, I got a job as front-desk clerk at Steamworks. Set behind a glass panel, with a slot for verbal and monetary interaction, the desk clerk is the first fleshy male body encountered by the lusty gaze of the client. Clients have, often, spent two or three hours thinking about sex, whether at a bar or at home in front of a laptop, before coming to stand on the other side of this window.

For my first shift, I was paired with a freshly 'turned' twenty-year-old who was mourning the end of a three-month relationship. I immediately recognized there was little room to share my news: the end of a ten-year relationship of life-changing moments: deaths of parents, testing positive, travel, growth, intense loving, and the legal confines of same-sex marriage (and divorce). My co-worker's melancholy was too dense to penetrate. I quickly scooted back to the chalkboard to peruse the menu, my dinner break in mind.

The chalkboards are not the only method to bridge the temporal and spatial gaps between the Barracks and Steamworks. There are bodies – hard, fleshy, and leaky – that emerge in the form of fuck buddies and 'sidewalk relationships.'

There was Todd. Built like a hockey player. Todd was beautiful. Todd – like Jason, Brock, and Blake – is one of those 1980s-era boy names that evoke a mythological, heroic male identity. Monolithic, monumental, monosyllabic. Sturdy and carved, Todd's hairless legs and ass were magnificent. Flawless arms and chest, and a warm and desirous twinkle in his eyes. Todd made curious facial expressions, twitchlike sparks in response to my tongue and mouth. These made me think he was straight, had a girlfriend, and was experiencing conflictive moments with the desire that coursed through his body and, inevitably, down my throat.

We first hooked up at the Barracks. Years later, I bumped into him in the dark at Steamworks, and our conversation picked up like it was only yesterday. Once I started working the front desk, it was inevitable I would know when Todd was in the house. As our hookups increased, so did our mutual interest. Todd revealed his true name: Bobby.

With our growing sexual closeness, I disclosed my HIV-positive status, which Bobby found challenging. We talked about what it means to be undetectable, but the complex entanglement of his sexual identity, conflicting desires and lifestyle, and hockey-loving buddies formed an impenetrable wall. In an extraordinary gesture, he revealed that our sex was the best sex he had ever had in his life.

Once, I saw Bobby standing near the corner of Yonge and Wellesley, unironically wearing a padded plaid jacket and toque, a three-legged German shepherd on a leash at his side. This image stays with me even now, a metaphor for Bobby's disabled desires. It's an entirely loving image.

Note to self: Next time at Steamworks, write a message to Bobby on the chalkboard, continue writing stories into imaginary futures.

I was married to a man, but we had started exploring bisexuality and non-monogomy within the marriage. He was good at it and I was terrible, but that's a whole other story. My husband and I discussed my going to Toronto's first Pussy Palace event at Club Toronto, on Mutual Street; he was almost overly enthusiastic that I should go and report back on the details.

But I had no one to go with, so I began to waffle. I wasn't even out yet, and here I was preparing to dive headfirst into a history utterly foreign to me. Not just queer history in Toronto, but queer history in general. The snail's pace at which I'd been exploring my sexuality was no longer self-determined. My then-husband demanded honesty about how I felt, but I couldn't resort to the usual avoidance measures that had served me, if not well, then at least efficiently for many years and through several relationships.

Monica Noy

Towel Service

It's unclear to me what I thought I might get out of the Pussy Palace. I had imagined some dark and sticky place where nobody knew each other, or cared to find out. I thought perhaps I'd get to have sex: after all, that was the goal of a bathhouse, where anonymous, dark, and sticky sex happened all the time.

The Pussy Palace, however, wasn't at all like I imagined. There was sex – oh yes, that happened, though not for me. There were also demonstrations of the use of dildos and strap-ons out by the pool. In some areas, it was shoulder-to-shoulder crowded. Lesbian porn played on strategically placed screens. The level of dress ran from stark naked to almost fully clothed. People seemed delighted to see each other. There were warm greetings, hugs, laughter. It was a party. The only anonymous thing was that I didn't know anybody, and nobody knew me. The only shadowy thing about it were the corners I backed into, clenching my white towel (provided, by the way) around me while trying to catch my breath.

Between the first and second Pussy Palace, my husband and I went our own ways. At the second Pussy Palace – yes, I went again, this time with a friend – I met, flirted with, talked for hours to, and then *finally* had sex with a woman. It was a wonderful experience at a raucous party full of variously clad queers, some of whom I even knew in passing. There were even more demos, and porn, an s&m room, and shoulder-to-shoulder dancing. A lovely young usher met us at the top of the stairs and showed us our room. The woman I met and had sex with has since become my wife. Our meeting at the Pussy Palace is a fond and strong memory for both of us.

Part One

For decades, lesbians have envied our gay male brethren, who on a moment's notice can have a soak and a steam, get their cock sucked, and enjoy a turkey buffet, all on Christmas Day.

And so it came to be that lesbians' desire to attain the anonymous sexuality of gay men created Pussy Palace. After all, there is nothing more transgressive and anonymous than lining up for three hours on Carlton Street with all your ex-lovers and all your ex-lovers' ex-lovers' thesis supervisors.

Fiona MacCool

The First Rule of Pussy Palace

On that fateful evening, after we paid our cover, we were met by a bathhouse Walmart greeter: 'Here is your personal lubricant and freshly laundered dishtowel. Now c'mon, girls, let's get out there and make this an experience I can write about you for *Xtra!* next week.'

There we all were in the hallway, like second-graders being helped out of our snow pants, eventually wrapped in our towels, shuffling down the hall in flip-flops for the guided tour.

After moving from the hot tub to the sauna, up to the pool deck, through the empty workout room, around to the s&m floor, down to the entertainment lounge, over to the photo booth, and back to the hot tub, I finally threw caution to the downwind and engaged in some skinny-dipping or 'fat-positive immersion' in the Javex-scented human keratin pit.

There I was with my pool noodle, trying to make conversation with the one woman I had not already talked to in lesbian bars for decades, when I realized everyone was watching Toronto's most famous strap-on model giving it from behind to a local academic of some notoriety. Watching a 2 per cent body fat man-woman doing the 'innie-outie' with his/her/their custom-made prosthetic only reminded me that most of us in a strap-on look like someone wrapped a black eighties mini-belt over a pink balloon.

I ended the night in a shame spiral as some gaggle of anorexic academic lesbians stole my towel, leaving me to cover my bearded clam with a soggy pack of du Maurier Special Mild.

Part Two

When the second Pussy Palace came to be, I planned ahead. This time, I wore a vintage men's silk dressing gown, avoided aquatic activities entirely, and brought a date. My girlfriend-of-the-month was this fabulously perverted creature with whom I was engaged in a ridiculous break-up-get-back-together pattern. That evening, we were on one of our weeks together. We were spouting off the 'free agents' crap while knowing we were at least going to get down each other's pants if nothing more interesting came along. This was a comfort as she wandered the halls complaining there were no butches, while I gave myself whiplash looking for anyone who would pass for a girl on the outside.

The real clincher that night was the fisting demo. A nearly identical-looking lesbian couple celebrating their hundred-year anniversary were introduced as 'professional sex educators.' Out they strolled into the middle of the lounge, stark naked with their little yoga mat. One plunked herself down with a preparatory exhalation, and the other basically parted her legs and slid the arm right up to the Timex. The crowd erupted in gasps like Shamu was being born at SeaWorld.

The night ended upstairs behind a locked door. The whole private-room thing was wild – like a vet-exam room, except with maid service provided by volunteers. Speaking of which, what motivates someone to forgo their usual community service serving soup at the women's shelter to volunteer to strip the bed and clean up the snail trail from lesbians all night? Is the ten-dollar cover charge really that prohibitive?

But in the end, the evening was delightful because there is nothing quite like having anonymous sex with someone who is also willing to share a cab home and walk your dogs together before bed.

Part Three

Rules of the Baths

I found these on a gay male website that explained codes of bathhouse behaviour. Of course, it raised for me a few subtle differences between the usual patrons of Club Toronto and, well, lesbians.

Rule 1: Conversations in the orgy room should be kept to a minimum.

Rule 2: Finish what you start.

Rule 3: If you see a man in a room with a can of Crisco, a thick belt, and a bottle of poppers, be certain you know the purpose of all three items before entering.

This rule in particular seems fitting, although in our case it would be a tub of hemp body butter, a fanny pack, and a bottle of time-release echinacea.

Rule 4: When it's past the wrist is not the time to say 'no.'

So many times after I first came out at the Women's Centre, a woman with slim forearms would catch my eye and within seconds she'd be fisting me on top of the breast self-exam pamphlets and I'd think … hmm … maybe I would have preferred to just cuddle?

Rule 5: It is considered embarrassing to make it with someone you already know.

Rule 6: If you are at the baths busily cheating on your lover, don't make a scene should you discover him there.

With lesbians who've been together for years, the Pussy Palace is an important arena to experiment with non-monogamy and revitalize your erotic connection. In other words, you are allowed to stare at women's tits in the lineup for a soda water while your wife is getting your flip-flops from the car.

Rule 7: Once in a while, do your good deed: let an old troll suck your cock. Such magnanimous gestures are duly recorded by the Great Faggot in the Sky. When you are an old troll, the favours will be returned in kind.

It is important our queer youth understand that it is their duty at Pussy Palace to come up to their sixtysomething Women's Studies professor and benevolently spread their cheeks for some good old-fashioned rimming … because, hey, it makes for compelling 'herstory.'

Rule 8: In the dark, all cats are grey, but ten inches is still better than six inches. Men with small cocks can be sexually tremendous if they are technically proficient, but men with big dicks don't have to know a damn thing.

After four dates with a woman who has introduced me to her thirteen closest friends and let me drive her cat to the vet, should I manage to get her pants off, I am so out of there if I discover her labia minora aren't symmetrical.

Rule 9: If you remember the title of the porno movie showing in the 'rest section,' you did not have a good time.

Or, in our case, if you didn't write an undergraduate paper on the film being shown in the porn room, you've hit the fucking jackpot.

Rule 10: Never try to explain the bathhouse to heterosexuals.

Try explaining to your promiscuous gay male friends that you lined up at the Toronto Women's Bookstore on a Monday morning to get tickets to have anonymous sex a week later with your girlfriend.

Written (and originally performed onstage) in 2002.

Hilary and Karleen are a middle-aged professional lesbian couple with three children who live in Toronto's Little Italy.

KARLEEN: I had come for Amy Marie. She towered over me, part bear, part cowboy, part gay man: 100 per cent proud butch, American, pervert. She hailed from Omaha, with a swagger and a grin. She wore leather chaps over her worn blue jeans, and a black vest with the International Ms. Leather (IMSL) 1993 title glittering on the back. A tattoo chain clasped her broad bicep. I wanted to lay my head across her chest and kiss the soft dark chain. But that wasn't so easy to pull off.

Hilary Cellini Cook and Karleen Pendleton Jiménez

International Ms Leather 2000 Comes to Toronto

HILARY: I wasn't thinking about Amy Marie. She had come to Toronto in November to scout for the upcoming International Ms. Leather contest. It was based in Omaha, Nebraska, and this was their first brave foray out of the U.S. You had stayed out late with her, dressed as a sailor boy, and gone to that leathermen's competition on Eastern Avenue. God knows what you got up to …

You drove her around in your Mustang while she visited venues and booked with the Colony Hotel on Chestnut Street behind City Hall. I got the kids up and dressed and off to school and daycare. You went out the door to follow Amy Marie. It was okay, I could see her appeal and I didn't think you'd be moving to Nebraska. That's the kind of non-monogamist I am, one who calculates the odds.

KARLEEN: I resembled a clean-cut twelve-year-old boy in my second-hand Marine uniform. The leathermen at the Toolbox complimented Amy for having such a fine boy. I liked being the object of their gaze, and Amy's pride. Lots of queers were drawn to her charisma, and to her appreciation for our perversities, showcased at IMSL competitions. Her event provided the setting and encouragement for the rest of us. She gave dykes access to play parties and casual sex; she gave Hilary and me access to Elise.

HILARY: Now it was July, and IMSL was coming to town. Amy Marie would be here, but also her wife, her slave, and a whole pack of unpaid staff descending on the Colony Hotel. You were working the competition, the kids were at their dad's, and we were invited to everything. There was also this butch called Elise, someone you met in Las Vegas at last year's event.

KARLEEN: Swimming pools can make you drop your guard. The limited clothing, sheer and stuck to the body, the direct connection between water and life. Elise had picked me up to tackle me or fuck with me or something. We had spent the week in competition, two brothers vying for a parent's attention at IMSL '99 in Vegas. Her dark red hair, green eyes, freckled cheeks, wide grin were six inches from my face, and a switch got flipped inside me. I realized I could sleep with her if I wanted to. Her closeness opened that up.

HILARY: Elise and you shared the drive back from Las Vegas, pulled into a motel, messed around, drove on. You came home from that trip pleased and a bit distracted. Now she was coming to town, and you were looking forward to seeing her again. And I was there, so there was some kind of deal, some kind of understanding: maybe she could 'hang out' with you and your girlfriend, or some such euphemism.

KARLEEN: I hadn't given myself over to a butch before. I had to hold in a laugh when she spoke the same lines on me I'd used a dozen times. The words faded away when we jumped each other with the glee of puppy dogs, rough and joyful. I thought, this is a new kind of sex for me, a boyish spree shaking up the motel room. She pinned me down with a determined crease in her brow, and pushed inside. I started plotting how to get more, even before it was done.

HILARY: You and I had one of those conversations, like, 'Is this cool with you?' And me, 'Yeah, probably.' Of course, you always have to see how these things pan out, but in theory it was or could be cool. Better than cool.

A few days before the show, I wanted to make things a bit more clear. I know you can wreck these things by trying to pin them down, but that doesn't always get in my way: 'So she's cool to "hang out" with you and me. But she's never met me.'

YOU: 'Yeah, so?'

ME: 'But we know that you and she like each other. So it is possible that the two of you are going to be more into each other, so … '

YOU: '?'

ME: 'So if that's how it works out, I can live with that. I don't want it to be this all-or-nothing deal, if you guys are not that into me and more into each other.'

The IMSL gang hit town, sort of a cross between a kinky gender-variant circus and an army platoon. They had matching black flight suits with the initials of Amy Marie's production company embroidered over the breast pocket. The first night they held an event on the patio at Zelda's, the drag hamburger joint on Church Street. Elise came over laughing and hugged you, leaned over to talk to me, looked me in the eye. 'Leather people are the last ladies and gentlemen,' I thought to myself, which was what Kate Bornstein [respected trans writer and activist] had said to you in the hot tub in Las Vegas the year before.

You, Elise, and the gang were running the conference over at the hotel. I shopped at the vendors. The IMSL group went out for a bite, or at least we tried.

Leatherwomen from Nebraska were freaked out by Cantonese food, Thai, sushi, Italian. We found a diner we could agree on, and they just ate there for every meal.

I was thinking about what to wear to the main awards gala. Black leather corset, velvet skirt, black stockings, and garters. I heard Amy Marie make a joke about s&m standing for Stand and Model. I could sort out my curls and make them cascade down my back. Bit of eyeliner, red lipstick. (When I got to the gala, one crew guy said, 'Wow, you clean up nice!' – a compliment I still carry close to my heart.)

At a party in the organizer's suite, Elise was still being wonderfully attentive. It was riveting how much she and you were similar, not physically, but in energy, focus, vulnerability. Elise told me her friends called her 'E Ticket' because that was the ticket that got you into the best rides at Disneyland. She was boasting, but maybe not without reason. One of Elise's friends said to me, 'You know what's going on here, don't you?' 'What?' 'She's really into you.' The story I had been telling myself was about you and Elise. In that story, she was overdoing it to make sure I felt included.

KARLEEN: When Elise smiled at Hilary, I knew we could take her away from the leather crowd and covet her in our bedroom. It was too hard bringing a femme home for a threesome, hard to split my focus and swallow the resulting sense of guilt. But a butch was different. Hilary was not threatened by butches, knowing I didn't fall in love with them. Hilary appreciated the beauty of masculine affection – two men or two butches kissing. To my mind, I could have it all: I could recapture the lust of wrestling with Elise, and simultaneously pleasure my observing girlfriend.

HILARY: We managed to get Elise over to our house and into our attic bedroom. The two of you blindfolded me, and you told me what to do. Elise leaned back against the headboard while I gave her a blowjob. You were behind me. Oh my god, the two of you were so in tune, it was transcendent. Much, much, much better than cool.

But the story had turned around. It wasn't about preventing me being left out. It was about her deciding she and you were going to make a fuss over me. You weren't boys wrestling. In her mind, you were going to be a team and please the girl. Shit, this had not occurred to me. I hadn't made us have that other boring strategic conversation – 'Baby, what if … '

KARLEEN: It didn't work out for me. Push down on one side of the triangle and another pops up. You lose your balance. Elise couldn't see me with Hilary in the room. Hilary would take everything Elise offered her. I was the one left watching.

HILARY: My transcendent moment, where did it go? Even with a blindfold half over my eyes, I could tell things were not right. I wanted to talk to you. Elise said,

'No, no, babygirl, I will talk to Karleen.' The two of you lay in bed and talked. I sat in the narrow stairway where I could hear your voices but not what you were saying. I hope that's the last time I let someone have a conversation for me that I should be having myself.

KARLEEN: Couldn't they think to include me? Not until the very end, when I was angered. Did Elise anger me on purpose? To cause me enough rage that I would pull her and pin her and fuck her. She needed this, too, from another butch, but the precarious strategy left us broken across the blue-green rattan couch. Hilary huddled in the bay window with her chin in her hands.

HILARY: That was the one that came for you, but went for me. That bittersweet weekend. That ecstasy and that discontent, that fun and that sadness. Damn it, love. Damn pleasure, damn bodies, damn butches, damn sex.

I've never had sex in a bathhouse. Or a park. Or most of the sex spaces that have been fixtures in Toronto's queer landscape.

Perhaps this reeks of my own prudishness toward public sex. Or maybe it's because the utility of these sex spaces has been usurped by the websites and apps that I, like so many others, use more often for sex. I came of age in the bars of Winnipeg in the 2000s, but these technologies have become more integrated into my sex life over time. One has not replaced the other; rather, queer space and apps intermingle, producing a more dynamic means of living a queer life.

When I first arrived in Toronto, I was drawn to the Church-Wellesley Village, but I soon ventured beyond the neighbourhood. As I met men online, Toronto's queerness became familiar through both my virtual and meatspace wanderings. In many ways, my sex life has expanded, taking in new spaces – both physical and virtual – within Toronto's thriving sex spaces, from clubs, parks, campuses, and street corners to apps, mobile phones, and image exchanges. Sex, for me, accounts for more than acts of penetration and orgasm, but also looks, chatter, pictures, and all the techno-social elements that now surround it. Physical and virtual sex spaces are two parts of spatial-technological architectures of queer sex.

Mathew Gagné
Geographies of Gay Sex in the Digital Age

Many have blamed hook-up apps for the slow death of queer space – an accusation that overlooks the redevelopment and gentrification of urban space that preceded these technologies. More specifically, some accuse hook-up apps of contributing to the loss of queer neighbourhoods that were centres of political activism and sexual liberation, as if these are the only spaces that make Toronto queer or that queer people inhabit. I have come to feel not a sense of loss, but rather a diffusion and expansion of Toronto's queer geography.

A friend tells me of having fucked and sucked some guys in the basement bathroom of a college at the University of Toronto on break from studying in the library. Upon hearing the story, I wonder: could I do that? And think: I should try it sometime. Then I see an empty profile on Grindr with the name 'Innis College Now.' From the tale of my friend, I surmise that the guy is in the cruising spot, waiting for someone to join him. My friend's sex experience comes full circle to the interface of my personal device. These various spaces become nodes in a network of different connections. Such is queer life: all those events that transform into collectivized meaning and shared experience. The effects of incoherent banalities and trailing ramblings congealed into meaningful geographies. For all those quick sexual releases, blurred faces, unknown names, random dicks, and splayed orgasms, there are things that linger, moments that pop up in tales and memories. There is a trace of queer meaning in retelling our sex stories, thereby turning private moments into collective experience.

I recall one night, out with a friend on Church Street, when I was feeling particularly randy and was on the apps in search of sex. I could have searched from among the crowd, but I was getting more attention online. The guy living across the street was chatting to me – sexting really – as we built an imaginary of the sex we might have. But his responses lacked commitment to meeting, and were coming slowly. I had a hurried feeling as I watched the battery of my phone gradually drain without a confirmation of meeting. My friend and I decided to leave, but I wasn't yet ready to stop. I stood out on the street, waiting for instructions to his apartment.

I waited silently on the corner in the minutes between his messages, the street becoming a site of anxiety and foolishness. I wanted that confirmation to come, but he, unaware of where I was, took his time to decide. My phone died on the cusp of getting his address, leaving me frustrated and cursing technological imperfections. Having lost contact, I returned home, charged my phone enough to inform him of the reason for my temporary yet untimely disappearance, and then I slept.

On another occasion, I saw a face at a particularly sexy party at the Black Eagle. I slightly recognized the features from a photo I had recently seen of a man I was chatting to on Grindr. From the angle of the image, and the blurry quality, I was initially uncertain if it was him. Feeling emboldened, I greeted him with an inside joke from our conversation. If he hadn't gotten the reference, it meant he wasn't the same guy. Instead, he laughed. 'Oh hey, it's you.' As the night wore on, our bodies got closer while those around us thumped and bumped to the music.

The awkward recognition of the scene in the Black Eagle is not unfamiliar in the techno-sexual age. We move among many different spaces, sometimes not seamlessly. He and I came together because there was a connecting thread between the online and offline, however tenuous. Our history over the app facilitated an encounter that the physical space moved forward. They are two parts of the same process that creates my sex life.

My queer-sex geography is banal and sometimes random, and it is entirely spread out over multiple places. Perhaps such qualities make this geography feel less coherent and less graspable due to its lack of a central focus. But it doesn't seem like loss. To think of my queer-sex geography as a loss fails to account for changing landscapes, new relationships, and the place of memory that bridge individual experiences to collectively shared mappings.

While I may not share my Toronto sex geography with others, we can at least share them as a collective experience of fucking in multiple places all around the city. My private encounters become public not because they are visible and accessible to others, but because we follow the same paths within this geography. The expressions of the city's horniness take multiple forms.

To look at Toronto's queer geography in the digital age entails considering the physical and the virtual, the public and the private, and the personal and the collective as shifting dichotomies that overlap. There are multiple kinds of spaces, some trodden by many, others only by a few. Each day I move within Toronto, the urban landscape becomes a living palette that ignites my queer life and gives it shape, meaning, memory, and attachment.

HE SACRED FIRE

2-SPIRITED PEOPLE
OF THE 1ST NATIONS

RIGHTS

AND RITES

Parliament St., Suite 202, TORONTO, Ont M4X 1P2 961-4725/FAX 961-87

On a bright, sunny summer day in 1985, I got married in the majestic Great Hall at Hart House, University of Toronto's nouveau gothic palace for student activities – a space elegant enough to add mystery to the event, with a courtyard splendid enough to embed it with romance. Though grand, this wasn't the standard sort of wedding ceremony you see in parks and churches all over Toronto each spring and summer.

Camp was the order of the day. A socialist-feminist manifesto grounded the program. The song 'It's Raining Men' accompanied the bridal entrance. A well-known openly gay minister officiated. My love, Jamie, was the outrageous maid of honour, and the acclaimed Sue Golding was the butch-fem best man. The wedding cake was topped ever so appropriately by a Barbie-like bride ceremoniously whipping a Ken-like groom oh-so-subtly bent over the cherry on top.

This subversive ridicule of patriarchal hegemony was the brainchild of the ever fabulous, politically committed Chris Bearchell, Canada's highest-profile lesbian.

Bob Gallagher

It Seemed Like a Gay Wedding To Me

I never considered the implications of my decision to move from the United States to Canada. My passion for political theory simply drove me to study in Toronto with the greatest living theorist of democracy – C. B. MacPherson.

It hadn't dawned on me that being a little bit queer, a political activist, and a Vietnam War protester would interfere with my leaving the U.S., getting a student visa, and studying at the University of Toronto. And, of course, it didn't.

It didn't even interfere when the police raided the gay bathhouses and I became heavily involved in anti-police protests, demonstrations, and countless queer and political organizations. And it didn't even seem to register when I got arrested for some of those activities.

It didn't interfere, that is, until I fell in love.

Once I fell in love with the city, with being queer, and with my soulmate, I wasn't willing to just leave Canada once my studies were finished. However, a common route for staying under such situations – heterosexual marriage to a Canadian citizen – wasn't available to me. And in my case, marrying my true love and settling down happily-ever-after was not an option Immigration Canada understood.

You see, 1985 was twenty years too early to get married as a gay man. And for me, it was twenty years too late to clean the record of my queer and political activities that clearly identified me as a gay man and a political dissident.

Hence, the only real pathway to permanent residency and citizenship that Immigration Canada offered – that of marriage – would prove to be a bit complicated for me. I knew of many closeted queers who had gone the route of a 'marriage of convenience.' But that's the thing about going the closeted route … you have to actually be closeted. And (un)fortunately, that closet door had swung open long ago.

Nonetheless, the cruelty of the state being blind to my love, the hypocrisy of criteria open only to heterosexuals, and the indignity of breaking up my family while at the same time not recognizing that family, seemed like ridiculous reasons not to proceed.

Then the persuasive and irrepressible Chris Bearchell convinced me the cheeky thing to do was to marry her and file for immigration.

Soon after we started the process, our lawyer brought our attention to Question 26F on the immigration form for sponsorship by a spouse: 'List each and every social or political organization, club or group you have been a member of in the last 10 years (use additional sheet if needed),' it read.

Any untruth or omission on this legal form would be a felony and grounds for deportation, our lawyer dutifully pointed out.

The words untruth and omission were very much on our minds as we listed the many organizations we had belonged to over the previous decade. My list of eighty-some groups proved to be nothing compared to the causes and campaigns in which Chris had been a central figure throughout the seventies and eighties.

And when we put our lists in alphabetical order, the Gs and the Ls dominated the three additional sheets of paper we attached to our form. As we submitted our documents, it seemed a defiant yet futile act. And it certainly felt surreal.

It was clear to Chris and me that the interview we were called into two months later would likely not be easy. We simply hoped it would go beyond a simple one-word meeting: Denied.

We were ready for an argument, ready to be indignant, and (as in so many political battles we had mounted over the years) we were prepared for spectacular failure.

However, amid all the anticipatory political posturing, we had overlooked the fact that we were filing for immigration in a distinctly Canadian bureaucracy. A system featuring some bureaucrats who were authoritarian, some compassionate, some dictatorial, some kind, and some just bored. The system was rule-based, but it was populated with the mosaic of Canadians.

I don't know how the processing of immigration papers works, or how someone gets assigned to manage a file and conduct the mandatory interview. However, we took it as a good sign that we were actually granted an interview, even if it was possibly set up to ridicule and embarrass us. The hope was definitely that they weren't conducting it to press charges against us.

As we waited in the sterile, washed-out-blue waiting room, we steeled ourselves for interrogation. When we walked into the tiny room with one metal desk and two guest chairs, we were greeted with the extended hand of the immigration officer and an emotionless 'Good afternoon.'

It wasn't the officer's meticulously pressed uniform that immediately struck Chris and me. It wasn't the precise formality of her movements. It was the slight hint of a smile on the corner of the mouth of this strong, heavy-set, short-haired, baritone-sounding woman. A look and a smile Chris had become familiar with decades earlier.

'I've looked over your file,' the officer said evenly. 'And I have only one question: why did you get married?'

'We want to raise a family,' we answered.

'Very good.'

She thanked us, and told us the formal decision would be in the mail within a couple weeks.

'**W**hy do you go *there?*'

My friend Martine (not her real name) told me she had been asked the question many times by her fellow Black queer Torontonians.

In this case, the 'there' that incurred so much incredulity was the Metropolitan Community Church of Toronto, a large Protestant church near Broadview and Gerrard that is predominantly LGBT. To be more precise, MCCT is an increasingly diverse congregation, but one that remains primarily composed of middle-class, cisgender white gay men and lesbians.

Besides the 519 Community Centre, there are few other LGBT institutions in Toronto with as high a public profile outside of LGBT communities as MCCT. But the church has also drawn critical attention and scrutiny from within LGBT communities. Indeed, while MCCT has been at the forefront of struggles around gender and sexual diversity for over forty years, many people of colour who have been involved describe a structural pattern of alienation, marginalization, and burnout.

David K. Seitz

'Why Do You Go *There?*'
Struggle, Faith, and Love at the Metropolitan Community Church of Toronto

I first began attending MCCT as a University of Toronto graduate student in early 2011, because I was interested in learning more about the work of the church's refugee program. I conducted intensive research at the church through 2013, including sixty interviews over the course of those three years. One afternoon over tea in June 2013, Martine explained to me the difficulty she experienced as a woman of colour at a queer church where she longed to see 'anyone who is not a gay white man' get a chance to lead. That question – 'Why do you go there?' – came not only from Black queer folks in Toronto who were skeptical of the church because of its reputation, it was one Martine told me she asked *herself* on a regular basis. While she continues to attend church, she told me, she does so without rose-coloured glasses.

'What, then, keeps you at the church?' I asked her.

She told me about a sign near the back of the worship space. It bore a version of Isaiah, chapter 56, verse 7: 'My house shall be a house of prayer for all people.' Martine told me she liked that sign because it suggested the work of social justice was not a fait accompli but an ongoing struggle. She saw that promise – my house *shall be* a house of prayer for all people – as an opening she could use to work to transform the church.

I open with her insights here because my conversations with Martine and other women of colour active in the life of the church have taught me a great deal about love and queer community in Toronto. Love in this sense is a sustained relation to an idea or place that you want to stay in the picture, which can also be an 'object' that pisses you off, an object you want to transform.

The Sisters of Perpetual Indulgence bless the old Bathurst Street Theatre, formerly home to the MCCT.

(As queer theorist Lauren Berlant puts it, 'When we talk about objects of desire, we are really talking about a cluster of promises we want someone or something to make us and make possible for us.')

Karen, a Black woman who serves as a deacon, helping to lead worship services and providing pastoral care and counselling at the church, described to me routine experiences of racialized misrecognition – confusion with another prominent Black woman in the congregation – by long-time white churchgoers. She told me she felt she was regarded with suspicion both by some whites, who seemed to be on guard for evidence of her 'acting out of line,' but also ambivalently by many queer people of colour, who viewed her as providing important representation for queers of colour yet also as a kind of 'whitewashed' token. Karen, however, described a remarkably generous political sensibility. Our conversation encompassed trans and disability rights and alliances with other communities of colour. With great respect for Karen's ministry, I asked her a similar question to the one I asked Martine:

> D: What keeps you at MCCT, given the kinds of barriers you've talked about to Black people staying for a long time?
> K: So what's kept me there? The other part of what I've done is I used to hold wellness workshops. So I'd have a wellness day; I'd have all different kinds of alternative therapists coming in, just to show people there are other ways of healing beyond the traditional sense, right?
>
> So what keeps me there are the possibilities. And the social justice work we do. I think we reach a lot of people. I do think we do good work, I just think we need to do more of it, and have our voice heard in different settings – and not just one voice, but many voices. So it's the possibility that keeps me there.

And it truly is a loving place. If you walk in there, you feel the love, right? And I know, for me, through all my stages of healing, MCC's always been there. However I've wanted to let MCC in, it's always been there. I think any church, any system, has its problems.

Many of the people of colour involved with the church told me they felt dismissed by whites as playing identity politics, as playing the race card or the gender card or both, rather than being taken seriously. Yet the critiques of the church that Martine, Karen, and others make are, in fact, an invitation to coalition, and an incitement to the productive mutual discomfort that necessarily accompanies it. As the Black feminist Bernice Johnson Reagon puts it, 'the first thing that happens [in coalition] is that the room doesn't feel like the room anymore ... and you can't feel comfortable no more.'

In a complex way, then, the answer to the question 'Why do you go *there*?' for Martine or for Karen might be 'love.' I make this argument not to naturalize the struggles that Martine, Karen, and their colleagues have experienced at the church, but rather to suggest that the emotional sophistication these leaders demonstrate is worth heeding when thinking about the life of queer political coalitions in this city.

It's not difficult to tell that the church is a normatively white space, often in exclusive ways. But actually talking to and learning from some of the women of colour who go there has helped me understand the tremendous savvy and sophistication with which (to invoke, of all people, Margaret Cho) they have chosen to stay and fight. Moreover, it reminds us that even 'mainstream' or 'big tent' LGBT organizations in Toronto – including faith communities – are contested terrain, places where people of conscience struggle over the meaning of community, and work for more meaningful forms of inclusion.

A Brief History of the MCCT

In October 1968, Rev. Troy Perry, a gay man who had been raised Baptist and Pentecostal and sought to integrate sexuality with spirituality, held the first worship service of what became known as the Metropolitan Community Church in his living room in Los Angeles. In the years that followed, MCC congregations, initially populated mostly by gay men, popped up in many major cities in the U.S., and soon in Canada and Mexico. In July 1973, Rev. Bob Wolfe, previously the pastor of the MCC congregation in San Diego, was dispatched to serve a fledgling congregation that had formed in Toronto. Four years later, Rev. Brent Hawkes, a former teacher from Bath, New Brunswick, who took part in the congregation during his time as a divinity student at Trinity College, became the pastor.

Over the following four decades, MCCT and Hawkes have played a prominent role in urban, provincial, national, and transnational LGBT political struggles. The church has been at the forefront of responses to the bathhouse raids and HIV/AIDS, campaigns for anti-discrimination and relationship-recognition legislation, and support for LGBT youth, people living with addiction, and seniors. While Toronto is home to a wide range of LGBT-affirming and, in many cases, LGBT-led communities of religious faith and/or practice, MCCT has occupied a relatively unique (though by no means exclusive) position, benefiting both from its status as a predominantly LGBT church and from what David Martin (2000) calls the 'shadow establishment' of Christianity in Canada – the often invisible, implicit sense of rightness conferred to Christians and especially Protestants in Canada. In other words, MCCT isn't the only game in town, but being mostly LGBT and being Protestant – in addition to its charismatic leadership and music leadership– has helped contribute to its size and influence.

Although many people have related to MCC churches in Toronto and globally as revolving doors – spaces that offer solace while these people wait and work for their 'home' religious communities to change their stance on sexual or gender diversity – many have stayed. While not without controversy or dissension, Hawkes's visibility and tenure, almost as long as the lifespan of the congregation itself, have served to keep the church in the spotlight.

For instance, Hawkes played a key role in the fight for same-sex marriage rights in Canada. When city and provincial officials were unable to grant marriage licences to same-sex couples, Kathleen Lahey, a feminist law professor at Queen's University, suggested Hawkes take an alternative – and legally binding – route by reading the banns, or proclamations of an upcoming marriage, in church, opening them up to public objection. Following this path, Hawkes performed a legally binding double wedding for two same-sex couples in January 2001, and the historic litigation that followed led to the nationwide legalization of same-sex marriage.

But the personal and political concerns that congregants bring to the church – racism, poverty, transphobia, disability, a precarious grasp on housing or citizenship status – go far beyond marriage or legal equality. Today, the average Sunday at MCCT greets six hundred in-person visitors at three worship services, and another two hundred viewers who tune in to a global webcast of the service over the following seven days. Those numbers make MCCT the largest predominantly LGBT faith community in Canada, and among the largest in the world.

On Tuesday, May 22, 2007, Edith Windsor and Thea Spyer flew to Toronto to get married in a small ceremony with six friends at a hotel near Pearson International, with Harvey Brownstone, Canada's first openly gay judge, presiding. 'Windsor wore white,' the *Guardian* reported later, '[Spyer] was in all black.'

Some years earlier, a same-sex marriage ceremony would have attracted reporters and perhaps even the mayor. But Windsor and Spyer's nuptials merited no such attention – at least, not on that day. After all, same-sex weddings by 2007 were commonplace in Toronto; the city had become a destination for American gay and lesbian couples who wanted to get married but couldn't do so legally in their own country.

John Lorinc

From Banns to DOMA

The legal process that led to their marriage began seven years earlier, in December 2000, when Rev. Brent Hawkes, of the Metropolitan Community Church of Toronto (MCCT), proclaimed banns declaring the weddings of two same-sex couples: Kevin Bourassa and Joe Varnell and Elaine and Anne Vautour. When no one objected within the response period, Hawkes performed the ceremonies, on January 14, 2001. He then sought to register both marriages. But the registry clerk had to refuse, as the definition of marriage at the time specified a man and a woman. (At least two other same-sex marriage ceremonies had taken place previously, including one in Toronto officiated that same year by Cheri DiNovo and another in Manitoba, in 1974.)

The MCCT appealed, and so began a judicial odyssey that led to the Ontario Court of Appeal decision, issued on June 10, 2003, which held that existing Canadian marriage laws violated the equal protection provision – Section 15(a) – of the Canadian Charter of Rights and Freedoms. (The landmark ruling, *Halpern et al. v. the Attorney General of Canada et al.*, was signed by then-Ontario chief justice Roy McMurtry, who, in a previous incarnation as attorney general in February 1981, had been a key player in Operation Soap, the bathhouse raids.)

The judges ordered the Toronto city clerk to issue the marriage licences, and so Ontario became the first jurisdiction in North America to recognize same-sex marriage. Michael Leshner, a veteran Crown attorney, and his longtime partner, Michael Stark, a graphic designer, became the first gay couple to marry after the decision. Other higher-court rulings followed, as did the Liberal government's same-sex marriage legislation, which received Royal Assent on July 20, 2005.

Windsor, a seventy-seven-year-old retired computer consultant, and Spyer, a seventy-five-year-old clinical psychologist, had been a couple for decades on the day they arrived in Toronto, two years later. According to a *New York*

Times wedding announcement, they met at a Greenwich Village restaurant in 1965, and the two women ended up at a friend's apartment. 'Dr. Spyer and Ms. Windsor danced until the impromptu party ended, finally "dancing with our coats on, and other people standing at the door, annoyed, waiting for us," Ms. Windsor recalled, adding, "She was smarter than hell, beautiful – and sexy." Dr. Spyer recalled of Ms. Windsor that night, "We danced so much and so intensely that she danced a hole through her stockings."'

By the time of their wedding, in 2007, Spyer was terminally ill with multiple sclerosis, and Windsor had become her full-time caregiver; she died in 2009.

Soon after her spouse's death, Windsor was ordered to pay $363,000 in estate taxes because federal marriage law prevented her from claiming the exemption for surviving spouses. She sued, challenging the constitutionality of the Clinton-era Defence of Marriage Act, and the case eventually made its way to the U.S. Supreme Court.

United States v. Windsor[1] was heard on March 27, 2013, with the judgment released three months later. In its landmark five-four decision, the court overturned DOMA, with the majority judges ruling that the law violated the equal-protection provisions of the U.S. Constitution – an argument anticipated by the Ontario Court of Appeal. Justice Anthony Kennedy, who cast the swing vote, began the seventy-seven-page judgment with a sentence that set the stage: 'Two women then resident in New York were married in a lawful ceremony in Ontario, Canada, in 2007 ... '

According to Statistics Canada, in its first such report, there were 64,575 'same-sex couple families' in Canada in 2011, including 21,015 married couples.[2]

1. The ruling is available at: www.supremecourt.gov/opinions/12pdf/12-307_6j37.pdf
2. www.statcan.gc.ca/eng/dai/smr08/2015/smr08_203_2015.

During World Pride 2014, a mass gay and lesbian wedding held at Casa Loma, Toronto's famous faux castle, drew intense media attention. The event featured fancy outfits, limousines, cake, and champagne for almost a thousand people, and a choice of twelve religious officiants. TV news crews, which had otherwise paid little attention to World Pride, featured heart-rending same-sex romances – stories about couples of long standing who, legally unable to marry at home, had travelled across oceans to obtain both a legal certificate and a stylish wedding.

Although most of the happy couples were either local or from the United States, it is telling that the stories focused on a few photogenic couples from afar, such as a young lesbian couple from Taiwan, and an older gay male couple from Australia who bemoaned that country's same-sex union rules. 'We're husband and husband now,' they told the *National Post*. 'That's what really matters to us.[I]

Maureen FitzGerald and Mariana Valverde

City of Love at the Castle on the Hill

Since 2000, sexual diversity had played an increasingly important role in the self-image of Toronto. Originally, the city's motto, 'Diversity Our Strength,' referred to ethnic, religious, and racial diversity. But in the early 2000s, sexual diversity came increasingly into view, with Toronto positioning itself as inclusive and tolerant (often by comparison, implicit or explicit, with the U.S.). Same-sex marriage burst into public view in January 2001 when Brent Hawkes, the pastor of a gay/lesbian Protestant congregation, used the old Christian tradition of reading banns in church to perform two marriages. A church wedding being the sort of thing only the most diehard homophobes could denounce, the coverage of those ceremonies was celebratory, and contributed to the legalization of same-sex marriage by provincial courts in Ontario and British Columbia in 2003.

That year, only two other countries and one U.S. state (Massachusetts) allowed gays and lesbians to marry. So Toronto leveraged its geographical position (close to millions of American gays and lesbians who could not marry at home) to boost tourism income and simultaneously burnish its diversity reputation. From 2003 to 2014, many non-Canadian same-sex couples travelled to Toronto to marry.[II] Fortunately for the emerging gay-wedding industry, which brought in hundreds of millions of dollars (though reliable figures are not available), the Province of Ontario does not have onerous residence requirements for marriage licences.

But Toronto's reputation as the gay-wedding haven suffered an unexpected blow after the 2010 election of redneck councillor Rob Ford as mayor. Ford became internationally famous for smoking crack cocaine in one of his

'drunken stupors,' as he himself put it. Locally, Ford's refusal to appear at the annual Pride Parade was seen as a threat to the city's reputation for tolerance.

In that context, the city-supported Casa Loma mass same-sex wedding became an important chapter in the history of the city as a whole, not only to its LGBT citizens.

The much-publicized ceremony could not have taken place without a particular alignment of political and economic interests not visible to the participants (or the viewing audiences), but that nonetheless revealed a lot about the city. In January 2014, a few months before World Pride, City Council approved a twenty-year lease of Casa Loma to entertainment-venue mogul Nick Di Donato. (Energy mogul Henry Pellatt built Casa Loma in 1914 as a private residence of great pretension, but after Pellatt's fortune collapsed, the city acquired ownership and, in the 1940s, assigned management responsibility to the Kiwanis Club.)

Di Donato, president and CEO of Liberty Entertainment, had a reputation for turning large heritage buildings into profitable event venues. His company is named for the Liberty Grand, located at the Canadian National Exhibition. After he persuaded Council to let him take over from Kiwanis, Di Donato set to work overcoming the castle's hackneyed reputation and outdated decor.

While Di Donato was trying to refresh Casa Loma, the city faced an even more daunting problem. Despite Ford's admissions about cocaine and drunken stupors, he refused to resign. By November 2013, Council had had enough, removing all non-statutory powers from Ford and delegating those to Deputy Mayor Norm Kelly.

One of over a hundred LGBTQ couples marrying at a mass ceremony at Casa Loma, June 24, 2014.

In the lead-up to World Pride, Kelly met with Parents and Friends of Lesbians and Gays, and then, above Ford's objections, had the rainbow flag raised at City Hall during the 2014 Sochi Winter Olympics (an important gesture because some LGBT activists felt Sochi should be boycotted due to Russia's homophobic policies). Meanwhile, Kristyn Wong-Tam, an openly lesbian city councillor whose ward includes the Gay Village, did her best to ensure official support for World Pride activities.

If Rob Ford had never been elected mayor, World Pride would likely have received rubber-stamp City approval and more modest publicity. But given the public relations debacle with Ford, Wong-Tam reckoned it made sense to dream up something big to restore Toronto's reputation.

And what could be bigger than a fancy-dress mass wedding at Casa Loma?

The event could easily have proceeded on a purely secular basis, with justices of the peace officiating. But it did not. While it is impossible to know how many of the couples that got married sought religious validation, the ceremony acquired a strongly religious flavour.

One might imagine that Toronto's own gay church, the Metropolitan Community Church located in Riverdale, would have presided over the religious aspects, but that did not happen. Instead, the mass wedding turned into an occasion for the strengthening of a loose interfaith coalition of gay-affirming congregations that had been quietly working to build a multiculturalism that, unlike the City's official policy, would be strongly spiritual.

In January 2013, John Joseph Mastandrea, the openly gay pastor at the Metropolitan United Church, at Church and Queen, began to think about forming a committee to organize an interfaith queer-positive fair just prior to World Pride.

In an interview, Mastandrea, chair of the Interfaith Committee, stressed that this plan had been developed in a city where, at the time, 'the mayor was as homophobic as the day is long.' But he and others recognized that Toronto had been known since 2001 as a same-sex marriage destination. So in 2013, Mastandrea approached David Lewis-Peart, of Sunset Service, a ministry for 'sexual minorities and members of marginalized racial and ethnic communities of all faiths.' A small interfaith group came together and grew quickly.

El-Farouk Khaki, a well-known gay activist and refugee rights lawyer as well as the leader of the Unity Mosque, then came on board. Khaki shared a hairdresser with Mastandrea; this accidental connection led them to share impromptu monthly conversations about expanding the scope of 'interfaith' beyond the usual Christian-Jewish-Unitarian alliance. They invited representatives of the Ismaili Muslim, First Nations, Hindu, Buddhist, and Pagan faith traditions, as well as a breakaway Catholic community that ordains gay and lesbian people.

In early 2014, Wong-Tam approached Mastandrea, saying her office wanted to organize a mass wedding with an interfaith component. As Mastandrea said, 'the universe had lined up.' The existing Interfaith Committee recruited twelve officiants to perform weddings for up to 130 couples and created a liturgy for the day.

While he had no direct link to the interfaith group, Di Donato offered his newly leased Casa Loma as a venue. To round out the offer, he threw in free champagne, hors d'oeuvres, and cake.

On May 5, 2014, just days after he took over mayoral duties when Rob Ford went into rehab, Norm Kelly threw his support behind staging the mass wedding during Pride Week. While Kelly, a right-wing councillor, had never been a particular friend of the LGBTQ community, he realized he had to save the city's reputation for diversity. At an event with Wong-Tam, he invited two hundred LGBTQ-Two Spirit couples to participate. 'Inclusiveness has to be the basic principle of any office that includes the title of mayor,' he said.

The story of how same-sex marriage came to be legal, in Canada and elsewhere, has been well documented. Various allies, from labour unions to the NDP to churches (especially the United Church of Canada), mobilized to help obtain legal victories for sexual-orientation rights activists. But the story has been told as a tale of law reform. This is an important dimension, of course, but marriages are more than legal relationships.

In particular, weddings are complex and emotionally powerful rituals that serve many larger social purposes besides making individual brides and grooms happy. The mass wedding at Casa Loma, partly by design and partly through chance, addressed many unrelated needs. For a city suffering from the unprecedented public relations disaster that was the Rob Ford mayoralty, the event helped restore Toronto's self-image as cosmopolitan and diverse. For minority religious leaders such as El-Farouk Khaki, who had long worked in obscurity to build queer-affirming congregations, the visibility and upscale arrangements provided an instant, positive media presence they could never have obtained on their own. And last, the event also helped consolidate the public-private partnership between Liberty Entertainment, a powerful local company, and the City of Toronto (though Di Donato later got in trouble with municipal officials in relation to other large parties his firm hosted).

We do not know what the Casa Loma extravaganza meant for those who got married.[2] But at the level of the city and its LGBTQ communities, the mass wedding was certainly pretty close to a fairy tale.

1. news.nationalpost.com/toronto/first-mass-gay-wedding-in-canada-draws-couples-from-around-the-world.

2. Or whether some of those marriages culminated in divorce. Some U.S. states now track same-sex divorce, although there's no consensus on whether LGBT marriages are more or less likely to end in divorce than those of straight couples. While Statistics Canada has begun counting gay marriages, it does not collect statistics on divorce. Yet.

T hanks to the work of Toronto-based activists, lawyers, litigants, and community animators, alongside those in other parts of the country, there has been a sea change in the world of LGBTQ2S parenting over the last thirty years in Canada. Where once queer and trans people had to deny huge parts of themselves in order to keep their children, it is now increasingly okay to claim our sexual and gender identities and our right to parent.

Rachel Epstein

LGBTQ2S

Parenting:

Some Milestones

Yet despite the enormous social and legal gains of the past three decades, we are haunted by the spectre of the conventional nuclear family and the ghosts of a recent past in which LGBTQ2S people were both denied the right to have children and had children taken away from them. Many LGBTQ2S people still feel unsure about their rights and abilities to parent, and most institutions, including daycares, schools, and health care facilities, struggle to be queer- and trans-inclusive. Trans people remain vulnerable to attacks on their parenting abilities and continue to be at risk of losing their children in custody battles. We can celebrate milestones and still recognize that change is rarely as simple as the linear narrative of progress suggests.

1980s & 1990s: Groups like Gay Fathers of Toronto, Gays & Lesbians Parenting Together, and support groups for lesbian moms meet at the 519 Church Street Community Centre.

1995: Lesbian couples are granted the right to second-parent adoption in Ontario.

1997: First Dykes Planning Tykes course is held, sponsored by the Centre for Lesbian & Gay Studies, held at the International Student Centre, University of Toronto. (Developed by Kathi Duncan and Rachel Epstein; later also facilitated by Rose Gutierrez and Nila Gupta.)

2001: The LGBT Parenting Network is created as a project of David Kelley Services (Family Service Toronto), with Rachel Epstein as coordinator. In 2007 moves to Sherbourne Health Centre.

2003: First Daddies & Papas 2B course developed and facilitated by Chris Veldhoven, held at the 519.

2004: Pride Toronto and the LGBTQ Parenting Network collaborate to create the Family Pride space at the Church St. Public School.

2004: Kevin Durkee wins Ontario court battle to register as the sole birth parent of his daughter (born via an anonymous egg donor and a gestational carrier).

2006: Charter challenge *Rutherford v. Ontario*. Lesbian parents in Ontario (who use an anonymous sperm donor to conceive) can put both women's names on the birth registration, without having to bear the cost (and indignity) of a formal adoption.

2007: First Trans Fathers 2B course developed and facilitated by Robin Fern, held at the Central YMCA (later further developed into Transmasculine People Considering Pregnancy and facilitated by j wallace and Andy Inkster).

2007: AA BB CC: The Ontario Court of Appeal releases its decision in the 'three-parent' case, ruling that judges in Ontario have the jurisdiction to declare more than two persons to be legal parents of a child.

2011: First Queer & Trans Family Planning course, held at the 519, facilitated by Rachel Epstein, Chris Vendhoven, and j wallace (and later others, including Andy Inkster and Nila Gupta).

2014: Dana Baitz heads up the Trans Family Law Project, a project intended to keep trans parents and their children together by providing Ontario family law information.

2016: Lawyer Joanna Radbord spearheads the fight for a family law that recognizes a broader range of LGBTQ2S family configurations, including families with known sperm donors and multi-parent families. The All Families Are Equal Act, which became law in Ontario in 2016, includes a degendering of language from mother/father to parent, protection for non-biological parents, and the possibility to include up to four people on a child's birth registration.

'The fact is, there are gay and lesbian and bisexual kids on our caseloads. They're really afraid to be who they are.' – Children's Aid Society of Toronto worker, speaking in 1994

John McCullagh

'We Are Your Children Too!':

How Toronto's Children's Aid Society Learned to Support Queer Youth

During the late 1980s and early 1990s, Toronto's queer community had become increasingly visible and successful at gaining recognition of its rights. But not everyone benefited equally, and this was especially true for many queer youth.

As a Toronto Children's Aid Society (CAS) youth worker, I had encountered many queer young people, most of whom were afraid to come out. They often internalized the negative values society at large held about queer people. Unable to talk openly to their families or friends, they often became isolated and withdrawn. Some were rejected, or forced to leave home, forced to survive on the city's streets. 'At school it was really tough,' one young person told me. 'In the cafeteria, I'd be pushed and shoved and asked if I was a boy or a girl. I never knew if I was going to be attacked after school one day.'

Many of these youths ended up in the care of the CAS. But even this was not always a refuge. As one young woman said, 'I don't see why I should be terrorized in a place that I'm forced to live.' Another youth in care put it this way: 'It gets dark, everybody's asleep, and the kid who's been labelled a fag gets beaten up.' It is no wonder that stress, anxiety, and depression mark the experiences of so many young queer people; the scars can often remain for a lifetime, which in some cases ends with a suicide.

I understood, from personal experience, what it meant to grow up gay. And from a decade spent as a volunteer with the Toronto Counselling Centre for Lesbians and Gays, I knew something about the strategies queer youth used to survive in a hostile environment and to develop an identity as a lesbian, gay, or bisexual person.

In 1992, I formed a CAS steering committee of youth, staff, and foster parents, and we quickly identified systemic barriers within the agency that prevented it from meeting the needs of queer youth. We recommended changes and found, not surprisingly, that the best advocates were the youths themselves. As one young woman described her experiences at a meeting of foster parents: 'The system has failed us in a fundamental way, in not providing a sense of family belonging and support to help us get through.'

In response, one foster parent shared her own dilemma: 'We were sitting at the table once, and the kids in Grade 5 or 6 in our foster home were taking sex education. We were talking about that over dinner and we were bringing up what they learned. One of the boys said, "Well, I sure look forward to kissing girls," and the other one said, "Yeah, I look forward to it, too." And another one quite innocently said, "I think I'd like to kiss a boy." The silence – you could have cut it. And that's because we didn't know how to deal with it, which made it worse.'

While queer youth commonly experience pervasive barriers, we carefully examined how these biases and risks played out in the lives of the young people the CAS served. We identified four key systemic barriers to equitable, accessible, and quality services:

• *Invisibility*. Most workers did not realize they worked with queer youth, resulting in a lack of policies and procedures promoting equal access to services. One youth in care described how he could never tell his foster parent how unsafe he felt at school: 'I was always late for class. I never went through a hallway where there were other students. That would have been stupidity, putting my life at risk.'

• *Pathologizing queer youth*. When these young people disclosed their same-sex orientation to CAS workers or foster parents, they were frequently treated as if they had a psychological disorder. 'It makes it harder to deal with our own issues when we're dealing with society telling us we're bad,' one said. 'Then our own worker tells us we might need to see a psychiatrist, reinforcing all of the problems society is handing us.'

• *Tolerance of anti-lesbian/gay behaviour*. 'When other peers in my group home would direct a homophobic remark to my face,' one lesbian youth said, 'staff would not comment or tell them they wouldn't accept that kind of discriminatory behaviour in the home.'

• *Denial of relationships*. While the development of interpersonal relationship skills was seen as an important activity for heterosexual youth, CAS staff and foster parents often responded with fear and dismay when it involved two individuals with a same-sex orientation. Workers and care providers often discouraged friendships and connections between queer youth. As one female group-home resident complained, 'Once I let out that I thought I was falling in love with one of the other girls. From that point on, the staff never let us out of their sight.'

The youth members of the steering committee challenged us all to find solutions. 'If we have been this strong to survive and share with you what we have learned,' one told us, 'then we trust you can be strong enough to create change.'

To create that change, we needed to advocate internally for the elimination of all forms of discrimination against queer youth. Lesbian, gay, and bisexual youth –

and, later, trans and gender-non-conforming youth – had to be able to see themselves reflected in CAS programs, services, and communications materials. And because so little was known then by most child welfare professionals about the needs of LGBT youth, we also recognized that comprehensive training in sexual orientation and gender identity issues was perhaps the single most important component in improving the quality of care.

In 1995, the Toronto CAS board accepted over thirty steering-committee recommendations in a report entitled *We Are Your Children Too!* The outcome was the establishment of a specialized Out and Proud Program, serving queer youth and their families, a pioneering effort to deliver safe, accessible, and supportive child welfare services. (Visit www.torontocas.ca/out-and-proud.)

Toronto CAS now has more than two decades of experience providing services and care for children, youth, and families who identify as queer. The real credit for this shift belongs to the young people who shared their stories and showed us the way.

As one told us, 'Not ever finding a gay or queer staff who was "out" in my journey of youth services, I jumped at the opportunity to offer up some sound advice on young queer issues in the service community. I felt I could open the eyes of service providers. I wanted them to protect the youth in care from the homophobia directed by other young people in their care. I wanted to make sure we mattered, and to ensure that no one else walked alone as I did, lost and making so many mistakes.'

The story of the Unity Mosque begins with a need. In 2004, I was faced with the reality that my common-law partner of fifteen years had died; he had wanted a Muslim funeral, but he also wanted to be cremated.

How was I going to go to a traditional or dominant Muslim community and say, 'Hi, this is my same-sex partner who wants to have a Muslim funeral but also wants to be cremated and not buried'? Our sexual orientation and his wishes made it difficult. My cousin connected me to the head of funeral services in her community to do the washing (*ghusl*) and funeral shroud (*kaffan*). He said they couldn't do these tasks because my partner wasn't a part of their community, and if they made an exception for him, how could they say no to others? But, the funeral official said, 'I can show you how to do it.' This man brought the fabric to my home, and a group of our friends and I did the body washing and the wrapping under his supervision.

El-Farouk Khaki

Building the Unity Mosque

The next day, we held a multi-faith service at Emmanuel Howard Park United Church, facilitated by Cheri DiNovo, the minister there. I led the traditional Muslim funeral prayer (*salat* or *namaz ul Janaza*) in the church's sanctuary, after which we led the procession to the crematorium at St. James Cemetery on Parliament Street.

By profession, I am a lawyer and I come from a family known in certain circles and communities within the Canadian Muslim community. After this experience, I thought, 'Wow, so if this is what I had to go through to have my late partner's wishes met, what do those who don't have the same kind of access do?'

I think a lot of racialized queer folk who don't come from a Christian background have no access to an affirming faith community. The notion of the merging of our spiritual, racialized, and queer identities is a process many of us are just embarking on. Those of us who are Sikh, Hindu, Buddhist, or Muslim, or follow an Indigenous path, have not had communities or spaces where we can access our spirituality – spaces that also affirm us as queer people. Like many queer Christians and Jews, many racialized LGBTIQ of other religious traditions have tried to purge religion and spirituality out of their individual and collective narratives. But we've seen that that doesn't actually work; many people still want and need a spiritual connection.

Through my activism with Salaam Canada and LGBTIQ people – especially Muslims – and through my own experience of loss, I saw those needs were not being met. I said, 'I can do this!'

People ask me, 'What special knowledge do you have to have to be an imam?' In Canada in the 1970s, 1980s, and 1990s, I would see men who were imams in communities in North America, whose claim to being an imam was that they knew the Quran by heart, or they had gone to a madrasa for a couple of years, or they spoke Arabic. I thought, 'So that's all?' Most of them have limited if any counselling or pastoral training. They don't know how to take care of people or care for their souls. They don't understand people's pain. They can't speak to that and they don't do any of that.

Technically, *imam* means leader. In the context of a mosque, it means somebody who leads prayers. Now, with the 'clergification' of imams in the West, the question is only about certification. I've been doing my master's in Pastoral Studies in the Muslim stream at the University of Toronto's Emmanuel College on a part-time basis. I have learned my theology through reading, conversations, mentorships, and lived experience. I know a lot of theologians and academics on a first-name basis, and I've dealt with them for a long, long time. My own path of reconciliation and the development of my own theology has been a many-decades process. I step into this not as somebody who is oblivious, but somebody who has lived experience and extensive practice in pastoral care working with LGBTIQ and gender-based refugee populations.

I am clergy who has risen to meet a need that is unmet by others. I try to bring to my ministry my politics, my human rights activism, and an anti-colonialist political and feminist narrative, which is one of the reasons El-Tawhid Juma Circle congregations tend to be predominantly female.

When I started my inclusive mosque work decades ago, I had a hard time getting women to lead prayer. The Muslim women who did step up were white women converts as opposed to women from historical Muslim backgrounds. Perhaps white convert women stepped up to lead prayer because, having grown up in North America or Western, they had not experienced some of the gender limitations many non-Western women face. And they often didn't have the ties that suffocated.

There are the ties that bind and the ties that choke. Often, women who are racialized, and women who were born Muslim or raised Muslim, would have to deal with their extended families and community for doing this audacious act of leading prayer. Whereas with a lot of the converts, both Black and white, the privileges and barriers are different. Many of these women actually use their privilege in a positive way when others are unwilling or unable to do so.

In 2016, I was ordained as a reverend in the Clergy Fellowship Memorial Church. I can now officiate at weddings, including same-sex marriages. Now we have to get the Unity Mosque registered and recognized as a religious organization. There are a few imams in the larger Canadian Muslim community with whom I have good relationships, but often they can only be allies in private because their circumstances are such that it is a challenge to be out as a Muslim ally to LGBTIQ Muslims. It is an articulation of a sad reality that we have people who are supportive of us but who feel they cannot be public about it because of consequences for them in the larger Muslim community.

Part of the strategy in the outreach of the Toronto Unity Mosque is to build a capacity and a profile so the Muslim community will eventually come to us because we can't be ignored. Once we have that, maybe our allies will have more resilience.

PRIDE

I n 2016, Toronto hosted Pride Month. An estimated 2.6 million people attended more than thirty days of programing. Prime Minister Justin Trudeau, Ontario premier Kathleen Wynne, and Toronto mayor John Tory all marched in the parade. With revenues of nearly $4.5 million, Pride turned a profit of almost $60,000. Yet the big news from the event was the Black Lives Matter Toronto sit-in that delayed the parade at Yonge and Carlton. The group made nine demands, including the end of police floats and booths at the event. With tens of thousands of participants waiting for the parade to resume, Pride's then-executive director Mathieu Chantelois agreed to BLMTO's conditions, then disavowed them, and resigned a few

Tim McCaskell

Pride:

A Political History

weeks later.

Why would an organization, on the surface so successful, be so embroiled?

Toronto's first Gay Pride Week was held in July 1972, and included a march that went to city hall, the federal immigration office, and Queen's Park. Similar events were held in August in 1973 and 1974 to celebrate the anniversary of the 1969 Criminal Code Amendments partially decriminalizing homosexual sex. A sign in the *Body Politic*/Gay Alliance to Equality storefront window in 1974 urged people to come out to protest police harassment, the Ontario Human Rights Code's failure to protect lesbians and gay men, and the lies by the schools and media about homosexuality. Pride began as a mix of celebration and protest. There were fewer than one hundred of us marching in 1974. It felt brave to be part of it.

That was the year, and the Pride, when I came out. Although various summer celebrations took place in the intervening years, it wasn't until after the bathhouse raids in 1981 that Pride in Toronto came to be celebrated on the anniversary of the Stonewall riots, the historic protest against a violent police raid on a gay bar in Greenwich Village on June 28, 1969. Organized by Gay Liberation Against the Right Everywhere and Lesbians Against the Right, a community fair took place in Grange Park behind the Art Gallery of Ontario, followed by a march. The event was pitched as more celebratory, relaxed, and welcoming to dykes with kids after the series of tense, largely male, and occasionally violent, nighttime demonstrations in response to the raids.

After another year at Grange Park and one at King's College Circle at the University of Toronto, in 1984 Pride migrated to the Gay Village and the park surrounding the 519 Church Street Community Centre. That was one of many changes. The 1982 Pride had been organized by a coalition of eleven community groups, but by 1985, Pride was its own organization with individual members. The first significant corporate advertising appeared in 1987. Ramses flogged its condoms to a community now shifting to safer sex. Re/Max sensed a new real estate market. And Molson's realized we drank a lot of beer. Government, however, was slower to respond. It wasn't until 1991 that city council successfully proclaimed the day. By that time, Pride had a board of directors and attendance was estimated at 80,000, eighty times the number that had turned out in 1981. To see this kind of growth was exciting. There were so many of us. Pride was the emotion we felt, not branding.

Demonstrators in front of federal office on University, calling for removal of homosexualism as grounds for rejecting immigrants. Aug 26, 1972.

Change was accompanied by increasing tensions as community unity around the bathhouse raids receded into history. By 1990, *Rites* reported that Pride had split into a 'party faction' and a 'political faction,' and noted an unsuccessful attempt by the party faction to restrict parade participants to organized floats and marching bands. Nevertheless, politics remained front and centre, with AIDS ACTION NOW! die-ins held in 1992 and 1993. The whole parade marched on Queen's Park in 1994 to protest the failure of the Bob Rae's NDP government to pass legislation recognizing same-sex partners or to establish a catastrophic drug plan to cover the spiralling costs of AIDS meds.

Despite those protest gestures, the underlying tensions persisted, and in early 1995 more than half the board resigned because of internal disputes, leaving Pride paralyzed. Councillor Kyle Rae stepped in, applied for the necessary permits himself, and pulled together a new board. While most of the other advocacy organizations spawned in the burst of energy after the 1981 raids had since disbanded, Pride had become too big to fail. Attendance that year was estimated at 650,000.

As a big tent seeking to bring everyone together, Pride found itself dealing with an ever more complex community. The first formal Dyke March occurred in 1996; that year, a 'T' for transgender was added to the list of initials Pride used to describe itself. During 1998, the first Pride in the newly amalgamated City of Toronto, *The Globe and Mail* reported, 'corporate cash [rained] down on gay parade: No longer a fringe festival, Pride Week becomes a marketer's dream.'

With this kind of company, Kyle Rae even convinced a reluctant Mel Lastman, the first megacity mayor, to attend. But the *Varsity*, U of T's student newspaper, noted that all that corporate cash was pricing out local community groups, widening the split between grassroots organizations and the board. The following year, Black queers, dissatisfied with the festival's overwhelming white programing, formed Blackness Yes! and the Blockorama stage in a parking lot across from the Wellesley subway station to celebrate and ensure visible Black communities within Pride. Other ethnoracial groups also began to demand more diverse programming.

In 1999, Frank Chester was hired as a part-time office manager, and by 2002 was executive director. His tenure coincided with a growth spurt – Pride's operating budget increased to just over $1 million by 2005. That same year, Rae had the festival reclassified as one of the city's eleven major cultural institutions, eligible for direct city funding. Both the provincial government and Ottawa made grants available. But this new acceptance, and all the corporate funding that flowed into the event, also brought heightened demands for acceptability. Pride itself had become a complex structure with competing interests, paid staff, a general membership, volunteer coordinators who did much of the organizing, and an elected board. And increasingly one heard the sentiment that success was not just numbers. It's certainly true that many continue to value Pride and those large turnouts for the solidarity they convey. But others have come to regard the parade as a giant, impersonal crowd that attracts tens of thousands of onlookers and plenty of corporate branding, but no longer evokes that earlier sense of belonging.

Pride's role as a big tent was tested in 2010 when Israeli lobbyists leaned on government and corporate sponsors to demand that the Palestine solidarity group Queers Against Israeli Apartheid be banned from the parade. Pride capitulated, and then faced protests by the Pride Coalition for Free Speech, the withdrawal of the local and international grand marshals, a mass return of awards by former Pride honorees, and a damning letter from the original 1981 festival organizers. By then, Pride had already alienated Blockorama organizers by moving the popular

University Avenue, south of Queen's Park. First Gay Pride March, August 26, 1972.

the gaydays raffle $1.00

1st Prize: Return airfare
for two to San Francisco

Draw held at Midnight,
August 26, 1978, at
THE BIGGEST GAY DANCE IN
THE HISTORY OF TORONTO
St Lawrence Market North,
Jarvis and Front Streets

gaydays by LIBERATED ENERGY 4 Collier St, Toronto

Lot. Lic. N°. 246401. Printing: Fabulous Quikprint

dance stage to ever more peripheral and inappropriate sites. The trans community was up in arms after Pride unilaterally took over the Trans March and stage without consultation. The Dyke March, in turn, split into an official march and a protest march, Take Back the Dyke.

At the eleventh hour, after an intervention led by Metropolitan Community Church minister Brent Hawkes, Doug Elliott, and Maura Lawless, the Pride board unbanned QUAIA and agreed to establish a community advisory panel to poll the community on how to resolve contentious issues. Tracey Sandilands, Pride's executive director throughout this fiasco, resigned before the report was released.

So the tensions revealed in 2016 by the BLMTO demands, board turmoil, and abrupt resignations at Pride are not without precedent. They reflect a city and a community that now exhibits far greater economic and racial disparity than when Pride was reconstituted in 1981. While Toronto queers may enjoy legal equality, social and economic inequality is far worse than in 1972, as University of Toronto sociologist David Hulchanski has shown in his Three Cities analysis (www.urban-centre.utoronto.ca/pdfs/curp/tnrn/Three-Cities-Within-Toronto-2010-Final.pdf). Those of us without money are not the preferred targets for corporate advertising and therefore don't see ourselves reflected. Disparity also means our experience of institutions such as the police are now profoundly different. While the cops once targeted all of us, white, middle-class queers today are largely immune. Yet racialized people, sex workers, and the poor still regularly taste the bloody end of the baton.

Pride may bring us together, but it is the crucible where such contradictions will continue to boil.

I magine three hundred women marching down Yonge Street chanting, 'We are the D-Y-K-E-S!' over and over. The year was 1981 and Toronto's first dyke march was winding its way through downtown. Organized by Lesbians Against the Right, the October 17 protest was a very public response to the rising anti-gay/anti-sex backlash sweeping across North America. I had been involved in lesbian, gay, and feminist activism since the 1970s, and the political context of that moment demanded a highly visible gesture.

Amy Gottlieb

Toronto's Unrecognized First Dyke March

The march, which I helped organize, was part of the gay/lesbian resistance to the growing tide of right-wing groups such as Renaissance Canada and Positive Parents, both of which started after the 1978 Toronto visit by Anita Bryant, the one-time Florida beauty queen turned orange-juice promoter who had become the face of the American opposition to gay rights. Bryant's visit followed the 1977 Emanuel Jaques murder, the police raid on *The Body Politic* magazine in the same year, and the homophobia swirling around the openly gay George Hislop's 1980 bid for a seat on city council.

In short, 1981 was a dangerous time to be visibly lesbian or gay in Toronto.

Despite those storm clouds, we printed posters with a thunderbolt across three women's symbols that read, 'Bring your balloons, banners and babies.' In fact, there were only a few babies of lesbians around then – maybe we were predicting the lesbian baby boom.

On the back of the poster was text that unpacked lesbian power, pride, and visibility: how it felt good to be strong, independent women, and how we needed to share the strength and collective power with other lesbians we knew.

More than all that, the demonstration was also meant to provide a specific response to police arrests of gay men in their own homes and police harassment of lesbians. 'Will your lesbian co-op be charged as a common bawdy house?' the poster asked. 'We're told we're not fit to be mothers or teachers. We're told we're not fit to be part of a family or neighbourhood. We can't be in the streets, in the schools, in the parks, on the TTC, in bars, in donut shops, even in laundromats. Lesbians are everywhere. And we have the right to be everywhere.'

The march started at the 519 Community Centre on Church Street and wove past what Lesbians Against the Right identified as Toronto's lesbian landmarks of that era. Here are the scripts that were read at each stop:

The Quest (Yonge at Charles) – The owner of this gay man's bar is Phil Stein, who also owns Stage 212 at Shuter and Dundas, which housed the Fly-by-Night, the one women-only space in the city. The lesbian-

Dykes on Bikes.

feminists operating the bar were kicked out when they had refused to reduce their wages any further. Sympathetic gay men have been boycotting the Quest, and we are here today to show our anger at being limited in our social lives.

342 Jarvis (at Carlton) – From 1976 to 1980 this house was a hub of lesbian social, cultural, and political life and housed the Lesbian Organization of Toronto. Active lesbians started meeting in the fall of 1976 and organized brunches, dances, demonstrations, parties, drop-ins, and, finally, the Bi-National Lesbian Conference in 1979.

McPhail Residence (Church at Granby) – The Board of the YWCA has been trying to make up for their losses and bad financial planning by cutting back on the services they have been offering to low-income women. By next year the McPhail Residence may be closed, which will limit low-rental living space to a great many lesbians, Aboriginal women, and women of colour living on welfare, going to school, or working in low-paying jobs.

Cinema 2000 (Yonge near Dundas) – This cinema and several others nearby are famous for their pornographic, anti-women movies. This section of Yonge Street has also become famous since fall 1977, when, during an anti-rape march, several hundred women occupied Yonge Street, demonstrating against the movie *Snuff*, which portrayed a woman being tortured and killed.

The Continental Hotel (Dundas at Elizabeth) – There are still many lesbians in the city, as well as on this march, who remember the Continental Tavern by the bus station. Ten years ago, gay liberation started to enter the Continental and other lesser-known places. The strong women who drank there were a part of lesbian culture we must begin to reclaim with pride.

Old City Hall (Bay and Queen) – We will wrap up the march with a speech exposing the legal system's unjust attitudes toward women and lesbian mothers, and the ongoing police harassment of lesbians and the attitudes that bar us from a full life.

Dykes in the streets declared our power and visibility, with many gay male allies marching along on the sidewalk. We walked down Bay Street near Old City Hall, with police escorts. There, in the middle of the street, we linked arms and chanted, 'Look over here, look over there, lesbians are everywhere.'

After more than two decades of Dyke Marches during Pride festivities, that first one reminds me how, in chilly political times, we need kick-ass radical energy. It is a reminder of the ongoing necessity of taking up public space in ways that radically reconfigure our city.

In the fall of 1981, I moved from Winnipeg to Toronto to attend medical school. As an isolated gay student in Winnipeg, I had searched high and low for any signs of gayness in the community, and eventually heard about a gay bookstore in faraway Toronto. So when I came to Toronto, one of the first places I visited was Glad Day. On the bulletin board was a poster advertising Chopsticks, an event held by Gay Asians Toronto to raise funds for the Right to Privacy Committee.

At that event, I discovered my community and quickly became actively involved. GAT had been formed a few months earlier by Richard Fung, Gerard Chan, Nito Marquez, and Tony Souza. They had connected after Richard became inspired by the People of Color caucus at the 1980 Washington LGBT conference, and then by an article by Gerard Chan – 'Out in the Shadows' – about being gay and Asian, published in the magazine *Asianadian*.

The following summer, I was volunteering at Glad Day one afternoon when a Pride Toronto organizer asked if someone from GAT would do the keynote on Pride Day and lead the parade. In 1981, after the bathhouse raids, the annual gay picnic had exploded in scale to become the first 'official' Pride parade, held at Grange Park, next to Chinatown.

Alan Li

The Only Time Gay Asians Led the Pride Parade

When the Pride organizers applied for the permit again in 1982, they ran into hurdles at city council, with claims there were complaints from the area's Chinese-Canadian communities that the public display of homosexuality was offensive. The Pride committee felt that GAT's leadership and active involvement was needed to counter those complaints – and also demonstrate there were gay Chinese, too.

The timing was tight, and the few more open activists in GAT (notably Richard and Pei Lim) were not able to accept that invitation. I became the final option to represent GAT. Despite my involvement, I had not come out to my family, at school, or within the Chinese communities. After much agonizing, I agreed to be Pride's keynote speaker – it was too important an issue for our group not to take a stand.

On June 27, 1982, over twenty gay Asians led the Pride parade through Chinatown. It was the first and only time the parade went through that neighbourhood, and the only time the gay Asian community was accorded leadership status in Pride's long history.

The keynote speech I gave was a group effort, with support from friends and mentors including John Linfield, Kevin Orr, Tim McCaskell, Brian Conway, Paul Cheung, Richard Fung, and Tony Chung. Here are some excerpts:

Alan Li's 1982 Pride key note speech.

When I was first asked to speak today, I was very scared. I realized that this would be a very valuable opportunity for my personal growth as a gay person and for the visibility of the gay Asian community. However, I was very worried about the exposure it would involve because it would mean an unconditional self-disclosure. I even decided to grow a moustache to alter my appearance.

Then, as I began to work on the speech, among the materials I read was a small book called *With Downcast Gays*. In reading this book, I became truly aware for the first time of my own self-oppression. I became very angry with the straight world and with myself for accepting their guidelines for oppression. I got really mad about all those times that I tried to pass for straight, repeated a heterosexual joke, changed the 'hes' into 'shes' when I talked with my straight friends about my love life, and put away all my gay magazines and books when a straight friend came to stay for a visit.

I looked at myself and saw all the wounds that I had inflicted upon myself every time I did something like that. I was deceiving myself more than I was deceiving the straight world. Anger and indignation welled up inside me, and I went into the bathroom and shaved the moustache that I had been trying to grow for three weeks. I felt an unimaginable sense of liberation and pride. I am so glad to be here today to share this with you, for this is truly one of the most exhilarating experiences of my life.

For me personally, today is therefore also a celebration of a breakthrough in my coming-out process. For some of my brothers and sisters here, today may be a first step in their coming out, and I admire your courage very

Gay Asians of Toronto lead the 1982 parade through Chinatown.

much. For all of us, today is one more step in showing ourselves as we are, a community united in our hopes and aspirations and a community with richness and strength in our diversity. I would like to give my warmest welcome to you in celebrating our presence.

But I am here today not only as a gay man but also as an Asian man. And, as an Asian, I have an additional battle in the fight for my own liberation and for the liberation of the Asian community. As gays, we have to fight for our right in the straight society; but Asian gays, like Black gays, Jewish gays, sexual minorities, the handicapped among us, and every other minority within the minority, have other battles to face as well.

Because the Canadian society as a whole is divided along racial lines and cultural differences, as gay Asians we have to face a triple source of rejection: rejection as Asian in the white community, rejection as gays in the Asian community, and rejection as Asian gays in the white gay community. Being gay alienates us from the larger Asian community and limits our resources and support base; this lack of a stable footing can restrict our ability to contribute to the gay community at large.

Our being Asian gives us an additional minority status within the gay community, and lack of understanding makes us end up fighting about issues that should very well be understood and acknowledged as cultural differences in perception. This establishes a vicious circle that keeps some minority groups in the subordinate position and can serve to reinforce feelings of isolation within the larger gay community. This problem is particularly harmful in the gay community because if we are divided we won't be strong enough to fight our battles together. It is therefore especially crucial that we realize that our common goals and our joint battles make all lesbians and gay men one common race.

In that sense we are all gay Asians. We, too, are everywhere, whether living free or suffering the most intolerable persecution. Black, white, Asian, we are one. There is strength in our numbers, as in our differences ...

[E]ven at this time of joy and celebration, we must also not overlook the unpleasant hurdles ahead. The police have now employed the strategy of divide and conquer. A great number of smaller charges were laid against individuals and gay businesses in their attempt to demoralize us so that we can be picked off one by one ... The battle we had to win before getting this park today for our celebration is yet another example of the city council's attempt to divide the lesbian and gay community and the Chinese community. Our victory today added to my pride in talking to you now ...

I would not be speaking here ... if it was not for the support and help of my group and my community. I hope, by actively participating and channelling all our energies into positive action, we will continue to be seen, to be heard, and to grow as one strong and united lesbian and gay community, proud to be who we are.

Our Pride involvement in 1982 was a watershed moment that brought together many previously apolitical members of the gay Asian communities to celebrate their gay identities in public for the first time. It helped created a strong sense of community and energized GAT. In the following years, GAT launched our signature event, CelebrAsian, and a magazine of the same name (1983); co-hosted an international gay conference in Toronto (1985); co-founded the first queer Asian organizations in Vancouver (1985) and in Hong Kong (1986); and launched the Gay Asians AIDS Project (1988), Asian Community AIDS Services (1994), the multicultural Coalition Against Homophobia (1996), and Asian Canadians for Equal Marriage (2002).

It would be twenty-eight years later, in 2010, before I was invited to lead the Pride parade again. By then, Toronto's Pride had become the largest festival in the country, with more than one million participants. I was selected as the grand marshal to lead the Pride parade, with a budget of $1,000 to put together a float or marching contingent to walk with me.

However, that same year, Pride Toronto decided to prohibit the participation of the group Queers Against Israeli Apartheid, in response to corporate and political pressures. In an ironic twist of fate, this time I took a principled stand for Pride by declining the role of grand marshal. Instead, I marched with our LGBT buddies in the Coalition for Free Speech at the end of the parade!

In 1991, I helped form Lesbians of Colour, a group that participated in that year's Pride. Afterwards, I joined forces with Anthony Mohamed, a fellow Trinidadian, to figure out how to make Pride more diverse. After many meetings at the Trinity–St. Paul's Centre in the run-up to Pride 1992, the Proud and Visible Coalition was formed, and ultimately carried a banner that proclaimed '500 Years of Pride: Celebrating Our Resistance.'

The following year, lesbians and dykes of colour reclaimed our space in the parade, carrying another banner: 'World Majority Lesbians: A Revolution of Colour.' By 1999, World Majority Lesbians decided it was time to do something big for that year's Pride by making a float with the banner 'Queer Womyn Colouring the Century.' I had always dreamed of having a big truck in the parade like the white boys. We requested a subsidy from the Toronto Pride Committee and rented a big truck with driver.

leZlie Lee Kam
The Encounter of a Brown, Trini, Carib, Callaloo Dyke with Police at Pride 1999

Two months prior to the parade, the Toronto Police Association started running ads on TTC billboards and posters featuring two Latino men with the caption 'Help Prevent Crime on the TTC!'

Community groups and people of colour across the city were appalled by this blatant example of racism and discrimination. The members of World Majority Lesbians decided immediately to use their truck as a platform of resistance to this outrageous act of oppression. We were going to Rage, Rant and Resist. We created a huge sign for one side of the truck that read, 'Stop Police Racism: End the Criminalization of People of Colour!'

The group appointed my friend Sil and me as spokeswomen. The truck and its six hundred followers drew the attention of the media and photographers. But we were also aware of the risk we were taking by putting up this sign of protest on the truck.

While we waited in line to enter the parade, two burly white cops approached the group. 'Who's in charge here?' they shouted. Sil and I stepped forward. The cops pointed to the sign and demanded we take it down immediately. We politely refused.

The cops then approached the driver. 'JP Towing has a contract with the police,' I heard them say. Then came the threat: the driver, the cops warned, should remove the sign or the company would face a penalty.

'The lesbians have rented the truck for the day,' replied the driver. 'I can't do anything.'

Knowing there could be retaliation from the police, the World Majority Lesbians organizers asked the media and photographers to quietly surround the truck. The two cops stormed off, threatening further action.

A few minutes later, two white women wearing pantsuits approached us and asked for the sign to be taken down. Sil and I were called over to deal with the women, who identified themselves as 'undercover police.' Their job, they said, was to 'protect your group today. It will be in your best interest to remove the provocative sign, which is degrading to the police and the City of Toronto.'

This conversation took place while they had their hands on their guns under the cover of their jackets. Again, we politely refused while many cameras recorded this unfolding scene. The two undercover cops did not seem to realize they were surrounded and were now the subject of hundreds of pictures.

After this last and not-so-veiled threat by the police, our big truck finally entered the 1999 parade, with the sign displayed. 'Queer Womyn Colouring the Century: Celebrating Pride, Love, Strength,' proclaimed another sign at the front of the truck.

The World Majority Lesbians had just struck a huge blow for justice!

I n 1998, Blockorama, a black queer diasporic space, made its debut in a parking lot across from the Wellesley subway station as the first Black Pride space in Toronto's Pride Festival. While the pilot event lasted for several hours, featuring DJs and live performers, Blockorama has now grown into an all-day dance party that celebrates Black queer pride.

Yet it continues to represent a site of struggle for Black diasporic queers to mark out a space and place in Pride by challenging the de-racialization of Pride. This conversation with founder Jamea Zuberi is an account of what led to the creation of Blockorama and the organizing committee Blackness Yes! Zuberi is a self-identified Trinidadian lesbian, feminist, educator, and activist. Her reflections offer a window into how Black queer/lesbian organizing is deeply intertwined with Toronto's Black feminist and Black cultural communities.

R. Cassandra Lord in conversation with Jamea Zuberi

Blackness Yes! Blockorama:
Making Black Queer Diasporic Space in Toronto Pride

RCL: Jamea, thank you for taking the time for this interview. I want us to begin the conversation by speaking about your community organizing.

JZ: My background in community organizing goes back almost thirty years, starting at the age of sixteen. Growing up in Jane and Finch, my sister and I founded a group called UMOJA, a young women's collective, and it then morphed into a young people's collective because there were young boys who defined themselves as feminists who wanted to join the group. At that time, I was coming into myself as a lesbian. I began to meet people through friendship circles who were Black lesbians, and I began to socialize and organize in those spaces. All my life, I existed in multiple spaces: Caribbean, queer, feminist. My family has a history of making Trinidad and Tobago Carnival and Toronto Caribana costumes, and playing the steelpan. I have also been involved in teaching the steelpan in community centres and feminist educational settings. Blockorama was a natural extension and a blend of my experiences.

RCL: Could we revisit the beginnings of Black queer organizing at Pride? What inspired you to start Blockorama?

JZ: As a yearly ritual, a group of my friends and I would visit a Jamaican restaurant on Pride Sunday to sit and watch the parade make its way south on Yonge Street. As we watched from the sidelines, we noticed at that moment that Toronto Pride was a white LGBTTI2Q celebration. Nothing about it drew us in or reflected our identity. Personally, I felt a void. I saw no representation

of us as Black queer people, or Blackness, reflected in the parade. I associated parades with Trinidad and Tobago (T&T) Carnival, and its diasporic export, Toronto Caribana, with 'masquerading' – people dressing up in costumes and parading and dancing together as a group in the street. In T&T we call this playing mas', where the performance extends to people moving their hips from left to right to the beat of soca music.[1] T&T Carnival represented a practice of freedom that emerges out of the history of African enslavement as a form of rebellion and celebration. I yearned for that same freedom and celebration in Pride.

I reached out to a close-knit group of four of my Black queer friends (David Junior Harrison, Angela Robertson, Douglas Stewart, and Courtnay McFarlane) to bring T&T Carnival to the Pride parade. Many of them were excited and agreed to participate. Simultaneously, I wanted to pitch my idea to the Pride Toronto organization that puts on the event to get funding, so I contacted them by phone and left numerous messages that remained unanswered. One of the challenges of Pride Toronto at the time was that they were understaffed.

In the meantime, I convened a formal meeting with my friends, and what arose were concerns about the lack of funding to put the event together, as well as buy-in to the concept from the larger Black queer community. We decided to shelve the idea of playing mas' in Pride, but we were determined that 1998 needed to be the year that Black queer people had a larger visible presence in Pride.

As an alternative, I drew on the experience of the Caribbean block parties (blockos) that I experienced growing up in Jane and Finch, and on my many sojourns to Brooklyn. These events involved dancing, listening to music, and sharing food, and took place in urban neighbourhoods where streets are blocked off for the entire day. While playing mas' was familiar to the group because of Caribana, the reception to the idea of a blocko was lukewarm.

1. People who play mas' are part of a Carnival or mas' band formed around a larger thematic concept that is translated into a number of smaller costume themes or sections.

RCL: Walk me through the process of transmuting Blockorama, a cultural tradition of Trinidad and Tobago, into a queer-specific event with its own identity.

JZ: The first meeting of Blockorama was in my living room. Later, we moved to a public space. A few months before Pride, the planning group divided tasks for the day's event into three groups: entertainment, logistics/set-up, and funding. We received some financial assistance from Pride Toronto, as well as access to the parking lot across from the Wellesley subway station to host the event. The process of re-adapting a Caribbean blocko into a Caribbean queer blocko was no easy feat, as there were two real challenges that emerged.

First, convincing the group that the concept of a Caribbean queer blocko was possible. Second, determining our identity as an organization. After the Pride parade, there are performance stages that feature musical guests, which attract large crowds. When I began to further explain how a blocko would work in Pride, people in the group began to refer to the event as a Black stage, thinking that the blocko would be a similar performance format. I explained that there was no stage and that the performers, music, and audience would all be at eye level. I wanted there to be a large presence of Black queer people visibly taking up and creating space for themselves.

I realized my experience of inhabiting multiple spaces (straight Black Caribbean spaces in terms of Carnival and steelpan) was not a similar experience for many Black queer people in the group, as they tended to inhabit predominantly Black queer spaces. I continued to explain that the word blocko was a short form for the word Blockorama, similar to T&T steelpan competitions and festivals that are called Panorama. Camille Orridge, a sister at the meeting, said, 'I am for this space celebrating diasporic people of African descent from planning to participation.' She continued, 'I am for Blackness, yes. I'm for that.' The room grew silent and then raucous as two words resonated: Blackness, yes. Our movement had its name, and here we are nineteen years later.

RCL: Could you describe Blockorama 1998?

JZ: We were all excited. The goal of the logistics committee was to transform a section of the parking lot by infusing symbols of Black queer culture. Colourful and vibrant fabric was used, and we inserted a blend of hand-painted African symbols with our own creative finishing. Tents for the DJs and a section where Black drag performers could prep were also set up. The program schedule allotted a specified time for Black drag performers, live steelpan, and DJs.

What I remember most is that the space was overflowing with large crowds of Black queer people all celebrating, dancing, laughing, and having fun. During the live steel-plan segment, I looked up from my steelpan to see my father playing right beside me. In that moment, I knew that Blockorama had exceeded my expectations far beyond what I could have imagined. I felt complete with my culture, family, friends, and sexuality all being in one space. We all came together as Black queer people to celebrate transforming Pride into a space for us.

1992: At Home

My daughter Sadie is born, surrounded by a labour team of twelve. We are not allowed to put her other parent's name on the birth registration, or even combine our last names to make Sadie's surname.

Almost a quarter of a century after Pierre Trudeau decriminalized homosexuality, lesbians, gay men, and trans people are still losing their children in custody cases. The majority of fertility clinics still won't serve lesbians. One fertility physician in Toronto requires queer women to write a 'letter to the doctor,' convincing him to allow them to become parents. Another clinic, at McMaster University, requires a psychiatric assessment.

Rachel Epstein

Pride Is Hot and Red and Political

Queer people who want to become parents have nowhere to go for information or support. Non-biological parents have no protection under the law. Most queer people still assume that being queer means forfeiting their desires to have children. Many have buried grief about this.

1997: University of Toronto, International Student Centre

I am at the University of Toronto's International Student Centre on St. George Street, an old building with high ceilings, thick wooden door frames, and scalding radiators. I've been here for ballroom dancing, political debates, and mediation skills sessions. Tonight, Kathi Duncan, the midwife who attended my daughter's home birth, and I are facilitating, for the first time, a course called Dykes Planning Tykes (DPT).

Twenty dykes show up at the door. People are pumped – hungry and grateful for information. We pass around a paper to share contact information so people can be in touch with each other. We talk a lot about sperm, and it is, if you will, a seminal moment in the growth of LGBTQ2S parenting community in Toronto.

Over the six weeks of the course, we talk about fertility, insemination, adoption, and co-parenting. We hear from a lawyer, a midwife, and queer parents. We role-play how you might respond to a doctor who denies you reproductive services. We laugh a lot and we all get a little choked up when visitors come in with their babies.

2004: Church Street Public School

Janis Purdy and I, she representing Pride Toronto, and I the LGBTQ Parenting Network, initiate a space at Pride for LGBQT2S people and their children. Family Pride becomes an oasis from the crowds and a community space that recognizes that children are part of our communities. Here, small grassroots parenting groups share information. People pick up the latest copy of the LGBTQ Parenting Network's newsletter and kvell over the birth and adoption announcements.

2007: Church and Hayden

It is late June. It is hot. I am perched atop the back seat of a red convertible, at the front of the Toronto Dyke March. Dykes Planning Tykes is the honoured group. We are marking the tenth anniversary of the DPT courses and celebrating that fact that, despite the historical assumption that being queer means being childless, many of us have figured out how to bring children into our lives. I am the Honoured Dyke because of my role in gestating the course.

Sadie, my now-fifteen-year-old daughter, sits beside me. I've dressed in red – a short frilly skirt, high heels, and a tank top with 'Hot Mama' emblazoned on the back. A bevy of butches in red fire hats surround us – fanning, fawning, squirting – a femme dream come true. The pickup truck behind us, decorated early that morning in the parking lot of the Sherbourne Health Centre, is now filled with gyrating women. Hundreds of queer women and their children, many in strollers, stream behind the vehicles. Hot Mama T-shirts are everywhere, and the kids wear shirts that say, 'Tyke of a Dyke.' Red balloons and glitter abound. We are celebrating our children and our sexuality and the communities in which we live and struggle. We finish the march back at Family Pride.

2008: Church Street Public School

Family Pride is in full swing. The LGBTQ Parenting Network has a table at the front, and I've put my girlfriend in charge of greeting people, helping them park their strollers and making sure they get a newsletter. However, she is being jostled out of the way by young people hired by Proctor & Gamble who are vying to greet the LGBTQ2S parents streaming into the space with gift bags filled with P&G products.

2010: 519 Community Centre

I am sitting with twenty-two other past Pride Toronto award winners at a press conference at the 519 Community Centre. We are collectively announcing our intention to give back our awards to Pride Toronto to protest the organizers' decision to ban Queers Against Israeli Apartheid from the parade.

I am no stranger to the heat of this issue. One of those Jews who cannot stomach what is done in my name by the state of Israel, I'm a founding member of the Jewish Women's Committee to End the Occupation of the West Bank and Gaza. It's not the most fun political work – when we show up to protest pro-Israel events, we are accused of self-hatred, even told we should have died in the ovens.

Pride Toronto's decision, in the opinion of this collection of award winners, is a bowing to pressure from conservative quarters and a denial of free speech in favour of funding for a festival that has increasingly become about delivering queer and trans bodies to corporate sponsors.

The 519's second-floor auditorium is packed. How appropriate that we are here, in a space emblematic of queer organizing in Toronto. This is where the Lesbian Mothers' Defence Fund held dances to raise money for women fighting for child custody, where people gathered to strategize about AIDS organizing, to square dance, to attend AA meetings. The twenty-three of us sit next to a large 'Shame Award' that we will deliver to Pride Toronto's office. I was proud to receive the Honoured Dyke award in 2007; today I am proud to stand with so many people who have given of their bodies and souls to make the world a better place for queer folk.

2015: Church Street Public School

I drop in to Family Pride to visit my friends with small children but I don't stick around. Family Pride has become a showcase for large institutions and corporations. The TD logo dominates the kids' mural-making space. Canadian Tire provides activities. The LGBTQ Parenting Network, and other more grassroots parenting groups, no longer participate in the event.

2016: At Home

I have stopped attending Pride on Sunday. The crowds are too large; the corporate sponsorships too apparent; the beer garden too gated, and the lineups too long. And I get bugged when Pride volunteers, resembling corporate police, are required to throw out good water at checkpoints. I'm at home, watching the parade on TV. Black Lives Matter Toronto is this year's Honoured Group. They have stopped the parade, refusing to move on until Pride Toronto agrees to a series of demands – about funding, about community control, about accessibility, about more involvement of Black people and people of colour at all levels of Pride, and, most controversially, about the removal of police floats from the Parade. I cheer.

NOT GAY
AS IN HAPPY

BUT QUEER
AS IN FUCK YOU

CONCLUSION

Ｔhe subtitle of our anthology makes a bold assertion: *How Toronto Got Queer*. Herein are stories of how people, daring to be themselves, have witnessed and shaped historical shifts in the city's social and physical spaces through their existence, resistance, cultivation, and creativity. But did Toronto really get queer?

The question yields others. What does it mean for a person, a community, or a space to be queer? What does it take for a city to become queer? Is that even possible?

Tatum Taylor and Rahim Thawer

Did **Toronto Get Queer?**

This book does not claim to hold the answers. We hope it will contribute to an ongoing dialogue, acknowledging queer Toronto voices that have been heard through the years and, even more importantly, those that have been silenced.

To spur that conversation, we posed a simple query to a sample of young Torontonians, circa 2017: Is Toronto a queer city?

What Does *Queer* Mean?

The word *queer* is both distinct and amorphous. It defies definition, and the connotations are evolving. In this book, we have tended to use it as an umbrella term, including all LGBTQQI2S+ (lesbian, gay, bisexual, trans, queer, questioning, intersex, Two Spirit) people. To identify as queer might imply same/multiple-gender attractions, non-normative ways of navigating sex and love, or living on the margins of a world that celebrates fixed heterosexual and cisgender identities. Perhaps becoming 'queer' is relief from the rigid limitations of a previous label. For some, it might simply be interchangeable with another identity marker. For others, it is imbued with deeper connotations of a politic that connects with social justice issues.

Eren, who is twenty and queer, explains: 'The term *queer* for me is a little complicated because I associate it with my gender and sexuality. I think of it as a big mix of everything, since there are so many different terms out there now … Most other people I know who refer to themselves as queer seem to have a similar idea, where it's just an umbrella term they go to instead of digging deeper. I know a lot of people whose gender or sexuality makes up a lot of who they are, but to me personally, I rarely even think about it since I'm generally more focused on hobbies or my future.'

Brian, twenty-nine, is a queer man who has only ever lived in Toronto. 'Gay is what I do,' he says, 'but queer is who I am. Reclaiming language is or can be difficult for some. Culturally it is an identity that includes academia and urban centrist politics. Toronto has developed into a hub where normalizing queer has been centralized in LGBT politics. *Queer*, where it is a word that offends an older population, is being reclaimed through their work in community. But I would not say Toronto is a queer city but one with a large LGBT community. The moment we start regulating and normalizing queer, the more we systematically segregate ourselves from the notion of being queer.'

'My struggles with my queerness and Toronto go hand in hand,' says S.Y., a young bisexual woman. 'I'm very sure of my bisexuality, but I often feel pressured to validate it, as I'm in a long-term relationship with a man. I never feel "queer" or "straight" enough, however those terms may be defined. The same could be said with my relationship with Toronto. I'm Chinese-Canadian, and similarly to my bisexuality, I feel like I exist both inside and outside the "Chinese" identity and the "Canadian" identity.'

What's a Queer City?

As queer identity evolves into multiplicities, so do the meanings of queer social, political, and geographic spaces. The understanding of what it means to become a queer city also varies by community. Some queer histories are well-documented; others have been marginalized in mapping and archiving processes. Many queer people in Toronto have seen a change in the city's spaces over time. But does that make the city queer?

'Racism, ableism, classism, fatphobia, femmephobia, and other oppressions force us to question what queer-friendly even means,' says Arti, a thirty-five-year-old artist, LGBTQ youth worker, aspiring therapist, and long-time advocate for queer/trans spaces. 'When my sweetheart – who is brown, trans, poor, and disabled – and I are walking down the street together, people assume that because I'm pushing their wheelchair that I'm their caregiver and not their lover. How can we say that Toronto is inherently a queer-friendly place if we are still dealing with basic ableism like that?'

'In the beginning,' observes Michael, thirty, a non-profit professional, 'it felt as if there was a critical mass of queerness; now it feels as if the queerness of these places has become less central, less defining, less overt. Just another ingredient in a neighbourhood mélange.'

Michael identifies as an occasional playwright and feminist killjoy. 'I don't think that for a place to be queer, it has to be inhabited exclusively by queers … However, just seeing an occasional smattering of queer people on the street doesn't seem to me to be enough either. If there aren't queer shared spaces, shared practices, shared culture or community, I don't think the "queer" label applies. If Toronto were a queer city, there wouldn't be this sense of queer or queer-friendly neighbourhoods. If these neighbourhoods were actually queer, the queerness of them would be more centrally defining … not just a queer night at the new hipster microbrewery with a concrete dance floor or a sticker pasted on the door of the gluten-free bakery.'

Rodney, twenty-seven, a community organizer and artist, disagrees: 'I think all cities are queer cities, because queerness, queer people, queer communities, queer culture, queer ideas/perspectives are universal human realities. They permeate all cultures and borders. Toronto, as a world city, a mélange of people, epitomizes that. Queerness has shaped the fabric of this city, its culture, its practices, its sense of identity. From Toronto's arts and culture scene, to commerce, to the political landscape, queerness has pushed the city beyond its comfort zone, allowing and challenging residents to expand their concepts of hegemony.'

'How is a city not queer?' asks Kristylea, a thirty-three-year-old 'DemiPanGurrrl.' 'Would that make it straight? We. Are. Everywhere.'

'Toronto is like your superqueer auntie who everybody in your family hated because she's unapologetically unashamed.'

For some, proof of Toronto's queerness lies in the visibility and energy of its queer communities.

'Toronto has a vibrant queer scene and is an important place in the history of queer liberation,' says a twenty-two-year-old queer student. 'It's a safer city than most for queer people and a place that celebrates diversity.'

Elise, thirty, agrees: 'You realize that Toronto is a queer city when you step outside of Toronto. As a Black trans Muslim tall woman, I feel like I won the lottery compared to all the other places I could have ended up in this cold, closed-minded world!'

'Most cities I've lived in or visited keep their LGBTQ2I events in one area (the gay village/district),' offers a thirty-two-year-old lesbian fashion designer. 'Toronto is also a pretty safe city where the queer community can exist all over without harm.'

'Every day I see at least one queer couple on the subway,' notes Robbie, a twenty-five-year-old 'aspiring hipster transguy.' 'I don't even see that in New York.'

Caitlin, twenty-seven, is a sex educator, feminist porn producer, queer, kinky, poly, cis-woman. 'There are a lot of us, and there are a lot of queer events. Almost everyone I meet has some queer vernacular under their belt, even if just some surface knowledge.'

Jassie Justice is a thirty-year-old intersex non-binary mixed femme poet, yoga teacher, porn performer, and 'gilded trash ho' who feels the city 'resists the overwhelming white colonial cis-hetness as much as possible. I have found queer pockets in the spaces I get coffee in Bloordale or wander through in the Village. I find it in clothing swaps and in the park, at protests and in conflict, even within community.'

Charm, thirty-three, an artist and astrologer, likens Toronto to 'your superqueer auntie who everybody in your family hated because she's unapologetically unashamed of her choices. I came out as a flaming femme queer when I was twenty-five. The transition from being a confused straight girl to being queer was a smooth and flawless process for me.'

'Toronto is queer, but not all of us are allowed the same queer experiences.'

While some queers equate Toronto with liberation, progress, and possibility, many others who live at the intersections of race, gender, class, and disability are still fighting for a kind of queerness that acknowledges multiple and interconnected oppressions. But will the urgent call for mobilization toward intersectionality be heard in Toronto's queerly divided communities?

'Growing up in the suburbs of Mississauga,' says Thompson, twenty-five, 'I coveted Toronto as an epicentre of queerness. However, as a young queer Asian, finding safe spaces that affirm the intersections of my queer and racial identities proved to be difficult in Toronto's predominantly white, cisgendered male, gay spaces ... The presence of a multiplicity of identities is Toronto's strength, but a queer future that we need to realize is one that prioritizes the visibility and inclusion of marginalized LGBTQ+ folks within our "queer mainstream" spaces, such as the Church and Wellesley Village.'

A thirty-year-old QPOC health professional offers this view: 'As I was coming out queer, prior to and many years after moving to Toronto, the Church-Wellesley Village and Pride were my deepest connections to this city. Away from my family home, I had the chance to live, breathe, and taste the rainbow. If you asked me five years ago if I thought Toronto was a queer city, my response would have been a resounding and enthusiastic YES! Now, I am not so sure. As a female-identified queer person of colour, I have found it challenging to stay rooted in the existing Toronto queer landscape.'

'I grew up in this city,' adds S.Y. 'However, my sense of belonging is often challenged, whether implicitly by those who ask where I'm from (and where I'm *really* from), or explicitly through racist slurs. I love and value Toronto's multiculturalism ... That said, I feel like Canadians can get very smug about their progressiveness and politeness, and this often overshadows our blind spots – e.g., Toronto's problems with anti-Blackness, lack of trans rights, Indigenous rights. We still have lots of work to do."

Laura, thirty-nine, says that when she first arrived to Toronto, in 2003, 'I did feel that it was a queer city. I lived in the Gay Village, which provides, I think, a sort of "micro-social environment." But then I lived in North York and now in Brampton where, as a lesbian, I don't feel that safe anymore. One day while I was holding hands with my partner in a North York supermarket, a guy (total stranger) started yelling us, saying how "disgusting" we were and how unnatural our relationship was. In Brampton, the experience has been pretty much invisibility. Since we moved to our house in the northwest part of the city, we have told our neighbours several times that we are a couple – we even have two kids. Yet neighbours keep talking to us as if we're sisters or friends. This invisibility will make me say no, Toronto/GTA is not a queer city.'

Craig, thirty-eight, who describes himself as 'a cis-Black man first, gay man second,' lives north of the Village. 'Toronto,' he says, 'ignores the intersections of its queerness. It is a place where if I walked down the street hand in hand with my lover, eight out of ten times we would be left alone. At the same time, however, being Black and six-four, if I walk alone and happen upon members of the queer community, I have often been regarded with fear and distrust. Not all of us are allowed the same queer experiences.'

Amandeep, a thirty-year-old queer Sikh, feels Toronto is 'not queer enough to celebrate and welcome the intersection of my identities. Not queer enough to dismantle that norm.'

'In thinking about queerness and its intersections with space and place in Tkaronto,' says Secwepemc, a Two Spirit social worker and educator, 'I think about scholar Scott Morgensen's assertion that since contact and settlement of this place now known as Canada, now known as Toronto, Indigenous bodies have been marked as queer and marked for death. It's interesting to me that those decrying "exclusion does not promote inclusion" are kept warm and safe in their unknowing and thus knowingly/unknowingly becoming agents in the naturalization of white queer settlement – free from the responsibilities outlined in the Truth and Reconciliation Commission.

'As a front-line activist,' he continues, 'I have yet to see queer collectives showing up for land and water protection (show up, please, we need you!). There are complex intersections of identity and intergenerational/historic trauma for both our communities, but LGBTQ social justice initiatives cannot be won on the backs of oppressed Others – assumed to be included, captured under the rainbow umbrella.'

'Diasporic realities are filled with difference, until you realize that the end that awaits your family's migrant dream is either disappointment or assimilation,' says a twenty-two-year-old who identifies as a 'crippled Jewish Trans Wxman, communist, and Lesbian.' They grew up in Eglinton West and now lives in Chinatown. 'A queer city would not reward the few able to assimilate into productive, upstanding, hard-working, boring citizens. This is not a queer city. This is a gunshot struggle on someone else's front lawn.'

Says Arti: 'If my whole self can't be seen, respected, and held with dignity, then I can't claim that Toronto is always a queer-friendly place. I can't take my brown gender-queer body out at Pride, feel alienated, and then feel that Pride is a place for me or my communities. So while there are beautiful moments of queer friendliness that I experience, I know those moments are based more on my access to privilege and less on blanket ideas of queer friendliness as a Toronto-specific identity.'

'Struggle occupies various spaces in Toronto,' observes Brian. 'Not only between queer and non-queer folks for legitimization and equity and justice, but within the queer communities as well, which I find deeply frustrating and disappointing ... Toronto has moments of queerness, and of queer struggle, queer resilience/resistance, and also I'd say a queer anti-queer backlash. Toronto is all these things for me.'

In conclusion: there is no conclusion. The stories in this anthology reflect Toronto's sprawling queer history and hint at the possibilities of its future. In a metropolitan area this diverse, we must make spaces for the intersections of our differences. And confronted with the shifting tectonic plates of identities – Toronto's and ours – we must also acknowledge the discomfort and creativity arising from this friction. Toronto's queerness is not an accomplished state of being, but rather a constant process of becoming.

Jackie Shane with Frank Motley (right) and a member of Frank Motley and His Motley Crew (left).

Works Cited

'A New Way of Lovin'' by Steven Maynard

Banks , Elaine. *I Got Mine: The Story of Jackie Shane.* CBC Radio, 2010.

Cabrera, Edimburgo. *DIVAS: Love Me Forever.* Anton Wagner Productions, 2002.

Churchill, David. 'Mother Goose's Map: Tabloid Geographies and Gay Male Experience in 1950s Toronto.' *Journal of Urban History* 30, September 2004.

Egan, Jim, *Challenging the Conspiracy of Silence: My Life as a Canadian Gay Activist*, ed. Donald W. McLeod (Toronto: CLGA and Homewood Books, 1998).

Reynolds, Sonya, and Lauren Hortie. *Whatever Happened to Jackie Shane?* (animated video). 2014.

Walcott, Rinaldo. 'Black Men in Frocks: Sexing Race in a Gay Ghetto (Toronto).' In *Claiming Space: Racialization in Canadian Cities*, Cheryl Teelucksingh, ed. Waterloo, ON: Wilfrid Laurier University Press, 2006.

———. 'Fragments of Toronto's Black Queer Community: From a Life Still Being Lived.' In *Our Caribbean: A Gathering of Lesbian and Gay Writing from the Antilles,* Thomas Glave, ed., Durham, NC: Duke University Press, 2008.

Yonge Street: Toronto Rock & Roll Stories. David Brady Productions, 2011.

Wood-Wellesley and the 'Mystery Block' by Mark Osbaldeston

City of Toronto Planning Board. 'Wood/Wellesley Redevelopment Area, Third Report,' April 1956.

'Effort to Save Firm Fails: Ridout Real Estate Ltd. Is Put into Bankruptcy.' *The Globe and Mail*, January 4, 1957.

Lewis, Robert, and Paul Hess. 'Refashioning Urban Space in Postwar Toronto: The Wood-Wellesley Redevelopment Area, 1952-1957,' *Planning Perspectives*, vol. 31, no. 4, 2016.

Osbaldeston, Mark. 'Eaton's College Street.' In *Unbuilt Toronto*. Toronto: Dundurn Press, 2008.

———. 'Simpson Tower/North American Life Building' and 'Spadina Gardens/Union Station.' In *Unbuilt Toronto 2*. Toronto: Dundurn Press, 2011.

Ridout Real Estate Limited. 'Proposals Submitted by Ridout Real Estate Limited to the Board of Control, Toronto ... ' February 15, 1956.

'Wood-Wellesley Plan Cancelled by Controllers.' *The Globe and Mail*, May 2, 1957.

Steps to Gentrification by Allison Burgess

Nash, Catherine Jean. 'Toronto's Gay Village (1969-1982): Plotting the Politics of Gay Identity.' *Canadian Geographer* 50, no. 1, 2006.

Walcott, Rinaldo. 'Homopoetics: Queer Space and the Black Queer Diaspora.' In *Black Geographies and the Politics of Place*, Katherine McKittrick and Clyde Woods, eds. Toronto: Between the Lines, 2007.

The World's Largest Lesbian Hockey League by Margaret Webb

Annett, Evan. 'Meet the Former Globe Columnist Who Almost Made It on Your Money.' *The Globe and Mail*, December 8, 2016. http://www.theglobeandmail.com/sports/bobbie-rosenfeld/article33264615/

McFarlane, Brian. *Proud Past, Bright Future: One Hundred Years of Canadian Women's Hockey.* Toronto: Stoddart Publishing Co. Ltd., 1994.

outsporttoronto.org/organisations

Watson,H. G. 'Moss Park Eyed as Home for LGBT Sports Centre: If Approved, Redevelopment of Entire Park Space Would Be Possible.' *Daily Xtra!*, April 17, 2015.

Theatre as Settlement by Sky Gilbert

Warner, Michael, editor. *Fear of a Queer Planet* Chicago: University of Minnesota Press, 2004.

Jewish Virtual Library, www.jewishvirtuallibrary.org/jsource/Peace/settlements.html.

Merriam-Webster Dictionary, www.merriam-webster.com.

Oxford Dictionary, en.oxforddictionaries.com.

Desh Pardesh: A Cultural Festival with Attitude by Sharon Fernandez

Ansari, Rehan. 'If Desh Were Founded Today.' *Avec Pyar*, August 1975.

Carvello, Nelson. *Xtra!*, June 3, 1999.

Fernandez, Sharon. 'More than Just an Arts Festival: Communities, Resistance, and the Story of Desh Pardesh,' *Canadian Journal of Communication*, 2006.

Khosla, Punam. Desh Pardesh opening address. *Rungh Magazine*, 1991.

Piepzna-Samarasinha, Leah. 'Artist, Rebels, Warriors: Desh Pardesh's Legacy and the Future of South Asian Art.' *FUSE Magazine*, 2005.

'Why Do You Go There?' by David K. Seitz

Berlant, Laura. *Cruel Optimism.* Durham, NC: Duke University Press, 2011.

Martin, David. 'Canada in Comparative Perspective.' In *Rethinking Church, State and Modernity: Canada between Europe and America*, David Lyon and Marguerite van Die, eds. Toronto: University of Toronto Press, 2000.

Reagon, Bernice Johnson. 'Coalition Politics: Turning the Century.' In *Home Girls: A Black Feminist Anthology*, Barbara Smith, ed. New York: Kitchen Table: Women of Color Press, 1983.

LGBTQ2S Parenting by Rachel Epstein

LGBTQ Parenting Network: lgbtqpn.ca

Gays With Kids: gayswithkids.com

LGBT Families of Colour: www.nbjc.org/sites/default/files/lgbt-families-of-color-facts-at-a-glance.pdf

The Contributors

Kamal Al-Solaylee is the author of *Intolerable: A Memoir of Extremes* and *Brown: What Being Brown in the World Today Means (to Everyone)*. He has written for the *Globe and Mail*, *The Walrus*, the *Toronto Star*, and *Chatelaine*, among others. Kamal holds a PhD in English literature and is an associate professor of journalism at Ryerson University.

Cathi Bond is a writer, podcaster, and crop farmer. In 2013 Bond published *Night Town*, a critically acclaimed novel about coming out on the mean streets of Toronto in the early seventies. Bond is currently working on *Invincible*, another novel featuring the considerable challenges of being gay in Toronto during the Great Depression through to World War II.

Allison Burgess works as the Sexual & Gender Diversity Officer at the University of Toronto. She has a PhD from the Ontario Institute for Studies in Education of the University of Toronto.

Alec Butler's play *Black Friday?* was a finalist for the Governor General's Literary Award for Drama in 1991. She is the author of *Rough Paradise*, a queer novella, and the writer/director of an award-winning animated film trilogy about growing up Two Spirit/Intersex, called *Misadventures of Pussy Boy*.

Karen B. K. Chan is a queerdo from Hong Kong. Her small, middle-class astronaut family emigrated to Toronto in 1987 during the mass exodus before the 1997 handover. Fluent in Cantonese but also someone who passes as Canadian-born, BK loves navigating between communities, stories, and meanings.

Elise Chenier is a queer historian and digital humanities specialist who teaches in the History Department at Simon Fraser University. She is the founder and director of the Archives of Lesbian Oral Testimony, alotarchives.org. Another recent project on the history of sexuality in Toronto can be found at interracialintimacies.org.

Alvis Choi is a Toronto-based artist, performer, and researcher. They were named in the BLOUIN ARTINFO 2014 list of Canada's 30 Under 30. Choi was appointed chairperson of the Chinese Canadian National Council Toronto Chapter in 2015. They obtained their master's in environmental studies from York University (2016).

Michèle Pearson Clarke is a Trinidad-born artist who works in photography, film, video, and installation. Her work, which has been shown nationally and internationally, explores queer and Black diasporic longing and loss. She holds an MSW and an MFA in documentary media studies. www.michelepearsonclarke.com.

Jennifer Coffey is a Toronto writer and editor. For five years, she served as co-editor and feature writer for the CLGA's *The Archivist*, where she conceived and edited the anthology *Keeping Our Stories Alive*. In 2010, she placed third in the *Toronto Star* Short Story Contest, and has been copy editor for Toronto's Inside Out Film Festival since 2008.

Keith Cole has a BFA from York University and an MFA from OCADU. His art career is vast and continues to ebb and flow. He ran for Toronto's top political job in 2010: mayor. His platform was art, bicycles, and civic engagement. He did not win. However, Keith did receive well over 1,000 votes. To him, this was a victory.

Susan G. Cole is an author, musician, and playwright. She has written two books on pornography and violence against women, and is the editor of *Outspoken*, a collection if monologues from Canadian lesbian plays. She is currently senior entertainment editor at *NOW* Magazine, lives in Toronto, and still can't get enough of women's music.

Hilary Cellini Cook is a Toronto lawyer, writer, photographer, cyclist, car camper, raiser of children, and lover of gizmos. Most recently, she has become obsessed with roasting and making the perfect coffee, even though she can't handle caffeine.

Mezart Daulet is a community educator who specializes in equity and inclusion, sexual health, and anti-oppression. When he is not actively involved with Toronto's queer Asian community, he publishes in various magazines, such as *Badi*, *Bits*, and *2Chopo*, as a Japanese queer columnist.

Jon Davies has worked as a curator at the Power Plant, Oakville Galleries, and the Art Gallery of Ontario, and has published widely on cinema and contemporary art. He is currently undertaking an art history PhD at Stanford University.

Debbie Douglas is executive director of the Ontario Council of Agencies Serving Immigrants, co-founder of Zami, Toronto's first political and support group for LGBTI Black and Caribbean people, and co-editor of *Máka Diasporic Juks: Contemporary Writing by Queers of African Descent*.

Rachel Epstein (PhD) is a long-time LGBTQ2S activist, educator, and researcher, and the founding coordinator of the LGBTQ Parenting Network at the Sherbourne Health Centre in Toronto. She is also executive director of the Morris Winchevsky School/Jewish People's Order, a secular, social-justice-oriented Jewish organization.

Sharon Fernandez worked at Desh from 1988 until 2000 in various roles, including volunteer, producer, programmer, graphic artist, community development advocate, and arts funder. She has been a diversity coordinator for the Canada Council for the Arts and is now the principal consultant at Creative Policy Consulting.

Dennis Findlay was born in 1947 on a Saskatchewan farm. He is a teacher and gay activist from the early 1970s who lived in a commune, and became a self-taught baker, establishing Altitude Baking. He was active in the Right to Privacy Committee, 1981–85. Now retired, Findlay volunteers at the Canadian Lesbian and Gay Archives.

John Forbes was a founding member of *The Body Politic*, creating the columns 'Twilight Trails' (as Twilight Rose) and later 'Tribal Rites.' Moving to Hamilton in 2003, he worked as a volunteer acupuncturist for the AIDS Network until 2013.

Elle Flanders is a filmmaker and artist living in Toronto. She has worked in the queer and feminist communities since the 1980's. After fighting the censorship wars, opposing gay marriage, and joining the deeply unpopular (but acutely necessary) Queers Against Israeli Apartheid, Flanders is a happily married self-described pessoptomist.

Richard Fung is an artist and writer, and professor in the Faculty of Art at OCADU. He has received the Bell Canada Award for video art, and the Kessler Award for 'significant influence on the field of LGBTQ Studies.'

Elaine Gaber-Katz is an enthusiastic bubbie to Noa and Eitan. She works as a feminist activist/facilitator for the non-profit sector. Elaine co-authored *The Land that We Dream Of: A Participatory Study of Community-Based Literacy* and writes on issues of violence, poverty, the marginalization of voices, and the inadequacy of the individual narrative.

Mathew Gagné is a PhD candidate in anthropology at the University of Toronto. His research examines the impacts of gay dating and mobile communications apps on sexuality and intimacy among men in Beirut. His work has been published in various online and academic sources, particularly speaking to Middle East studies.

Bob Gallagher co-founded the Campaign for Equal Families, Canadians for Equal Marriage, and the Lesbian Gay Bi Youth Line, and served as a director of Buddies in Bad Times. He has taught social theory and political economy at Trent University. Bob also managed election campaigns and served as chief of staff for NDP leader Jack Layton. Currently, he is director of communications and political action for the United Steelworkers.

Chanelle Gallant is an activist-writer with a focus on sex and justice, a long-time leader in the sex workers' rights movement and a queer femme powerhouse. Her writing has appeared in *MTV News, The Rumpus, The Establishment, Huffington Post, The Walrus.* and more. She is working on her first book.

Jake Tobin Garrett is a writer, urban planner, and park nerd in Toronto. He works as manager of policy and research for the charity Park People and often writes about parks for *Spacing Magazine*.

Sky Gilbert is a writer, director, teacher, and drag queen extraordinaire. He has had more than forty plays produced and has written seven critically acclaimed novels. Sky is also a professor in the school of English and theatre studies at the University of Guelph. A street in Toronto is named after him: 'Sky Gilbert Lane.'

Amy Gottlieb is a butch lesbian and lifelong activist and educator for social and economic justice. She teaches photography and art at a Toronto high school. Her video and photo-based art explores the intersection of personal and historical memories.

John Greyson is a Toronto film/video artist whose features, shorts, and transmedia works include *Pink:Diss, Murder in Passing, Covered,*

Fig Trees, Proteus, Lilies, Zero Patience and *Urinal.* A board/advisory member of Vtape, Cinema Politica, and Toronto Palestinian Film Festival, he teaches film at York University.

Andrew Gurza is a Disability Awareness Consultant and Cripple Content Creator working to make the lived experience of queerness and disability accessible to all. His writing has appeared in *Huffington Post, This Magazine, The Advocate, Everyday Feminism, Mashable,* and Out.com. Find out more at www.andrewgurza .com or via @andrewgurza.

Vince Ha is a writer-director who questions our moving-image heritage on issues of class, gender, race, and representation. He is currently pursuing an MFA in documentary media studies at Ryerson University.

Gerald Hannon, a retired journalist and sex worker, was a writer, editor, and principal photographer for *The Body Politic* for most of its fifteen-year history. After the paper's demise in 1987, he turned to mainstream journalism, winning, before his retirement, thirteen National Magazine Awards.

Jin Haritaworn is associate professor at York University. They have published numerous articles (e.g., GLQ, *Society & Space,* and *Sexualities*), four co/edited collections, and two monographs (*Queer Lovers* and *Hateful Others and Queer Necropolitics*). Jin has made forerunning contributions to several trans-Atlantic fields, including queer of colour, critical ethnic, and urban studies.

Jarett Henderson is an associate professor of history at Mount Royal University in Calgary. His current research explores the relationship between same-sexuality and settler self-government in 1830s British North America within the context of empire-wide debates about race, freedom, and colonial governance.

Tom Hooper is an historian of queer Toronto in the 1970s and 1980s. His research interests include the 1981 bathhouse raids, and the intersection of morality, law, and political resistance.

Karleen Pendleton Jiménez is a writer and a professor. She is the author of *How to Get a Girl Pregnant, Tomboys and Other Gender Heroes*, and the short film *Tomboy*. She lives with her girlfriend Hilary and kids in Toronto.

El-Farouk Khaki is a spirituality activist, human rights and social justice advocate, and refugee lawyer. He is founder of Salaam: Queer Muslim Community (1991) and co-founder of el-Tawhid Juma Circle (2009). El-Farouk is the imam of the ETJC Toronto Unity Mosque. He spearheaded the representation SOGIEG (Sexual Orientation, Gender Identity/Expression & Gender) and HIV status-based refugee claims. A public and media speaker on issues including Islam, LGBTIQ and human rights, refugees, race, politics, and HIV, El-Farouk is also co-owner of Glad Day Bookshop and recipient of numerous awards.

leZlie Lee Kam is a world majority, brown, Trini, callaloo DYKE, differently abled, and an elder. 'i have been OUT as a DYKE community activist since 1976. i advocate for queer people of colour and live my life from an anti-oppression perspective. i enjoy a cold beverage and a hot 'LIME' anytime!!'

Alan Li is a physician, community organizer, researcher, and advocate who has worked with many diverse and marginalized communities, including immigrants and refugees, LGBT, and people with HIV/AIDS. Chair of Gay Asians Toronto from 1983–1986, Alan co-founded the Gay Asians AIDS project, Asian Community AIDS Services, and the Committee for Accessible AIDS Treatment in Toronto. In the early 1990s, he became the first publicly gay national president of the Chinese Canadian National Council.

Sarah Liss is an award-winning writer, editor, and occasional music columnist, and the author of *Army of Lovers* (Coach House Books, 2013), a community history of the late artist and civic hero Will Munro. Her work has appeared in *The Walrus, Toronto Life*, Hazlitt, the *Globe and Mail*, and *Maclean's*, among other publications. She lives in Toronto with her family.

R. Cassandra Lord is an assistant professor, sexuality studies, at the University of Toronto, Mississauga, specializing in Black diasporic queer culture. Lord is currently working on her book manuscript *Performing Queer Diasporas: Friendships, Proximities and Intimacies in Pride Parades.*

Michael Lynch (1944–1991), author of the book of poetry *These Waves of Dying Friends*, taught English at the University of Toronto until his death from AIDS. He was a founder or early organizer of numerous LGBT organizations in Toronto: Gay Academic Union, Gay Fathers of Toronto, AIDS Committee of Toronto, Toronto Centre for Lesbian and Gay Studies, AIDS ACTION NOW! and the Toronto AIDS Memorial, where his poem 'Cry' is memorialized on an engraved plaque.

Stefan Lynch is a father of two and nurse who lives in Philadelphia. He was the first director of COLAGE, which unites people with lesbian, gay, bisexual, transgender, and/or queer parents.

Fiona MacCool is a retired stand-up comedian, exhausted parent, extroverted shut-in, lounge singer, and social media addict. She lives in Toronto with her patient wife and two impatient children, does not have a book coming out, nor will you be seeing her doing anything interesting in public other than protesting and looking at her phone.

Steven Maynard has been researching and writing queer history for nearly thirty years. Published in numerous academic journals and in the queer press, Steven lives in Kingston, where he teaches the history of sexuality at Queen's University.

Alexander McClelland was born and raised in downtown Toronto. He has developed a range of collaborative writing, academic, and artistic projects on issues of criminalization, sexual autonomy, surveillance, drug liberation, and the construction of knowledge on HIV. He was a drag queen in his past life.

Derek McCormack's most recent book is *The Well-Dressed Wound* (Semiotext(e), 2015). His other books include *The Haunted Hillbilly* and *The Show That Smells*. He lives in Toronto.

John McCullagh is a counsellor, youth worker, and educator. He has worked for over thirty years with queer people of all ages, and with those living with and affected by HIV.

Donald W. McLeod has been a volunteer at the Canadian Lesbian and Gay Archives for more than thirty years. His latest book is *Lesbian and Gay Liberation in Canada: A Selected Annotated Chronology, 1976–1981*, accessible here: hdl.handle.net/1807/74702.

Philip McLeod (1923-2010), a World War II RCAF veteran, was a quiet but avid behind-the-scenes volunteer with gay community organizations in Toronto for many years, including Gay Court Watch, the Committee to Defend John Damien, and Came Out Decades Ago.

Diana Meredith works as an independent artist, writer, and critical thinker. The body is at the centre of her practice. Her work is informed by second-wave feminist ideas about embodiment. Until a cancer diagnosis in 2015, she taught digital art at Humber College. www.dianameredith.com.

Shawn Micallef is the author of *Stroll: Psychogeographic Walking Tours of Toronto*, *The Trouble with Brunch: Work, Class and the Pursuit of Leisure*, and *Frontier City: Toronto on the Verge of Greatness* (2017). He's a weekly columnist at the *Toronto Star*, co-founder of *Spacing*, and teaches at the University of Toronto.

Jearld Frederick Moldenhauer is a Canadian-American born in Niagara Falls, N.Y. in 1946. His career as a gay activist began in 1967, during his student days at Cornell University. He founded many gay liberation organizations, including student groups at both Cornell and at the University of Toronto, the Glad Day Bookshops (Toronto and Boston), *The Body Politic* journal, and the CLGA (Canadian Lesbian & Gay Archives). His website, jearldmoldenhauer. com, includes much material about gay history as well as his personal life.

Ghaida Moussa is doctoral candidate in Social and Political Thought at York University, where she interrogates chronic unidentified illness and gendered, racial, and neoliberal regimes of knowledge. She is co-editor of *Min Fami: Arab Feminist Reflections on Identity, Space, and Resistance*, and recipient of the 2010 Lambda Foundation for Excellence Award.

Kurt Mungal is a Toronto-based event planner, marketer, and reality TV addict. He works as senior account manager for YellowHouse Events, a boutique agency located in the Distillery District, and actively supports the development and growth of queer spaces in Toronto.

Pat Murphy (1941–2003) was vice president of the Community Homophile Association of Toronto in the early 1970s, later involved with Women Against Violence Against Women, and managed Fly By Night, a popular lesbian bar.

Faith Nolan is a Canadian social activist folk and jazz singer-songwriter of mixed African, Mi'kmaq, and Irish heritage. Her music is her political work, a politics firmly rooted in her being working-class, a woman, African-Canadian, and queer.

Stephanie Nolen is the Latin America correspondent for *The Globe and Mail* and the author of *28 Stories of AIDS in Africa*. She has reported on conflicts, humanitarian crises, and social change from more than eighty countries around the world. She lives with her partner and children in Rio de Janeiro.

Monica Noy was born in Australia and came out in Canada. She is a manual therapist working with people experiencing pain. On the side, Monica is a pain-science geek shackled to professional social media groups while trying to find time for an online MSc in rehabilitation at McMaster University.

Michael Ornstein teaches sociology at York University. His research includes work on corporate elites, political ideology, and socioeconomic differences between ethnoracial groups in Toronto and other cities. Currently he is working on labour market inequality. Tim and Michael met in the mid-1970s when they were members of the Marxist Institute, a radical group that gave courses and sponsored talks.

Mark Osbaldeston has written and spoken extensively on Toronto's architectural and planning history. He is the author of three books that explore unrealized building, planning, and transit proposals: *Unbuilt Toronto, Unbuilt Toronto 2,* and *Unbuilt Hamilton.*

Amandeep Kaur Panag is a queer Sikh Punjabi parent, community organizer, sexual health educator, and counsellor living in Toronto. They are currently completing a master's degree at York University. Amandeep loves being mom to two amazing kids and is working on reclaiming and creating radical queer and Sikh family legacies.

Yvette Perreault comes with Prairie roots and migrated to Toronto in 1980. She has been a community organizer and counsellor for four decades, first in the area of violence against women and children, then in the AIDS sector – always as a tough pretty working-class lesbian feminist.

Kyle Rae was born in Ottawa in 1954, raised in Oakville, and came out while in grad school in England. He returned to Toronto in time for the 1981 bathhouse raids. Rae organized the first annual Pride that year, and continued until 1987, when he became executive director of 519 Church Street Community Centre. Elected as Toronto's first openly gay City Councillor in 1991, Rae represented Ward 6 and then Toronto-Centre Rosedale until retiring from public office in 2010. He now teaches at Ryerson University, precariously.

Rupert Raj has been a Eurasian-Canadian, pansexual, trans activist since 1971. As a gender specialist/psychotherapist in Toronto from 2000 to 2015, he counselled transgender, genderqueer, intersex, and Two Spirit people, and as an expert witness, testified at human rights hearings. In 2013, Rupert was inducted into the Canadian Lesbian and Gay Archives, where 'the Rupert Raj Collection' is housed. He co-edited (with Dan Irving) *Trans Activism in Canada: A Reader*. His memoirs, *Dancing the Dialectic: True Tales of a Eurasian-Canadian Trans Activist*, will be out in 2017.

Gillian Rodgerson, a freelance writer and editor, is a former member of *The Body Politic* collective and a current member of the board of directors of Pink Triangle Press, publishers of DailyXtra.com. She lives in Toronto. Visit her at www.gillianrodgerson.com.

Río Rodriguez is a latinx educator and health worker whose work is based in queer, trans, and POC communities. Río's master's in environmental studies from York University examined key moments in Toronto's Gay Village history, highlighting how urban planning has promoted white gay safety while displacing and criminalizing queer and trans bodies of colour.

janet romero-leiva is a queer, feminist latinx writer, performer, and visual artist inspired by wood, paper, nature, love ... and her lived experience. her work mostly focuses on (but is not limited to) issues of displacement, denied aboriginality, queer identity, and living en dos lenguas.

Sly Sarkisova is a queer and trans writer and therapist. He has been working intimately doing mental health and emotional labour for far too long. He enjoys whimsy, photography, and holding people's experiences alongside his own with the utmost of care.

David K. Seitz teaches sexual diversity studies, women and gender studies, and human geography at the University of Toronto. His book about the Metropolitan Community Church of Toronto, *A House of Prayer For All People*, is forthcoming.

John Sewell was a member of Toronto city council from 1969 to 1984, and mayor of Toronto from 1979 to 1980. He has engaged in politics in Toronto as a community activist, city councillor, journalist, writer, housing administrator, and social entrepreneur, often speaking for and representing those who do not have access to the levers of power in society. He has written a dozen books, most recently *How We Changed Toronto, 1969–1980*. Sewell was awarded the Order of Canada in 2005.

Makeda Silvera is a Jamaican-born writer and publisher who has 'always been partial to living outside the margins – those places where conversation and exploration buck up 'gainst each other. It's where we can shout and hear the echoes of our own voices.'

Christine Sismondo is researching Toronto's gay and lesbian bars in the Cold War era for her history doctorate at York University. She is a frequent contributor to the *Toronto Star* and the *Globe and Mail* and the author of *America*

Walks into a Bar: A Spirited History of Taverns, Saloons, Speakeasies and Grog Shops.

Nicole Nanku Tanguay is a community arts worker. 'I am a mixed race, Two Spirit person. However, I am a lot more comfortable being with people from the same cultural heritage and having to deal with queerphobia than having to deal with racism. It is painful, but in the end our spirit comes first.'

Mariana Valverde was very active in feminist and gay politics in Toronto in the 1980s. Currently a professor at the University of Toronto, she researches urban law and city governance, writing both for academic journals and the general public.

Anu Radha Verma is a queer diasporic sometimes-femme with a complicated relationship to 'south asia,' a survivor, and someone with lived experience of mental health issues. She has lived, worked, studied, played, and agitated in Canada and India.

Syrus Marcus Ware is an artivist, educator, and PhD student in environmental studies at York University. He has authored many book and journal chapters on disability, museums, and trans parenting and sexual health. He was voted Best Queer Activist by *NOW* Magazine (2005) and received the Steinert & Ferreiro Award (2012) and the Sylff Fellowship for Academic Distinction (2014).

Margaret Webb is an author (*Older, Faster, Stronger* and *Apples to Oysters*), screenwriter (*Margarita*), and journalist who has written for Canada's leading publications.

Kristyn Wong-Tam made history in 2010 by becoming the first out lesbian to be elected to Toronto City Council. She is a long-time human rights activist and energetic champion for new urbanism.

Natalie Wood is a multimedia artist and curator whose work – drawing, painting, printmaking, video, and web-based – cohabits the areas of art and historical research. She studied at OCADU and received her MA in art education from the University of Toronto in 2000. Her work has been shown nationally and internationally. In 2006, she won the New Pioneers Award for her contribution to the arts in Toronto.

Andrew Zeally is an artist, educator, and lover. He lives in the sky with his feline companion, Roland Grey, and creates sublime noise.

Kate Zieman is a volunteer at the Canadian Lesbian and Gay Archives (for love) and a reference librarian at CBC (for love *and* money). She lives in the east end with her wife, son, and requisite cat.

Art Zoccole is Anishnawbe ogokwe from Lac des Mille Lacs First Nation in Ontario. Former executive director of 2-Spirited People of the First Nations in Toronto, and an HIV/AIDS activist for three decades, he recently retired.

Jamea Zuberi (BEd, York University) has been transforming the lives of others through education and community development for over thirty years. Her passion for the carnival arts led her to contribute in the Panatics Steelband Network, the Toronto North Stars Children Steel Orchestra, Blockorama, and Pelau MasQueerade.

The Editors

Stephanie Chambers is a news researcher at *The Globe and Mail* and teaches investigative reporting at Humber College. She has been a researcher for many *Globe* stories, from investigative to business and beat reporting, including some that have gone on to win National Newspaper Awards and most recently a 2015 Michener Citation of Merit. She has a Master of Information from the University of Toronto.

Jane Farrow is a curious Torontonian who has immersed herself in urban affairs as a city hall staffer, community animator, CBC radio broadcaster, and writer. She was the first executive director of Jane's Walk, a global movement of free, citizen-led walking tours celebrating urbanist Jane Jacobs's ideas. For ten years she worked as a CBC Radio One host and producer on such programs as *The Sunday Edition*, *This Morning*, *Workology*, *Sometimes Y*, and *Wanted Words*. She co-edited the bestsellers *Wanted Words* and *Wanted Words 2* and *The Canadian Book of Lists*, including an edition forthcoming in fall 2017.

Maureen FitzGerald is an urban anthropologist and a Fellow of the Mark S. Bonham Centre for Sexual Diversity Studies at the University of Toronto. She is a co-editor of *Queerly Canadian: An Introductory Reader in Sexuality Studies* and *Still Ain't Satisfied: Canadian Feminism Today*. In the 1980s, she was managing editor of Women's Press and a member of Lesbians Making History, a collective that did oral history of 'gay women' in Toronto in the fifties and sixties. She is fascinated by all things Toronto.

Ed Jackson was a long-time member of the editorial collective of *The Body Politic* and co-editor of *Flaunting It!: A Decade of Gay Journalism from The Body Politic*. He was one of the founders of the AIDS Committee of Toronto, where he managed prevention education in the crisis years, and later served as Director of Program Development at CATIE until his retirement in 2015. An ongoing supporter of the Canadian Lesbian and Gay Archives, his enduring interest is queer local history.

John Lorinc is a Toronto journalist, author, and editor. He is a regular contributor to numerous publications, including the *Globe and Mail*, the *Toronto Star*, *Spacing*, *Walrus*, and *Canadian Business*. Lorinc is the author of three books, including *The New City*; contributed to every edition of the Coach House uTOpia series; and co-edited two other Coach House anthologies, *The Ward: The Life and Loss of Toronto's First Immigrant Neighbourhood* and *Subdivided: City-Building in the Era of Hyper-Diversity*.

Tim McCaskell is a long-time gay activist. He worked on *The Body Politic*, the Right to Privacy Committee after the 1981 police raids on gay baths, the Simon Nkodi Anti-Apartheid Committee, AIDS ACTION NOW! and Queers Against Israeli Apartheid. His first book, *Race to Equity*, a history of the struggle for equity in Toronto public schools, is widely used in teacher education. Tim is also the author of *Queer Progress: From Homophobia to Homonationalism*.

Rebecka Sheffield is an archivist and archival educator. She has held teaching positions at the University of Toronto and Simmons College, Boston. Rebecka has worked with the Canadian Lesbian and Gay Archives since 2008, and served as the organization's first executive director and archives manager. She completed a graduate degree in archives and records management and completed a PhD at the University of Toronto in collaboration with the Mark S. Bonham Centre for Sexual Diversity Studies.

Tatum Taylor is a writer, heritage planner, and Texan transplant currently working in Toronto. She holds a master's degree in historic preservation from Columbia University, where she wrote her thesis on interpreting the heritage of marginalized groups, specifically the LGBTQ community. She is also a co-editor of *The Ward: The Life and Loss of Toronto's First Immigrant Neighbourhood* (Coach House Books, 2015).

Rahim Thawer is a registered social worker, consultant, post-secondary instructor, and mental health counsellor. He has worked at multiple HIV/AIDS service organizations in Toronto as an outreach worker, resource writer, program coordinator, tester, and counsellor. Rahim continues to work in direct practice settings with newcomer, racialized, and LGBTQ communities. He is also an active community organizer with Salaam: Queer Muslim Community and is co-founder of Ismaili Queers: Advocates for Pluralism.

Acknowledgements

This anthology is the product of the creative efforts of an incredibly diverse group of contributors who have summoned their voices, connections, experiences, and communities in a collaborative effort to capture part of the living history of an ever-evolving queer Toronto. We thank them for their memories, passions, and insights.

Any Other Way has also benefited enormously from an informal partnership with the Canadian Lesbian and Gay Archives (www.clga.ca). Founded in 1973 as a project of the early lesbian and gay newspaper The Body Politic, the collection has grown beyond its initial store of queer-movement print media to become the largest independent LGBTQ archives in the world. From a succession of cramped quarters in individual homes and drafty warehouses tended purely by dedicated volunteer labour, the CLGA has expanded to a prominent place in the archive community, with a home of its own at 34 Isabella Street.

The CLGA collects a wide range of materials, including personal papers, photographs, moving images, sound recordings, oral histories, periodicals, clipping files, reference texts, and ephemera such as buttons, T-shirts, and protest banners. Its mandate is to acquire, preserve, organize, and give public access to information and materials in any medium by, for, and about LGBTQ+ Canadians. It has become a core reference source for researchers interested in the city's queer history. We are grateful for the generous assistance of staffers Reagan Swanson, Jade Pichette, and Caitlin Smith and dedicated volunteers Alan V. Miller, Don McLeod, and Paul Leatherdale.

Queer archiving efforts are now taking many forms, particularly in communities that have been previously under-represented in the archival records drawn primarily from white queer communities. The editors of Any Other Way have benefited from the efforts of Marvellous Grounds (www.marvellousgrounds.com), a collective dedicated to documenting and creating the collective history of space-making by queer and trans Black, Indigenous, and people of colour, as well as from Invisible Footprints, a project focused on collecting the history of queer Asians activities in Toronto.

Coach House Books has been a champion of this project from its beginning, led by chief cheerleader and editorial director Alana Wilcox. Norman Nehmetallah, Jessica Rattray, Kate Barss, Rick/Simon, Stuart Ross, and the rest of the Coach House team supported us in our quest to transform a vague concept into a wonderful final physical product. Ingrid Paulson created yet another striking design for this anthology. This book could never have come together without the skilled and committed editorial coaching and coordination of John Lorinc, already practised in the art from facilitating two other Toronto-focused anthologies.

We'd like to thank the librarians and archivists at Toronto Reference Library, the Globe and Mail, York University, and the City of Toronto Archives, as well as ERA Architects for generously providing the editors with access to its boardroom for meetings.

Finally, the editors would like to thank their partners, friends, and families (chosen and otherwise) for their support and encouragement while working on this important project.

Credits

p. 12. Photographer: Russ Strathdee.

p. 14. *Toronto Star*, 22 February 1967.

p. 16. City of Toronto Archives, Fonds 2032, Series 841, File 17, Item 22.

p. 21. Canadian Lesbian and Gay Archives, 1982-175-01P.

p. 23. Courtesy of Ottie Lockey.

p. 33. Courtesy of AA Bronson and the Art Gallery of Ontario.

p. 38. Courtesy of J. D. Doyle/Queer Music Heritage.

p. 40. Black Coalition for AIDS Prevention. CGLA File: Black CAP 2012 Vert Files.TIF

p. 42. Illustrator: Maurice Vellekoop. Courtesy of the AIDS Committee of Toronto and John Maxwell.

p. 43. Courtesy of John Chuckman.

p. 44. With permission from Natalie Wood.

p. 46. City of Toronto Archives, Fonds 1526, File 61, Item 78.

p. 48. Courtesy of Pink Triangle Press.

p. 56. Photograph reprinted with permission by Estate of Ken Bell.

p. 59. Courtesy of John Chuckman.

p 60. Designer : Graham Campbell. Courtesy of Alan Miller.

p. 64–65. Courtesy of Pam Gawn.

p. 74. Memorial service poster reprinted with permission of Maureen FitzGerald.

p. 81. Photographer: Heather Pollack.

p. 82. Photographer: Gerald Hannon.

p. 85. Library and Archives Canada, RG1 E3, State Submissions to the Executive Council of Upper Canada, Volume 50, File M.

p. 89. Photographer: Nathaniel Currier, 1813-1888, Toronto Public Library, JRR 292 Cab II.

p. 91. Alexander Wood Statue. Courtesy of Ed Jackson.

p 93. City of Toronto Archives, Fonds 200, Series 372, Subseries 1, Item 1601.

p. 94. Public domain.

p. 97. Canadian Lesbian and Gay Archives, File: 2001-009. Permission obtained by Kate Zieman.

p. 99. City of Toronto Archives, Fonds 2032, Series 841, File 46, Item 35.

p. 103. York University Libraries, Clara Thomas Archives & Special Collections, Toronto Telegram fonds, ASC14964.

p. 111–113. Canadian Lesbian and Gay Archives, Flash 1951-1956.

p. 117. Canadian Lesbian and Gay Archives, File:2001-009. Permission obtained by Kate Zieman.

p. 122. Photographer: Stephanie Chambers.

p. 128. Canadian Lesbian and Gay Archives, Handbill for Music Room drag show, File: musicroom.

p. 129. Public Domain. Canadian Lesbian and Gay Archives file: tabloid cover 4.pdf

p. 130. Courtesy of Estate of Philip McLeod (Ed Jackson).

p. 135. Photographer: Gerald Hannon.

p. 137. Canadian Lesbian and Gay Archives, File: 1998-126/01(15).

p. 149. 'High School Confidential' lyrics courtesy of Carole Pope.

p. 151. Courtesy of True North Records and Carole Pope.

p. 156. Canadian Lesbian and Gay Archive, File: F0021.

p. 153. Courtesy of Pink Triangle Press.

p. 160. Photographer: Jearld Moldenhauer.

p. 163. Photographer: Jearld Moldenhauer.

p. 166. Courtesy of Dennis Findlay.

p. 173. Courtesy of Pink Triangle Press.

p. 174. Courtesy of Pink Triangle Press.

p. 181. Photographer: Gerald Hannon.

p. 182. Courtesy of Norman Hatton. Canadian Lesbian and Gay Archives, 2004-029.

p. 183–184. Photographer: Gerald Hannon.

p. 186. Photo by Barrie Davis / The Globe and Mail. Reprinted with permission.

p. 198. Courtesy of Kyle Rae.

p. 206. Photographer: Nigel Dickinson. Canadian Lesbian and Gay Archives.

p. 209. Courtesy of Alec Butler.

p. 217. Canadian Lesbian and Gay Archives.

p. 224–225. Courtesy of Gay Asians of Toronto.

p. 229. Photographer: Ed Jackson.

p. 231. Photographer: Peggy McOmie. Courtesy of Stefan Lynch.

p. 241. Canadian Lesbian and Gay Archives.

p. 243. Courtesy of Holly Dale and Janis Cole.

p. 245–246. Courtesy of Lisa Kannako.

p. 248. Courtesy of Michael Comeau.

p. 249. Courtesy of Alon Daniel Freeman.

p. 252–253. Photographer: Alejandro Santiago.

p. 255. Courtesy of John Greyson.

p. 262. Desh Pardesh Postcard 1994 by Rachel Kalpana James.

p. 275. Courtesy of Alec Butler.

p. 277. Courtesy of Keith Cole.

p. 286. Photography by Andrew Zealley. Steamworks chalkboard (2012-2016).

p. 301. Canadian Lesbian and Gay Archives.

p. 306. Photographer: Kyle Rae. Canadian Lesbian and Gay Archives.

p. 312–313. Photographer: Nick Di Donato. Photo courtesy of Liberty Entertainment Group.

p. 325–328. Photographer: Jearld Moldenhauer.

p. 329. Canadian Lesbian and Gay Archives.

p. 331. Photographer unknown. Canadian Lesbian and Gay Archives.

p. 334–335. Courtesy of Gay Asians of Toronto.

p. 340. Canadian Lesbian and Gay Archives.

p. 345. Courtesy of Daryl Vocat.

p. 352. Courtesy Numero Group.

Every effort was made to contact rightsholders of the images included in this book. If we've missed something or erred, please notify us at mail@chbooks.com and we'll correct it.

Typeset in Aragon, Aragon Sans, and Knockout.

Edited by Stephanie Chambers, Jane Farrow, Maureen FitzGerald, Ed Jackson, John Lorinc, Tim McCaskell, Rebecka Sheffield, Tatum Taylor, and Rahim Thawer

Copy edited by Stuart Ross
Cover design by Ingrid Paulson
Design by Alana Wilcox

Coach House Books
80 bpNichol Lane
Toronto ON M5S 3J4
Canada

416 979 2217
800 367 6360

mail@chbooks.com
www.chbooks.com